Understanding
Contemporary

INDIA

THIRD EDITION

Understanding Contemporary

INDIA

edited by
Neil DeVotta and
Sumit Ganguly

LYNNE
RIENNER
PUBLISHERS

BOULDER
LONDON

Published in the United States of America in 2021 by
Lynne Rienner Publishers, Inc.
1800 30th Street, Suite 314, Boulder, Colorado 80301
www.rienner.com

and in the United Kingdom by
Lynne Rienner Publishers, Inc.
Gray's Inn House, 127 Clerkenwell Road, London EC1 5DB
www.eurospanbookstore.com/rienner

Library of Congress Cataloging-in-Publication Data
Names: DeVotta, Neil, editor. | Ganguly, Sumit, editor.
Title: Understanding contemporary India / edited by Neil DeVotta and Sumit
    Ganguly.
Description: Third edition. | Boulder, Colorado : Lynne Rienner Publishers,
    2021. | Series: Understanding: Introductions to the states and regions
    of the contemporary world | Includes bibliographical references and
    index. | Summary: "Sheds light on the paradoxical nature of the world's
    largest and most diverse democracy"— Provided by publisher.
Identifiers: LCCN 2021015775 | ISBN 9781626379404 (Paperback ; alk. paper)
Subjects: LCSH: India—History—1947– | India—Civilization—1947– |
    India—Politics and government—1947– | India—Social conditions—1947–
Classification: LCC DS480.853 .U54 2021 | DDC 954.05—dc23
LC record available at https://lccn.loc.gov/2021015775

British Cataloguing in Publication Data
A Cataloguing in Publication record for this book
is available from the British Library.

Printed and bound in the United States of America

The paper used in this publication meets the requirements
of the American National Standard for Permanence of
Paper for Printed Library Materials Z39.48-1992.

5   4   3   2   1

To the memory of Ainslie T. Embree
January 1, 1921–June 6, 2017

Contents

Illustrations

Photographs

Preface

The first edition of *Understanding Contemporary India* was published in 2003 and the second in 2010 with six new chapters. This third edition likewise includes six new chapters.

The book is designed to introduce students to contemporary India and as such follows the template of the other titles in the Understanding series by providing overarching accounts dealing with India's geography, history, politics, economy, international relations, caste, religion, women, and the environment. No comparable text on India deals in a single volume with the multiplicity of issues discussed here, and from that standpoint this book, like the others in the series, fills an important niche.

This noted, no single volume could do justice to a country as extraordinary and complex as India. Thus, each chapter in the book could be expanded into a hefty tome. Students interested in broadening their understanding of the issues covered in these essays should begin by consulting the reference list that begins on page 293.

Ainslie T. Embree, who wrote excellent chapters on India's religions in the first and second editions, passed away in 2017. We are grateful that Chad Bauman could combine his work with that of Ainslie to write a thoroughly updated and expansive chapter for this edition. Professor Embree was an Indologist who contributed immeasurably to our understanding of India. In appreciation for all he did for numerous students and colleagues, we dedicate this volume to his memory.

—*Neil DeVotta and Sumit Ganguly*

1

Introducing India

Neil DeVotta

Every time India holds a general election, it turns out to be the largest-ever exercise in democracy. Mind-boggling electoral statistics have been the norm in India, beginning with the country's very first general election of October 1951 to February 1952 (the logistical challenges involved in conducting general elections in India mandate that they be held in stages, with different regions going to the polls at different times, although elections today last around a month). That first general election saw 176 million Indians, of which 85 percent were illiterate, qualifying to vote at 224,000 polling booths presided over by 56,000 election offices, 280,000 assistants, and 224,000 policemen (Guha 2007b: 133–134).

When the country held its seventeenth general elections in April and May 2019, another record was shattered. This time nearly 900 million Indians qualified to vote, of which 15 million were first-time voters. The election required the services of around 12 million officials at over 1 million polling booths. As per Indian law, voters should not have to travel more than 2 kilometers (1.24 miles) to cast their vote. Election officials, therefore, had to visit the most remote parts of the country so citizens could exercise their franchise. In Ladakh, officials were equipped with oxygen tanks to get to twelve voters living at an altitude of over 14,000 feet, while others waded through crocodile-infested swamps in the Andaman and Nicobar Islands to reach voters. A polling booth was even set up in the Gir Forest National Park so just one person, a Hindu priest, could cast his vote (Quraishi 2019). Ultimately, over 600 million people cast votes, with turnout exceeding 67 percent. High turnout is a feature of eletions held in South Asia, and India clearly contributes to this standard.

India's unique democracy upends arguments made by scholars about prerequisites for ensuring a successful democracy. For instance, it is generally true that the more educated and economically better-off people are, the more likely they are to vote. In India, however, the less educated and poor vote in greater numbers (often after standing in queues for hours) than those who are better educated and economically well-off. Furthermore, in Western countries especially, minorities tend to vote in lower numbers. In India, on the contrary, minorities vote in higher numbers. In the most recent election, not only did the poor, low castes, and minorities vote in large numbers, but they (with the exception of Muslims) also voted in higher numbers to reelect Narendra Modi and his Hindu nationalist Bharatiya Janata Party (BJP) for a second consecutive term (Suri 2019; Chhibber and Verma 2019).

Figure 1.1   Political Map of South Asia

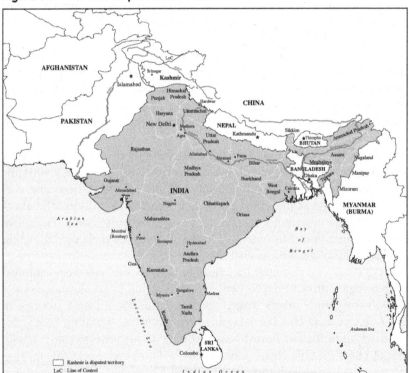

Democracies, more than any other form of government, are better at reforming and adapting. This process, however, is rarely neat, and India proves the point. Parties and politicians contest to win; so, absent strong rules, they will resort to electoral shenanigans to capture and stay in power. Thus, by one estimate, over 120 million Indians, mainly Muslims and women, were denied the chance to vote in the 2019 parliamentary elections because their names, for whatever reason, did not appear on voting lists (Shankar 2019). Ultimately, there are no perfect democracies in the world, and India needs to shed some troubling communal features in order to prevent democratic backsliding.

Thus far, however, India's democratic structure has remained sufficiently robust that various Indian nongovernmental organizations (NGOs) and citizens groups utilize the country's constitution and institutions (especially the courts) when trying to confront injustices committed against the most marginalized citizens—including the lower castes, women, and children. By some accounts these civil society organizations number over 500,000, and anyone spending sufficient time in rural and urban India can speak to their valiant efforts.

This triumph of democracy, however, represents a paradox, in that the deepening of democracy has been accompanied by political fragmentation and increased malgovernance (Sharma 2010: 68). Since Narendra Modi was elected prime minister in 2014, communalism rooted in Islamophobia and authoritarianism has contributed to this malgovernance (DeVotta 2019). But this is merely one paradox in a country that is in many ways a paradox. For India is both a young state and one of the world's oldest civilizations; it is a potential superpower, yet more than 300 million of its citizens live in abject poverty; it is the proud land of the peaceful Mohandas Gandhi, yet it brandishes nuclear weapons and hosts one of the world's largest militaries; its rivers are revered for embodying deities, yet are among the world's most polluted waterways; its infrastructure in many areas is abysmal, yet its information technology workers, engineers, scientists, and academics are in demand the world over; and it is a country led by powerful women at various ranks, yet its women are among the most marginalized in the world. The chapters in this volume confront such paradoxes in seeking to explain contemporary India.

Diverse India

India's ability to combine relatively free and fair elections with diversity is what many find commendable. It is with good reason that Robert

Blackwill, upon completing his tenure as US ambassador to India in 2003, noted that "India is a pluralist society that creates magic with democracy, rule of law and individual freedom, community relations and diversity. . . . I wouldn't mind being born ten times to rediscover India" (Phadnis 2003).

Indeed, one would need to be born at least ten times to discover India. This is why there are no "experts" on India. Notwithstanding the plethora of knowledgeable commentators on specific subjects pertaining to India, only those who are arrogant or ignorant dare claim to be an expert on this maddeningly diverse country comprising 325 functioning languages (including twenty-two official languages), hundreds of dialects, twenty-five scripts, six major religions—Hinduism, Islam, Sikhism, Buddhism, Christianity, and Jainism—4,500 caste groups, hundreds of tribal groups, and their resulting traditions and cultures encompassed in twenty-eight states and nine territories (see Table 1.1).

India's diversity ranks among the country's greatest strengths. What we now call Hinduism has played a huge role in fostering this diversity. The term *Hinduism* is of recent origin and was popularized by the British in the nineteenth century as they sought to understand the varied religious traditions among India's Hindus (Hawley 1991). Given their Christian background, the British were nonplussed when confronted with the different "Hinduisms" in India that embraced numerous gods, rituals, and traditions, all of which had evolved over 4,000 years.

Unlike in the monotheistic (and most other) religions, Hindus do not have an official canon, a stated doctrine, an overarching leader, or an institution. In short, one could be a monotheist, a polytheist, or an atheist (who may merely devote her- or himself to the study of the Upanishads—ancient, abstruse philosophical texts—yet never visit a temple) and still be considered a good Hindu. Unlike the monotheistic texts that mandate fundamental beliefs, the Hindu texts promote varied beliefs and practices and come across as contradictory.

As US scholar Wendy Doniger (2009: 688) has noted, one could use these texts and argue for almost any position in contemporary India: that Hindus have been vegetarians, and that they have not; that Hindus and Muslims have gotten along well together, and that they have not; that Hindus have objected to suttee (or sati, whereby widows are burned on their husband's funeral pyres), and that they have not; that Hindus have renounced the material world, and that they have embraced it; that Hindus have oppressed women and lower castes, and that they have fought for their equality. One can see why the British, who possessed a predilection for categorizing and cataloging the territories and peoples they conquered, got confused.

Table 1.1   India's States and Territories

State	Year Created	Major Languages
Andhra Pradesh	1956	Telugu and Urdu
Arunachal Pradesh	1987	English, Miji, Honpa
Assam	1947	Assamese and Bodo
Bihar	1950	Hindi and Bhojpuri
Chhattisgarh	2000	Hindi
Goa	1987	Marathi and Konkani
Gujarat	1960	Gujarati
Haryana	1966	Hindi
Himachal Pradesh	1971	Hindi and Pahari
Jharkhand	2000	Hindi
Karnataka	1956	Kannada
Kerala	1956	Malayalam
Madhya Pradesh	1956	Hindi
Maharashtra	1960	Marathi
Manipur	1972	Meiteilon
Meghalaya	1972	English, Garo, Khasi
Mizoram	1987	English and Mizo
Nagaland	1963	English
Orissa	1949	Oriya
Punjab	1956	Punjabi
Rajasthan	1956	Hindi and Rajastani
Sikkim	1975	Nepali, Bhutia, Limbu, Lepcha
Tamil Nadu	1956	Tamil
Telangana	2014	Telugu, Urdu
Tripura	1972	Bengali, Kokborok, Manipuri
Uttar Pradesh	1947	Hindi and Urdu
Uttarakhand	2000	Hindi, Kumaoni, Garhwali
West Bengal	1960	Bengali
Territories		
Andaman and Nicobar Islands	2001	Nicobarese, English, Bengali, Tamil, Hindi, Telugu, Malayalam
Chandigarh	1953	Hindi and Punjabi
Dadra and Nagar Haveli	1961	Marathi and Gujarati
Daman and Diu	1987	Marathi and Gujarati
Delhi	1947	Hindi, Urdu, English, Punjabi
Lakshadweep	1956	Malayalam
Pondicherry	1963	Tamil, Telugu, Malayalam, French
Jammu and Kashmir[a]	2019	Kashmiri, Urdu, Dogri, Pahari
Ladakh	2019	Ladakhi

Note: a. Jammu and Kashmir, including Ladakh, operated as a state from 1947 to 2019, when it became two union territories: Jammu and Kashmir, and Ladakh.

India's diversity partly stems from the country not being a single political entity until recently. For while one can speak of an Indian civilization, India's present territorial borders represent a historical accident. British India consisted of nearly 600 principalities, and it was British ambitions and malpractice that gave the country its current boundaries. Britain's biggest mistake may have been to clumsily partition the subcontinent in

August 1947, which led to hundreds of thousands being killed and an estimated 15 million people displaced, as it created Pakistan and, inadvertently, Bangladesh (Talbot and Singh 2009: 2). Postindependence India's challenge has been to try to get the variegated peoples who ended up within its borders to embrace and celebrate a common Indian identity even while nurturing their distinct cultures and traditions. This is a continuous challenge, and it is manifested in the periodic communal violence (especially between Hindus and Muslims) and secessionist violence the Indian state has experienced since independence.

Muslim elites like Mohammed Ali Jinnah had justified Partition by promoting a "two nation" theory claiming that Hindus and Muslims were different nations no matter how they were evaluated, and that the subcontinent's Muslims therefore qualified to have their own country. This was the basis for creating Pakistan. Indian elites like Jawaharlal Nehru were determined not to position their country as a Hindu entity in opposition to "Muslim Pakistan" and staunchly promoted India as a state in which all religious groups could live amicably. Notwithstanding the grotesque violence that accompanied Partition, Gandhi and Nehru encouraged Muslims to make the country their home; and Gandhi's campaigns on behalf of Muslims, his assassination in January 1948 at the hands of a Hindu extremist, and the reflection this promoted among both Hindus and Muslims influenced many among the latter to stay on in India (Husain 1965: 134).

Given especially the communal violence that led to Partition, it is understandable why some Hindus felt their religious community ought to dominate the state's affairs. But it was the pluralist and secular approach that Gandhi, Nehru, and others within the Congress Party championed that initially held sway.

The idea of secularism is influenced by Europe's Protestant Reformation. In the United States it led to the separation of church and state given the Founding Fathers' aversion to any established state religion. But throughout South Asia's history, princely rulers had functioned as patrons of religions; so defining secularism in the newly independent India became problematic. Nehru felt that the irrational influences of religion would vitiate as society developed; India should therefore not privilege religious identities but instead emphasize individual rights rooted in public law. Gandhi, on the other hand, felt all religions were true and valid and could be the basis for sustaining communities (Rudolph 1987: 747). Given the contradictions associated with secularism in an Indian context, the constitution, which took effect in January 1950, avoided branding the state as secular. That took place in 1976, when a government under Prime Minister Indira Gandhi introduced the forty-second amendment to the constitution. Yet the state modern India's founding fathers sought to create was undergirded by a secular ethos.

This was evidenced by how India sought to accommodate religious minorities and groups who were discriminated against for centuries based on caste and tribal identities. Thus Muslims and Christians were allowed to create and oversee educational institutions. Independent India also decided not to institute a uniform civil code, which meant that Muslims could utilize their own law when dealing with issues of marriage, divorce, and inheritance.

The Reservation System

The reservation (or quota) system put in place so Dalits (formerly called Untouchables), Tribals, and Other Backward Classes could overcome discrimination and secure employment represents a significant instance of accommodation on the part of the Indian state. Whatever reasons may have justified the creation of the caste system, it morphed over the ages into an institution that oppressed and denigrated millions of Indians. The periodic violence ranging from rape and murder associated with caste represents a major blemish on Indian society. Dalits continue to face the brunt of this oppression.

Forced into lives of servitude, drudgery, and humiliation, it is only in postindependence India that many Dalit communities have been able to assert themselves, and the main reason for their being able to do so is the right to vote. Chapter 7 describes the caste and reservation systems, but what bears repeating is that the rise of the Dalits and lower castes in India represents a social revolution. The reservation system put in place over the years now ensures that 22.5 percent of all central government jobs and university placements are set aside for Dalits and Tribals. Similarly, 27 percent of all government jobs are placements in government-run universities reserved for caste groups that fall under the Other Backward Classes category.

In January 2019, partly as a sop to its higher-caste base, the ruling Bharatiya Janata Party engineered the 104th amendment to the Indian constitution and thereby ensured a 10 percent quota for so-called economically weaker sections (EWS) of society. As a result, those who are not from Dalit, Tribal, or Other Backward Classes families and making less than 800,000 rupees (around $11,000) per year qualify to compete for jobs and educational placement through this EWS quota. The quota will likely weaken opposition among the upper castes toward the reservation system (as they too now benefit from it), but it also muddies the criteria for reservation since quotas have hitherto been justified based on centuries-long caste oppression, not economic hardship. This new quota was established despite the Supreme Court having ruled that total reservations in India should not exceed 50 percent. Those who consider the 50 percent reservation cap to now be a basic structure of the constitution have brought cases against the new quota, although the apex court has refused to issue any stay orders. So the quota is being implemented in most central universities and other government establishments.

India also has quotas in place for Dalits and Tribals in parliament. Currently, out of the 543 seats in parliament's lower house, 84 are reserved for Dalits and 47 for Tribals. Dalits and Tribals also have seats reserved for them in the respective state legislatures. The Congress Party–led governments have even considered imposing job quotas on the private sector to increase Dalit and low-caste representation, but have been forced to back off.

Beginning in 1952, two representatives from the Anglo-Indian community (those of European and Indian ancestry) were nominated to serve in parliament (as the community is relatively small and too scattered to compete for any seats). But the 104th amendment to the Indian constitution, passed in January 2020, did away with this reservation at both the national and state legislature levels.

While the number of women winning elections to the Lok Sabha (lower house) of parliament has been inching up—45 women were elected in 2004, 58 were elected in 2009, 66 in 2014, and 78 in 2019—a movement to pass the Women's Reservation Bill, which would set aside 33 percent of seats in the lower house, state legislatures, and local governments for women, is yet to become a reality.

Women and Panchayati Raj

Indian women, however, do enjoy reservation at the local government levels. Panchayats are the five-member local governing bodies in India's federal system. Comprising three levels (gram panchayats, block panchayats, and district panchayats), there are over 250,000 entities at the lowest (gram panchayat) level. Not only does the Indian constitution reserve positions for Dalits and Tribals (in line with their population within the panchayat), it also reserves one-third of the seats for women. Consequently, at present over a million women get elected to these councils every five years. In 2009 the Congress Party–led Union Cabinet recommended that reservation for women in panchayati institutions be increased to 50 percent. Some states had already taken the lead in this regard, and at present over half of India's states reserve 50 percent of seats for women in panchayati institutions. The evidence of whether such decentralization has improved governance is mixed (Mullen 2013: 78), but the fact remains that there is no electoral exercise of this magnitude designed to empower women anywhere else in the world.

Dealing with Regions

The political process in India typically unfolds amid great tumult, and students of India cannot be blamed for thinking that Indian elites are better at ruling than governing. One can rule by diktat, but governance requires compromise and tact. Nehru, who was instinctively drawn toward accommodation as opposed to confrontation, stands out with regard to the latter, and this is evident in how he dealt with regional leaders and their various demands. It is especially evident in his instructions to the Indian army regarding how to deal with the Naga tribes even after Naga rebels had ambushed homes, burnt houses, "looted shops . . . kidnapped teachers . . . raided railway stations and sniped trains" (Elwin 1961: 60).

> You must remember that all the people of the area in which you are operating are fellow-Indians. They may have a different religion, they may pursue a different way of life, but they are Indians, and the very fact that they are different and yet part of India is a reflection of India's greatness. Some of these people are misguided and have taken to arms against their own people, and are disrupting the peace of this area. You are to protect the mass of the people from these disruptive elements. You are not there to fight the people in the area, but to protect them. You are fighting only those who threaten the people and who are a danger to the lives and properties of the people. You must, therefore, do everything possible to win their confidence and respect and to help them feel that they belong to India. (Elwin 1961: 60)

This was the same tact that Nehru used with the leaders of south India when they demanded separate states and later threatened secession (in what was branded the Dravidian Movement) due to Hindi being made the official language. The demand to create states along linguistic lines first led to the creation of Andhra in 1953 (and renamed Andhra Pradesh in 1956). With Andhra's Telugu speakers having won their state, other regions also began demanding statehood. This led to the States Reorganization Act of 1956, which created a number of states along ethnolinguistic lines. Nehru and the Indian elite were initially averse to creating such states, believing it could lead to India's balkanization, but by giving into the popular will of the masses, these states "consolidated the unity of India" (Guha 2007b: 189, 199–200). Since then, new states have been periodically created along regional lines (but never on religious grounds), with Chhattisgarh, Uttarakhand, and Jharkhand being made states in 2000 and Telangana in 2014 (see Table 1.1). The state-creation process and their ethnic composition have played no small role in ensuring India's relative stability as a federal setup (Adeney 2007).

It is a testament to Indian democracy that it remains one of the few countries (another being Nigeria) that can continue to add to its list of states (Tillin 2012). Given extant demands, one should not be at all surprised if the India of the future included states called Vidarbha, Gorkhaland, Harit Pradesh, Bhojpur, Mahakaushal, Poorvanchal, Bodoland, Marathwada, Rayalaseema, Bundelkhand, Seemanchal, Avadh, and Kongu Nadu. One author has even suggested that India should be divided into fifty or sixty states (Kashyap 1998). While this may sound excessive, it is useful to consider that the United States, as currently constituted, with about 325 million people, has fifty states, while India, with four times as many people, has just twenty-eight states. For instance, Uttar Pradesh, India's largest state, has nearly 205 million people (which is over 60 percent of the US population), and is bound to be reorganized in the future.

The manner in which Nehru and others dealt with Hindi becoming the national language also speaks to these early leaders' accommodative spirit. The Indian constitution, which was adopted in November 1949 and became operational in January 1950, said that Hindi would become the national language within fifteen years, until which time English could also be used for all official purposes. As the date approached to implement Hindi as the sole national language, southerners especially turned hostile. In 1963, India under Nehru passed the Official Languages Act, which said English may continue to be used for official communication even after 1965. When debates over verbiage led to the act not being implemented, violent protests erupted in Tamil Nadu, leading to rioting and self-immolation. Lal Bahadur Shastri, who became prime minister following Nehru's death in May 1964, soon thereafter declared that states will be allowed to maintain their regional languages and also continue to use English as an official language when communicating with each other and the central government.

This thus far continues to be the case in India, where the sense of being Indian is not associated with any particular language. Indeed, the popularity of Hindi and English has grown to the point where both languages now are spoken interchangeably, leading to a fusion called "Hinglish." Indian authors today are among the best writers in English, and their literary success has led some to claim that the "empire is striking back." At the same time, nearly 40 percent of Indians now speak

Hindi, and Bollywood no doubt has played a major role in facilitating this. Even regions that rebelled against Hindi being imposed are now gradually accepting it, and this would not have happened if the Indian government had refused to compromise on the language issue and sought to impose Hindi on the entire population. Like Nehru, who was averse to creating linguistic states but relented in order to ensure India's territorial integrity, Prime Minister Shastri was averse to continuing with English as an official language (Guha 2007b: 395). But he too gave in to the popular will of the south, and polyglot India is, consequently, a culturally richer country. And thanks to such accommodation, it is also one where "loyalty first and foremost to the regions is in steady decline" (Mitra and Pehl 2010: 53). The rise of Hindu nationalists, under Narendra Modi, who want to superimpose Hindi on the rest of India and institute policies that will empower the north over the south of the country will test these gains in the years ahead.

Nehru's predilection for accommodation as opposed to confrontation extended to the region as well, and this was especially so in his dealings with China—which arguably took advantage of Nehru's camaraderie and humiliated the prime minister—and smaller states like Sri Lanka, which had attracted a large number of Indian laborers whose plight Nehru took a deep interest in.

Nehru and his sister Krishna Hutheesingh with A. Vittal Pai (agent to the government of India) and his wife, Tara Pai, Sri Lanka, July 1939. Photo courtesy of Sharada Nayak.

Accommodating Separatists

India has experienced dozens of separatist attempts since independence. While the northeastern area that comprises seven states has undergone the most numerous and longest-lasting secessionist attempts, the movement by extremist Sikhs in the Punjab and Kashmiri separatism have generated the most coverage. The quest to create a state of Khalistan for Sikhs ended violently when Indira Gandhi sent the Indian army into the Golden Temple, Sikhism's holiest shrine, to force out insurgents hiding within its compound. Operation Blue Star culminated in her Sikh bodyguards assassinating her in October 1984, which in turn unleashed murderous riots against Sikhs (Tully and Satish 1985). There remain elements within Punjab who glorify pro-Khalistan leaders and clamor for a separate state for Sikhs, but Punjab, in the main, now operates as a solid unit of the Indian union.

Kashmiri secessionism, on the other hand, is complicated by the India-Pakistan rivalry and attendant communalism (Chowdhary 2016). When the Hindu ruler of Kashmir decided to join India, Nehru assured his predominantly Muslim population that they would be treated as equal citizens even as India and Pakistan battled over Kashmir. In an attempt to buy their loyalty, Kashmir was provided certain privileges that did not apply to other states (i.e., its own constitution and flag, and the provision that only Kashmiris could purchase land in Kashmir). This was in line with India's asymmetrical federalism, whereby some states are afforded certain rights so as to ensure their adoptability within the Indian union. Such accommodation did not prevent tensions between the state and center over numerous issues, but when (just as in the Punjab) Indira Gandhi, and thereafter her son Rajiv Gandhi, resorted to electoral meddling in the state in the 1980s, it contributed to the Kashmir insurgency (Ganguly 1997; Bose 2003). Pakistan-sponsored terrorist activities and Indian troops' violence with impunity caused much carnage in Jammu and Kashmir (DeVotta 2012: 35; Tankel 2013). The Modi government's policies—splitting the state into two territories, enforcing a lengthy communications blockade that prevented Kashmiris from accessing the internet and using phones, and keeping Kashmiri politicians under house arrest while promoting Hindu nationalism—have further exacerbated tensions in the region.

Since the late 1960s, India has also experienced an insurgency movement that has sought to overthrow the state. This so-called Naxalite Movement (which gets its name from a 1967 revolt in the village of Naxalbari) is influenced by Maoism, although it is linked to long-standing communist party activism in India (Joshi and Josh 2011). In the past few years, nearly 200 of India's over 600 districts have dealt with Naxalite violence. In most instances recently, the violence stems from attempts to uproot tribal people especially from their land (so states and private companies can extract various natural resources), the scarcity of government services and employment among rural youth, and the impunity with which police and paramilitary forces perpetrate violence against India's most marginalized populations (Guha 2007a; Miklian and Carney 2010; Sundar 2016). Naxalite violence is not separatist, because the Naxalites seek to take over the state.

Successive Indian governments have adopted a carrot-and-stick approach when dealing with forces threatening to undermine the Indian union. In the latter instance, the Indian state has resorted to brute violence to put down separatist forces, and its tactics have rightly generated condemnation both within and without India. But if India today functions as a stronger state with Indians taking pride in their nationality even as they celebrate their regional diversity, it is due to the mainly accommodative spirit that India's postindependence leaders promoted.

Democratic Vibrancy and Backsliding

There were dozens of countries in Africa and Asia that gained independence in the two decades following World War II, yet India is among the few that successfully nurtured and maintained its democracy even though it was considered among the most likely to fail. Why is this so? Nobel laureate Amartya Sen (2005) has argued that Indian civilization has long tolerated, encouraged, and celebrated an argumentative tradition that has been conducive to democracy and secularism.

Others suggest that there is nothing inherently democratic about India's past, and that the consolidation of democracy is mainly due to the conscious decisions made by Indian leaders like Jawaharlal Nehru who championed the idea of representative government for all citizens (Khilnani 1997). There is no gainsaying how important Nehru especially was in ensuring India adopted a democratic trajectory. Not only did he serve three full terms as prime minister, but among his first responsibilities was helping to forge the Indian constitution, which one scholar thinks may represent "the greatest political venture since that originated in Philadelphia in 1787" (Austin 1999: 308). This is because the world's longest written constitution, which Nehru together with Dalit leader Bhimrao Ambedkar and others engineered, has taught Indians how to operate within a democracy (Khosla 2020).

There was also a practical reason for democratic consolidation in India, and it concerns India's ethnic, linguistic, religious, and regional diversity: people strongly identify with their regional identities. In this context, authoritarian governance was bound to lead to secessionist pressures, while devolution of power to local regions as part of a federal political structure was more likely to maintain unity and territorial integrity. This meant granting everyone in the polity the right to vote (as opposed to countries like the United States and United Kingdom where the franchise was introduced gradually) even if the state lacked the capacity to accommodate people's basic needs (Ramanathan and Ramanathan 2017). If India has chugged along and defied the odds of disintegration that some believed likely (Harrison 1960), it is in no small measure due to this devolutionary culture.

Political scientists consider a democracy to be consolidated if all stakeholders therein are committed to changing governments through free and fair elections. From this standpoint, India is a consolidated democracy. Except for a two-year period between 1975 and 1977 when Indira Gandhi imposed emergency rule, the country has changed governments via the franchise. Indeed, elections in India are akin to carnivalesque celebrations, and the Indian word *tamasha* (which the *Oxford English Dictionary* now defines as "an entertainment, show, display, public function" and "a fuss, a commotion") best captures the accompanying spirit and milieu of political campaigning. The closest comparable atmosphere in the United States is the tailgating revelry that takes place prior to football games. Depending on their wherewithal, candidates aspiring to political office campaign using aircrafts, helicopters, trains, tractors, automobiles, bullock carts, elephants, and camels.

But a country could be democratically consolidated yet operate in illiberal fashion. Being a liberal democracy requires a country to go beyond merely holding free and fair elections. It must also uphold civil liberties for all citizens irrespective of ethnicity and religion, ensure an independent judiciary that fearlessly enforces the rule of law, tolerate civil society, minimize corruption, and balance against executive overreach (Diamond 2019: 19). Becoming and maintaining a liberal democracy is a constant work in progress, and this is evidenced by how even established democracies like those in Western Europe and that of the United States have experienced backsliding due to recent right-wing populist movements. Indeed, the backsliding that has taken place in the United States is sufficiently severe that some scholars wonder if democracy as we know it is being threatened (Mickey, Levitsky, and Way 2017).

The pro-Hindu politics of the BJP have long worried those who are committed to seeing India being a pluralist and secular country. The party, however, had governed relatively moderately when it headed the government from 1998 to 2004. This was partly due to its then leader Atal Bihari Vajpayee but also due to it being part of a coalition. When the party won a clear majority in 2014 and Narendra Modi became prime minister, many felt that notwithstanding Modi's anti-Muslim history he too would be pushed to govern moderately. Ashutosh Varshney (2014), a leading scholar of India, noted that the need to develop India economically and appeal to moderate voters, constitutional constraints, and the country's first-past-the-post electoral system, among other issues, would nudge Modi and the BJP to tone down their Hindu nationalist agenda. Varshney had echoed others before Modi became prime minister, saying: "No political party [in India] can come to power without putting together multi-religious, multi-caste, multilingual coalitions. Barring entirely unpredictable shocks to the system, a rightwing takeover of Indian politics is inconceivable" (2013: 131). And just before Modi's reelection, another knowledgeable authority on India's political economy likewise pointed to the country's varied regional and local dynamics and caste politics and argued that the BJP's goal to create a state rooted in Hindu nationalism will "remain aspirational, as India's complex ecosystem of identities will continue to act as a powerful break on a descent into outright ethnonationalism" (Sharma 2019: 106). Yet following the anti-Muslim agenda that was instituted within six months of Modi's May 2019 reelection, it is clear the country is becoming increasingly illiberal (Ganguly 2020). Within the context of democratic consolidation, it is now an electorally vibrant polity that is mired in illiberal majoritarianism (Varshney 2019). Hindutva is the ideology undergirding this majoritarianism.

Hindutva

India's success in defying the odds and staying democratic caused democracy scholar Robert Dahl to say that "democracy . . . is the national ideology of India" (1998: 162). But the ramping up of Islamophobia and majoritarian politics, especially since Narendra Modi became prime minister in 2014, allows one to argue that it is Hindutva that is now the national ideology of India.

Hindutva refers to "Hindu-ness" and is the ideology associated with the Rashtriya Swayamsevak Sangh (RSS, National Volunteer Organization). Its principal originator, Vinayak Damodar Savarkar, associated Hindutva with "Hindu blood," the Sanskrit language, and its attendant culture. While the term *Hindutva* can connote different meanings (Andersen and Damle 2018: 77), it generally holds that no matter an Indian's religion, she or he should subscribe to a Hindu ethos (Hardgrave 2005).

Hindutvadis may claim their ideology seeks to protect and promote Hindu culture and is not hostile toward non-Hindus, but the Hindu domination they subscribe to threatens minority rights, and the Islamophobia they wallow in similarly threatens the country's nearly 200 million Muslims. This sense of majoritarianism stems from the notion that Hinduism is the subcontinent's oldest religion and India is its home; while all Indians may consider the country their *pitribhu* (fatherland), only Hindus—plus groups like Jains, Buddhists, and Sikhs whose religions originated in India—possess it as a *punyabhu* (holy land) (Savarkar 2003: 115–116). Minorities must thus appreciate their subordinate position and not make undue demands on the majority, who are the authentic *bhumiputra* (sons of the soil).

The RSS was organized in 1925 with the goal of uniting and strengthening a divided Hindu community, although its rhetoric from the beginning was majoritarian and Islamophobic. The RSS incorporates nearly forty other pro-Hindu affiliates—with the BJP operating as its political wing—and seeks to create an India that is contrary to the secular country Gandhi and Nehru aspired toward. Indeed, it was a member of the RSS who killed Gandhi because he, like fellow Hindu extremists, believed the Mahatma appeased Muslims and the newly created Pakistan. Among Hindutva advocates, Gandhi's murderer is today hailed as a "patriot" (Kazmin 2019: 8). This is especially ironic given that the RSS played no oppositional role in India's quest for independence from the British.

While the RSS and its political affiliate the BJP have sometimes experienced tensions between them, the rise of Narendra Modi helped minimize differences. Modi was a *pracharak* (a full-time RSS volunteer) before being allowed to enter politics in the state of Gujarat. Postindependence India had experienced episodic Hindu-Muslim rioting (Berenschot 2011; Brass 2003), but soon after his election as Gujarat chief minister the state erupted in the worst anti-Muslim violence since Partition (Sarkar 2002). This caused Modi to be shunned by the international community (with the United States refusing to grant him a visa for a number of years), but his pro-Hindu credentials, coupled with Gujarat's relatively vibrant economy, made him all the more popular among Hindutva advocates.

The influence of the RSS now reaches to the far corners of India, and when Modi headed the BJP ticket in 2014, the organization's cadre campaigned on his behalf in ways they had not done for other BJP candidates. They did so again in 2019, even as the Indian diaspora and industrialists once more funneled vast amounts of money toward the BJP campaign and most media provided uncritical coverage. The lackluster leadership of the Congress Party was a major reason for BJP dominance (Hasan 2018), but the so-called three Ms—money, machine, and media—made stymying Modi's reelection prospects a formidable task (Jenkins 2019).

Modi's election and reelection as prime minister emboldened Hindutvadis determined to create a Hindu Rashtra (Hindu polity) that stands in opposition to the secular ideals upon which India's democracy has been built (Aiyar 2004; Bhargava 1998). They have long accused the Congress Party of mollycoddling minorities (especially Muslims) and have expressed their detestation for the party's secular claims by routinely spelling the word as "sickular." Congress Party leaders have occasionally pandered to pro-Hindu sentiments, a development some call "soft-Hindutva," but the party has consistently stood in opposition to violence against Muslims. Such violence and marginalization of Muslims, however, is a major manifestation of Hindutvadis' contempt for India's secular republic.

Since Modi's rise to national power, Muslims (and some Dalits too) have been assaulted and killed for eating beef even as they are accused of resorting to "love jihad" (a conspiracy to seduce Hindu girls and convert them to Islam) and "population jihad" (an attempt to overtake Hindus, who are nearly 80 percent of the population as per the 2011 census). This is despite evidence that fertility rates for both Hindus and Muslims are related to educational and economic circumstances (Jeffery and Jeffery 2006) and population growth is declining faster among Muslims ("Poison of Demographic Prejudice" 2015: 7). The anti-Muslim violence and agitprop coincide with attempts to convert non-Hindus to Hinduism (Gupta 2018) even as it appears to be part of a calibrated attempt to eventually disenfranchise Muslims by branding them noncitizens (discussed further in Chapter 11).

Following Partition, most prominent and accomplished Muslims migrated to Pakistan. Most among those who decided to stay in India were extremely poor, and according to the 2006 Rajindar Sachar Committee report, India's Muslims lag behind other communities when it comes to government employment, access to health facilities and bank credit, education, and their overall economic condition (Prime Minister's High Level Committee 2006). Demonizing an already downtrodden population is a sure way to radicalize them, and in a region where Islamic fundamentalism is in sway and Islamic terror groups are looking to attack India, it is akin to playing with fire.

Muslim incursion into South Asia starting in the eighth century, Muslim-Mughal influence that led to Hindus converting to Islam, and violence associated with Partition all combine to promote the Islamophobia

undergirding Hindutva ideology. The inability to reconcile with the subcontinent's Islamic legacy and the subsequent British presence is what
causes Prime Minister Modi and other Hindutvadis to talk about 1,000
years of slavery.

This sense of humiliation has led to ridiculous claims designed to
portray Hinduism as part of a civilization par excellence. For instance,
Hindutvadis assert that the Taj Mahal is not a Mughal creation but was
originally a Hindu temple built by a Hindu king in honor of Shiva and
that prayers to Lord Shiva should therefore be allowed on its premises;
and that cars, plastic surgery, in vitro fertilization, stem cells, and air-
planes (traveling between planets around 7000 B.C.E.) were all invented
in ancient India. Recently a BJP member of parliament claimed that
"speaking in Sanskrit every day boosts the nervous system and keeps
diabetics and cholesterol at bay" (quoted in "Ganesh Singh's Statement
in Parliament" 2019: 11).

This attempt to reconstruct and rewrite history in ways that burnish
everything related to Hinduism is a long-standing Hindutva goal that is
now well under way. Consequently, new textbooks vilify non-Hindu
elements throughout Indian history and disregard the labors of Jawaharlal Nehru and Congress Party leaders while magnifying the roles of
Hindu heroes and nationalists (Traub 2018). Other Hindutva objectives
include banning cow slaughter (which is illegal in a number of states)
throughout India, banning Hindus from converting to other religions,
and instituting a uniform civil code (which will end the special rights
especially Muslims enjoy when it comes to marriage, divorce, and
inheritance). Two other long-standing goals, repealing Article 370 of the
constitution and building a temple for Lord Ram in Ayodhya (located
within the state of Uttar Pradesh), have now come to fruition.

The temple dispute is based on a dubious claim that the mosque
honoring the first Mughal emperor, Babur, was constructed on the spot
where the Hindu god Lord Ram was born. While the god Ram is a celebrated and venerated figure, there is no evidence that he was born in Ayodhya or anywhere else. But the dispute led to a Hindu mob demolishing
the early-sixteenth-century mosque in 1992 as part of a well-orchestrated
RSS campaign (Kaw 2010: 56). In November 2019, in a victory for Hindu
extremists, the Indian Supreme Court finally gifted the disputed site where
the mosque stood to Hindu entities, and in August 2020 the prime minister
ceremoniously laid the foundation stone to build a grand temple to Lord
Ram. One can expect the temple to be completed before the next general
elections, so that Modi and the BJP can benefit from it politically.

Article 370, on the other hand, took effect in 1949 and allowed the
only majority-Muslim state, of Jammu and Kashmir, to design its own

laws except on issues pertaining to foreign affairs, defense, and finance. In the process, it granted the state the right to its own constitution and flag, which other Indian states are not entitled to. Together with a subsequent addition (Article 35A), the state legislature was empowered to determine who qualified to be a permanent resident and own property in the region. This prevented non-Kashmiris from owning land and obtaining state scholarships and government jobs. As noted earlier, the policies were designed to accommodate predominantly Muslim Kashmiris within the Indian union when Pakistan claimed all of Kashmir. But the residential restrictions have long galled Hindu extremists, who would like to settle Hindus in the region and thereby transform its demographics. In August 2019, Prime Minister Modi's government annulled the statehood of Jammu and Kashmir and created two union territories that are directly governed from New Delhi. This is another victory for Hindu supremacists, for they can now gradually transform the region's demographics by flooding the area with Hindu settlers. These recent developments question the extent to which India will function within a secular ethos.

In 2001, a decade after India began gradually opening up its economy, an influential US scholar wondered if "India is destined always to be 'emerging' but never actually arriving" (Cohen 2001: 2). Two decades later, with India being the fifth largest economy in the world and expanding military ties to the United States, one may argue that the country has indeed "arrived" and will play a leading role in the twenty-first century. But India's ability to be a consequential and even indispensable player on the global stage will depend on internal cohesion. That in turn mandates camaraderie, especially between its Hindus and Muslims, which is more likely to be achieved in a pluralist and secular, as opposed to majoritarian Hindu, India.

The Chapters Ahead

The chapters that follow, by prominent scholars of India, seek to provide especially undergraduates an overarching understanding of the country. They provide context while emphasizing the most important aspects of the topic that is covered. Thus Chapter 2, by Douglas Hill, not only maps India's geographical features but also discusses how people's socioeconomic, political, and environmental lives are shaped by them. There are many Indias and Hill highlights how India's variegated geographies are linked to livelihoods, for "the outcome of economic, political, or social processes depends on where it occurs; whether it is in a town in the fertile Gangetic areas, a small village in the middle hills of the Himalayas, or a prosperous neighborhood of a bustling megacity."

Chapter 3, by Benjamin Cohen, provides an overview of India and South Asia's major historical periods, events, and some themes from the Indus Valley era (c. 2500 B.C.E.) to India's independence in 1947. Neither settled nor fixed, India's history is constantly being added to, challenged, and revised as new discoveries are made and new theoretical insights are applied to its lengthy past. The chapter divides India's past into a more nuanced scheme rather than the traditional tripartite ancient, medieval, and modern periods. Cohen brings to the fore the major dynasties and empires that have held sway over the subcontinent while alluding to some of the scholarly debates that have intervened in their narratives. Although far from comprehensive, this chapter provides a broad introduction and contextualization for modern India's history.

In Chapter 4, Eswaran Sridharan explains the resilience of democracy in India in the face of a low-income economy, widespread poverty, and immense religious and ethnic diversity; how the country's federal system is structured; and how political parties have evolved and their leaders have operated over the decades within the system. Sridharan discusses Arend Lijphart's notion of consociationalism (sharing power within democracy) to explain India's ability to function as a relatively stable polity. He also points to the country's sense of unity in diversity as another major reason for such stability. The latter, as noted earlier, is now being challenged due to Hindutva advocates feeling emboldened, and the dangers this poses for the country are discussed briefly in the final chapter.

Chapter 5, by Rahul Mukherji and Seyed Hossein Zarhani, discuss India's socialist economy and why and how the country embraced globalization and private entrepreneurship. In doing so, they point to a number of policies the Indian state has adopted in order to try to alleviate poverty. But they emphasize that, unlike in certain other states that developed in dramatic fashion, Indian leaders typically come to major decisions gradually. In short, extant policies get jettisoned only after alternative options tried incrementally prove more useful. When this happens amid a degree of institutional consensus, a tipping point is reached, upon which new policies become embedded. According to Mukherji and Zarhani, the successful transformative changes that take place economically in India are not based on the whim of a prime minister; they result after issues have been debated over time.

Chapter 6, by Sumit Ganguly, evaluates the key drivers that have influenced the country's external relations since it gained independence. Ganguly discusses specific events that conditioned India's foreign policy posture, the institutional sources that have influenced its foreign policy trajectories, and certain challenges it faces in the twenty-first century. In doing so, he emphasizes how the Indian independence movement and beliefs and practices of Prime Minister Jawaharlal Nehru impacted the country's postindependence foreign policy trajectory. China's rise and expanding tentacles in South Asia challenge India's influence in the Indo-Pacific. While the country participates in military exercise with the United States, Japan, and Australia to ensure its continued influence in the region, Ganguly suggests India may need to join the United States in a strategic partnership to balance meaningfully against a dominant China.

Chapter 7, by Christophe Jaffrelot, discusses the origins of the caste system and how both Dalits and the Other Backward Classes have used their numbers and the franchise to gradually organize, mobilize, and assert themselves in Indian politics. Jaffrelot discusses how Kanshi Ram gave rise to the Bahujan Samaj Party and the party's progress and impact on Indian politics (especially in Uttar Pradesh) over the past few elections. Caste was most salient when the *jajmani* system (which specified services across caste groups) operated and perpetuated hereditary caste-based employment. But that is less and less the case today. As Jaffrelot notes, caste still exists and is especially important when it comes to marriage, but the caste system is undergoing significant change, at least in urban areas.

Chapter 8, by Chad Bauman and Ainslie Embree, highlights how many religious systems have contributed to the complex mosaic of contemporary Indian life. Four of them—Buddhism, Jainism, Hinduism, and Sikhism—originated in South Asia and constitute over 80 percent of India's population. Three had their origins outside the subcontinent—Islam (by far the largest), Christianity, and Zoroastrianism. Bauman and Embree offer brief surveys of the historical development of these religions in India and emphasize their interaction with each other and their contributions to the larger society. These interactions have unfortunately been characterized by hostility, especially before and after Partition in 1947 and by the development of political parties stressing the dominance of Hindu culture over the religious groups that had their origins outside the subcontinent.

In Chapter 9, Lisa Trivedi looks at Indian women and identifies some of the common pitfalls in our thinking about women in modern India even as she introduces the turning points in the emergence of women as historical subjects and actors. Beginning with a discussion of the common misconceptions and paradoxes of women's position in contemporary Indian society, Trivedi explains how colonialism, nationalism, and the family have contributed to the particular political, social, and economic positions in which women live today. Her chapter also explores the roles of Indian women themselves in transforming society and their position within it over the course of more than a century. Finally, the chapter considers women's position in society in terms of education, politics, and work in the period following independence. New opportunities in the work force made possible by India's liberalized and growing economy are today challenging social roles and customs that have heretofore been the single most important influence on women's lives in India. Just how much women's social status will be changed by women themselves and how much it will change due to forces brought to bear upon society by the economy are questions for the century ahead.

Poverty, development, and urbanization have degraded India's air, land, and water to the point where it is today one of the most polluted counties. Indeed, fourteen of the world's fifteen most polluted cities are in India ("Dirty Work" 2018: 14). And this despite the country's constitution enjoining citizens to protect the environment. Chapter 10, on population, urbanization, and the environment, by Kelly Alley, discusses how ecological, hydrological, and planetary cycles impact Indian livelihoods and how India's National Green Tribunal and judiciary have dealt with challenges stemming from urbanization, environmental strains, and public health. Alley's chapter points to how citizen and judicial activism operate as a check on government even as certain authorities may seek to put development ahead of environmental well-being. The chapter also discusses how Indians at multiple levels are seeking to deal with environmental challenges in purposive and consequential ways.

Finally, Chapter 11 looks ahead to the challenges facing India. These challenges include the assault on democracy by Hindu nationalist forces. They certainly include Covid-19 and the way the coronavirus has exacerbated the difficulties facing the country economically.

At the end of World War II, no serious student of international affairs could afford to ignore the United States. Similarly, no serious student of international affairs today can afford to ignore India, for its actions too will increasingly affect the rest of the world for better or worse. The chapters that follow go a long way in helping students better comprehend the extraordinary and complex country that is India.

2

A Geographic Preface

Douglas Hill

The geography of India is as diverse and as interesting as the people that inhabit its varied landscapes. As well as being an extraordinary example of different landforms and ecosystems, India is also an important country to understand in terms of its economic, political, and social variations. In this chapter, a description of the physical geographies of India is complemented by an examination of the different dimensions of human development (including in terms of literacy, nutrition, and housing). In capturing the diversity of India's people, a significant focus of this chapter is the social and spatial characteristics of uneven development. Even though the Indian economy has been growing rapidly in recent years, the country continues to have very high levels of inequality, which means that there are strikingly different levels of well-being throughout the population. Indeed, it is a sobering reality that despite having a growing number of billionaires and other high-net-worth individuals (Credit Suisse 2018), India remains the country with the highest number of poor people anywhere in the world. As we will see, these variations can be understood broadly, although imperfectly, by describing people's livelihoods, where they live, and the social groups they belong to, including their gender, caste, class, and ethnicity.

This chapter uses the phrase "geographies of India" to describe how social, economic, political, or environmental processes shape and are shaped by interactions between people and environment. To use the term "geographies" rather than "geography" of India means that we are considering how these interrelated interactions occur in a way that is dynamic and accordingly changes over time. This is particularly important in a country as vast and varied as India because the outcome of economic, political, or social processes depends on where it occurs—whether it is in a town in the fertile Gangetic areas, a small village in the middle hills of the Himalayas, or a prosperous neighborhood of a bustling megacity.

The first part of the chapter describes some of the most important physical aspects of the environment in India, including climate, the influence of the monsoon on precipitation, and the characteristics of its major river basins. This part also presents a simplified typology of India's agro-ecological regions. The second part of the chapter extends the insights of the first part by illustrating some modifications to relations between people and environment, with a specific focus upon the postindependence period. This part includes examples from forests and agriculture. These two parts are useful not only for demonstrating the dynamic relationship that people have with the environment over time and space, but also for showing how forests and agriculture continue to be extremely important for rural people's livelihoods. As such, understanding the changes that have taken place in these areas also helps us to understand something of the rural environment and its relationship to poverty and employment.

The third part of the chapter turns more explicitly to an engagement with the human dimensions of India's geographies. It begins by examining population trends across India. One striking feature of contemporary India is the social and spatial unevenness of development across the country. This part of the chapter explores some of the social characteristics of uneven development across India, noting the continuing significance of caste, class, and gender in predicting levels of well-being among different segments of the population. It also notes that different regions of India have varying levels of poverty, wealth, and human development, reinforcing the necessity to spatialize the description of uneven development. I ultimately assert that these social and spatial dimensions need to be brought together (an approach geographers call socio-spatiality) to analyze patterns of India's uneven development.

The fourth part turns our attention to changes occurring in where people live throughout the country. Specifically, this part explores the rates of urbanization and describes these patterns in terms of different size categories of cities and towns. While the future of India clearly means a much greater proportion of the population living in urban centers than what we have seen in the past, I argue that changes to the economy, polity, and society in the post-liberalization era have resulted in an increasing socio-spatial segregation within India's cities. As such, the urban geographies of India's future are likely to include continuing poverty and deprivation for many people, while the growing middle and upper-middle-class segments of the population live in conditions that are closer to those that we historically have associated with countries of the global North.

The Physical Geography of India

India's varied landscapes encompass deserts in the west, alpine tundra and glaciers in the far north, large alluvial floodplains, as well as humid tropical regions supporting rainforests in the southwest and the island territories. As such, it is a country that defies easy generalization, and understanding this incredible diversity requires an examination of some of its major geographical features.

Climate and Precipitation

According to a globally recognized and frequently used system of classification for subclimates called the Köppen system, India hosts six major climatic zones, as well as many regionally specific, and starkly different, microclimates. These six zones are shown in Figure 2.1.

An important influence on India's climate is its mountains, including the Himalayas, which dominates the northern part of the country, as

The arid landscape of Rajasthan. Photo by Lynne Rienner.

Lush fields on the way from Chennai to Kodaikanal in Tamil Nadu. Photo by Joost Kaptijn.

well as smaller but significant ranges in the Eastern and Western Ghats of South India. Around 50 million years ago, the Indian plate, which had split off from the Pangea supercontinent and was moving northward, collided with the Eurasian plate, and the resulting folding and faulting by compressional forces led to what is known as the Himalayan uplift, creating the Himalayas and Tibetan Plateau.

This collision shaped the climate of the region in profound ways (Zhisheng et al. 2001). The Himalayas draw warm, moisture-laden air from the oceans and, as these systems move toward the mountains, they fall across different parts of the country as precipitation in a reasonably predictable temporal sequence, so that rain arrives in the southern regions before shifting northward. At the same time, the presence of these mountains acts as a barrier to the cold katabatic winds that would otherwise flow down from Central Asia. Together with the Thar desert in the northwest, the presence of the Himalayas moderates the climate of the Indian subcontinent significantly, which means that northern parts of the country are much milder in winter than they otherwise would be, while in summer this region becomes extremely hot. Figure 2.2 shows the process of the Himalayan uplift.

The interaction of the monsoon and the Himalayas is not uniform across all of India. Indeed, the monsoon weakens from east to west.

Figure 2.1   Major Climatic Zones of India

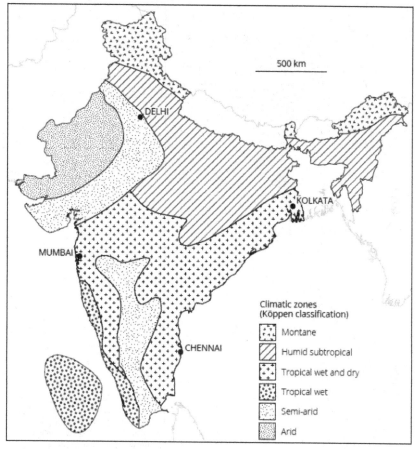

Source: Cartography by Chris Garden School of Geography, University of Otago. (Creative Commons License, Saravask, based on work by Planemad and Nichalp, March 2007.)

While parts of the east frequently receive more than 3,000 millimeters of rain annually, the far-western parts of the subcontinent often receive less than 300 millimeters. In contrast, snow and glacial melt is a far more important contributor to annual discharge in the Indus basin than it is in parts of the eastern Himalayas, such as the Brahmaputra subbasin.

The seasons in India are frequently categorized as falling into four distinct periods throughout the year, namely winter (January and February), summer (March to May), a monsoon season (June to September), and a post-monsoon (October to December). Much of western and central India receive more than 90 percent of their total annual precipitation

Figure 2.2   Himalayan Uplift

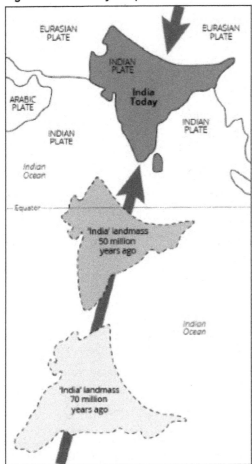

Source: Cartography by Chris Garden, School of Geography, University of Otago. (Adapted from *US Geological Survey*, https://pubs.usgs.gov/gip /dynamic/himalaya.html.)

during the summer monsoon, while the southern and northwestern parts of India receive about 50–75 percent of their total annual rainfall during the same period. The northeast monsoon (October–December), also known as post-monsoon rainfall, provides 10–20 percent of India's rainfall.

Unsurprisingly, then, the monsoon has played a vital role in the livelihoods of people living on the Indian subcontinent for millennia. Indeed, many cultural festivals in different parts of India are tied to agricultural cycles, including Baisakhi (April, especially in Punjab and Haryana), Pongal (mid-January, especially in Tamil Nadu), Bihu (April in Assam) and Onam (August–September in Kerala). Despite the tremendous increase in irrigation across different parts of India, the monsoon continues to be vital to agriculture and those whose liveli- hoods depend upon it. Even in the present day, at least 60 percent of total net sown area continues to be only rain-fed and thus largely dependent upon rain from this period. When the monsoon fails, it is a primary reason for much distress in rural India.

Water Resources and River Basins

Another important aspect of India's geography is its large river basins, which provide the water resources to sustain both the environment and a variety of human activities. Typically, Indian rivers are classified according to whether they originate in the Himalayas or the peninsular parts of the country. The northern part of India is dominated by two very large river basins, the Indus and Ganges-Brahmaputra-Meghna basins. Each of these basins takes their name from the largest and most impor- tant rivers flowing through the respective basins, although in each case the watersheds contain many smaller rivers that feed into each other as they progress from the high Himalayas across the floodplains before emptying out into the sea through extensive deltas. The Himalayan rivers actively shape the land they move through. Flowing down extremely steep gradients in the upper reaches near the headwater streams, they continually cut through rocks and erode new pathways, while continually shifting and meandering when they reach the floodplains.

The rivers of southern India originate from the peninsular and cen- tral highland regions and tend to be part of comparatively smaller basins, even though they still support huge numbers of people, as well as extensive biodiversity. These river systems are highly seasonal and dependent on monsoon rainfall. While Himalayan rivers are active, the peninsular rivers tend to be less prone to significant changes in their shape, moving as they do through a more fixed course in well-adjusted valleys. Figure 2.3 shows the major basins in different parts of the country and indicates where they discharge their waters into the ocean. It also indicates that large portions of the country face water scarcity problems, either occasionally or on an ongoing basis.

A feature of these river systems, particularly the Himalayan ones, is that they carry an enormous sediment load. As the rivers slow upon reaching the plains area, they deposit a huge amount of silt every year that significantly invigorates the fertility of the rich soils of northern India. This process is intensified because flooding is a regular part of the annual hydrological cycle, and as the rivers break their banks they deposit sediment across a still larger area, replenishing the existing soil.

Figure 2.3   Major River Basins in India and Water Scarcity

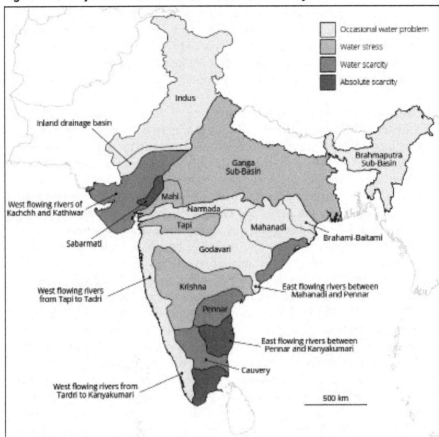

Source: Cartography by Chris Garden, School of Geography, University of Otago. (Based on Singh and Kumar 2018: 37.)

Indeed, about 40 percent of India's total land mass has rich alluvial soils, making this the predominant soil type in the northern plains of India, with other deposits found in the southern deltas of the Krishna, the Godavari, and the Mahanadi.

In contrast to the Gangetic plain to its north, much of the Deccan Plateau of the central part of India contains soil that is volcanic in origin. This black cotton soil, as it is frequently referred to, retains moisture very effectively, meaning that it is ideal for reducing the impacts of extended drought for farmers. Other parts of the country are marked by soil that is far less suitable for cultivation, with the saline soils of the Rann of Kutch in western Gujarat, for example, carrying very few nutrients. Similarly, only hardy crops like barley and millet can be grown in the arid soils of much of Rajasthan. Clearly, then, the livelihood strategies adopted by people in different parts of India reflect the need to respond to these variations. At the same time, in recent decades people have tried to supplement the fertility of soils in different parts of the country through the addition of synthetic fertilizers. While in the short term this has led to significant gains in yields, in the longer term it has stripped the soils of much of their fertility; as much as one-third of India's soil can now be classified as degraded.

Agro-Ecological Zones in a Changing Climate

With a huge variety in its geology, precipitation patterns, and soil types, as well as variations in the topography of different parts of the country, it is clear why India is home to some of the world's greatest biodiversity.[1] Table 2.1 summarizes some of the major features of India's diversity by dividing the country into five zones, following the simplified typology of the Central Research Institute for Dryland Agriculture (CRIDA). Several states feature in more than one agro-ecological zone.

The major features of each of these agro-ecological zones are listed in Table 2.2. It is evident that there are significant differences between these areas in terms of the size of the populations, the extent of urbanization, how heavily cultivated the land is and how much is under forest cover, and the relative importance of agriculture as a primary livelihood source compared to the service sector.

Unfortunately, as the climate changes, precipitation is becoming less reliable in many parts of India, including during the monsoon period. While there is significant variation between different parts of the country, in general a changing climate means that the rain that falls during the monsoon period does so over far fewer days, with significant consequences for agriculture (Taenzler et al. 2011). When the rain comes, it is more likely to be much heavier and intense than has been normal in previous eras. Unsurprisingly, in terms of the potential impacts of a changing climate, India is ranked among the most vulnerable large countries worldwide.

Extended periods of drought, as well as more frequent and intense flooding, are likely to become more common as the climate changes, with significant impacts for people and the environment. To take just one (albeit important) example, by 2050, glaciers in the Hindu Kush Himalaya ranges (of which India is a significant part) are projected to lose between one-third and two-thirds of their ice (Wester et al. 2019). These changes will have significant impacts for the Indo-Gangetic Plain, which will create issues for hundreds of millions of people in India, as well as those in neighboring countries.

Table 2.1   Simplified Typology of India's Agro-Ecological Regions

Agro-Ecological Zone	General Comments	States
Coastal areas and islands	The Indian coast is 7,517 kilometers long. It can be divided into the west coast, the eastern coastal plain, and the biodiversity-rich Indian islands.	Tamil Nadu, Karnataka, West Bengal, Odisha, Kerala, Maharashtra, Gujarat, Goa, Andhra Pradesh, Lakshadweep, Andaman, and Nicobar
Indo-Gangetic plain	The Indo-Gangetic plain is one of the most populous and productive agricultural ecosystems in the world. The region is a 400- to 800-kilometer-wide, low-relief, east-west zone between the Himalayas in the north and the peninsula in the south.	Punjab, Haryana, Uttar Pradesh, Bihar, and West Bengal
Central and peninsular India	The region covers most of India's rain-fed areas, contributing more than 40 percent of the country's food grain production.	Tamil Nadu, Karnataka, Madhya Pradesh, Jharkhand, Chhattisgarh, Odisha, Maharashtra, Andhra Pradesh and Telangana
Desert region	The Thar desert, covering 10 percent of the total geographic area of India, is the seventh largest desert in the world. Thar is also the world's most thickly populated desert.	Gujarat and Rajasthan
Himalayas	The Himalayas, which represent about 16.2 percent of the total area of the country, are not only a key watershed of India but also play a crucial role in the monsoon system.	Jammu and Kashmir, Himachal Pradesh, Uttarakhand, Sikkim, Arunachal Pradesh, Meghalaya, Mizoram, Manipur, Assam, Tripura, and Nagaland

Source: Derived from "How Vulnerable Are We?" 2019.

While the physical geography of India must be considered influential in how people have chosen to pursue their livelihoods, we should not be too deterministic in trying to attribute too much about contemporary India to its geographical features. Indeed, as much as geography has shaped people's lives, people have considerable agency in how they respond, and the adaptability of people in transforming the physical conditions of the country is a consistent theme throughout India's rich and varied history, including in the contemporary period.

Geographies of a Changing Environment

Describing the geography of India only in terms of the physical characteristics of climatic zones, patterns of hydrogeology, or biodiversity has limitations if analysis does not also consider the role of people in shaping their environment. In the postindependence period, India has built

Table 2.2   Characteristics of India's Agro-Ecological Regions

Agro-Ecological Region	Coastal Areas and Islands	Indo-Gangetic Plain	Central and Peninsular India	Desert Region	Himalayas
Population (millions)	201	433	452	50	47
Percentage rural/urban	53/47	73/27	69/31	70/30	80/20
Percentage net sown area/forest cover	42.3/21.7	68.0/7.3	45.3/23.1	45.7/23.8	14.5/47.0
Percentage livelihoods derived from agriculture/service sector	48.5/26.0	53.0/25.0	54.0/24.0	50.0/22.7	61.0/20.5

Source: Derived from "How Vulnerable Are We?" 2019.

many roads and railways, large-scale dams have diverted water and displaced many people, and the land has been extensively mined for coal, bauxite, and many other things. New cities have been built and existing urban areas have been extended. The ideology of state-led development under Nehru and beyond believes that the environment should be harnessed for the national good. In the contemporary era, the activities of the state have been supplemented by large-scale private sector companies. At the same time, local people often over-exploit the natural resource base as a form of small-scale livelihood.

Geographies of Forestry

We can see the way that people have interacted with and modified the environment through examining changes taking place in the forest sector. Historically, many people living in rural India relied upon forests for a significant part of their livelihoods, including for fuelwood, fodder, medicines, and a range of ecosystem services. This dependence was greater among women and the poorest people within the society. At the same time, in many parts of India there was a tradition of certain parts of the forest being designated as sacred groves, which afforded these areas special significance in the religious and cultural life of villagers and also placed restrictions on how these parts of the forest could be utilized.

Although forests underwent significant changes at different points of time over hundreds of years with successive empires (Habib 2015), there was an unusually important shift accompanying British colonialism. Initially, the arrival of the British into India brought little change to the way that forests were utilized or valued. However, with the desire to extend the railway system across the Indian subcontinent, forests were soon incorporated into a bureaucratic system of management based on

Western understandings of silviculture. Indeed, the formation of the Indian Forest Department in 1864 and legislative changes in 1865 and again in 1878 meant that vast swathes of biodiverse forests were henceforth collapsed into three different categories of forests that were applied throughout British India (Gadgil and Guha 1995).

Within these three categories, most forests were for immediate use and were classified as reserved. A smaller, yet still significant, proportion were classified as protected. These areas were typically difficult to access and some of them were set aside because of their high conservation value. As the protected forests became more accessible through road-building and the extension of other infrastructure, a great deal of them were reclassified as reserved forest. By far the smallest of the forested area belonged to the third category, forest set aside for use by villages. In all cases, the state maintained a right to restrict access to these resources and held a monopoly on any species deemed valuable.

The institutionalization of Western scientific knowledge (Cohen 1996; Guha 1996) clearly altered the trajectory of forestry within the Indian subcontinent. Forests were thought about in instrumental terms as a resource to be scientifically managed to ensure maximum yields.[2] On the other hand, the reclassification of forests in this way also significantly negatively impacted the livelihoods of villages adjacent to forests, particularly if they had historically depended upon resources from these forests but were no longer able to access them because of this reclassification.

The geographies of forestry did not remain static in postindependence India. Significant civil society mobilization in the 1970s refocused attention upon how forests were being used and the difficulties this created for local people. The Forest Act of 1980 was intended to reduce the potential for inappropriate activities and to promote conservation, but these aspirations were not realized in practice. In response to a perceived fuelwood crisis, the World Bank established its Social Forestry Programme in the early 1980s, focused on seeding deforested areas with nonindigenous eucalyptus plantations.

The understanding and use of forests shifted again from 1988 when participatory forest management became more significant through a scheme called joint forest management. Under this scheme, villagers assist in the protection and rehabilitation of degraded forests and in return receive a share of the timber harvest and access to nontimber forest products. This kept the focus on forests as a resource to be utilized for the broader economy but also tried to incorporate local livelihoods by getting villages to participate in the regeneration and upkeep of forests near to them in co-management with the forest department. Since this time, there have been further legislative changes by governments of different ideological persuasions to either enable or constrain the rights of poor people to access and utilize forest resources. When these rights have conflicted with the interests of mining companies or hydropower developers, the forest-dependent people have frequently seen their access removed (Oskarsson 2013).

Another fault-line evident in how forest should be utilized relates to those habitats for endangered wildlife. As the most prominent advocates of wilderness areas are sometimes middle-class urban dwellers, forests are often treated as a rarefied category of the natural world, to be managed by different strategies than those areas of settled agriculture that are fringed with forests. While the environmental movement is an important aspect of how biodiverse parts of India are contested, some forested areas demonstrate the divisions within this movement, as wildlife advocates seek to reduce the access of forest-dependent peoples (but not eco-tourists) to India's national parks.

Modifying the Agricultural Environment

A similar shift in people's relationship to their physical environment as has been outlined in the case of the forestry sector can be seen if we trace changes to agriculture in the postcolonial era. In the early twentieth century, while the British continued to rule much of the Indian subcontinent, agriculture was growing at a relatively modest rate. Many scholars have argued that the relative stagnation of agriculture during this period is because rents were able to be collected by those who held various forms of title rather than for a need to invest for changes in productivity.

Agriculture took on a different character in the immediate postindependence and land use changed accordingly. Again, however, the structure of society influenced how land was distributed and utilized. Specifically, the political difficulties associated with initiating significant land reform or land redistribution meant that most of the initial growth of agriculture came from reclaiming wasteland (Corbridge and Harriss 2000). Indeed, even fifty years after independence, the total area of land under cultivation increased by little more than 20 percent, while India's total population increased by about three times during the same period.

Early experiments with intensifying agriculture occurred in the northwest of the country (particularly in the Punjab and Haryana) and in coastal Andhra Pradesh in the southeast. These regions were chosen for these initial experiments in changes to agricultural productivity because they already had existing irrigation. The Green Revolution, which began in the late 1960s and became more widespread as the decades progressed, was also built upon the necessity for irrigation, with the government constructing canals and sinking tube wells, and eventually private operators began to do the same (Sathyamurthy 1995). The utilization of groundwater revolutionized agriculture within India, and other parts of the country subsequently began to undertake similar intensification. The eastern state of West Bengal, for example, did not see this transformation to a great extent until the mid-1980s onward, despite highly favorable potential conditions for agriculture (Rogaly et al. 1995). The intensification of agriculture as a consequence of the Green Revolution resulted in significant increases in the amount of food that has been able to be produced within India, so much so that the country now has reasonable food security and is emerging as a major exporter of many crops.

While the impact of the Green Revolution has been profound in terms of increasing food production, there have clearly been some drawbacks as well (Vaidyanathan 2010; Shah 2008). High-yielding varieties of seeds, fertilizers, and pesticides meant that the cost of inputs for farmers skyrocketed. This particularly became the case as the land lost some of its productivity and the amount of fertilizer, pesticides, and water that needed to be added grew more significant as time went on. The strains of the intensification of agriculture have intensified further in recent years, to the extent that it has been common to describe the sector as at a point of agrarian crisis (Narasimha Reddy and Mishra 2010).

As the country has grown richer, agriculture is diversifying, although this is not always based on the most appropriate crops for the regions concerned. For example, in Maharashtra, sugarcane is grown on only about 4 percent of farmed land but consumes 72 percent of the state's irrigated water. Bolstered by patronage from state politicians who benefit from the industry, 79 percent of this water-intensive crop is grown in drought-prone regions such as Marathwada (Mohan 2015).

Sugarcane farming in areas inappropriate to the conditions is just one example of the significant environmental cost of the changing geographies of agriculture. Close to half of India's total geographical area is affected by serious soil erosion through ravines and gullies, shifting cultivation, cultivated wastelands, sandy areas, deserts, and water logging. Groundwater is now over-extracted in many parts of the country to an extent that is among the worst of anywhere in the world (Shah 2010). Further, the quality of surface water is extremely poor in many parts of the country, with significant implications for health. Despite agricultural surplus and shifting food preferences among the wealthier sections of society away from staple foods (Amarasinghe et al. 2007), India has among the highest rates of stunting and malnutrition in the world, reminding us that these are issues of distribution within the population rather than just about how much food is being produced.

The Geographies of Uneven Human Development
Population Growth and Future Prospects

India is the world's second most populous country after China, with approximately 1.34 billion people calling the country home in 2017. Because China's population has stabilized and is now growing older, India is on track to become the world's most populous country in the coming years. Figure 2.4 shows the projections of how India's population will age upward until 2050.

There is little question that the rapid growth of population in the postindependence period has created many challenges for India, including in terms of employment, infrastructure, health, and well-being. At the same time, some commentators are optimistic about what they describe as the potential for a demographic dividend in the future as the country's young population matures into a large work force, at the same time as many other countries around the world are struggling with aging populations. However, other commentators suggest that

Figure 2.4   Comparison of India's Demographic Profile in 2014 and Projected Profile in 2050

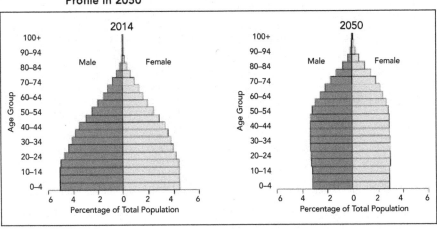

Source: Bloom and Eggleston 2014: 3. (Adapted by Chris Garden, School of Geography, University of Otago.)

India's changing demographic composition will not become a dividend, but rather a burden, if it cannot ensure that this population is skilled and healthy and has meaningful employment. Table 2.3 gives population totals for twenty-one of the major states. Note that Andhra Pradesh figures include the area that has become the state of Telangana.

As well as illustrating how quickly the population has grown in a comparatively short period of time, the table also gives a sense of the enormity of India's population and how it is dispersed across the country. The most populous state in India, Uttar Pradesh, had a population of more than 220 million in 2016, meaning that it is larger than all but a handful of countries worldwide. Just as significant, it demonstrates that population growth is quite uneven across states. Indeed, while some of these major states are continuing to grow quickly, the population growth of many other states has considerably slowed. Demographers have pointed to a significant variance in total fertility rates between states, such that only a handful of states are now above the 2.1 children per woman that is considered replacement level for a population. Table 2.4

Table 2.3   Population of Major States, 2001–2016

State Name	2001	2011	2016
Andhra Pradesh[a]	79,226,000	87,072,000	89,773,000
Assam	27,758,000	32,115,000	33,973,000
Bihar	86,627,000	107,219,000	117,311,000
Chhattisgarh	21,730,000	26,361,000	28,554,000
Goa	1,400,000	1,498,000	1,524,000
Gujarat	52,801,000	62,259,000	66,489,000
Haryana	22,038,000	26,147,000	28,009,000
Himachal Pradesh	6,322,000	7,055,000	7,330,000
Jammu/Kashmir	10,583,000	12,956,000	14,099,000
Jharkhand	28,103,000	34,023,000	36,817,000
Karnataka	55,016,000	62,961,000	66,240,000
Kerala	33,037,000	34,264,000	34,318,000
Madhya Pradesh	62,904,000	74,879,000	80,345,000
Maharashtra	100,858,000	115,750,000	121,951,000
Orissa	38,294,000	43,180,000	45,094,000
Punjab	25,343,000	28,516,000	29,749,000
Rajasthan	58,919,000	70,802,000	76,330,000
Tamil Nadu	64,962,000	74,297,000	78,143,000
Uttar Pradesh	173,227,000	205,839,000	220,671,000
Uttarakhand	8,846,000	10,431,000	11,140,000
West Bengal	83,419,000	94,031,000	98,182,000

Source: World Bank Subnational Population Database, https://datacatalog.worldbank.org /dataset/subnational-population-database.

Note: a. The numbers for Andhra Pradesh include the population of Telangana, a region of Andhra Pradesh that became a state in 2014.

showcases the nine major states that are above replacement level fertility. Although all have seen their fertility rates drop rapidly compared to previous decades, none of these states have yet to fully undertake the demographic transition toward lower birthrates and low death rates that are now characteristic of many other parts of the world.

Clearly, the population will continue to increase most rapidly in the northern and central parts of the country, an area that includes several states with very large existing populations (such as Bihar or Uttar Pradesh). While parts of southern India have seen rapid increases in the past, the populations in states like Kerala, Goa, or Tamil Nadu are likely to move more quickly to a profile resembling a middle-income country.

What might explain the differences in population growth in different parts of India? Certainly, India's significant reduction in poverty has contributed, although this is only part of the explanation. A wealth of evidence suggests that women have fewer children when they marry later, allow greater time between pregnancies, and have reliable access to basic services. Those states that have seen a significant stabilization of the population, such as Kerala, also typically have higher literacy levels of women and greater gender equality.

Uneven Development as a Spatial Phenomenon

In comparing the differences between states in India, a significant feature of the geographies of India has been uneven development (Hill 2013). Indeed, while much of India's inequality of opportunity is due to historical legacies, the continuation of these inequalities reflects contemporary biases within society. Opportunities for social and economic mobility differ significantly depending on whether the family one is

Table 2.4   Total Fertility Rates of Selected Indian States, 2016

State	Total Fertility Rate	Region of India
Uttar Pradesh	3.3	Northern
Bihar	3.3	Northern
Madhya Pradesh	2.8	Central
Rajasthan	2.7	Northwestern
Jharkhand	2.6	Northern
Chhattisgarh	2.5	Central
Haryana	2.3	Northern
Gujarat	2.3	Western
Andhra Pradesh	2.2	Southern

Source: Government of India, Niti Ayog, https://niti.gov.in/content/total-fertility-rate-tfr -birth-woman.

born into is from a tribal community, a middle-class professional, or a wealthy industrialist family, and whether one is a man or a woman.

Attempts to understand differences between people in India have historically relied upon a poverty line, which measures the percentage of the population who are below a certain income level thought to be the minimum necessary to be able to acquire basic necessities. In recent years, the suitability of such poverty lines has been questioned, not least because of disagreements about the appropriate income level that such a line should be set at, with India's poverty line frequently significantly below those used in other parts of the world (Deaton and Kozel 2005).

Increasingly, the development community around the world has taken to understanding levels of poverty in terms of a human development index or the multi-poverty index (Alkire and Seth 2008). These approaches are based on the idea that there are significant limitations to thinking about poverty only in terms of income levels.[3] The most prominent example of this approach is the Human Development Index (HDI) of the United Nations Development Programme. In 2019, India was ranked 129th in the world with an overall HDI score of 0.647. Table 2.5 provides some illustrative variables that are used to calculate this index and how India fares under these measures. These measures are linked to the Sustainable Development Goals (SDGs) of the United Nations.

A significant finding from this table is that India is richer than would be expected for a country of its comparatively low HDI ranking. The inequality-adjusted HDI suggests that, as India's economy has grown, the gains from increases in gross national income have not been effectively translated into widespread gains in aspects of human development, such as health, education, or sanitation. A clear factor in these failures is India's consistent levels of inequality. Indeed, according to the World

Table 2.5   Selected Variables of the Human Development Index

	Life Expectancy at Birth	Expected Years of Schooling	Mean Years of Schooling	Gross National Income per Capita (2011 purchasing power parity US dollar equivalent)	Inequality-Adjusted HDI
Related Sustainable Development Goal (SDG)	SDG 3	SDG 4.3	SDG 4.6	SDG 8.5	
All-India total	69.4	12.3	6.5	6,829	0.538

Source: United Nations Development Programme, *Human Development Reports*, http://hdr.undp.org/en/countries/profiles/IND#.

Bank's database of 2005 to 2015, there were only five countries in the world with higher income inequality than India. Perhaps just as troubling is the fact that of these most unequal countries, only India has seen an increase in inequality over the past decade (Himanshu 2019).

Table 2.6 provides examples of Human Development Index scores for different parts of India, with a higher score indicating a higher level of human development. This is broken up into statewide demarcations of the HDI and clearly demonstrates some significant differences between parts of the country.

Clearly, assessing changes to the HDI within India over time demonstrates that most states have made significant improvements, particularly since 2001. However, Table 2.6 also illustrates some big differences between the major states in terms of the HDI rankings. To put these figures in perspective, if Kerala, Goa, or Himachal Pradesh were individual countries, they would be classified as having high human development and would globally rank approximately 76th, 86th, and 103rd respectively. These HDI rankings are like those of countries such

Table 2.6 HDI for Selected Indian States, 1991–2017

Region	1991	2001	2011	2017
All-India total	0.435	0.502	0.590	0.643
Andhra Pradesh	0.428	0.484	0.590	0.646
Assam	0.415	0.493	0.574	0.610
Bihar	0.382	0.440	0.524	0.572
Chhattisgarh	0.567	0.564	0.571	0.609
Goa	0.557	0.621	0.749	0.756
Gujarat	0.475	0.533	0.612	0.668
Haryana	0.471	0.554	0.643	0.704
Himachal Pradesh	0.484	0.596	0.671	0.721
Jammu and Kashmir	0.498	0.536	0.652	0.684
Jharkhand	0.567	0.564	0.572	0.595
Karnataka	0.449	0.524	0.613	0.678
Kerala	0.550	0.610	0.719	0.774
Madhya Pradesh	0.410	0.465	0.546	0.602
Maharashtra	0.498	0.563	0.652	0.692
Orissa	0.404	0.462	0.545	0.602
Punjab	0.501	0.581	0.665	0.719
Rajasthan	0.406	0.474	0.556	0.625
Tamil Nadu	0.476	0.549	0.656	0.704
Telangana	0.622	0.628	0.635	0.665
Uttar Pradesh	0.401	0.468	0.542	0.593
Uttaranchal	0.634	0.631	0.638	0.680
West Bengal	0.445	0.508	0.579	0.636

Source: Global Data Lab Subnational Human Development Index, https://globaldatalab.org /shdi/shdi/?levels=1%2B4&interpolation=0&extrapolation=0&nearest_real=0.

as Sri Lanka, China, and Samoa. In contrast, the HDI values of Orissa, Jharkhand, Madhya Pradesh, or Uttar Pradesh would see them classified as medium human development, with a global ranking around 141st, like countries such as Kenya, Laos, and Vanuatu.

The Subregional Dimensions of Poverty in India

A significant issue with understanding the spatial distribution of poverty throughout India is that there are infrequently classifications that include subregions within states. This can be a problem because the overall ranking of the state does not capture the extent of deprivation occurring within specific regions. For example, one of India's wealthiest states, Maharashtra, includes India's commercial capital, Mumbai, as well as much poorer inland areas.

An exception to this general problem is the work of Mehta and Shah (2003), whose focus is on those who have been in poverty for five years or more—those whom they refer to as living in chronic poverty. Although the data they use are now somewhat dated, this remains a significant example of the spatial unevenness of development within and between states in India. Each of the regions listed in Table 2.7 have a large percentage of the people living there classified as poor. Within that category, there is a further subcategory of those that might be considered very poor, that is those whose incomes are less than three quarters of the poverty line. Since these calculations pre-date the more recent bifurcation of some states, they include regions that in the contemporary period belong to new states that did not exist at that time (such as Jharkhand and Chhattisgarh).

Table 2.7   Rural Regions with High Concentrations (in percentage) of Severe Poverty, 1993–1994

State/Region	Very Poor	Poor	Severely Poor
Southwestern Madhya Pradesh	42.24	68.20	2.04
Southern Uttar Pradesh	39.70	66.74	2.19
Southern Orissa	34.08	69.02	1.77
Inland central Maharashtra	28.91	50.20	3.01
Southern Bihar	31.57	62.44	5.66
Northern Bihar	27.62	58.68	9.99
Central Uttar Pradesh	26.79	50.20	5.15
Central Bihar	24.66	54.03	5.95
Southern Madhya Pradesh	22.37	46.36	1.55
Eastern Uttar Pradesh	23.20	48.60	11.05
Total			48.36

Source: Mehta and Shah 2003.

Table 2.8 is also derived from the work of Mehta and Shah (2003), but this time shows the ten urban regions that contain the most significant concentrations of the poor. Taken together, these ten rural regions and ten urban regions accounted for more than three-quarters of India's total numbers of those classified as severely poor in 1993–1994. Although we should not discount the fact that there are poor people living throughout different parts of the country, clearly it is overwhelmingly these regions that have the greatest numbers of those living in severe poverty. Unsurprisingly, these subregions continue to contain large numbers of people in these conditions, despite the time that has passed and the economic growth that India has experienced since 1995.

The Social Geographies of India's Uneven Development: Caste and Class

While the preceding discussion has established the spatial characteristics to the uneven geographies of development in India, this analysis needs to also be refined by describing the social geographies of this unevenness. For example, there have been (and continues to be) significant differences in the quality of life and the opportunities for different people in India depending on the social group they belong to. People who are born into the lowest rungs of the caste hierarchy (including Dalits, the erstwhile Untouchables) and tribal people (Adivasis) are disproportionately represented in the proportion of poorest people. Indeed, for 2011–2012, in rural areas the highest level of poverty (43 percent) was seen among Adivasis, followed by Dalits (29 percent), compared to 22 percent for all classes (Himanshu 2015: 32).

Table 2.8   Urban Regions with High Concentrations of Severe Poverty (in percentage), 1993–1994

State/Region	Very Poor	Poor	Severely Poor
Inland central Maharashtra	42.62	60.13	3.69
Southwestern Madhya Pradesh	36.60	57.14	2.28
Inland eastern Maharashtra	38.99	59.32	5.32
Southern Uttar Pradesh	37.54	72.52	1.67
Inland northern Karnataka	36.49	57.63	5.92
Central Madhya Pradesh	32.93	53.68	2.25
Inland northern Maharashtra	32.28	56.94	2.76
Southern Orissa	33.53	45.64	0.51
Southern Madhya Pradesh	27.90	57.23	1.09
Southern Tamil Nadu	24.82	48.13	3.62
Total			29.11

Source: Mehta and Shah 2003: 495.

There is clearly a class dimension to the deprivation of Dalits and Adivasis. Most poor people from these backgrounds work in the unorganized sectors such as small-scale industries or as casual agricultural laborers or marginal farmers, who are involved in low-wage, unskilled, or semi-skilled occupations. Significantly, the greatest number of those who are both lower-class and lower-caste are largely concentrated in those parts of India outlined in Tables 2.7 and 2.8. Indeed, the difficulty of moving out of poverty for people in these areas is intensified by the fact that they often have few assets and are trapped in exploitative and adversarial social relations (Harriss-White 2003). In these areas, agriculture is frequently only for subsistence crops and low level of input use. Diversification into nonagricultural occupations is limited and frequently involves outmigration to other parts of the country. Public services, such as those related to education, nutrition, health, or the public distribution of food are limited, and where they do exist, governance issues and corruption frequently mean that the intended beneficiaries are not able to access them (Swaminathan 2000).

Significant changes have occurred throughout Indian society with regard to the prominence of caste relations as a determinant of quality of life, and in many places this is arguably not as significant as it once was. However, India still clearly suffers from entrenched social inequalities that can be broadly, if imperfectly, understood with reference to caste categories. Indeed, those who belong to higher castes typically have higher rates of literacy, live longer, and are healthier than those who belong to the very bottom of the caste hierarchy. Similarly, Muslims (particularly those in urban areas) tend to have poorer outcomes in terms of measurements of human development than do Hindus, although these are like the poor outcomes of Hindus in the bottom of the social strata.

Therefore, in addition to spatial differences in uneven development we can also see that there are social categories of disadvantaged groups within the population. However, in joining these two approaches together to consider the socio-spatial dimensions of uneven development, we can see that in most places there are differences in the HDI of different social categories even in those places that have comparatively better outcomes. Thus, people born of a lower caste are typically still worse off in Kerala than those born of a higher caste in that state, even though those differences between social groups are not as significant in Kerala as they are in a northern state such as Uttar Pradesh.

Uneven Development and the Geographies of Gender

Along with class and caste, another significant point of geographical difference within India can be seen with regard to gender relations.

Throughout the country, women face a range of barriers to the full realization of their capabilities to a greater extent than their male counterparts. They tend to have fewer assets and lower levels of nutrition and education, and are frequently denied a voice in decisionmaking institutions. Their employment opportunities are constrained and therefore they find themselves working in jobs that are poorly paid and physically demanding. At the time of marriage, a woman often must leave their home and go and live with their new husband (and frequently his parents). In those parts of India that have exogenous marriage patterns, this often means that the new bride is relocating to an area a considerable distance from her own family home. Because of the combination of all these interrelated vulnerabilities, women are disadvantaged relative to men (Dasgupta 1993).

Unsurprisingly there is also a substantial difference between men and women when it comes to human development. Indeed, in 2018, India's overall Human Development Index was 0.574 for women compared to 0.692 for men (United Nations Development Programme 2018). Many authors who try to understand the extent of gendered bias within society use an indicator called the sex ratio. This is the number of women in the population for every 1,000 men. In societies with comparatively little gender discrimination, the number of women to men in a population is frequently at parity or even slightly above. In India, there are several reasons why gender discrimination leads to fewer women in the population: these may include the prevalence of female infanticide, or that girl children receive less access to healthcare or nutritious food. Table 2.9 gives a sense of these differences in the sex ratio in selected states.

One of the clearest findings from Table 2.9 is that the sex ratio in many parts of India is not necessarily improving, and even in some high-performing states (such as Kerala) these ratios have stalled over time and in some cases are becoming worse. An important distinction evident in the table is that there are very different patterns of gender relations in northern India compared to southern India. Specifically, the female-to-male ratio in northern India is very low by global standards, reflecting significant discrimination against women within this part of the country. In contrast, the sex ratio in southern India is comparatively better, particularly in states such as Kerala and Tamil Nadu.

It is also important to note that there are some perhaps counterintuitive aspects to the dimensions of gender inequality across different parts of India. Specifically, some of the wealthiest parts, including the agriculturally prosperous part of the northwest in states such as Punjab and Haryana, also have some of the worst sex ratios. Patriarchal norms, female infanticide, and son-preference are all significant here. On the other hand, states with high proportions of Tribal populations (or

Table 2.9   Sex Ratio in Selected Indian States, 2005–2007 to 2013–2015
(number of females per thousand males)

Region	2005–2007	2007–2009	2009–2011	2013–2015
Chhattisgarh	969	980	991	961
Gujarat	891	904	909	854
Haryana	843	849	854	831
Karnataka	926	944	950	939
Kerala	958	968	965	967
Odisha	933	941	946	950
Punjab	837	836	841	889
Rajasthan	865	875	878	861
Tamil Nadu	944	929	926	911
Uttar Pradesh	881	874	875	879

Source: Derived from Government of India, Niti Ayog, https://niti.gov.in/content/sex-ratio
-females-1000-males.

Adivasis, as they are known), such as Chhattisgarh and Odisha, frequently have less gender discrimination than other states, despite being poorer and having worse human development overall.

Similar patterns can be observed with regard to literacy rates among women, which also display significant disparities between parts of the country. The average literacy rate for women was 65.5 percent, and for men it was 82.1 percent according to the census of India in 2011. Again, literacy rates in the southern states are in general far better than in the northern ones, including within similar social groups.

A huge range of literature has argued that the levels of female literacy within society are a powerful driver of social change and can have impacts upon many facets of human development, including health, nutrition, mortality, and morbidity (Dreze and Sen 2002; Dasgupta 1993). The continuing discrimination against women in different parts of the country regarding literacy levels should therefore be read as a significant inhibitor of the potential of those societies.

The Urban Geographies of India's Future

Another important aspect of the changing geographies of India relates to where people live and the conditions under which they do so. Indeed, the country continues to have comparatively low levels of urbanization, but in coming years this will shift significantly. Official estimates put the rate of urbanization at only 31 percent; however, many scholars argue that this figure is too low, because the methodology used to estimate who is living in an urban area underestimates changes in the boundaries between the rural and the urban areas. Certainly, the percentage of the total population who are living in urban areas has increased over the long term (see Table 2.10). Nevertheless, what is striking in examining the long-term trends in urbanization is that recent years have not seen a seismic shift in the number of people moving to urban areas.

Urbanization in Comparative Perspective

Even if the exponential annual population growth rates have not shifted that much, what is certainly significant is that the size of towns that they are moving to, and living in, is changing. Table 2.11 gives a sense of different categories of cities in India according to the size of their population. It is striking that cities with more than 100,000 people are now home to more than two-thirds of the urban population.

Projections from the McKinsey Growth Institute suggest that India's urban population will grow from 340 million as of 2008 to 590 million in 2030, with sixty-eight cities having a population of more than 1 million (Sankhe et al. 2010). Similarly, the United Nations estimates that by 2030, India will have seven megacities, as Mumbai, Delhi, and Kolkata are joined by Ahmedabad, Bangalore, Chennai, and Hyderabad (United Nations Department of Economic and Social Affairs 2014).

If we disaggregate the patterns of urban growth according to the states that are urbanizing fastest, we see that recent decades have seen a changing trend whereby it is the wealthiest states that are urbanizing the quickest. In the early years of the postindependence period this was not the case; it was the poorer states that were urbanizing fastest (although it must be understood that they were coming from a lower base of urbanization). In contrast, in the post-liberalization era it is the wealthier states where urbanization is most significant. States like Tamil Nadu, Gujarat,

Table 2.10   Number of Towns and Percentage and Growth of Urban Population in India, 1901–2001

Census Year	Number of Towns/Urban Areas	Urban Population as Percentage of Total Population	Annual Exponential Growth of Urban Population
1901	1,827	10.84	
1921	1,949	11.18	0.79
1941	2,250	13.86	2.77
1961	2,365	17.97	2.34
1981	3,378	23.34	3.83
2001	4,368	27.78	2.73

Source: Kundu 2011: 8.

Table 2.11   Urban Population in Different Size Towns, 1901–2001 (percentages)

Census Year	Class I	Class II	Class III	Class IV	Class V	Class VI
1901	26.00	11.29	15.64	20.83	20.14	6.10
1921	29.70	10.39	15.92	18.29	18.67	7.03
1941	38.23	11.42	16.35	15.78	15.08	3.14
1961	51.42	11.23	16.94	12.77	6.87	0.77
1981	60.37	11.63	14.33	9.54	3.58	0.50
2001	68.67	9.67	12.23	6.84	2.36	0.23

Source: Kundu 2011: 19.
Note: Class I = 100,000 or more population; Class II = 50,000–99,999 population; Class III = 20,000–49,999 population; Class IV = 10,000–19,999 population; Class V = 5,000–9,999 population; Class VI = under 5,000 population.

and Maharashtra are all above, or at least equal to, the national average. The poorest states, like Orissa, Bihar, and Jharkhand, are mainly below the national average (Kundu 2011).

Geographies of the New Urban India: Socio-Spatial Differentiation Within Cities

India's economy has been growing rapidly in the past two decades and much of this growth has been centered in its major cities. While manufacturing has not reached the heights that many had hoped it would, much of India's economic growth has been spurred through consumption and service sector growth. The much vaunted middle class has propelled much of this growth (Hill 2016). Analysis by Himanshu (2019) suggests that in 2011–2012, the top 20 percent of the population were responsible for 45 percent of consumption expenditure, compared to 8 percent for the bottom 20 percent. The government of India, and particularly state governments, have facilitated growth in cities through a range of different regulatory changes designed to stimulate investment. These have included extended tax holidays for the information technology sectors and special economic zones for software parks and high-end retail and residential areas. Since land acquisition within already crowded large cities is problematic (Levien 2012), much of the new infrastructure that has emerged in the past twenty years has taken place in satellite cities strategically located on the outskirts of New Delhi, Mumbai, Kolkata, Hyderabad, Bangalore, and Chennai (Hill and Athique 2013; Shaw and Satish 2007). As prices in these areas have risen, this growth has spread to smaller cities.

However, a range of commentators have argued that the fruits of this growth have been only narrowly distributed and that the spatial transformation of India's cities reflects these biases. Those such as Chatterjee (2004) and Fernandes (2004) have argued that cities are becoming refashioned in the image and desires of the middle and upper-middle classes, and that this is leading to a socio-spatial segregation of India's cities. Commentators such as Hill and Athique (2013) and Gooptu (2009) have documented the cultural changes that have accompanied the liberalization era to argue that prosperous groups within the city are consciously attempting to distance themselves from the poor through the creation of exclusivist residential, retail, and leisure infrastructure. Shopping malls, multiplex cinemas, and theme parks have become social spaces in which the culture of the new India is being played out by the consuming classes. The photo of Crown Plaza shows an example of this built environment.

In contrast to these additions to the built environment reflecting a "new India" of prosperity, many parts of India's cities have struggled to keep up with the demands of growing populations. Adequate access to water, sanitation, transport, and housing is difficult for a large proportion of people in India's cities (D'Souza 2019; Wankhade 2015;

Crown Plaza, Faridabad, National Capital Region. Photo by Adrian Athique.

A common-looking slum. Photo by Adrian Athique.

Athreya et al. 2010). Indian cities also continue to be highly gendered, as women have fewer rights to public space than men (Phadke 2007).

Successive governments have tried a range of urban renewal programs to combat some of these issues, including the Jawaharlal Nehru National Urban Renewal Mission (JNNURM) of the Congress Party–led United Progressive Alliance (UPA) government and the Smart Cities Mission of the current BJP-led (National Democratic Alliance (NDA) government.[4] Critics have argued that these schemes have been poorly coordinated, and their implementation has often served to reinforce the elite bias of urban transformation in India. As the photo of a slum demonstrates, low-income housing often exists near these new facilities. Clearly, if India's future is to be increasingly urban, as looks likely, there are no guarantees that the cities of the future will be inclusive or sustainable.

Conclusion

The diversity of India—a vast and varied subcontinental-scale country—is astounding. But a changing climate has created increased uncertainty, particularly for the most marginalized and vulnerable people within the population. We can think about this uneven development both in social and spatial terms. At the same time, thinking about the socio-spatial differences in development outcomes within India only in terms of differences between states is deceptive, because many of these states also have significant differences within them. In a general sense, the areas of the country where there are the most significant pockets of chronic poverty and deprivation are the inland areas of central and northern India. People living in areas that continue to depend upon rain-fed agriculture rather than improved irrigation are typically worse off than those living in areas where livelihood opportunities are more diverse. Similarly, people living in remote mountainous regions with poor connectivity usually have fewer livelihood opportunities and less access to healthcare and other basic services than their compatriots in other parts of the country.

We should not think that these uneven outcomes are naturally occurring and therefore somewhat inevitable, but instead see them as reflecting ongoing power relations between these different social groups whereby some are more powerful than others. Indeed, as many other contributors to this book argue in different ways, variations in development outcomes are socially embedded and as such reflect social, economic, and political power.

An important focus of this contestation in the future will be India's cities. Indeed, as the country becomes more urbanized, its cities may become an even stronger engine of economic growth. Making these cities inclusive and sustainable is a significant challenge both for policymakers and society at large. In a similar way, ensuring that the dynamism of these urban areas creates opportunities for rural settlements and for the most marginalized social groups is likely to be one of the defining challenges that India faces in the twenty-first century.

Notes

1. In particular, the Western Ghats region in the southwest and the eastern Himalayas in the northeast stand out for their extensive and globally important range of endemic flora and fauna. Although many other parts of the country have historically also played host to distinctive plants and animals, the impact of humans over the centuries has been such that many habitats have been adversely affected. Traces of this rich biodiversity now largely remain in isolated pockets, including in reserves that have been set up by the government of India.

2. The growth of the railways also had very significant other impacts. On the one hand, the growth of the railway system radically altered the interconnectedness of different parts of the Indian subcontinent. Most of this initial investment was for infrastructure linking natural resources to ports or major cities, so interconnectivity was primarily intended for natural resource extraction. However, there were other impacts on the extension of rail connectivity. People from different parts of the subcontinent were able to travel to areas that had hitherto been too far away to realistically visit. Many scholars have argued that this inadvertently went some way toward fostering a shared sense of imagined community. See Kerr 2007.

3. Indeed, a great deal of literature has demonstrated that there are overlapping deprivations, including housing, child and maternal health, literacy, and access to nutritious food. Just as significant, this literature points out that different people may experience greater depths or intensity of deprivation; because of this, classifying populations according to the poverty line may have limitations in terms of understanding the potential mobility of different people. See, for example, Alkire and Seth 2008.

4. JNNURM targeted sixty-three of the largest cities. The Smart Cities Mission requires cities to tender for the opportunity to gain central government funding. In the first tranche there were twenty-three cities selected, with a much broader range of sizes of cities from throughout India. For a critique of the JNNURM, see Kundu 2014.

3

The Historical Context

Benjamin B. Cohen

India's history is long, complex, and vibrant. Humans have inhabited the Indian subcontinent for at least 7,000 years and have used script for much of that time. Over the millennia, countless political and social formations have emerged, prevailed, and then either have been dramatically vanquished or have gradually faded from power. Thus India's history presents a complex and lively array of people, places, and events scattered over time as well as diverse social, political, and economic processes. Further, far from being settled fact, with new discoveries, new theoretical insights, and new trends in scholarship, India's history is constantly undergoing reappraisal. What follows then is a whirlwind tour of the major historical developments in India, beginning with the Indus Valley civilization c. 2500 B.C.E., where the earliest script has been found, and ending with modern India's independence from colonial rule in 1947.

One legacy of British rule in India, the Raj, was that British and European historians neatly divided India's history into three eras: ancient, medieval, and modern. Historians borrowed this template from much of Europe's own history and applied it to India. They believed that India once had a great ancient period that saw Hinduism and Buddhism at their social, political, and cultural peaks. That era was violently ended by the arrival of Muslim conquerors, which ushered in a darker medieval period. To reinforce and justify their own rule in India, European scholarship marked the modern period with the beginning of their own rule. This historical trilogy has largely been dismissed, and what follows is a more nuanced periodization of India's history.

The Indus Valley, 2500–1500 B.C.E.

In the early nineteenth century, British East India Company officials visited what appeared to be ancient sites at Harappa, located in the Indus Valley system and now within modern-day Pakistan. Slowly, over the nineteenth and early twentieth centuries, men like Daya Ram Sahni uncovered bricks and other artifacts at Harappa that were clearly from an ancient civilization. With advances in technology and increasingly sophisticated archaeological tools, scholars have dated the Indus Valley civilization to roughly 2500 B.C.E.

Large urban settlements are key markers of the Indus Valley civilization. Urban settlements at Harappa, Mohenjo-Daro, and Ganweriwala each covered an area approximately 160 to 200 square acres. Each city had an outer wall that was likely used both to demarcate the urban core from the periphery, as well as for defensive purposes. Within the city, streets fanned out in a clear grid pattern with different sectors conceivably for residential and official areas. Residential homes were often two or three stories in height and had such technological advances as indoor plumbing linked to drains and a sewer system. Within official or business areas, all three cities have a "citadel" or large raised dais, located in the center of this area, perhaps on which locals performed ritual or political functions. Unique to Mohenjo-Daro is the Great Bath—a structure scholars believe contained water for ritual purposes. Also found at the cities are structures that archaeologists speculate might have been for grain storage. Many of the buildings uncovered within the Indus Valley were constructed from bricks that are uniform in size. This uniformity indicates large-scale and sophisticated brick-making technology, and as these bricks have been found at multiple locations, it alludes to links between Indus valley sites and cities. When British officials and scholars visited Harappa in the late nineteenth century, they found that many of the bricks on the surface—that would have revealed a great deal about Harappan architecture and society—had been crushed and carted off to form the ballast for the Lahore-Karachi railway line.

The clearly articulated form of Indus Valley cities indicates highly developed social and political structures. Indus Valley inhabitants also had a script. This script is composed of geometric shapes interspersed with animals and other natural symbols. The script is likely pictographic, but has not yet been deciphered. Archaeologists have also recovered sophisticated household items from the sites. These include jewelry, tools, ceramic pots and shards, and children's toys. Perhaps most visually striking, several highly detailed and beautiful sculptural pieces have been unearthed. These include one sculpture of a man dubbed the "priest-king," and another of a stylized woman dubbed the "dancing girl." Finally, at the Indus Valley sites, and discovered as far away as Mesopotamia, a large number of "seals" have been discovered. These seals, carved in soapstone or other rock types, depict script along with an animal or other scene. Many have one particular animal resembling a unicorn. Scholars believe that merchants of the Indus Valley used the seals to identify particular families or businesses: the seal could have been pressed into soft clay or mud to identify a particular parcel with its sender.

The Indus Valley is rich in natural resources, and its residents incorporated this wealth into their economy. They grew rice, barley, and wheat as well as sesame and mustard seed. Cotton was also within their agricultural repertoire. Inhabitants combined some agriculture with pastoral practice, raising goats and sheep. From their environs, copper, gold, ivory, pearls, and crucially timber were all available and were traded both eastward toward Rajasthan and westward to Mesopotamia. Archaeologists have uncovered a system of standardized weights in different sites, used to help regulate the economy. This allowed trade between Indus Valley locations to be carried out with some degree of uniformity.

What happened to the inhabitants of the Indus Valley is much-debated. By 1900 B.C.E., it is clear that the area was in decline, and somewhere between 1700 and 1600, much of the Indus Valley civilization disappeared completely. Several theories exist to explain this civilizational collapse. The first theory posits that the area suffered a massive and hostile invasion by Aryans who came from the Central Asian steppe. This Aryan-invasion theory rests upon references in later Vedic literature that allude to some form of invasion. (The word *arya,* meaning "noble," does not actually appear in Sanskrit literature.) However, archaeological evidence does not support the invasion theory. What human remains that have been found show no sign of trauma, nor do local structures. A second, "internal" theory suggests that local Indians who came from either the north (Kashmir) or the south incorporated the Indus Valley people into their society. However, clear linguistic differences that mark the end of the Indus Valley period, and further links to Central Asian languages, do not support this theory. A third theory, accepted by most serious scholars of South Asia, suggests a combination of social and environmental changes that led to the gradual decline of the Indus Valley civilization. This idea suggests that Central Asian Aryans migrated into the Indus Valley and intermingled with its inhabitants. Evidence suggests racial mixing as well as cultural borrowing between the Aryan and Indus peoples. Thus, migration—not invasion—is currently accepted as the most likely explanation for the arrival of

Aryans in South Asia. In addition, scholars have uncovered significant evidence for a concomitant change in the environment that likely added to the demise of the Indus Valley people. The region is subject to earthquakes that have shifted the Indus River and its tributaries. These shifts led to flooding in some areas and significant water shortages in others. Many of the homes at Mohenjo-Daro were rebuilt and raised on the same plot, indicating a rising water table and periodic flooding. Water shortages or surpluses would have stressed the health of the region's inhabitants, lowered their immunity, and opened the door to possible pandemics. Indus Valley ceramicists fired bricks using timber, and by the late Indus period, widespread deforestation—affecting flora, fauna, and the hydrological cycle in the area—likely sped the civilization's decline. Environmental changes might also have strained the Indus Valley people's agricultural and economic systems, forcing them to abandon their location in search of more hospitable environs.

The Vedic Era, 1500–500 B.C.E.

The period from 1500 to 500 B.C.E. is called the Vedic or Indo-Aryan period. As with all periodization, these dates are approximate. This Vedic age takes its name from the *Rig Veda* (among the world's oldest texts), which was compiled during this time. During this era, Indo-Aryans slowly moved east into the Gangetic plain and as far as Bengal. These people increasingly refined their use of iron technology—as weapons, for felling the thick Gangetic forests, and later for tilling the earth for agricultural purposes. They also moved south, perhaps extending their influence to the Godavari River in India's high central plateau, the Deccan.

In the early Vedic era, 1700–1400 B.C.E., Indo-Aryans occupied an area now concurrent with parts of Afghanistan and Iran. Scholars believe that these peoples eventually split—the Indo-Aryans coming to India, and the second group, the Avestan, moved into Iran. Similarities in language and ritual practice between the Indo-Aryans and Avestan suggest they derived from a single people. In the centuries that followed, and certainly by 900 B.C.E., the Indo-Aryans began establishing themselves across north India's Gangetic plain.

Vedic literature, composed in the Sanskrit language, was memorized and the texts were orally transmitted over generations. Sanskrit was related to the larger Indo-Aryan linguistic family, which itself was derived from the Indo-European languages. Scholars have established links between Sanskrit and English, for instance *nava* and "nine" or *matr* and "mother." *Veda* translates as "knowledge," but the *Rig Veda* might better be thought of as a compilation of hymns, rituals, and sacrifices—or in other words a manual on how best to please the gods that Vedic-era peoples worshipped. The *Rig Veda* consists of 10,600 verses, and it was likely composed along with its newer counterparts from 1700 to 1500 B.C.E., but not committed to a written form until closer to 500 B.C.E. The text refers to these people's earlier homes, including an area that best describes the Swat Valley, now in Pakistan, but generally is more concerned with various rituals. The *Rig Veda* describes rituals to appease the gods, especially Indra, the god of war. Scholars believe that the Vedic people engaged in repeated conflicts with the inhabitants of the Gangetic plain, who are referred to as the "dark skinned" or "black" people (*dasas*). Three other works are part of the core Vedic literary tradition: the *Sama Veda, Yajur Veda,* and *Artha Veda.*

The *Rig Veda* mentions both pastoral and agricultural practices. During this time the Indo-Aryans slowly transitioned from pastoral lifestyles where horse, sheep, and cattle were highly valued, to an agricultural lifestyle—in part learned from the earlier inhabitants of the Gangetic plain who taught them to grow crops such as wheat and barley. At home, Vedic society was highly patriarchal. Fathers or grandfathers were heads of the house, and sons—even after marriage—stayed at home to help their fathers and families. Large families merged into clans and became subcastes. For women, life inside the home was bearable, as families honored and respected women within the home, but once outside they had little if any social power. It is during the Vedic period that sati—widows performing self-immolation on their husband's funeral pyres—came into practice. Vedic society had its lighter side. The *Rig Veda* mentions horseracing, dancing, music, and the consumption of a power-giving drink (*soma*), and even warns against the vices of gambling.

An agricultural society led to greater stratification within Vedic culture, giving way to ever-increasing social complexities. Early forms of social organization revolved around clans with a kind of chieftain as their head. Over time, these chieftains acquired greater power and became rulers, called rajas. As rulers or kings, these men oversaw progressively larger territories, and their power grew more autocratic, marking a shift from clan-based society to state-based society. With the rise of kingship, so too did the power of the priests (Brahmans). This religious adviser was an important component in the king's authority. Priests oversaw elaborate sacrifices that enforced the king's authority. At the same time, the king granted the priest temples, lands, and other boons to secure merit. Perhaps none is more striking than the horse sacrifice (*ashvameda*). In this event, one of the king's horses was set free to wander for a year. Wherever the horse went, the king's army proclaimed that territory as part of the king's realm. When the year was over, with the king's realm significantly increased, priests oversaw a complex practice whereby they sacrificed and ritually consumed the horse.

From the *Rig Veda* comes the earliest explanation of India's caste system. The term *caste* itself comes from the Portuguese word *casta,* which refers to ideas about blood purity. Early Portuguese explorers in India believed caste to be about blood—which is correct to some extent—but more accurately it is about birth and occupation. The *Rig Veda* explains that there are four caste groups. Visitors to India who inquire about caste often hear this oversimplified explanation. This idealized caste quartet placed individuals in their particular occupational pigeonhole. At the top are Brahmans, who worked as priests and scholars. Beneath them are the Kshatriyas: the kings and warriors. Vaishyas follow, being the money lenders and traders. At the bottom are the Sudras: artisans, laborers, and slaves. Within caste groups are social communities (*jatis*) that further diversified society. Brahmans, who controlled rituals and sacrifices carried out within temples, used the concepts of duty (dharma) and merit (karma) to explain why people were poor and must not seek social advancement. Their duty was to perform their occupational tasks, thus acquiring merit so that when reborn, they might advance up the caste ladder, eventually finding deliverance (*moksha*) from the cycle of birth, death, and rebirth. Woven into the caste system is color (*varnas*), thus leading scholars to believe that early fair-skinned Indo-Aryans discriminated against darker-skinned pre-Aryan inhabitants, the *dasas* of the *Rig Veda.*

The Buddhist Period, 500 B.C.E.–700 C.E.

Before proceeding, we must take a brief tour through India's encounter with Grecian powers. Early Greek conquerors pushed into Afghanistan between 550 and 330 B.C.E. and were part of the Achamenid Empire. They were followed by Alexander the Great, who extended Greek authority up to the Indus River basin. In 326 B.C.E., Alexander defeated King Porus after the latter refused to bend his knee in submission. However, Alexander's troops refused to push farther into India and thus he turned and began his trek homeward. All along his path, Alexander installed generals to maintain his holdings. Descendants of these sentinels formed the Seleucid dynasty (364–312 B.C.E.). The Seleucid kings signed a treaty with Indian ruler Chandragupta Maurya, agreeing to make the greater Hindu Kush the border between them. Later, the Bactrians, under Menander (r. 160–130 B.C.E.), extended their authority into India to the Maurya capital of Pataliputra (modern-day Patna). In the last century before the common era, the remaining Greek forces found themselves attacked from the west first by the Scythians (c. 80 B.C.E.), and finally by the Shakas and Parthians. This brought a close to the last remaining Greek stronghold, Bactria, around 50 B.C.E.

In central India in the fourth century B.C.E. the Mauryan Empire emerged, rising from the Magadha Empire in the Gangetic plain. The Mauryan Empire was the first to cover nearly the entire subcontinent under one dynastic rule, from the Arabian Sea to the Bay of Bengal, and from the Vindhya mountains in the south to Kashmir in the north. During the Magadha period, as the nearly 550 smaller states that lined the Gangetic plain clashed over power and resources, two kings, Bimbisara and Ajatashatru in the fifth century B.C.E., rose to power. The latter king constructed Pataliputra (Patna) as his capital. The rich environment surrounding Patna provided pre-Mauryan and Mauryan rulers with an ample supply of elephants, timber, and iron.

In the year 321 B.C.E., Mauryan ruler Chandragupta Maurya defeated the last of a minor and weak Nanda regime. The Nanda kings ruled for only two decades and are notable for being from the lower Sudra caste. As noted earlier, Chandragupta Maurya also engaged and defeated Greek forces who held territory west of the Mauryan base. The battle had not been a lengthy one, and Chandragupta and his Greek adversary Seleucus quickly made peace: the former marrying the latter's daughter, and Seleucus receiving 500 elephants as a gift from Chandragupta. Aiding Chandragupta's rise to power, and crafting one of India's most important texts, was a Brahman courtier named Kautilya. This adviser to the king wrote the *Arthashastra* (a treatise on power), which stands today as among the world's best texts on power, politics, statecraft, and war. Kautilya explored concepts such as "the enemy of my enemy is my friend"— a classic strategy in statebuilding and war craft. Under Chandragupta, the Mauryan Empire devised an efficient and elegant system of ministers who held different ranks and were responsible for distinct functions of the empire's life. Yet political realities sometimes intervened, and Chandragupta—to protect his own power—simultaneously developed an elaborate network of spies to keep him informed of his empire's doings. Further, he built a large and powerful army, used repeatedly to expand his holdings out from the Gangetic plain. Chandragupta was followed by his son, Bindusara (r. 297–272 B.C.E.), who is best known for his use of the army in taking large portions of the Deccan. Bindusara was in turn followed by his son, Ashok (r. 268–232 B.C.E.).

In the history of Indian rulers, Ashok holds a special place. Not only was he a brilliant military commander who expanded the Mauryan Empire to its greatest extent, but he also underwent a moral-spiritual awakening. Early in Ashok's reign (261 B.C.E.) he launched a massive war against the recalcitrant people of Kalinga, on India's southeast coast, roughly contiguous with the modern state of Odisha. They had resisted earlier attempts to bring them into the Mauryan fold. A legend recounts that after winning the battle, Ashok toured the bloodied field and was so overcome with grief and remorse at the loss of life that he converted to Buddhism on the spot. Facts show that after the battle of Kalinga, Ashok became an even greater patron of Buddhism. He embarked on a plan of erecting inscribed pillars as well as crafting other inscriptions throughout his domain. His patronage of Buddhism, and the inscriptions with their emphasis on duty (*dhamma,* or dharma), are considered Ashok's greatest contributions. The building of the pillars and their edicts marked the second half of Ashok's rule. In addition, in support of Buddhist tenets, vegetarianism and a new sense of ethical rule were added to the Mauryan imperial character. Little or nothing of Ashok's rule would have been known without the work of a British official, James Princep, who in 1837 deciphered the language (Pali) of the rock and pillar inscriptions. Ashok and the Mauryan influence are recognized today in the Indian flag with its wheel of law (*dharma-chakra*).

After Ashok's death, the Mauryan Empire quickly faded. Theories abound as to the reasons for its demise. One suggests that Ashok's patronage of Buddhism slighted powerful Brahmans, who took their revenge by unsettling his successors. Alternatively, Ashok's successors were weak and thus unable to maintain the empire's vast holdings. Or perhaps the empire was unable to collect enough revenue to maintain itself. Finally, as the Mauryas maintained a second capital at Taxila that siphoned resources away from Patna, a theory suggests that it bred cultural and economic differences that weakened the empire. Most likely, it was some combination of these events that ended the Mauryas.

From the end of the Mauryan Empire (c. 185 B.C.E.) for nearly five centuries, an interregnum settled over north India marked by a few smaller kingdoms. The Mauryas were followed by the Shunga dynasty (185–173 B.C.E.), led by King Pushyamitra. He is known for restoring favor to Brahmanical Hinduism at court—he himself performed the *ashvameda* ceremony twice. In the Deccan, the Shatavahana dynasty arose sometime in the late second century B.C.E. spanning a region from Nashik in the west to Dhanyakataka in the east. India also witnessed two "invader" states during this period, the Shaka and Kushana dynasties. The

Shakas came to rule in northwest India up to about 400 C.E. Borrowing from the earlier Greek regimes in the region, they too used local governors (*satraps*) to administer their territories. The Kushanas, like the Shakas, were of Central Asian descent, and ruled from Kashi in the east to Sogdiana in the west. Their king, Kanishka, is remembered as a great patron of Buddhism. The Kushana Empire collapsed by 225 C.E.

The Gupta Empire, 320–550 C.E.

In the year 320, the second great encompassing empire arose, the Guptas. The Guptas, like the Mauryas, are known for having unified almost the entire subcontinent under one political regime. They accomplished this both by force and through diplomacy, incorporating lesser rulers as their vassals—a political strategy used in India up through the British period. The Gupta period is often considered the Golden Age of Indian culture, as philosophy, art, architecture, and literature all flourished. However, recently scholars have begun rethinking the Golden Age idea, suggesting instead that some of the cultural boons might have occurred in the less imperial post-Gupta age. Regardless of these debates, there is no doubt about the importance of the Gupta rulers and their social and political contributions.

Chandragupta I (r. 318–330) expanded his empire outward from the Gangetic plain, near modern-day Uttar Pradesh. He had coins minted to mark his coronation, and later took the title "great king of kings" (*maharajadhiraja*), a practice not known before, but used frequently within Indian polities in the time to come. Samudragupta followed (r. 330–375), further expanding the empire south to the Deccan and east to the Naga hills. He in turn was succeeded by Chandragupta II (r. 375–415), who after winning a brief succession struggle, took on and defeated the Shakas of northwest India. He also erected a great iron pillar in what is now a suburb of modern Delhi. Such was the metallurgic skill of the Gupta craftsmen that the pillar has never rusted. Kumaragupta (r. 415–454) followed and was in turn succeeded by Skandagupta (r. 454–467). Under Skandagupta's reign, Central Asian Hunas challenged the Gupta Empire on its western front in what is modern-day Afghanistan. Skandagupta also faced a series of internal revolts and dissensions. These combined to see the empire collapse by 550 (see Figure 3.1). Scholars have argued about the impact of the Huna battle, some believing that it was the cause of the Gupta collapse, while more recently others believe that the Gupta Empire, not unlike the Mauryas, simply collapsed under its own weight.

Figure 3.1   **Map of South Asia at the Time of the Guptas, 320–500 C.E.**

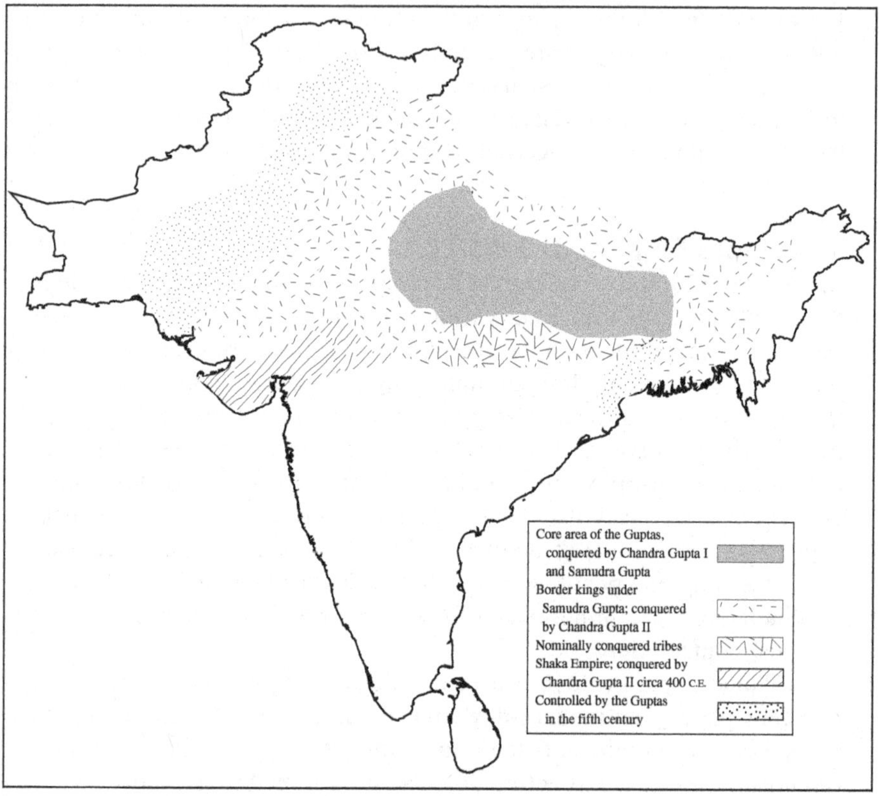

Source: Based on Kulke and Rothermund, 1998: 366.

The Gupta period witnessed numerous cultural developments. Literature flourished, perhaps the most famous text from this period being Vatsayana's manual on love, the *Kama Sutra*. Painting and sculpture also reached new artistic heights, as seen in the cave paintings and carvings at Ellora and Ajanta. The Guptas received income from trade between Southeast Asia, famous for its precious spices and textiles, and Central Asia and Arabia, known for their horses. Such wealth aided artistic and architectural developments; for instance, followers of Hinduism were able to construct greater and more ornate temples. At this time members of the Sudra rank gained in stature as their work in land-clearing became more important in an era of imperial expansion, while those beyond the caste system (Untouchables) fell further—relegated to scavenging, cremation duties, and leather working. Hinduism shifted toward a modified monotheism wherein a few major deities took on greater importance (for instance, Vishnu and Shiva), while a concurrent movement encouraged individuals to practice a personal devotion, called bhakti, over older Vedic-style sacrifices. More is known about life during the Gupta period, as two Chinese pilgrims, Fa-hsien and Hsuan Tsang, visited India in search of Buddhist texts and left written accounts of what they saw.

The Southern Dynasties

Shifting momentarily back in time, we must pick up the trail of events in southern India, below the Narmada River. From about the second to fourth centuries, the Satavahana Empire continued to expand from the Narmada River southward. The Vakatakas (fourth to sixth centuries) replaced them in the northern Deccan. Farther south, the Kadambas (in the west), Pallavas (in the east), and Ganga and Pandya Empires (in the deep south) all took hold. After the mid–sixth century and the decline of Gupta control over the Deccan, the Western and Eastern Chalukya Empires arose in the central Deccan. By this time, the three major contestants for power were the Chalukyas, Pallavas, and Pandyas.

The greatest of the Chalukya rulers was Pulakeshin II (r. 610–642). Under his tenure, he defeated the Kadambas of the south as well as making the nearby Gangas his vassals. He further expanded Chalukyan territory by launching a naval attack up the east coast to Puri. After his death, the Chalukyas continued for roughly a century before finally collapsing. Their demise was typical of many Indian empires: overextension, internal dissension, and (new for the south) external Arab aggression.

Farther south, the Pallavas inherited the remains of the Satavahana dynasty in the third century. Holding the territory between the Krishna and Kaveri Rivers was Mahendravarman I (r. 600–630). This wealthy region stood in the way of Pulakeshin II in his efforts to expand south and marked the beginning of what would be nearly three centuries of both skirmishes and major assaults between the Pallava and Chalukya rulers on each other's territories. Exhausted, the Pallava dynasty all but came to an end with the death of its last king in 912. At Madura, the Pandyas—the smallest of the three deep-south empires—initially opposed Pallava expansion, but later joined them in an uneasy alliance against the more threatening Chalukyas to the north. The growing Chola dynasty largely absorbed the Pandyas early in the tenth century, but they would rise to glory once more some 300 years later.

As the Pallava and Pandyan states collapsed in the late tenth century, the Chola Empire emerged out of the ruins of both. The Chola kings employed a common strategy for stability and expansion. Using a large army, they would attack their neighbors, accomplishing three things. First, this kept the army busy and focused on an "enemy" so it would not turn on the ruling king. Second, loot retrieved from such activities was redistributed to the army, thus keeping its soldiers paid and satisfied. Finally, subdued neighbors were often made tributary vassals and then woven into the larger state system and made to pay revenue.

The Cholas reached new levels of sophistication in their art and administration. Chola king Rajaraja I (r. 985–1012) beautified his capital at Tanjore by constructing a massive temple. As an example of his wealth and power, the top stone of the temple he sanctioned weighed eighty tons and was hauled up a four-mile-long ramp to put it in place. If the Cholas excelled in artistic endeavors, so too did they ably manage their domestic administration. For instance, Chola officials carefully divided land into three socioeconomic types: at the top were merchant elites, beneath them were commercial villages and towns, which in turn rested on the base tier of village agricultural units. Fueling their success, the Cholas also conducted two "overseas" expeditions. The first was to Sri Lanka, and the second, under Rajaraja's successor, Rajendra I (r. 1012–1044), was to Southeast Asia and Srivijaya. This contact with Southeast Asia explains why even today parts of that region are influenced by Indian and Hindu language, myth, and culture. By the thirteenth century, the once-defunct Pandyas had regained considerable strength, and by 1279 they had all but incorporated the remains of a depleted Chola Empire. In addition, from the eleventh to fourteenth centuries, the Telugu speaking Kakatiya kingdom, with its capital city at Warangal, took root and provided a buffer between empires and ideologies developing north of the Narmada and the feuding dynasties of the deep south.

By the mid–fourteenth century, two new empires arose in south India that dominated the political scene for the next two centuries. In about 1340, two brothers, Bukka and Harihara, established the kingdom of Vijayanagar. Over time, Vijayanagar came to dominate the peninsula south of the Krishna River. The empire incorporated new cavalry technology, new fort-building, and overseas trade. The successive kings of Vijayanagar also further incorporated subordinate rulers into their realm, rewarding them with robes of honor and other gifts while at the same time requiring annual revenue payments and contributions to the army. Under Vijayanagar's greatest king, Krishnadevaraya (r. 1509–1529), the city and empire took on a syncretic feel as Krishnadevaraya constructed a mosque for his Muslim citizens and he himself often wore Islamic-styled dress. Thus, notions of a Hindu-Muslim "clash of civilizations" in

the Deccan are largely unsubstantiated. The chief rival to the Vijayanagar Empire was that of the Bahmanis. This sultanate began under Bah-
man Shah in 1347. The Bahmanis consolidated several polities north of
the Krishna River. The Bahmanis and Vijyayanagar kings repeatedly
fought for control of the rich agricultural lands between the Krishna
River and Tungabhadra River, the Raichur *doab* (two waters). Eventually, in January 1565, after the Bahmani dynasty had splintered, its rene-
gade smaller sultanates reconvened in a large-scale assault on Vijayanagar. The rulers of Bijapur, Golconda, Ahmadnagar, and Bidar joined
forces and defeated the Vijayanagar forces near the village of Talikota.
Vijayanagar never recovered from this defeat.

Islam in South Asia, 700–1206
From the seventh century onward, north India witnessed two concurrent
processes. First, in the post-Gupta period the area again devolved into a
series of smaller regional kingdoms. Second, these kingdoms increasingly encountered raiders and rulers, energized by the new faith of Islam,
who pushed their way east from the Arabian Peninsula both into Central
Asia and through Afghanistan down to the Indus River basin. After the
Guptas, the Gangetic plain came under the rule of Harsha Vardhana (r.
606–647). Harsha's rule is considered the last "indigenous" north Indian
empire. Those that followed would be led by so-called foreigners from
Afghanistan and beyond. Harsha expanded southeast toward Patna, then
shifted his efforts to the Deccan, where he met with defeat at the hands
of the Chalukya rulers in 633. Returning northward, his final expansion
extended from Thaneswar in north-central India to the Bay of Bengal.
This was accomplished in 636. Harsha was a gifted poet and author as
well as patron of Buddhism, while he himself was Hindu. His tolerance
of other faiths extended to his support of Hsuan Tsang, the Chinese pil-
grim who visited India from 633 to 643. Unfortunately, Harsha's empire
did not last beyond his own lifetime. After his demise, north India came
under the Gujara-Prathiharas between the eighth and eleventh centuries,
while Bengal came under the Pala rulers. Smaller regional empires
replaced the Gujara-Prathiharas: Mahmud of Ghazni in Punjab, the
Chauharas in Rajasthan, and the Paramaras in central India.

One community, the Rajputs, emerged in the post-Gupta era and came
to play a vital role in both the ensuing Muslim-led era as well as that of the
British Raj. The Rajputs established themselves in northwest India and
comprised a series of royal families. Each defended itself against the other
unto death, thus marking the community as noble, fierce, and talented in

battle. The Chauhan branch of the larger Rajput community helped establish the city of Dhillika, modern-day Delhi. From this clan and location, Prithviraj emerged as among the most famous Rajput warrior-kings. In the year 1191, he struck a blow against Muhammad Ghuri, but suffered defeat and death against that same foe the next year. The Rajputs continued to play an increasingly important role in north Indian political formations as Muslim dynasties established themselves in north-central India. While the initial relationship was contentious, the Mughals later came to count on Rajput alliances to protect their western flank.

In the seventh century, the new religion of Islam caught hold in the Arabian Peninsula and began a rapid expansion both east and west. In the east, the first contact with India came in 710 when travelers crossed the Hindu Kush and entered the Punjab. At the same time, Arab Muslim merchants sailed the Arabian Sea and made landfall along India's west coast, establishing small outposts in port towns. Early in the eighth century, Muhammad bin Qasim captured Sind and Multan—now in modern-day Pakistan and Afghanistan. This became a small Muslim-ruled corner of South Asia but had little overall impact on the rest of the subcontinent. One practice that was established, and continued in later regimes, was that of a head tax (*jizya*) levied on non-Muslims. Its application and repeal are often markers by which particular rulers have been judged. Over time, the bulk of Afghanistan came under Muslim control, and from this came Mahmud of Ghazni (r. 998–1030).

The Ghaznivid Empire began under Alptigin in 962. He and his descendants eventually took control of the area near modern-day Peshawar in Pakistan. Around the year 1000, from the city of Ghazni, Mahmud commenced a series of raids into India. In the process, he defeated not only local kings, but also Ismaili Muslims in Multan and Sindh. Over the next few decades, he conducted some seventeen raids. These occurred in the spring season, when snow that blocked passes between the Afghan mountain ranges and the Indus Valley region melted. The raids were concerned not with faith or territorial acquisition, but rather with an eye toward loot. Mahmud looted Hindu temples not because of their Hinduness per se, but rather because they were sites of extraordinary wealth and not heavily guarded. He did, however, take some time to deface Hindu carvings and slay resistant priests. He returned to Ghazni with immense wealth and set about beautifying that city. Mahmud's raids illuminate two facets of this early contact between the growing Islamic world and India. First, Mahmud was not concerned with acquiring territory or religious jihad; rather, he was most interested in accumulating wealth. Second, that Mahmud strode into north India with little resistance demonstrates the relatively weak position many Indian rulers were in at this time. For them, he was simply another advancing enemy that had to be met.

The Ghaznivids were followed by Muhammad Ghurid (r. 1173–1206) of the Ghurid Empire. The Ghurids were different from Mahmud's reign in that they sought territorial acquisition in India, or in other words they came to India and stayed. The Ghurids laid the groundwork for the Delhi sultanate, and the eventual Mughal dynasty in India. Muhammad Ghurid swept through the Gangetic plain as far east as Bengal, and brought under his control parts of Punjab and the Indus River basin. In 1193, he captured the city of Delhi. Muhammad used a tactic similar to that of other rulers before him: he placed trusted individuals at key captured locations to defend and maintain his holdings, while he himself retreated to the cooler climes of Afghanistan.

The Delhi Sultanate, 1206–1526

The Delhi sultanate consisted of five unrelated dynasties, largely centered in north India and variously expanded and contracted east, west, and south. An increasingly complex and sophisticated bureaucracy marks the sultanate period. Accounting and recordkeeping systems helped track revenue, which was the prime motivator of the sultanate rulers, not religious conversion. Yet during the sultanate period many individuals became Muslims. Scholars attribute some of this conversion to the work of Islamic mystics, Sufis, who traveled and preached at the edges of sultanate territorial control, especially in Bengal, where large numbers of Muslims came to exist. The first sultanate dynasty was the "slave dynasty" established by Qutb-ud-Din Aybeck (r. 1206–1210). "Slave" here refers to a system whereby Muslim rulers would take a youth captured in war or purchased in slave markets, and train him in the arts of governance and military strategy. A ruler's own family and courtiers were often among the first to double-cross him and seize power, yet a slave owed his life to the ruler and would—ideally— remain loyal. Further, coming from obscure origins, slaves could claim no royal blood. Aybeck himself had been a slave of Muhammad Ghuri, and when the latter died, he seized power. His territories stretched from western Punjab down to an area past Benares. Aybeck's rule was cut short when he died from injuries sustained from a fall while playing polo. He was succeeded first by Iltumish, then Raziya—the only woman to rule during the Delhi Sultanate—and later Balban. Balban expanded his territories up to the Indus Valley, where he was checked by Mongol forces.

The second sultanate dynasty was that of the Khaljis (1290–1320). The Khaljis had six sultans in all, the greatest of them being Allauddin (r. 1296–1316). To secure power, Allauddin killed all claimants to the throne. Once secure, he instituted administrative reforms, including a revenue-collection system based on land measurement, and repealed hereditary perks given to village leaders. Four times he repulsed Mongol thrusts into India, while at the same time expanding his own territorial claims into Gujarat, Rajasthan, and the Deccan. In 1307, he sent Malik Kafur to subdue the Deccan kingdom of Devagiri, the defeated raja becoming an ally of the Khalji regime.

The Tughluq dynasty (1320–1413) followed the Khaljis. Under its second ruler, Muhammad (r. 1325–1351), the Delhi sultanate reached its greatest extent. Muhammad was not only a supreme military leader, but also a philosopher intrigued by India's Hindu faith. His liberal and curious outlook led him to go so far as to participate in the Hindu holiday Holi. For Muhammad, the Deccan continued to be an elusive prize, so much so that he shifted his capital to Daulatabad (c. 1326) in the Deccan to better oversee expansion there. However, southern ambitions left the north open to revolt and internal dissensions. Further, a vast domain required greater manpower, and circumstances forced Muhammad to

One of the many tombs in Lodi Gardens, Delhi, of a member of the Lodi dynasty (1451–1526). Photo by Ainslie T. Embree

put local leaders in place in far-flung locations. Their loyalty was suspect and left him further open to revolt. As the Tughluq regime shrank, it was dealt another blow by the swift incursion of Timur in 1398. Timur, or Tamerlane, a Turco-Mongol warrior king, swept all the way to Delhi, where he sacked the city before returning to his Central Asian home. The Tughluqs never recovered from Timur's strike and left a shrinking realm to the fourth Delhi sultanate, the Sayyids (1413–1453). The Sayyids were the weakest and smallest of the Delhi sultanates, their territory at one point not extending much beyond Delhi city limits.

The final Delhi sultanate was that of the Lodis (1453–1526). This dynasty was Afghan in origin and once again expanded the sultanate's territory to Punjab, Rajasthan, and what is now Uttar Pradesh. In Delhi, the Lodis created elaborate gardens (in Islam, heaven is said to be a garden), which are extant in modern New Delhi. Yet what early Lodi rulers gained was lost by the last Lodi sultan, Ibrahim (r. 1517–1526). In 1526, he engaged a young prince on the battlefield of Panipat. Ibrahim lost, bringing to a close the Delhi sultanate period and allowing the victorious prince, Babur, to establish the Mughal dynasty.

The Mughals, 1526–1707

The young prince Babur succeeded his father at the age of eleven. At the time, while ruler of Ferghana (in modern-day Uzbekistan), he sought to extend his power to Samarqand. Unable to hold Samarqand, and in the process losing Ferghana, Babur made his way to Kabul. From Kabul, after further failed attempts to reclaim cities in his Central Asian past, Babur looked east to "Hind"—India and South Asia—for his next conquest. Babur's success in defeating Ibrahim Lodi at Panipat and securing for himself the important cities of Delhi and Agra (home of the Lodi treasury) can be attributed to several factors: better rifles, cannons, and shields as well as talented Turkish artillerymen and cavalry.

With the Lodis defeated, Babur began to secure his tentative holdings in north India. He sent his son, Humayun, to secure the treasury at Agra. There, so the legend goes, Humayun came across a stunningly large diamond, which he presented to his father. Babur, bouncing the stone in his hand, realized that its wealth was so great it would feed the world for two days; he then casually handed it back to Humayun for safekeeping. The stone was the famed Koi-i-noor diamond, now part of the Queen of England's jewels and held in the Tower of London. Babur went on to defeat the Rajput king Rana Sanga in 1527, and then settled down to enjoy a relatively peaceful period of his life.

Babur and his daughter worked to compile his memoirs, later published as the *Baburnama*. He was fascinated with India's flora and fauna, and the text provides an early environmental styled account of India in the sixteenth century. Babur also designed gardens, bringing a sense of order to India's unruly natural surroundings. In 1528, one of Babur's nobles, Mir Baqi, constructed a mosque, the Babri Mosque at Ayodhya, in honor of the Mughal ruler. This mosque, demolished in 1992 by Hindu nationalists, would later come to haunt modern India. Just four years after establishing a foothold in north India, Babur died in 1530. He was first buried at Agra, but later his body was shifted to Kabul—its weather and climate always a source of nostalgia for the first Mughal.

When Humayun assumed power, he made changes to early Mughal administration. However, being exceedingly superstitious, these changes were not entirely in line with building a strong empire. For instance, Humayun rearranged the Mughal administrative departments according to the elements: earth, water, wind, fire, and air. He further doled out punishment based on the day of the week and its astrological character, without any sense of justice, thus letting murderers go free on one day, and dismembering pickpockets on another.

Humayun faced three sets of foes: Sultan Bahadur of Gujurat, Sher Shah Suri of Bihar, and his own brothers. Humayun initially sacked Sultan Bahadur but soon thereafter restored him to power, only to continue to be menaced by the young ruler. Bahadur was then sacked by Portuguese forces (who had arrived on India's shores in 1498) and did not live to bother Humayun again. Sher Shah posed a much greater problem for Humayun. In 1539–1540, Sher Shah advanced against the Mughal ruler. Humayun met him in battle and in a comical misstep was taken by surprise and forced to retreat first to Delhi, and then back to Lahore. This marked the beginning of a fifteen-year exile by Humayun out of India. His journey took him to Sind (where his wife, Hamida, gave birth to a son, Akbar), then to Persia, and finally back to Afghanistan and into India. By 1555, Humayun returned to power at Delhi. Sher Shah had built an impressive administrative system, but his weaker son, Islam Shah Sur, was unable to keep Humayun at bay and relinquished north India back to the Mughal ruler. Blinded, enchained, and otherwise subdued, Humayun's brothers no longer bothered him. He lived in relative peace until the next year, 1556. In January, while spending time in his second-floor library, Humayun tripped on the stone steps as he made his way to prayer. After a few days in a coma, he died.

Humayun's son Akbar is considered the "great" Mughal. Not only was he an able administrator—despite being illiterate—but he was also a

Humayun's Tomb in New Delhi. Photo by Neil DeVotta.

fine military commander and, perhaps most notable, possessed a tolerant mind that translated into a more liberal style of governance. Akbar began his tenure by reorganizing the Mughal administrative system into sensible units such as departments of finance, military, household, and religious affairs. Next, having conquered Gujarat, Akbar battled several holdout Rajput kings who had refused to acknowledge Mughal suzerainty. In victory, he brought much of Rajasthan into the Mughal fold, thus ensuring that allies now protected his western flank. To further secure this alliance, Akbar married more than one Hindu Rajput princess, and allowed them to maintain their religious practices while living in his home.

Akbar foremost forged a Mughal-Rajput alliance that helped him secure much of north and northwest India. Further, his administrative changes not only related to governmental departments, but also included new ways of ordering his nobility by assigning them ranks (*mansab* and *zat*) and including them in court rituals. In his own spiritual quest, he created a new faith (Din-i-Ilahi) based on the worship of light. He invited his nobles to join him and in doing so bound them closer to himself. Akbar's tolerance included not only interfaith marriages and spiritual curiosity, but also religious debates and dialogue between scholars of other faiths. In his policy, he repealed the head tax (*jizya*), thus making him popular with a Hindu-majority populace.

Seeking a male heir, Akbar patronized a shaikh who correctly predicted that he would have three sons. To honor this miracle, Akbar constructed a new Mughal capital at Fatehpur Sikri, the home of the shaikh. Masons drawn from local communities carved into red sandstone what they had formerly done with wood, thus creating a hybrid of pre-Islamic and Islamic architectural styles. However, Fatehpur Sikri did not have sufficient water and so Akbar abandoned it fourteen years after it was complete. By 1580, Akbar expanded Mughal holdings to include Gujarat, Bihar, and Bengal. He shifted his attention to Kashmir, and took that region in 1585, beginning what would become a Mughal love affair with Kashmir. Akbar's first son Salim was born in 1569 and survived to succeed his father. The other sons both died of alcoholism. Akbar himself died in 1605, thus bringing to an end a reign of nearly fifty years.

Salim took the name Jahangir, "seizer of the world," and began his reign on October 24, 1605. The first years were largely peaceful except for the disobedience of his eldest son, Khusrau. To keep Khusrau from intrigues against his father, Jahangir had him blinded. From this point on, a pattern emerged of contested and often bloody succession battles between Mughal fathers and sons. In 1616, Jahangir sent his third son, Khurram, to the Deccan to replace the elder and hapless second son, Parwiz. Khurram was successful in bringing portions of the Deccan under Mughal control, and when he returned with the spoils of victory, his father proclaimed him Shah Jahan, "emperor of the world." Jahangir faced rebellions in the latter part of his reign, first by the Mandu ruler Nasir-ud-din in Gujarat, then by Malik Ambar of Ahmednagar, and finally by Shah Abbas of Khandahar. Each of these was dealt with in turn. Further, Jahangir faced constant intrigues by his sons. Weary from battle and alcohol, Jahangir died in 1627.

Jahangir's life and legacy are better documented than those of his predecessors because of artistic advances and external accounts of his reign. The emperor was deeply interested in scientific inquiry and technical experiments; for instance, he observed the casting and firing of new cannons. These he not only recorded in his own diary, the *Jahangirnama*, but also had recorded by court painters. Painters were also used to portray special events (battles, family reunions, etc.). In the paintings, Jahangir was the first Mughal to employ the nimbus. This glowing halo signified who in a crowded scene was the ruler. Jahangir also minted coins with his own face on them, a somewhat un-Islamic practice. This was made further repulsive to his religious advisers when the coins portrayed him drinking from a wine glass.

During Jahangir's reign, an ambassador from the British East India Company, Sir Thomas Roe, made his way to the Mughal court and left behind an important narrative of his travels. In December 1615, Roe arrived at Ajmer, where he met Jahangir. He had already met Jahangir's son Parwiz, at which meeting the latter had relieved Roe of several bottles of wine. Roe presented Jahangir with several gifts: books whose leather bindings had rotted, a mirror whose silver backing had rubbed off, and other trinkets. The Mughals were unimpressed with the shabby gifts and lone trader. Desperate to impress the Mughal ruler, Roe presented him with a miniature painting of the Virgin Mary. Fascinated by this new miniature style of art, Jahangir ordered his court painters to imitate it, thus beginning the Mughal miniature-painting style. Roe remained at Jahangir's court for three years, perhaps even becoming Jahangir's drinking partner, but was ultimately tasked with securing Mughal protection for early British East India Company bases in Surat.

Following Jahangir, his son Shah Jahan is best known for constructing the Taj Mahal. Shah Jahan married a woman who received the name Mumtaz Mahal, "chosen one of the palace." Theirs was a love marriage and Mumtaz bore Shah Jahan fourteen children. She died in childbirth in 1631, and legend states that she asked her husband to erect a monument for her that would rival any in the world. Thus, the Taj Mahal ("Taj" being a form of "taz") is Mumtaz and Shah Jahan's tomb. It remains modern India's greatest tourist destination.

The structure itself took twenty years to complete, and Shah Jahan was intricately involved with its design and construction. The building is a synthesis of several styles. From Babur's time and his life in Kabul come the divided symmetrical gardens with water cascading through them. (The current gardens are actually an imagined Mughal garden constructed during the British period.) From Akbar's time comes the use of minarets (which are purely decorative at the Taj), and the use of white marble with precious-stone inlay. The small "kiosks" and inverted lotuses are Indic motifs. Moreover, from Persia comes the use of the dome. The dome possesses a slight swell in its midsection that adds to its beauty and was a wholly Indian idea. Shah Jahan constructed several other noteworthy architectural and public works projects. Under his rule, the Grand Trunk Road was built, linking Agra at the Mughal imperial core to Lahore, a gateway to Afghanistan and the west. He also constructed marble palaces at Agra and Lahore, and transferred the Mughal capital to Delhi, where he laid the groundwork for a new capital, Shah Jahanabad. This has since become Old Delhi.

Of his sons, Shah Jahan favored Dara Shukoh, whom he kept close to him throughout much of his life. Aurangzeb, the less favored son, was sent off to the empire's periphery to suppress one rebellion or another. This tactical mistake allowed Aurangzeb to develop military

The Taj Mahal. Photo by Lynne Rienner.

acumen and leadership skills, while Dara Shukoh remained "soft" and largely untested. By 1657, Shah Jahan was ill and retired to Agra. He left Dara Shukoh in charge while the three other brothers all made plans to return and take power for themselves. As Aurangzeb made his way back to Delhi, he defeated his brother Shah Shuja, who had been in Bengal. Aurangzeb and Murad Bakhsh (the other brother) formed a pact and were able to defeat Dara Shukoh, who fled Delhi. Aurangzeb and Murad became increasingly wary of each other, with the latter finally being tricked into capture and escorted to jail. With his father imprisoned and his brothers suppressed, Aurangzeb proclaimed himself emperor on July 21, 1658. After Shah Shuja died, Aurangzeb had Dara Shukoh beheaded. In a fit of acrimony, he sent to his father his brother's severed head on a platter.

Aurangzeb is not widely beloved by scholars of the Mughal period, as he is perceived to have been spiritually conservative and overly harsh in his rule. Several changes that he made have fueled this perception. First, Aurangzeb reimposed the *jizya* that Akbar had abolished nearly a century before. Second, several recently constructed Hindu temples were dismantled, and Aurangzeb forbade the construction of new temples. Third, he ended the practice of showing himself (*jharoka*), or being viewed by the people of Delhi. In addition, at court he discontinued music, forbade any history-writing of his reign, and insisted on more somber dress by his nobles. All of the previous practices he deemed un-Islamic. In 1666, Aurangzeb's father, Shah Jahan, died at Agra fort, overlooking the Taj Mahal. The two had carried on an acrimonious relationship to the end, but Aurangzeb allowed his father to be buried next to Mumtaz Mahal in the central rotunda of the Taj Mahal; his sarcophagus is the only off-centered feature of the space, as it was added later.

Aurangzeb's son, Prince Akbar, rebelled against his father and fled from Rajasthan—where the two had been involved in suppressing Mewar—to the Deccan. Aurangzeb pursued him to the Deccan, never again returning to Delhi and north India. In the Deccan, Aurangzeb and the Mughal forces faced several challenges. The Maratha chief, Shivaji, constantly harassed Mughal forces by use of light, fast, guerrilla-style attacks. These were successful against the larger, cumbersome Mughal army. Second, the sultan of Golconda—once a part of the Bahmani sultanate—refused to submit to Aurangzeb's authority. An eight-month siege ensued, all the while Aurangzeb's forces plundered the city of Hyderabad while the sultan remained at Golconda fort. Finally, in September 1687, a Golconda general betrayed his master and opened the fort's gates. The Mughals incorporated Golconda into their political tapestry.

Golconda Fort. Photo by Neil DeVotta.

However, Aurangzeb and his forces were constantly harassed by minor Deccan kings who refused to submit to Mughal authority, and Aurangzeb wasted precious time and finances suppressing recalcitrant kings across the Deccan. Meanwhile, with his attention focused on the Deccan, north India slipped into rebellion.

Aurangzeb died in 1707 and was buried in a simple grave at Khuldabad in the Deccan. After him, a series of eight Mughal rulers held power for a sum total of fifty-two years. Adding to the chaos, in 1738 Nadir Shah of Persia marched into north India, camped outside of Delhi, and sacked the city. A small group of Delhi's citizens resisted his attack, and for this some 30,000 Delhites were slaughtered in revenge. Shah carried off the famed Peacock Throne, built by Shah Jahan, and took with him 1,000 elephants and some 400 carpenters and masons back to Persia. His attack on Delhi thus mirrored that of Timur's centuries earlier. The last Mughal, Bahadur Shah II, was deposed by the British and exiled to Burma after the events of 1857.

European Arrivals, 1498–1600

Before Babur's arrival in India, while the Lodi dynasty was protecting its assets at Delhi and Agra, far to the south a Portuguese captain-explorer named Vasco da Gama waded ashore on May 18, 1498 at Calicut. The Portuguese were the first European power to successfully navigate to India by sea, with da Gama completing the mission that Christopher Columbus attempted six years earlier. Da Gama and subsequent Portuguese explorers established control of several port towns along India's western coast: Cochin, Diu, and Daman. Da Gama sought spice, textiles, and reconnection with the "lost" Christian community of Prester John, believed to be somewhere in the east. So strong was da Gama's desire to find Christians in the east that in a colossal misunderstanding, convinced he had set foot in a far-flung corner of Christendom, da Gama stopped to offer prayers at what he believed to be a church but was instead a Hindu temple.

The Portuguese were successful in establishing a bridgehead in India for several reasons. First, they arrived at a time when the Bahmani sultanate was collapsing and no Indian power maintained a navy to defend itself from a sea-based attack. Second, as such, the Portuguese were able to control sea lanes—often by force—and dictate trade. Third, they used a system of passes required by local seamen to trade, thus carefully controlling trade and establishing a monopoly in places. Fourth, they constructed fortresses in their new territories and defended themselves by cannon and rifle. Fifth, Portuguese sailors were encouraged to marry local women, who were excellent ambassadors to local culture and its commodity production as well as a way to propagate Roman Catholicism. And finally, the Portuguese began to drill and train local Indian infantry—a practice adopted by the French and British with great success.

After da Gama, men such as Afonso de Albuquerque arrived to expand Portuguese holdings, establishing in 1510 the stronghold of Goa. Goa remained a Portuguese possession until 1961, when the Indian army wrested it from their control. Albuquerque was followed by those more interested in faith than trade, such as St. Francis Xavier and Roberto de Nobili. De Nobili, who arrived in India in 1605, found converts from some lower-caste Hindu communities and through the practice of intermarriage. By the seventeenth century, Portuguese power at home and in India had waned, leaving space for Dutch, French, and British powers to fill the vacuum.

The Dutch East India Company began in 1602. The Dutch were generally more focused on controlling the spice trade in Southeast Asia, where they had forced early British merchants out of the region and back to India. In India, the Dutch established bases at Pulicat, Masulipatam, and Surat. Unlike the Portuguese, the Dutch were not interested in pursuing religious conversion and instead concentrated on establishing monopolies over certain spices and textiles. However, the Dutch century in India lasted only until 1713, when the Treaty of Utrecht largely ended their presence in India (they remained a force in Southeast Asia), leaving only the French and British to contend for trade and power.

Under approval from Louis XIV, the French East India Company began in 1664. While this postdates the British and Dutch companies, we can address its history out of chronological order, as French power peaked early in India. The French established bases at Chandernagore, near modern-day Calcutta (now Kolkata), as well as at Pondicherry, established in 1674. From Pondicherry, the French—under the leadership of men such as Joseph Dupliex—expanded their territorial possessions while at the same time trading blows with British forces established nearby. Dupliex served as governor-general of Pondicherry from 1742 to 1754, before being recalled under charges of ineptitude.

French forces in India, however, were vibrant members of the political complexities unfolding in the eighteenth century. This post-Mughal period witnessed many local rulers, released from Mughal control, all vying with each other for power. For instance, the Nizam of Hyderabad proclaimed his independence and courted both French and British military support in his vast dominions. Into this mix, the French added their own interests as well as their armed forces, including Indian soldiers (*sepoys*) trained in European military styles. However, as the eighteenth century wore on, the French faced mounting difficulties. The French East India Company never enjoyed secure financial footing. French naval forces struggled for manpower (often hiring Dutch crews) and were eventually overcome by superior British forces. Finally, the French found themselves engaged in a series of prolonged conflicts with the British both in India and at home that drained their ability to sustain their Indian efforts. The company's war in India (1744–1748), war of Austrian succession (1740–1748), and Seven Years War (1756–1763) all sapped their energies. Thus, by the mid–eighteenth century, French power in India was all but finished.

Company Ascendancy, 1757–1857

The eighteenth century in India's history has been viewed as a "chaotic" time of Mughal decline and European—especially British—ascendancy. However, this view has been reappraised, and scholars now see the century as a transitional period replete with pockets of Indian cultural efflorescence, and with European dominance by no means a foregone conclusion. Aurangzeb's death in 1707, his weak successors, and Nadir Shah's romp through north India were not the only factors that contributed to Mughal decline. While Aurangzeb was in the Deccan, he faced a series of landlord (*zamindar*) revolts. These country lords-turned-rebels both exploited the peasantry beneath them and took up arms against overlords above them. Higher up the social chain, the Mughals faced revolts by different princes from India's indigenous ruling castes. For instance, the Rajputs staged a series of successful revolts against Mughal rule, causing cracks in the Mughal facade. Finally, governors of large territories who had been appointed by the Mughals also revolted, taking with them the loyalty, military, and revenue of their vast states. One example of this is the Nizam of Hyderabad, who declared independence in 1724.

In addition to various revolts in the early eighteenth century, different regional rulers came to prominence, further challenging Mughal rule and asserting their autonomy. In addition to Hyderabad, in modern Maharashtra, for example, the warrior Shivaji (1630–1680) created the Maratha Empire. Shivaji's power and that of successor Maratha rulers was based primarily on local loyalties from farmers and laborers. The Maratha rulers incorporated powerful Brahmans who were skilled bureaucrats, a skill they brought with them into the expanding Maratha Empire. Their empire was based largely on a sense of Maratha identity carved out of shared language, territory, and cultural practice. After Shivaji, a series of Brahman prime ministers (*peshwas*) oversaw the administration, allowing it to grow into four regional royal houses (Baroda, Gwalior, Indore, and Nagpur).

The eighteenth century also witnessed competition between the French and British companies in India, and by the century's end, the British emerged triumphant. The British East India Company formed as a joint-stock company in 1600. The joint-stock company allowed several investors to each make a small investment in the company, thus raising capital and spreading the risk—and rewards—among more people. Initially, its investors hoped that the spice islands of Southeast Asia would provide them profit from trade in clove, nutmeg, mace, and some textiles. However, Dutch forces repelled the British, sending them back to India. There, they created factories—more like warehouses and forts combined into a single structure or compound—at Surat (1612), Fort St. George at Madras (1640), Bombay (1661), and Fort William at Calcutta (1690).

In the early decades of the eighteenth century, as local and regional rulers vied for power, they forged partnerships with the French and British East India Companies. Company officials were interested in securing greater access to textiles and spices. When local Indian rulers battled with each other, it could decimate spice and textile production, so company officials had a stake in either preserving peace, or acting in such a way that trade and profit could resume as soon as possible. As such, they offered to "loan" their European-trained troops to different Indian parties, in return for a share of the profits from a successful campaign. At the same time, British and French forces lined up in opposition to each other as an extension of conflicts being fought in Europe. Through these military-financial arrangements ("military fiscalism"), European companies expanded their powers and enlarged their footprint in India.

In 1756, the nawab (ruler) of Bengal, Siraj-ud-Daula, became suspicious of the British factory located in his territory. The British had reinforced their fort, not in preparation to attack the nawab (as he feared), but rather to protect themselves from possible French attack. The nawab struck—capturing the British fort and placing 146 prisoners in a small room. Bengal was sweltering and the next day, 123 were dead from suffocation and dehydration. In British literature, this became the "Black Hole of Calcutta." The event continues to generate controversy; for instance, some historians have questioned, if not dismissed as propaganda, the lone (British) account of events, while others have identified the role that the "Black Hole" played as a colonial rallying cry for greater British intervention in India.

In 1757 in response to events at the time, a young company officer named Robert Clive marched from Madras to Calcutta. Through advance trickery, he defeated the Bengal nawab at the battle of Plassey. Clive placed the weak Mir Jafar on the throne as a pliable puppet for British interests, while the British East India Company assumed responsibility for much of Bengal. Bengal's wealth subsidized the company's activities in India; it no longer needed to import specie from Britain, but could pay its bills derived from profits taken from the region. In the early decades after 1757, and even before, company employees took the opportunity to engage in trade on the side, earning vast fortunes for themselves (while company profits plummeted), and earning the sobriquet of "nabob"—a corruption of nawab.

To clean up the company's affairs, its board of directors sent Warren Hastings to India in 1772 as the first governor-general. In addition to reforming trade practices, Hastings believed that Hindus and Muslims had separate legal codes, and that if the company better understood them, this would facilitate rule and trade. He worked to codify this idea, setting in motion a long process whereby the two communities came to increasingly identify as separate, a practice not necessarily followed in earlier times. Under Hastings, the company expanded the military to 100,000 strong by 1789. Further, it sought to better understand its Indian subjects through the creation of societies devoted to studying India. Enamored with Indian cultures, Britons took the lead in many of these organizations and associations. Their work led to the discovery of links between English and Sanskrit, the creation of numerous Indian-language dictionaries, and the Western-style writing of India's history by Britons. Thus, much of the eighteenth century was marked by cultural curiosity, crossovers, and hybridity.

Upon return to England, Hastings was charged with corruption and impeached, only to be later acquitted. In India he was followed by Lord Cornwallis, who served as governor-general from 1786 to 1793, and again briefly in 1805. Cornwallis established the Indian Civil Service, which became the "steel frame" that supported the Raj. He also experimented with land reforms that in one system supported the Indian landlord class (*zamindars*), or in a different system favored direct relations with cultivators (*ryots*). The zamindari system gave middlemen rights to collect taxes from cultivators, and anything above the fixed amount was profit. This system encouraged the abuse of cultivators to maximize profits. The *ryotwari* system, used mainly in south India, allowed cultivators to directly pay the company, thus eliminating the middleman. Its critics suggest that it introduced a form of private property and created a large cohort of landless laborers. In some places, the company employed both systems, which largely canceled each other out.

The company acquired territory either through treaty or military force (see Figure 3.2). However, about one-third of India never came under direct rule, but rather was indirectly controlled by British residents assigned to native princely courts. The residents reported to the company and were used as a check on the princes. Often, company officials placed a resident at a prince's court through the system of subsidiary alliance. In this system, a prince—strapped for cash from warring with neighboring princes—would accept military support and protection from the company. In return, rulers had to bear the cost of troops posted in their capital and allow residents at their court. The company annexed princes who fell into financial trouble or were generally considered unfit—a practice that in the mid–nineteenth century would have serious repercussions.

The tone and tenor of change in India shifted as different governors-general came to India. Each brought their own ideas about how far the pendulum of change should swing, if at all. For example, William Bentinck was governor-general from 1828 to 1835 and sought greater education reform. The law member of his cabinet was Thomas Babington Macaulay. In 1835, Macaulay drafted a "minute" (a kind of memorandum) seeking to create "a class of persons Indian in blood and colour, but English in taste, in opinions, in morals, and in intellect." This shift away from using and respecting India's cultural riches toward those of Europe (and specifically Britain) had far-reaching impact, not the least being India's subsequent tradition of English-speaking authors, poets, artists, politicians, and so on.

The early decades of the nineteenth century saw numerous social reforms pushed through by the company. In 1802 and 1829 the practices of infanticide and sati (widow immolation) were outlawed. Throughout the 1830s, the ritual robbery and occasional murder of travelers (*thugi*) was slowly and successfully stamped out. (The English word *thug* comes from this.) By 1856, widow remarriage was made legal, as was inheritance for converts to Christianity. These and other changes found both advocates and critics within the Indian community. For instance, Raja Rammohan Roy (1774–1833) was an early advocate of British rule in India and an especially outspoken critic of sati.

From 1848 to 1856, the Earl of Dalhousie served as governor-general of India. Dalhousie pursued a policy of expansion vis-à-vis the princes

Figure 3.2   Map of British Expansion in South Asia

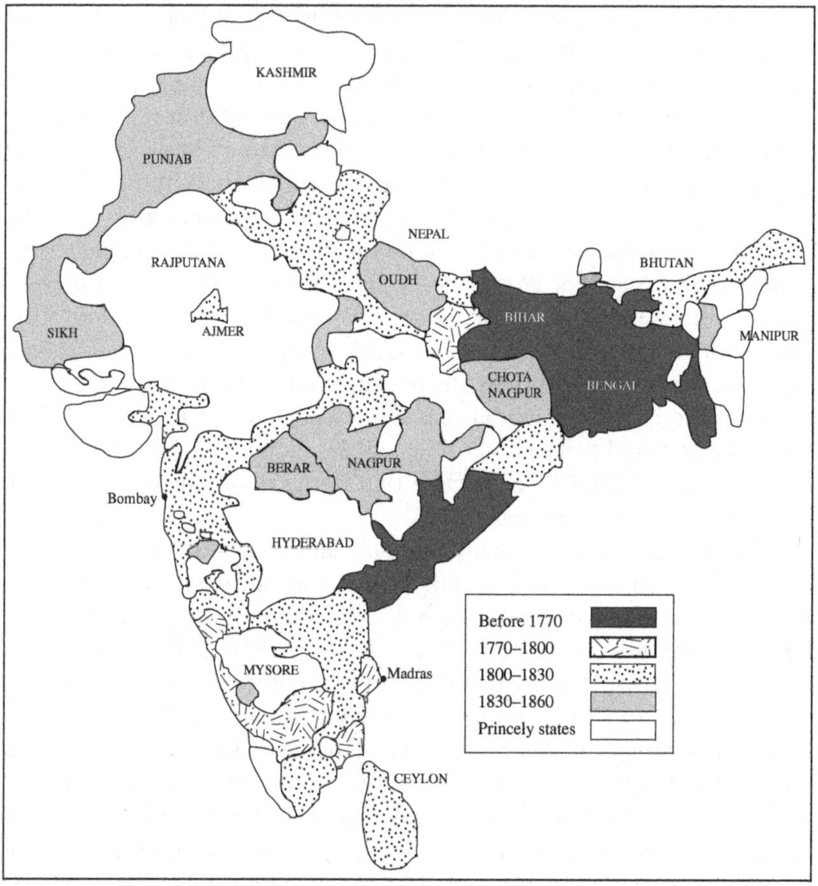

Source: Based on Kulke and Rothermund, 1998: 371.

of India. During his early tenure, he successfully concluded the second Sikh war (1846 and 1848), thus bringing the Punjab under company control. To further help consolidate the company's holdings, Dalhousie implemented the Doctrine of Lapse. This doctrine stated that if a prince failed to have a male heir, or was in some other way unsuitable to continue his rule, the state would "lapse" to the company. Women rulers were subject to the same policy. The doctrine did not allow the adoption of an heir, a practice common among the princely states. Under the doctrine, the company annexed several populous north Indian princely states: Satara (1848), Jaitpur and Sambhalpur (1849), Baghat (1850), Udaipur (1852), Jhansi (1853), Nagpur (1854), Karauli (1855), and finally Oudh (1856). Dalhousie combined political change with technological change. He believed that the railway could help improve the company's ability to extract raw materials (for Britain's growing industrial revolution) and to suppress any challenge to its rule through the speedy transport of troops. He also oversaw the expansion of the postal and telegraph systems in India.

In 1857 Indian troops employed by the British East India Company, first in Bengal and then spreading up the Ganges River basin, mutinied against their commanding officers. This event has been called "The Mutiny," "The Rebellion," "The First War of Independence," and other names all indicating a particular reading of history. Several reasons led to the events of 1857, which raged for over a year across north India. First, soldiers were made to use a new kind of greased cartridge for their Lee Enfield rifles. The grease was composed of both pig and cow tallow. When a soldier bit open the greasy packet with the bullet inside, they were bound to ingest some of that grease. Pork being offensive to Muslims, and beef to Hindus—the cartridge offended the entire army. Second, some British commanders used their position of authority to preach Christianity to their soldiers. Standing at attention in the hot sun while being read to from the Bible was more than these soldiers could take. Further, some soldiers were shipped overseas to help fight hotspots within Britain's empire. For devout Hindus, crossing the ocean was ritually polluting; thus the voyage caused fears of religious decline. Dalhousie's policy of annexation also added to Indian discontent. During the events of that year, massacres took place on both sides. At Kanpur, Nana Sahib murdered a group of British men, women, and children to whom he had promised safe passage. At Lucknow, a group of besieged Britons and Indians spent a horrific season within the residency compound watching as sniper fire, disease, and cannon shot slowly decimated their numbers. By late 1858, British forces regained control of north India. The events of 1857 were complex and defy simple explanations; for instance, much of India did not rise up, and many Indians fought with the British against the mutineers.

The Raj, Nationalists, and Independence, 1858–1947

Several changes took place in light of the events of 1857. First, in the following year Queen Victoria dismantled the East India Company's rule in India, and officially made India part of the growing British Empire. In doing so, she helped usher in an era of conservatism that saw greater respect for Indian religious practices and a new support for India's princely states and their rulers. Second, reforms took place in the army. The ratio of Britons to Indians increased, and recruitments and regimental compositions were reformulated along ethnic lines. Thus, if one part of the army were to mutiny again, a different part could be brought to suppress the trouble without fear of pitching fellow ethnic members against each other. This was an early form of "divide and rule." Third, despite any hard evidence of their leading the revolt, Muslims were increasingly discriminated against. They found that gaining access to highly sought government positions became more limited. Fourth, across India and extending back to London, a new sense of racial prejudice emerged. For instance, a large number of private British social clubs opened from the 1860s to 1880s across India. In these secluded spaces, Britons could retreat from their imperial duties. Yet, as with much of India's history, these clubs were far more complex than at first blush: many were staffed by Indians, were supplied by Indian business houses, and made numerous exceptions to allow Indians to attend the club. Adding to a sense of racial superiority on one side, and growing frustration among India's educated middle classes on the other, in 1884 the Illbert Bill passed. This bill allowed that a Briton could request a majority British jury to decide their fate, rather than allowing Indians to do so. For Britons, the thought of the ruled deciding the fate of the rulers was repugnant, while for Indians the Illbert Bill controversy was belittling and added to a growing frustration with British rule.

The next year, 1885, is often marked as the beginning of India's nationalist period. In this year, a group of Indians and Britons gathered in Bombay to form the Indian National Congress. This organization eventually became the Congress Party—one of modern India's major political parties. However, the congress in its early years was created more to work with the British government than against it. Its founder was A. O. Hume, and W. C. Bonerjee was its first president. The congress was part of India's growing associational life. As imperial tools like the census (first conducted in 1871) took hold, Indians began to organize themselves in new associational forms and make greater use of public space and a growing print culture. For instance, caste groups that had been enumerated in the census now began to form groups, societies (*samajas*), and clubs to better articulate their identities and concerns. The Brahmo Samaj, founded in 1828; the Arya Samaj, in 1875; the Indian National Congress, in 1885; the Muslim League, in 1906; and others were all part of this process. These were in turn coupled with pamphlets and newspapers that further articulated political as well as social views. These tools were also used to foment scandals and innumerable "cases" (petty lawsuits) launched between Indians and Britons alike.

One result of growing associational life and imperial tools like the census was an increased awareness, and slow divergence, between the greater Hindu and Muslim communities of India. Early meetings of the Indian National Congress tried to bring prominent Muslim leaders such as Sayyid Ahmad Khan and Sayyid Amir Ali into the fold, but these and other leaders had come to the position that Muslims and Hindus composed two distinct communities. Other events added to this new communal tone. Riots over cows (and beef consumption) occurred in the 1880s, and more broadly in 1905 Lord Curzon partitioned the massive Bengal province, thus upsetting a balance between Hindu- and Muslim-majority districts. Responding to the changing political winds, in 1909 the Morley-Minto Reforms created provincial legislatures that included separate Muslim electorates. The Muslim League further argued that Muslims represented a nation within a nation. When the partition of Bengal was annulled in 1911, Muslims felt threatened as the further reconstituting of Bengal portended the possibility of a minority Muslim community being drowned in a Hindu-majority India. This was the same year as the last Delhi Durbar—a great imperial spectacle modeled after Mughal practice whereby all of India's princes were gathered together—and the creation of India's new capital, New Delhi.

In 1915, Mohandas Karamchand Gandhi returned to India from two decades of work in South Africa. Gandhi was born in the princely state of Porbandar in Gujarat in 1869. He was deeply influenced by his mother's adherence to Buddhist and Jain beliefs in nonviolence (*ahimsa*). The family invested in Mohandas, and he attended law school in Britain before taking up work in South Africa. While there, Gandhi was subject to discrimination and began developing his own style of nonviolent responses. Influenced by Leo Tolstoy, Henry David Thoreau, and the teachings of Jesus, Gandhi developed the concept of passive resistance or noncooperation, summarized in the term *satyagraha,* defined as "truth-force" or "soul-force." This concept required one to stake out the moral high ground, love one's opponent, and through nonviolence show the true path. Gandhi returned to India and became politically active when he led a campaign to aid the farmers of Champaram in 1917, and by 1920 had made the call for self-rule (*swaraj*). By working toward self-rule through noncooperation, Gandhi was able to erode whatever moral claim British imperialists had for remaining in India.

Gandhi's call for self-rule in 1920 was in part a response to three events that occurred the year before. In 1919, the government passed the Montagu-Chelmsford Reforms and the Rowlatt Bills, and witnessed the Amritsar massacre. The Montagu-Chelmsford Reforms introduced the concept of diarchy in India, allocating some responsibilities to local Indian councils while retaining the lion's share of power and control for the central government. The Rowlatt Bills allowed Indians to be arrested and detained without trial. This draconian act was in response to growing revolutionary and terrorist activities coupled with postwar uncertainties. Finally, on April 13, 1919, British general Reginald Dyer ordered his troops to open fire on an unarmed, peaceful gathering in an enclosed garden in Amritsar called the Jallianwalla Bagh. Some 370 men, women, and children were killed and over a thousand were injured.

In response, Gandhi launched the first noncooperation movement. In this national effort, Indians were encouraged to stay home, thus bringing offices, factories, schools, courts, and other public entities to a close. He encouraged the boycotting of English manufactured goods. However, this movement ended after some of Gandhi's followers turned to violence in the town of Chauri Chaura. They beat and burned to death several Indian police officers who—it was claimed—interfered with their demonstration. Gandhi was punished for the event and sentenced to six years in prison.

Gandhi was a master of using symbols to make larger points. Among his campaigns was encouraging Indians to make homespun cloth (*khadi*) to exercise self-rule, show patriotism, and economically hurt Britain. In another symbolic act, the 1930 salt march, Gandhi led followers to the sea to make salt. The British taxed salt and controlled its production. Gandhi recognized that salt—essential to human life— could be a powerful point around which to protest British rule and demand independence. He carefully orchestrated a 230-mile march to the seaside, where in defiance of the law he made salt. Gandhi made sure that newspapers and news cameras covered the event, all of which raised India's independence movement to an international level. In addition, during the 1930s, Gandhi engaged in an extended debate with B. R. Ambedkar over the rights of India's Untouchables. Ambedkar wanted Untouchables to have separate electorates, which Gandhi objected to. Gandhi fasted until Ambedkar withdrew his request.

In 1935, the Government of India Act came into law. This act allowed for widespread elections that saw Congress sweep into power in all but two predominantly Muslim areas on India's eastern and western flanks. While sweeping in its breadth, the 1935 act ultimately offered Indians very limited franchise. A few years later, the outbreak of World War II marked another turning point for India's relationship with Britain. On September 3, 1939, Lord Linlithgow decided on India's behalf that it too was at war. This infuriated the Congress leadership, who saw it as a return to high-handed imperialism. During the war with

Indian children celebrating Gandhi in song. Photo by Neil DeVotta.

much of the Congress Party jailed, in 1940 the Muslim League passed the Pakistan Resolution. This called for a separate homeland for South Asia's Muslim community in the shape of a new nation-state, Pakistan. Britain increasingly depended on India's financial, military, and material contributions throughout the war period. To recognize this, the government sent Sir Stafford Cripps to India to offer "dominion status" to India after the war's end. The Cripps mission failed and Gandhi and the Congress launched the nationwide Quit India movement.

The Quit India movement (also known as the August Rising) took place in August of 1942. Students and peasants led the movement while much of the Congress leadership was in and out of jail. However, Quit India spiraled into violence as mobs vented their anger and frustration on government infrastructure. Not all Indian leaders sided with Gandhi. Men like Subhas C. Bose left India in 1941 to join the Japanese, and in 1942 he founded the Indian National Army, which he hoped would fight with the Japanese against the British to liberate India.

Adding to the tension within the subcontinent, the next year a devastating famine struck Bengal that saw nearly 2 million people starve. The famine was largely human-made, and the British government came under heavy criticism for its failure to stave off the loss of life.

At the war's end in 1945, Lord Archibald Wavell met with Gandhi, Muhammed Ali Jinnah (leader of the Muslim League), and Jawaharlal Nehru (leader of Congress) at Simla. Wavell proposed an executive council for India's independent government with equal numbers of Hindus and Muslims. Jinnah and the Muslim League repeatedly demanded a disproportionate number of Muslim representatives in any scenario to prevent that community from becoming a permanent minority. Jinnah, however, wanted to choose all the representatives for the council, even those that should technically have been chosen by Congress. The plan failed. The next year saw the proposed Cabinet Mission. This plan suggested a three-tiered independent government responsible to a union government at the center. Elections the previous winter had given the Muslim League a resounding victory in the east and west of the subcontinent, and the Cabinet Mission would have included these two regions, plus a largely Hindu center in the middle of the subcontinent. While Jinnah accepted this plan, Nehru rejected it. With both plans rejected, some form of partitioning of the subcontinent became all but certain.

In February 1947, Lord Louis Mountbatten came to India as the last viceroy. His job was to extricate the British from the subcontinent and hand over power to newly independent India and Pakistan. Mountbatten announced that Pakistan would gain independence on August 14, 1947, and India the day after. Working on an extremely short schedule, Mount-

Subhas Chandra Bose. Photo courtesy of Government of India Press Information Bureau.

batten, Jinnah, and Nehru painstakingly divided the appropriate assets. At the same time, a Briton named Sir Cyril Radcliffe drew the new border between the two nascent countries. With the border becoming ever clearer, a massive migration of Hindus, Muslims, and Sikhs began. This migration, referred to as Partition, remains the world's largest human migration. Some 12 to 15 million people crossed the borders, leading to massive displacement and up to 2 million deaths due to communal violence.

In the months leading up to independence, all but a few of India's princely states joined with either India or Pakistan. However, at independence, Hyderabad and Kashmir had still not made their decision. Hyderabad was ruled by the Nizam, a Muslim, whose vast state was predominantly Hindu. He flirted with joining Pakistan as well as becoming an independent nation-state. However, the Nizam's dominions, also known as Hyderabad State, was landlocked within the south-central heartland of India, and anything short of merging would have been difficult if not impossible. After a year of protracted negotiations—including an appeal at the United Nations (UN)—the Nizam and Prime Minister Nehru had still not reached an agreement. Nehru lost patience and launched a "police action" to forcibly bring Hyderabad into the Indian fold. The action lasted only three days, and Hyderabad merged with India.

Kashmir was more difficult. First, the state was on the border between India and Pakistan, and thus could have been included in either new nation. Second, the state's populace was predominantly Muslim. According to the logic that saw Pakistan's creation, Kashmir "belonged"

Mohammed Ali Jinnah, president of the Muslim League and later the first president of Pakistan, August 1945. Photo courtesy of the National Archives.

to Pakistan. However, third, the state's ruler, Maharaja Hari Singh, was Hindu and under intense pressure to have Kashmir join India. Finally, as Nehru embraced India's secular status and guaranteed the protection of all religious communities—Muslim or otherwise—the inclusion of Kashmir in India with its majority Muslim population was key to "proving" India's secularity.

Shortly after independence, Hari Singh faced an insurrection within his state that was aided by Pakistan. His own forces about to be overrun, Singh asked for help from Nehru. Nehru offered the Indian army, but only if Singh signed an instrument of accession to bring Kashmir into the Indian fold. Singh did so (although there is some debate about the exact timing of this), and Nehru airlifted Indian soldiers into Kashmir. Here, they fought a brief war against Pakistani forces, with India securing about two-thirds of the state, and Pakistan the rest. In its first peacekeeping mission, the UN brokered a ceasefire, and the two-third/one-third division of Kashmir remains much the same today. Among many reasons the conflict remains unending, Kashmir "makes" India's claim to secularity, while it also "makes" Pakistan incomplete as the homeland for South Asia's Muslims. A third minor princely state, Junagadh, also held out at independence, but eventually joined with India.

Late in 1947, Gandhi announced a visit to Pakistan. On January 30, 1948, as he was walking to attend a prayer service in a New Delhi garden, he was assassinated by Nathuram Godse. Godse was a militant Hindu and member of the Rashtriya Swayamsevak Singh (Association of National Volunteers). Godse and other Hindu fanatics believed that Gandhi was too "soft" on the Muslim community and were deeply opposed to his visit to Pakistan. Thus, contradicting much of Hinduism's claim to peace, Godse resorted to the ultimate in violence.

The rise of Hindu nationalism, the creation of Pakistan and the pivotal place of Kashmir, and the legacies of British colonialism are just some among many factors that shape modern India today. India is thus a country built upon a historical platform that stretches back at least 7,000 years. "History" is usually dated from the Indus Valley period, when the first script emerges, yet the Indian subcontinent had been inhabited for millennia before that time. Over time, succeeding empires have added layer upon layer to India's diverse and rich historical makeup. Far from being settled, India's history continues to be written, rewritten, challenged, and rewritten again. Debates come and go (Aryan "invasion" or "migration"? *Ryotwari* or *zamindari* success? Benevolent or violent Raj?), but as with any civilization, the debate itself is part of India's historical vibrancy and a critical component of its greatness.

4

The Political System

Eswaran Sridharan

India became independent on August 15, 1947—after close to two centuries of British colonial rule—when British India was partitioned along territorial religious lines, leading to the Muslim-majority areas of eastern Bengal, western Punjab, Sindh, Baluchistan, and the Northwest Frontier province becoming Pakistan. In 1971, eastern Bengal, called East Pakistan after Partition, seceded to become Bangladesh. The violence that accompanied Partition meant India's independence comprised both liberation and trauma.

British colonial rule evolved by limited incorporation of Indian participation in the regime due to repeated rounds of agitation and negotiation by the umbrella party of the Indian freedom movement, the Indian National Congress (henceforth Congress or Congress Party). There were three landmark moments, the Government of India Acts of 1909, 1919, and most importantly 1935, that saw an incipient quasi-federal structure of relatively strong provinces and a relatively weak central legislature put in place with limited Indian franchise subject to property qualifications, and with limited powers, the British Viceroy having the final word.

The Indian independence movement had been led by the Indian National Congress, a broad umbrella party with a base in all parts of India. Founded in 1885, it was led by the emerging professional middle class, and followed a gradualist strategy of increasing Indian representation and participation in the British colonial government in stages. It evolved from a group of urban-based notables asking for better representation in the colonial power structure into the early twentieth century into a mass movement for independence after World War I. The leadership of

Mahatma Gandhi was responsible for this transformation. Influenced by Gandhi's thinking, the Congress became both a party and a mass movement, including peasants and workers, after World War I. It also sought to include all religious communities, castes, linguistic and regional groups and classes, as well as a variety of ideological strands ranging from soft Hindu nationalism, social conservatism, and pro-Indian business on the right to socialist thinking on the left.

The Congress developed an organization led by local notables with roots in nearly all parts of the country. It should, however, be noted that despite the Congress's encompassing and secular character and its accommodative politics, its major failure during the independence movement was to prevent the rise of alienation among the Muslims of the subcontinent that led to the growth of the separatist Muslim League from 1906 and eventually to India's Partition and the birth of Pakistan in 1947. It tried to incorporate the Muslims, but it succeeded only partially. In 1947, two-thirds of India's Muslims who were natives of the Muslim-majority provinces of the northwest and eastern Bengal became citizens of Pakistan.

India's Social Diversity

Before attempting to understand Indian politics it is necessary to understand India's social diversity. It is one of the most socially diverse countries in the world. The social cleavages that are politically important are those of religion, language, caste, and tribe. In addition to these diversities and overlapping with them is considerable regional diversity. Racial diversity is present, though it has virtually no importance in politics.

India's religious mix is constituted of Hinduism, Islam, Buddhism, Christianity, Sikhism, Jainism, and Zoroastrianism, of which Hinduism and Islam have the biggest number of adherents. There is also a microscopic Jewish community. Hindus, tremendously diverse internally, were 79.8 percent of the population in the 2011 decennial census. Muslims were next at 14.2 percent and constitute India's biggest minority. They are spread all over the country as a minority everywhere except Jammu and Kashmir, which was split into two union territories in 2019, and the Lakshadweep Islands. Only about 15 out of 543 Lok Sabha constituencies have a Muslim majority, although Muslim representation in that house has always been much higher than that, reaching 49 in 1980 and 45 in 1984, which indicates that Muslims won a number of major-party nominations followed by electoral victories in considerable numbers of non-Muslim-majority constituencies. Though a smaller minority overall at 1.7 percent, Sikhs are a majority in one state, Punjab, and Christians (2.3 percent) a majority in the three small northeastern states of Nagaland, Mizoram, and Meghalaya.

Linguistic diversity is even greater than religious diversity. Hindi, the most widely spoken language, is the native tongue of 44 percent of the population. Four other languages—Bengali, Marathi, Telugu, and Tamil—are spoken by between 5 and 10 percent of the population, and the rest of the twenty-two languages in the eighth schedule of the constitution are spoken by under 5 percent each. Most languages, though not all, have a state of their own. Each state in the federation is thus a linguistic homeland; however, most states also contain linguistic minorities, although these tend to be very small except for Assam and some other northeastern states.

The Scheduled Tribes, or tribes so listed in the constitution, refer to about 8.6 percent of India's population who live in central and northeastern India; they themselves are racially diverse, and are largely dependent on subsistence agriculture and forestlands for livelihood. The tribes are considered economically and educationally backward and subject to discrimination historically and are thus eligible for affirmative action, which in India means quotas in parliament and in government employment and college admissions.

Of all social cleavages in India, caste distinctions are the most varied and most prevalent almost all over the country. Caste is a defining feature of the Hindu social order. In its original form going back centuries, the caste system had an occupational hierarchy based on birth. At the top were the priests (the Brahmins), who could also be landowners, the warriors (the Kshatriyas), typically landowners, and the businessmen (the Vaishyas). Peasants and artisans and other manual workers were the lower castes (the Sudras). A further category, the Untouchables, stood outside the caste system: they were placed at the bottom of the hierarchy. Each caste had different rights and privileges: the lower the caste, the fewer the privileges. After independence, the Brahmins, Kshatriyas, and Vaishyas came to be known as the upper castes, and the ex-Untouchables as Scheduled Castes (the constitution abolished untouchability). The Sudras, an extremely diverse category ranging from landowning small farmers to manual workers, was given a new name: the Other Backward Classes, which were defined in caste terms. Numerically, upper castes at this point roughly constitute 17.6 percent of the population, the Scheduled Castes about 16.6 percent, and the Other Backward Classes 42 percent. The rest are intermediate castes that fall between the upper castes and Other Backward Classes, and religious minorities.

The constitution, adopted in 1950, abolished untouchability and caste privileges by equal citizenship, and introduced reserved quotas in political representation (in both federal and state legislatures), in public employment, and in college admissions for the Scheduled Castes and Scheduled Tribes. These two groups then made up 22.5 percent of the total population (now 25.2 percent). As a result, 22.5 percent of the entry-level positions in public sector jobs, educational institutions, and seats in legislatures were reserved for the Scheduled Castes and Scheduled Tribes. This was revised upward by the Delimitation Commission in 2008, based on the 2001 census, so that there are now eighty-four seats reserved for Scheduled Castes and forty-seven for Scheduled Tribes in the Lok Sabha, based on their proportions state by state, with intrastate reservation of seats based not only on the electoral district proportions of Scheduled Castes and Scheduled Tribes but also on the principle of geographical spread of reserved seats. In the original draft of the constitution, religious minorities were also supposed to be granted quotas, but this idea was dropped during the deliberations as it was felt, against the backdrop of the past half century of growing religious divisions ending in Partition, that reservations for minorities would accentuate such separate identities and political divisions.

The Other Backward Classes—a later term that came into widespread usage in the 1980s onward—were originally excluded from the list of beneficiaries. There were two arguments: one, that the Scheduled Castes and Scheduled Tribes, not the Other Backward Classes, had historically suffered the worst discrimination; and two, that the Other Backward Classes, at over 40 percent of the population, had numbers on their side. They could use their numbers to influence the distribution of political power in a democracy as they in fact had done in many states in south India in the twentieth century.

In the 1970s, faced with pressures from below, the government constituted the Mandal Commission to investigate afresh whether affirmative action should cover the Other Backward Classes as well. In 1980, the commission gave its report, recommending extension of affirmative action to the Other Backward Classes. The commission said a quota of 27 percent should be added to the 22.5 percent already reserved for the ex-Untouchables and tribesmen. Half of public employment and seats in institutions of higher education would thus be reserved, and roughly two-thirds of India—Scheduled Castes, Scheduled Tribes, and Other Backward Classes—would be eligible for reservations. It is these three groups that today's "lower caste" parties have mobilized as a new political constituency. They are not fully united because the caste hierarchy is highly state-specific and these groups are also divided by state boundaries and by language, but caste bloc-based regional parties have emerged in many states and have successfully challenged erstwhile upper-caste dominance. The Mandal Commission recommendations were adopted in 1990.

The Constitution and the Basics of the Political System

At the time of independence India adopted a liberal-democratic, parliamentary, and federal framework of government in the form of the Indian constitution, which was adopted on January 26, 1950. The constitution was debated threadbare, draft article by draft article including those borrowed from or building on the 1935 Government of India Act, for almost three years, from November 1946 to November 1949 by a constituent assembly elected from the provincial assemblies and consisting largely of Congress Party legislators, of whom a large number had gone to jail in the struggle against British rule.

India's constitution defines it as a union of states—that is, an implicitly federal arrangement without using the word "federalism." It is a parliamentary system with a ceremonial president and vice president, with real power in the hands of the prime minister and cabinet, drawn from either house of parliament. The Lok Sabha, or popularly elected lower house, is the more powerful chamber, compared to the Rajya Sabha, or upper house, which consists of members elected by proportional representation from the state legislatures. However, unlike the US Senate, it is more or less proportional to population like the Lok Sabha. Legislation needs to pass both houses by a simple majority, with the Rajya Sabha only able to delay but not block money bills if passed again by the Lok Sabha. Constitutional amendments require a two-thirds majority of those present, and voting in both houses is subject to a simple majority of the membership of each house. Some articles affecting center-state relations require a simple majority in half the state assemblies. And the final guardian of the constitution is the judiciary, a pyramidal structure with the Supreme Court at its apex, which is independent of the other two branches and has the power of judicial review—that is, can strike down legislation that is unconstitutional in its view.

At the level of India's now twenty-eight states (not to speak of the eight union territories directly governed by the center) the parliamentary system is reproduced. There is a governor appointed by the president, and the government is headed by the chief minister and cabinet, drawn from the majority party or coalition in the state assembly. Most states have unicameral legislatures, with some having an upper house.

Since 1993 there is a third tier of government that became constitutionally mandatory: urban and rural local government, consisting of the municipal and panchayat governments (the latter itself has three tiers), thus resembling the federal-state-local levels in the United States. However, while the states have become stronger since the 1990s, local governments are still relatively weak in the division of powers. One-third of the seats in village-level panchayats are reserved for women.

The executive consists, apart from a council of ministers drawn from parliament, of a permanent civil service or bureaucracy, recruited by competitive examinations. These consist of the All India Services (the Indian Administrative Service, a follow-on of the colonial Indian Civil Service), the Indian Police Service, and the Indian Forest Service, who are recruited by the central government but are allotted to state governments, under whom they serve for a large part of their careers, alternating between state and central governments. There are also the Indian Foreign Service and various central services like the tax collection services, the audit and accounts service, the postal services, the railway services, and others, whose officers can be transferred around the country.

India's constitution was revolutionary given that despite the country's deeply unequal and hierarchical society—largely rural, agrarian, illiterate, and poor—India adopted universal adult franchise, something that had come into being only in stages over centuries in most Western democracies. It ensured citizens of a set of fundamental rights including the usual democratic freedoms of speech, expression, conscience, religion, and so forth, and the right to equality and nondiscrimination before the law. Citizenship was based on birth in India or to Indian parents and not on blood, race, ethnicity, religion, language, or culture.

India's Federalism

How democratic and how federal is the Indian system? India has had democratic elections, increasingly free and fair, since the first national elections in 1952, and has maintained its record of uninterrupted democracy except for one break—the emergency rule of 1975–1977 imposed by Prime Minister Indira Gandhi under the emergency provisions of the constitution. At the state level likewise, there have been state assembly elections at intervals mandated by the constitution plus a large number of midterm elections when governments formed at the state level fell due to lack of a majority in the assembly, often due to party splits and defections, one of the occupational hazards of a parliamentary form of democracy. However, between the late 1960s and 1994 there was frequent imposition of central rule on a number of states by the use, and very often misuse, of Article 356 of the constitution, under which central rule could be imposed if the state governor was convinced that the government of the state could not be carried on in accordance with constitutional provisions. States ruled by opposition parties were the typical targets. This was substantially remedied by the Supreme Court's 1994 judgment (in the Bommai case) that made imposition of central rule much more difficult. It had led to Article 356 being rarely implemented and within legitimate contexts.

While India is considered quasi-federal by some scholars due to provisions that allow imposition of central rule in extreme circumstances and the right of parliament to break up states into smaller states or change their boundaries, India is substantially federal if one considers how greater financial devolution has led to well over 60 percent of total government spending being overseen by states.

Most states were reorganized along linguistic lines in 1956, thereby breaking up the arbitrarily carved-out British Indian provinces. This state creation process was extended to Punjab in 1966, with some union territories like Goa and the northeast also becoming states over time between 1963 and 1987. Three new states were added in 2000, while the large southern state of Andhra Pradesh was split in 2014 to create the newest state of Telangana. Currently India comprises twenty-eight states, of which nine are Hindi-speaking, two Bengali-speaking, and two Telugu-speaking, with the others having their own unique language. India's federalism is primarily language-based and can be considered a case of what is often called ethno-federalism. While ethno-federalism has acquired a negative reputation in the literature given the disintegration of ethno-federal states like the former Soviet Union, Yugoslavia, and Czechoslovakia, linguistic federalism in India in the context of considerable devolution of resources plus power-sharing in the central government has proven to be a stabilizing factor in India's democracy.

Political Parties and the Evolution of the Party System

We now turn to a brief overview of the main players in the Indian political landscape (for more detailed accounts see Gowda and Sridharan 2007; Sridharan 2002). Historically, the Congress dominated the party landscape, building on its legacy as the all-encompassing movement that led

India's struggle for independence from the British. Postindependence, the Congress won seven of the first eight general elections from 1952 to 1984, except 1977, and has governed India for fifty-four of seventy-three years. It had an unbroken domination for the first thirty years of free India, and won pluralities of the vote of 40 percent and above against a fragmented and regionalized opposition. Even since 1989 it has remained the single largest party by vote share, though not by seats, in each of the seven elections from 1989 to 2014, losing that status in 2014 and 2019. The Congress is a secular party that believes in a linguistically and cultur-ally diverse notion of Indian nationhood and remains broadly acceptable to all segments of the population.

There are four other major categories of parties (though these groups of parties do not necessarily constitute a coalition, by any means). These are, first, the Hindu nationalist parties (the Bharatiya Janata Party [BJP], and the Shiv Sena); second, the communist parties, also termed the Left Front (including the Communist Party of India (Marxist) [CPI(M)] and the Communist Party of India [CPI]), and the various Communist Party of India [Marxist-Leninist] splinters); third, the agrarian/lower-caste populist parties (the Janata Party, the Janata Dal, and its offshoots like the Sama-jwadi Party, Rashtriya Janata Dal, Rashtriya Lok Dal, Biju Janata Dal, Janata Dal [Secular], and Janata Dal [United]); and fourth, the ethno-regional or ethnic parties based on particular regional linguistic groups or lower-caste blocs or tribes (in the northeastern states in particular). Exam-ples of such ethno-regional parties are the Dravida Munnetra Kazhagam (DMK) and the All India Anna Dravida Munnetra Kazhagam (AIADMK) of Tamil Nadu, the Shiromani Akali Dal of Punjab, the National Confer-ence and People's Democratic Party of Jammu and Kashmir, Asom Gana Parishad of Assam, the Telugu Desam Party (TDP) of Andhra Pradesh, the Jharkhand Mukti Morcha of Jharkhand, various small ethnic parties of the northeastern rim states, and the Scheduled Castes–based Bahujan Samaj Party (BSP).

In some states are regional parties that have been founded by influ-ential leaders. The Nationalist Congress Party of Maharashtra and the Trinamool Congress of Bengal are examples. Most of these, and a large number of even smaller parties, are single-state parties, and are offi-cially termed regional parties.

In terms of the electoral performance of various parties, since the end of Congress dominance in 1989 the pattern of Congress majorities based on vote pluralities has broken down. The Congress plurality fell from 40 percent to as low as 19 percent, and this low share did not enable it to obtain a majority of seats. The three electoral mega-trends since 1989 are, first, the decline of the Congress vote share from 40 percent to 19 percent, though it still won a plurality of votes except in 2014 and 2019; second, the rise of the BJP's share from 11 percent in 1989 to a high of 25 percent in 1998, and then to 37 percent in 2019; and third, the rise of mostly single-state-based regional parties such that the combined vote shares of the Congress and the BJP were less than 50 percent in 1996, 1999, and 2004, and barely 51 percent in 2014, with a rise to 57 percent in 2019. With the communist parties' vote share stagnant at about 8 percent, and crashing to 2 percent in 2019, the bulk of the non-Congress, non-BJP vote goes to ethnic or regional parties organized on the basis of regional, linguistic identities or state-specific lower-caste coalitions. The rise of regional parties is even more pronounced in state assembly elections. Both the BJP and the Congress rule only a minority of states, even as part of coalition governments until the Modi term of 2014–2019.

In terms of seats, both the Congress and the BJP have fallen well short of the 272 seats that are required to form a majority government until 2014. In 2004 both major parties won under 150 seats. Thus coalition and minority governments have been the order of the day since 1989. All coalitions have been large, multiparty minority coalitions (of nine to twelve parties in government), often cobbled together after the elections, and dependent on external support. In 2014 the BJP won a majority of 282 (or 52 percent) of seats based on 31 percent of votes, and in 2019 a majority of 303 seats based on 37 percent of votes. In both cases, it formed what is termed a surplus-majority coalition government by including its preelectoral allies, although their seats were strictly not necessary to demonstrate a majority. Going by vote and seat share it is evident that the number of political parties that have become and remained viable is increasing. Over time, India has clearly emerged as a multiparty democracy despite the BJP becoming the dominant party since 2014. However, its dominance is still not quite that enjoyed by the Congress from 1947 to 1989, either in parliament or measured by its spread across the nation.

Underlying Drivers of Party System Evolution

What are the underlying drivers behind these electoral mega-trends and the emergence of large, multiparty coalitions? There are, broadly speaking, two classes of explanations for the configuration of party systems in the comparative literature. One can be called the social cleavage theory of party systems, and the other the political-systemic theory of party systems, of which the most well-articulated is the electoral rules theory of party systems. The electoral rules theory has been enhanced by influential recent theorizing based on the division of powers among various levels of government.

The social cleavage theory postulates that the party system will reflect the principal cleavages in society, as for example between capital and labor in ethno-culturally homogeneous industrialized societies, with parties positioned on a left-right spectrum. In the Indian context, this theory would predict that political parties would emerge to capitalize on several politically salient cleavages, for example caste or ethnicity, religion, language, and region (such parties are said to be indulging in "identity politics"). Yogendra Yadav (1999) argues that the rise of identity-based parties represents the political empowerment of historically marginalized groups and reflects favorably on the vibrancy of political entrepreneurship. In the Indian case, political fragmentation has not led to significant instability because of the political system's ability to include these diverse parties in power-sharing arrangements.

The political-systemic theory, particularly the electoral rules theory, postulates that the larger political system's features, and more specifically the electoral system's rules, will be reflected in the number, relative weight, and ideological positioning of political parties.[1] Principally, these rules include the size of constituencies (number of representatives elected from each constituency), the structure of the ballot (choosing a party list, an individual candidate, or a mix of the two), and the decision rule or electoral formula (proportional representation, first-past-the-post, variants of each). These features interact to create varying disproportionalities between votes and seats, and hence incentives for the coalescing or splitting of political forces.

A leading electoral-rules theory, Duverger's Law, would predict that the single-member constituency, first-past-the-post electoral system will result in a two-party outcome, at least at the constituency level. In a first-past-the-post system, small parties would have an incentive to merge into larger formations to aggregate votes to obtain the winning plurality or alternatively to form preelectoral coalitions for the same purpose.

From 1967 onward, a consolidation of the non-Congress opposition took place, state by state, in tandem with such consolidation in state assembly elections. This bipolar consolidation was the key feature and driving force of the fragmentation of the national party system.[2] But this bipolar consolidation has been one of multiple bipolarities (e.g., Congress-BJP, Congress-left, Congress–regional party, in different states), thereby contributing to fragmentation at the national level. Duvergerian dynamics were the drivers of these multiple bipolarities.

In India's federal polity, states are typically linguistic and cultural entities, and parties that reflect such social cleavages flourish therein. Duvergerian dynamics can lead to bipolar systems at the state level due to the consolidation of the state-level opposition to the principal party at the state level, whether it is a national or regional party. This leads to a multiparty system nationally because the state-level two-party systems do not consist of the same two parties (Rae 1971). Indeed, they can consist of a variety of parties, some national, some purely state-level. The delinking of national and state elections since 1971 has reinforced the systemic properties of the first-past-the-post electoral system. Further, because the division of powers between the center and states makes it sufficiently attractive to achieve power at the state level alone, this too drives the bipolarization of state-level party systems.[3] The playing out of the Duvergerian dynamic has resulted in the consolidation of regional/linguistic- or caste/ethnic identity–based parties in a large number of states.

For explanations emphasizing the division of powers between levels of government—national, state, and local—the argument goes as follows (see Chhibber and Kollman 1998, 2004). Other things being equal, the greater the political and economic powers of state governments in federal systems over decisions that most affect the lives of citizens, the greater a political prize the capture of power at the state level represents. Hence, the greater incentive there is for political entrepreneurs to form state-level political parties, and for voters to vote for such parties. Conversely, the more centralized the powers are over decisions that most affect citizens, the more incentive there is for political entrepreneurs to coordinate to form nationwide political parties and for voters to vote for such parties and to ignore state-level parties. Hence, a more multiparty system can be expected under the former circumstances and a less multiparty system can be expected under the latter circumstances. It is the former situation that prevails in India. Regional parties have also benefited from the fact that the national parties have developed highly centralized "high command" decisionmaking cultures that are renowned for their opacity. In contrast, it is easier in regional parties for local level leaders to access their party leaders and to influence their decisionmaking.

Leadership: Key Leaders and Their Impact

India's trajectory has been shaped before and since independence not only by parties but also by their leaders. India has had towering political leaders over the past century. The greatest and internationally best-known was undoubtedly Mohandas Karamchand Gandhi (1869–1948), better known as Mahatma (Great Soul) Gandhi. He was the undisputed leader of the

Congress Party (not always the party president; the latter was elected every year) and transformed the Congress from an elite party into a mass party through his nonviolent mass mobilization and civil disobedience campaigns against British rule in a gradualist process that extracted increasing concessions from the colonial power. A British-trained lawyer, originally from Gujarat but transcending provincial boundaries, he emerged as a pan-Indian leader soon after he returned from two decades in South Africa in 1914. He preached nonviolence, which he saw as a moral force apart from a political strategy, and launched a noncooperation movement in the early 1920s and a civil disobedience movement in the early 1930s, which had the effect of turning the Congress into a mass movement and mobilizing a very broad swathe of Indian society into the independence movement. It made the Congress an umbrella party encompassing the diversity of Indian society. Gandhi was a devout Hindu but believed in a secular and inclusive state that included all as equal citizens. He was tragically assassinated by a Hindu extremist in January 1948, less than six months after India's independence.

Mahatma Gandhi, leader of the independence movement. Photo courtesy of Indian National Congress, https://www.inc.in/en/inc-timeline/1925-1935.

India has had fourteen prime ministers since independence, not counting acting/interim holders of the office, and some of them have served two or three terms, sometimes in different spells, with the longest-lasting serving seventeen years and the shortest ones less than a year (five of them).

The first prime minister and best-known and impactful leader after Mahatma Gandhi was Jawaharlal Nehru (1889–1964), a leader of the Congress Party who became India's prime minister for seventeen years (1947–1964), during which time he deepened the foundations of India's parliamentary federal democracy, shaped its foreign policy as he held the foreign affairs portfolio throughout that period, and launched India's postindependence economic development. Under Nehru's leadership the Congress Party won three consecutive elections in 1952, 1957, and 1962 by large majorities, as well as winning by majorities the state assembly elections in almost all states except Jammu and Kashmir and Kerala in that period when state elections and national elections were held simultaneously. This gave him the political stature and strength to undertake major initiatives that shaped the subsequent political economy and policy framework of India's democracy.

Under Nehru, the constitution was debated and adopted in the Constituent Assembly by 1950, and the linguistic reorganization of India's states was accomplished in 1956. Social reform in the form of the reformation of Hindu marriage and succession was accomplished by 1956. Economic development took off, with the rate of economic and industrial growth during his rule reaching new heights compared to the

Jawaharlal Nehru, prime minister from 1947 to 1964. Photo courtesy of Indian National Congress, https://www.inc.in/en /inc-timeline/1935-1945.

stagnation of the last fifty years of the colonial period, although these growth rates were not high compared to those achieved by postwar recovering economies or by many newly industrializing postcolonial economies. The centerpiece was a drive to create a basic and heavy industrial base in the Second Plan of 1956–1961 and Third Plan of 1961–1966 and the creation of a base in science and technology education and research. This included the setting up of the Atomic Energy Commission as early as 1948 and early initiatives in the space and missiles areas. In foreign policy the paradigm adopted along with some other leading developing countries was that of nonalignment, which meant not being part of either the United States–led Western or Soviet-led communist blocs in the Cold War of the 1950s and 1960s.

Nehru also vigorously supported continued decolonization worldwide. Nehru has been critiqued for a too-trusting attitude to China, specifically for accepting the Chinese takeover of Tibet without negotiating explicit boundaries and for a post–World War II military build-down. On economic policy he has been critiqued for neglecting agriculture, primary education, and health and creating a state-led, protectionist model of industrialization that did not create internationally competitive products. His major achievement was to stabilize India's democracy and federalism based on repeated free and fair elections and launch industrialization and build a scientific base. His major failure was India's defeat in the October–November 1962 border war with China.

The next best-known Indian leader is Indira Gandhi (1917–1984), Nehru's daughter, who was prime minister for sixteen years in two spells, 1966–1977 and 1980–1984. While she is regarded as an achiever for India's victory in the Indo-Pakistan war in 1971, which led to the carving out of an independent Bangladesh from Pakistan, and for India's first nuclear test in 1974, she is also remembered for negative developments like the emergency rule of 1975–1977, in which democracy and fundamental rights were suspended. Her rule saw two major splits in the Congress Party, in 1969 and 1978, and the centralization of power and suspension of internal democracy within the party.

She also misused Article 356, imposing central rule on opposition-party-led state governments many times on flimsy pretexts. In response to the food and foreign exchange crises of the late 1960s, she intensified state-led development, nationalizing the major banks in 1969, and insurance and coal in the early 1970s, and placed restrictions on big business and foreign companies. However, under her rule parts of India benefited from the green revolution and India became increasingly self-sufficient in food production. Her rule saw India's nonalignment acquire a slant

*Indira Gandhi. Photo courtesy
of Government of India Press
Information Bureau.*

toward the Soviet Union, particularly from the Indo-Soviet accord of 1971 just before the Bangladesh war to hedge against a perceived US tilt toward the Pakistan-China axis. However, she began liberalizing imports and improving relations with the United States in her last term, which also saw the rise of a Sikh separatist insurgency in Punjab. After a long period of slowdown from the late 1960s to 1980, gross domestic product (GDP) growth picked up to over 5 percent in her final term. She was assassinated by her Sikh bodyguards in October 1984.

Seven other prime ministers who were impactful in their own ways were, in chronological order, Lal Bahadur Shastri, Morarji Desai, Rajiv Gandhi, V. P. Singh, P. V. Narasimha Rao, Atal Bihari Vajpayee, and Manmohan Singh. Lal Bahadur Shastri's brief nineteenth-month rule saw the India-Pakistan war of 1965 fought to a draw, but with India initiating the doctrine of counterattack at any point of its choosing across the border in response to Pakistani aggression in Jammu and Kashmir. He also pacified the anti-Hindi agitators in the non-Hindi-speaking states in 1965 by adopting an accommodative stance on the issue of Hindi as the official language of the union by retaining English as long as the non-Hindi states wanted it, and thereby contributed to India's unity.

Morarji Desai (r. 1977–1979) was a former Congress Party leader and cabinet minister who became the prime minister of the Janata Party, formed in 1977 by the unification of several non-Congress opposition parties that fought against the period of emergency rule. Though technically a single party, it was in effect a hastily put-together coalition and marked India's first experiment in coalition government. Desai was responsible for reversing the authoritarian measures taken during the emergency period by Indira Gandhi and restoring democracy and fundamental rights and the independence of the judiciary.

Rajiv Gandhi (r. 1985–1989) was catapulted to prime minister at the age of forty by the assassination of his mother, Indira Gandhi. The Congress Party he led won the biggest ever electoral victory in 1984, a three-quarters majority in the Lok Sabha based on a 48 percent vote share. In his five years in office he launched an early attempt to liberalize the economy, started a computerization drive that led eventually to the creation of a vibrant information technology industry, presided over five years of high growth, took initiatives to modernize the armed forces and weaponize nuclear capability, and tested the first in the Agni series of ballistic missiles. He also pacified separatist movements in the states of Assam and Mizoram with accords in 1985 and 1987. He further took steps to improve relations with the United States and China. His term was marred by the Bofors arms-import payoffs scandal, which led to the Congress Party losing the 1989 election.

Vishwanath Pratap Singh, prime minister for eleven months of 1989 to 1990, came to power as part of a broad National Front coalition in pre-electoral alliance with both the Hindu-nationalist BJP and the left, conceding a large number of seats to the BJP in northern, central, and western India, which played a decisive role in boosting the BJP to national party status. He also implemented the Mandal Commission report of 1980, which created quotas in government jobs and college admissions for the caste-defined Other Backward Classes, a development that impacted Indian politics across the board in that it created politician consciousness and mobilization around Other Backward Classes identities in broad swathes of India, as well as upper-caste and Scheduled Caste mobilizations in reaction. His government was also India's first true coalition government, and also a minority government, inaugurating a twenty-five-year period of minority and coalition governments from 1989 to 2014.

P. V. Narasimha Rao (r. 1991–1996), a former cabinet minister, was catapulted to prime ministership in May 1991 after being hauled out of retirement due to the assassination of Rajiv Gandhi. He took charge at a time of a desperate balance-of-payments crisis in which India had to approach the International Monetary Fund (IMF) for a bail-out. He appointed Manmohan Singh as his finance minister and launched an economic liberalization program that led to a consistently higher growth rate, causing India to become one of the world's fastest-growing economies. He also prepared the ground for testing a nuclear device in 1995, but called it off because the preparations were detected by US satellites; in the process he created the foundation for subsequent nuclear testing by the Vajpayee government in 1998. However, he continued to improve relations with the United States and China in the early post–Cold War era and launched new initiatives such as the Look East Policy (toward Asia) and established diplomatic relations with Israel. The major failure in his term was his inaction that allowed a frenzied Hindu nationalist mob to demolish a sixteenth-century mosque built on a site in the town of Ayodhya in north India that was believed to be the specific spot where the Hindu god Rama was born. This triggered waves of rioting and bloodshed, resulting in a large number of deaths and religious polarization of society. This is possibly a reason why the Congress Party downplays his legacy despite his record in turning the economy around to a higher growth path.

Atal Bihari Vajpayee (r. 1998–1999 and 1999–2004) was India's first prime minister from the Hindu-nationalist BJP. He ran a short-lived government in 1998–1999 followed by a full-term government over 1999–2004. Both were minority coalitions dependent on external supporting parties, and hence the Hindu nationalism of the BJP was moderated by these circumstances. Vajpayee continued the process of economic liberalization and technological modernization, extending it to the beginnings of a limited privatization of public enterprises and self-imposed fiscal rectitude. However, his signature initiatives were the conducting of five nuclear tests in May 1998 and the declaration of India as a nuclear weapons power, and following that the overture to Pakistan that resulted in the February 1999 Lahore Declaration, which included an agreement on notification of missile tests to stabilize deterrence and prevent war by miscalculation or misperception. The brief Kargil border war with Pakistan in the then state of Jammu and Kashmir also took place when he was prime minister. It led US president Bill Clinton to intervene and arrange for an unconditional Pakistani retreat from the Kargil sector, which in turn led to improved India–United States relations and a long, drawn-out dialogue on India's nuclear status with the United States. This laid the ground for the Indo-US civil nuclear deal signed by the subsequent Congress-led government.

Manmohan Singh (r. 2004–2014) was an Oxford PhD in economics and a longtime government economist who had held top economic advisory and administrative positions before he became finance minister under Prime Minister P. V. Narasimha Rao in 1991 and launched India's economic liberalization. His ten years in office make him the third-longest-serving prime minister after Nehru and Indira Gandhi. During his two terms India enjoyed an economic boom, riding out the world-wide economic downturn of 2008. As prime minister, however, he was considered weak in two senses: one, in that the Congress Party did not enjoy a majority on its own but headed a coalition called the United Progressive Alliance, which was dependent on other parties, particularly on the left in its first term, 2004–2009; and two, that Congress president Sonia Gandhi, the widow of former prime minister Rajiv Gandhi, and Congress vice president Rahul Gandhi, were thought to have held the real reins of power. Manmohan Singh was also the only person from a religious minority (Sikh) to become prime minister.

The current prime minister, Narendra Modi (first term 2014–2019, now in his second term, beginning May 2019), has also been impactful in both domestic and economic policies and in foreign and defense poli-cies. Riding to power on the basis of his reputation as an incorruptible and effective chief minister of the economically dynamic state of Gujarat, he is the first prime minister to lead a majority government in Lok Sabha after Rajiv Gandhi, and the first prime minister from the BJP to enjoy such a majority (although the BJP-led government continues to retain pre-electoral allies and is technically a coalition called the National Demo-cratic Alliance [NDA]). Modi has continued India's economic reforms by undertaking some structural reforms that have long-term benefits even at the cost of short-term dislocation, such as a code on insolvency and bank-ruptcy that helps loss-making companies shut down; and a goods and services tax, a major reform of indirect taxes in line with international patterns, and with trying to reduce the fiscal deficit. However, his reforms have not extended to privatization of public enterprises.

He has brought extraordinary energy to foreign policy, making an unprecedented number of foreign visits and meetings with major world leaders. He has extended past initiatives toward East and Southeast Asia, particularly with Japan and China, and in adroit balancing acts with the Israelis, Gulf Arabs, and Iranians, as well as improving rela-tions with the United States under both the Obama and Trump adminis-trations while maintaining ties with Russia. He has shifted the emphasis away from South Asia to the Bay of Bengal region, taking a hard line with Pakistan by conducting surgical strikes into Pakistan-held territory in response to terrorist strikes in 2016, and authorizing an air strike in response to similar provocations in February 2019, both of which have redefined India-Pakistan escalation dynamics.

Prime Minister Narendra Modi sworn in, 2019. Photo courtesy of Government of India,
https://www.pmindia.gov.in/en/pms-profile.

Modi came to power with a fearsome reputation as a hardline Hindu nationalist who was hostile to India's minorities, particularly Muslims, and this was mainly because of his association with the Hindu right and the anti-Muslim 2002 pogrom, which lasted weeks when he was chief minister of Gujarat. Although the Supreme Court cleared him of culpability, he is widely considered not to have intervened sufficiently to stem the riots. While no major riots took place in his first term as prime minister, a number of Muslims were lynched and attacked at various places for allegedly participating in cow slaughter. Modi has been slow to condemn such anti-Muslim attacks, and many associate his behavior with the desire to change the ideological center of gravity of Indian politics from constitutional secularism to Hindu nationalism. The manner in which the BJP and its allies have sought to capture and control the activities of the media and universities adds to the fears of India's secular supporters. These fears erupted in widespread mass protests across India led by students against a law called the Citizenship Amendment Act, passed in December 2019, under which non-Muslim illegal immigrants from Bangladesh, Pakistan, and Afghanistan, principally from Bangladesh and mostly in Assam state in the northeast, would be granted citizenship on the grounds that they were persecuted minorities in Muslim-majority and officially Islamic countries, whereas illegal Muslim immigrants would be denied citizenship. The protests were broad-based and not limited to the Muslim community. The fear was that the act, when linked with the proposed National Register of Citizens, for which every resident would have to produce documents proving citizenship, something large numbers might not be able to do in a largely rural country still characterized by widespread poverty and illiteracy, would render large numbers of Muslim citizens stateless while non-Muslims without the requisite documents would be saved from such a fate by the Citizenship Amendment Act. While no rules had been framed for the National Register of Citizens as of early 2021, the BJP's perceived anti-Muslim ideology, the pronouncements of some BJP leaders including Home Minister Amit Shah, and a feeling that linking the grant of citizenship to religion went against the secular character of the constitution, fed the protests. As of now, it looks like Modi will have to grapple with such perceptions and their consequences well into his second term.

Party Structure and Functioning

While leadership is important, it is also important to look at how parties select leaders and the processes of internal democracy.[4] Broadly speaking, following Lars Bille, there are six types of nomination processes in political parties in Western European parliamentary democracies, ranging from completely top-down to completely bottom-up at the two extremes, with four intermediate levels of decentralization or participation by the party rank-and-file, or in other words by levels of inclusiveness of the selectorate for nominations. These fall, from the most to the least centralized, into the following six broad categories:[5]

1. Candidate selection is completely controlled by the national party leadership.
2. Subnational party organs propose names but national leadership makes the final decision.
3. The national leadership provides a list of names from which the subnational party organs make the final selection.
4. Subnational party organs make nomination decisions, but need the final approval of national leaderships, and the latter can add or delete names according to various criteria.
5. Subnational party organs control the entire process and make the final decisions.
6. Nomination decisions are based on membership ballots, which are not the same as an open primary, but nevertheless the closest to grassroots participation.

The United States represents the decentralized extreme, that of party primaries for presidential and congressional elections. However, it needs to be noted that these party primaries are conducted by state and local officials, publicly funded and under law, and not by party officials under party rules and with party funds. This system came into effect for presidential primaries from 1912 to 1968, running in parallel to the party convention, and since then has become the determinant of candidacy for public office.

India lies near the other extreme in that most of its major parties are at the completely or near-completely top-down of the six types of party nomination processes, with the national party leadership having the final say. The two major Indian parties, the Congress and the BJP, fall into the second-most-centralized category.

In the Congress Party, there was an elaborate system consisting of observers sent to each of 543 Lok Sabha constituencies to prepare reports on potential candidates in their constituencies for the district Congress committees and the pradesh (state) Congress committees. These committees give inputs to the state election committees, which send a panel of names listing the pros and cons and relevant details of each potential candidate to the All India Congress Committee (AICC). The AICC appoints a screening committee for each state, which consists of important party leaders including a senior member of the Congress Working Committee; two senior leaders who do not belong to the state; the chief of the state Congress committee; and the leader of the state Congress Legislature Party. The screening committees prepare a docket listing the pros and cons and relevant details of each potential candidate and send these to the central election committee of the party, the highest organ in the process, which makes the final decision. Although the process is supposed to begin and be completed early, well ahead of the election campaign, in actual practice the screening and nomination process begins late and drags on to the last moment. This is deliberate, because early nomination is feared to lead to disappointed nominees either leaving the party or sabotaging the nominee's prospects. The process is one in which the central party organization makes the final selection based on the dockets sent up by the state election committees and centrally appointed screening committees for each state, although even at that level there are senior leaders for each state who do not belong to that state and hence are supposed to play the role of neutral arbiters.

In the BJP, there are just two formal levels of decision, the State Election Committee and the Central Election Committee. The former is the final authority for municipal- and local government–level elections in each state, with there being no need for names of potential candidates to be sent to the latter. For state assembly and parliamentary elections, the Central Election Committee plays a recommendatory role, suggesting names of candidates for each constituency, but the committee makes the final selection.

What this means is that the top leadership in both parties is much more able to influence the rise of personnel through the party than if the process were more decentralized and bottom-up. Leadership therefore plays a role in Indian politics that is more than just about policies while in power; it is also about influencing succession to the top levels.

Conclusion: The Stability of India's Unity and Democracy

Many have found it puzzling how a country as diverse as India has managed to stay united and avoided secession, despite some attempts among groups to separate. Equally puzzling to observers is how, except for emergency rule between 1975 and 1977, India has operated as a stable democracy despite enduring poverty and low levels of literacy. For it appears being diverse and poor would seemingly work to India's disadvantage.

Arend Lijphart (1999, 2007), the originator of the concept of consociational (power-sharing) democracy, has outlined ten major characteristics that distinguish a majoritarian democracy from a consensus democracy. Arguing that "the main institutional rules and practices of modern democracies—such as the organization and operation of executives, legislatures, party systems, electoral systems, interest groups and the relations between central and lower-level governments—can all be measured on scales from majoritarianism at one end to consensus on the other," Lijphart (2007: 16) says that in diverse societies democracy boils down to the questions of who will do the governing and to whose interests the government should be responsive to when there is disagreement. The answer to these questions is the majority of the people in majoritarian democracies and as many people as possible in consensus democracies.

Lijphart then divides the ten characteristics into two clusters of five each—the executives-parties dimension and the federal-unitary dimension. The first cluster "groups together five characteristics of the arrangement of executive power and of the electoral, party and interest group systems":

(1) majoritarian and disproportional electoral systems versus various forms of proportional representation (PR);
(2) two-party versus multi-party systems;

(3) concentration of executive power in single-party majority cabinets versus executive power-sharing in broadly multi-party coalitions;
(4) executive-legislative systems in which the executive is dominant versus executive-legislative balance of power;
(5) pluralist interest group systems . . . versus coordinated and corporatist interest group systems aimed at compromise and concertation. (2007: 16–17)

The second cluster—the federal-unitary dimension—consists of:

(1) unitary and centralized government versus federal and decentralized government;
(2) concentration of legislative power in a unicameral legislature versus division of legislative power between two . . . houses;
(3) flexible constitutions that can be amended by simple majorities versus rigid constitutions that can be changed only by extraordinary majorities;
(4) systems in which legislatures have the final word on the constitutionality of their own legislation versus systems in which laws are subject to a judicial review of their constitutionality by supreme or constitutional courts;
(5) central banks that are dependent on the executive versus independent central banks. (2007: 17–18)

In each point in each cluster, the first-mentioned characteristic is the more majoritarian one and the second-mentioned the more consensual one.

Lijphart's argument (1996), which he reiterated (2007), is that India has survived as a democracy and become an (increasingly) united country due to its being a consociational democracy—one that has most of the above-mentioned power-sharing features, particularly in the post-Congress dominance era of coalition politics after 1989. In examining his ten variables, one would note that India lies toward the consensus end in at least six of the ten—numbers 2 and 3 in the first cluster and numbers 1 to 4 in the second cluster. India's political system thus amounts to an effective power-sharing system.

The second factor that has contributed to India's unity and the stability of its democracy is the widely held and deeply internalized notion of what the Indian nation is. This is the notion of what Nehru termed "unity in diversity" rather than one of a homogenous nation. The traditional European-origin notion of a nation is one that is defined by objective characteristics such as race, ethnicity, language, religion, and culture, with these engendering a sense of political community. Ideal-typically, such nation-states would have a single, overwhelmingly dominant ethnic group with a common language and culture and established religion (church). Such identification can be described as ethnic nationalism. Sweden, the Netherlands, Japan, and Portugal are good examples of ethnic nation-states.

However, nations are political—not just ethno-linguo-religio-cultural—communities defined not only by objective (racial, ethnic, linguistic, religious, and cultural) characteristics but also by subjective identification—that is, by a shared sense of belonging to a political community by groups who may differ on racial, ethnic, linguistic, religious, and cultural lines but who nevertheless identify with the state that is built on the territory they live on due to a sense that the state represents or reflects their interests and ideals and includes them in who it is responsive to. This can be called civic or territorial nationalism and is exemplified by countries like the United States, Switzerland, and India. In these countries, the population overwhelmingly identifies with the state, as it and its diverse groups feel that it includes and is responsive to them in both symbolic and material terms.

Juan Linz, Alfred Stepan, and Yogendra Yadav (2007) apply the concept of state-nation against nation-state to India by building on the work by Linz and Stepan (1996). As the former put it, "The old wisdom holds that the territorial boundaries of a state should coincide with the perceived cultural boundaries of a nation" (2007: 50). They argue:

> The states we would like to call state nations are multicultural, and sometimes even have significant multinational components, which nonetheless still manage to engender strong identifications and loyalty from their citizens, an identification and loyalty that proponents of homogeneous nation states perceive that only nation states can engender. (Linz and Stepan 1996, quoted in Linz, Stepan and Yadav 2007: 52)
>
> By contrast, "state nation" policies stand for a political-institutional approach that promotes multiple but complementary sociocultural identities. "State nation" policies recognize the legitimate public and even political expression of active sociocultural cleavages, and they involve mechanisms to accommodate competing or conflicting claims made on behalf of those divisions without privileging or imposing any one claim. "State nation" policies create a sense of belonging (or "we-feeling") with respect to the state-wide political community, while simultaneously creating institutional safeguards for respecting and protecting politically salient sociocultural diversities. (2007: 54)

State-nations succeed by having power-sharing political systems and practices with constitutional underpinnings. Linz, Stepan, and Yadav (2007) argue that India is a state-nation rather than a nation-state, the nation being created by an inclusive and encompassing freedom movement led by a Congress party that could be so described and then cemented by an inclusive and power-sharing constitution that has over time strengthened identification of people in all states of the country, with India so defined despite a number of sometimes bloody stresses and strains. They stress the role of an inclusive, constitutionally defined power-sharing political system in nation building, specifically state-nation building. In sum, India's unity and democratic stability have been mutually reinforced by the fact of a power-sharing political system as well as by a widely held inclusive notion of the nation as inherently diverse but nevertheless united by threads of commonality.

Finally, to end with some speculation about how the Covid-19 pandemic that broke out in early 2020 will affect India's politics, one can venture to say the following. First, the stability of the Modi government, which has a solid majority and which has a term until 2024, will probably not be affected. Polls in the summer of 2020 showed majority support for the government, and that the opposition is disunited and unable to come up with a convincing alternative narrative and policy package. Second, however, one needs to qualify this conclusion, since the scale of economic contraction due to the pandemic's associated lockdown has been considerable, pushing millions into joblessness and poverty, and if these effects last well into 2021 there could be a popular discontent whose political shape is unpredictable. Third is the risk of a centralization of power, since central government's battle against the pandemic has tended to become almost rule-by-decree in some instances and has tended to bypass institutions like parliament and the opposition parties; the contraction has weakened the states fiscally as well. An overcentralization of power could affect the quality of democracy and could set off unpredictable reactions. However, all this is merely informed speculation and much depends on the speed and scale of recovery of economic and public health.

Notes

1. Taagepera and Shugart (1989) emphasize ballot structure, district magnitude, and electoral formula as the basic variables. Lijphart (1994) emphasizes, in addition, a derivative variable, effective threshold of representation, and assembly size, and considers the special cases of presidentialism and apparentement (linking of party lists).

2. For an account and explanation of the Duvergerian dynamic of bipolarization at the district and state level, see Chhibber and Murali 2007.

3. See Sridharan 2002 for a detailed account of the bipolarization of party systems.

4. See Farooqui and Sridharan 2014 for a detailed account of party structure and functioning in India.

5. This categorization paraphrases Bille 2001: 367.

5

Economies and Development

Rahul Mukherji and Seyed Hossein Zarhani

India was an extremely poor country when it gained independence in 1947. A region that had contributed a large share toward global GDP prior to British colonial domination, the country now experienced poverty and illiteracy while trying to recover from the grotesque violence that accompanied Partition. Alleviating poverty and growing the economy thus became the foremost goals of India's postindependence leaders.

India's first prime minister, Jawaharlal Nehru, and others associated colonialism with capitalism, and it was therefore not surprising that they embraced the mixed-economy option when seeking to develop India. The private sector would increasingly come under government control and planning, and the state would launch its own enterprises. The sense that India's challenges were so vast that only the central government could successfully oversee resource allocation to develop the country was also a powerful reason for promoting such a trajectory. In what follows we discuss India's mixed economy and the country's subsequent transformation rooted in globalization and private entrepreneurship. This growth, along with direct measures to alleviate poverty, has certainly made an impact on citizen well-being.

India is not a classic developmental state where powerful state authority disciplined the industrial classes or the landed gentry. Comparative political economists have produced much literature on how powerful states in East Asia, such as Japan, South Korea, Singapore, and Taiwan, guided industrialists to become globally competitive (Herring 1999; Evans 1995; Mukherji 2016). This demanded firm and often authoritarian oversight. The rapid economic growth these states experienced led to substantial socioeconomic transformations, denoted by their being branded "tiger" economies.

India has instead muddled through. Between 1956 and 1975, which marks the most intensive phase of economic planning, India's economy grew haltingly at about 3.4 percent annually. This was a period when the country emphasized the role of government-owned industries as opposed to private ownership. The state was also heavily involved with directing investments during this period. The ensuing dismal performance led to the epithet "Hindu rate of growth." This was a term first used by the famous Indian economist Raj Krishna in the late 1970s to connote the idea that India was not performing like the rest of the rapidly growing East Asian economies.

This reputation has changed in recent times, with the economy growing annually at 4.8 percent between 1975 and 1990 and accelerating furthermore to 6.3 percent between 1991 and 2018.[1] This most recent growth surge has made India the third largest economy in terms of purchasing power parity. Purchasing power parity is considered a better indicator of how much can be purchased on the basis of national income than on nominal gross domestic product.[2]

India's citizens, however, face many challenges, with the Covid-19 crisis exacerbating these challenges. The Human Development Index (HDI), which was established by the United Nations Development Programme and takes a multidimensional view toward deprivation by assessing factors such as health, education, gender equality, and income, illustrates the extent of the difficulties facing India. The country ranks 130th on the HDI despite being the seventh largest economy in nominal terms. Neighboring Sri Lanka and China rank 76th and 86th respectively.[3] Given the multidimensional nature of deprivation, the poor Indian HDI rank reveals that India's spectacular growth has hardly reached its citizens.

It is for these reasons that the rights-based approach to development was initiated around 2005, with powerful laws dealing with the right to information, education, work, and, for forest dwellers, the right to forest resources. The rights-based approach to development stresses that every Indian has certain basic rights.

India represents a gradual developmental model where dominant ideas propelled the state to transform institutions only after reaching a tipping point. For instance, it took India over a decade and a half to move beyond the mixed-economy paradigm and embark on globalization in 1991. Similarly, subnational states such as Andhra Pradesh and Tamil Nadu in southern India successfully implemented the right to work after years of policy learning when they realized that catering to most citizens was a surer way of ensuring electoral success than appeasing certain groups in exchange for support at the polls (see Figure 1.1 for the map of India). The most poverty-stricken subnational states, such as Bihar and Jharkhand, on the other hand, could not effectively implement this transition.

The first section of this chapter demonstrates the tipping-point model of policy and institutional change that typifies change within India's democratic framework (Finnemore and Sikkink 1998; Keck and Sikkink 1998; Capoccia and Kelemen 2007; Mukherji 2013, 2014a; Jha 2018b).

The second section, on economic growth and industrialization, deals with the politics of India's growth. It discusses how the dominant idea of economic independence governing the state led to a long period of slow growth (1956–1975) that discouraged trade and private enterprise (Bardhan 1984). The closed economy created a powerful group of industrialists, farmers, and professionals lobbying against opening the economy to the private sector and trade. The next period (1975–1990) constituted a time when India criticized its past policy formulations, until it reached a tipping point in 1990. By then the country had experimented with private sector involvement and was keen to depart from the old path, when a balance of payments crisis opened the door to globalization. In the face of powerful vested interests, the balance-of-payments crisis of 1991 allowed the state to effectively deal with those opposed to globalization. Globalization has produced one of the most rapid, sustained rates of economic growth. India's trade-to-GDP ratio rose from a low figure of 16.9 percent in 1991 to 55.7 percent in 2012. That figure has declined somewhat in more recent years but is substantially greater than in 1991.[4] The second section ends with some cautionary words about recent developments, even though India's growth is on a firm footing.

The third section deals with India's attempts to alleviate poverty by focusing on the rights-based approach and details the transition the country has made toward taking its responsibility for citizens more seriously. How did this occur in the case of the right to information, the right to work, and the right to forest resources? Here too there was a gradual and evolutionary story at work. The section ends by pointing to certain recent developments that could erode the rights-based approach to development.

Finally, the chapter factors in the extent to which Covid-19 has affected India and what this means for the country's economy in the years ahead.

Gradual Evolution of Policy Ideas

How the state in India thinks about policies is important for understanding what kind of policies will be deployed to deal with issues connected with economic development. Policy paradigms are a cluster of theories that explain economic phenomena such as economic growth or, for that matter, how the poor in India can be lifted out of poverty.[5] Policy paradigms reveal why policies and institutions persist. Fundamental policy change such as the transition from the closed economy to globalization has much to do with how old policy ideas are challenged when economic results do not meet expectations. The closed economy model, for example, emphasizes the exploitative nature of trade, whereas globalization theories suggest that trade and foreign investment are critical for economic growth.

India's closed economy policy model depended on high tariffs, an overvalued exchange rate, and a large number of import and production controls. The government also took complete control over investment over many sectors of the economy. Private companies were disallowed from investing in sectors such as iron and steel, coal, and airlines. These controls gave substantial powers to the state, which could decide which industrialists to favor when pursuing industrialization. A trade-oriented and globalizing economy, on the other hand, mandated fewer controls over trade and investment and greater emphasis on private initiative. The policy paradigm favored at a given time reveals how the state intends to develop its economy.

Most economic change in India was incremental—be it globalization or implementing welfare through the rights-based approach. Incremental change accumulated over time to counter the incumbent policy paradigm or the basic theory on which old policies were based. For instance, if economists believed that the closed-economy model would deliver growth with equity, countervailing ideas emphasizing globalization needed to evolve before they could be put into practice. In short, the country had to reach a tipping point in order for drastic change to take effect.

The tipping model involves gradual change in ideas and policies in a certain direction over a period of time. When policy change has reached a threshold building on new ideas, the system tips abruptly and discontinuously. The tipping model requires us to demonstrate three stages of policy evolution. The first stage is when a certain old policy idea is dominant. The second is when the old policy idea is substantially challenged over time to reach a tipping point. Finally, at the threshold or tipping point, change from the past is discontinuous.

The metaphor of boiling water is useful here. Water begins to boil suddenly at 100 degrees Celsius—but only after sufficient heat is supplied for a certain amount of time. Even though boiling appears like a sudden phenomenon, it is the result of heating a vessel of water over time. It is when water reaches 100 degrees Celsius after the continuous application of heat that water begins to boil. In terms of the tipping analogy, water reaches a tipping point at 100 degrees Celsius, when it changes its state from water to vapor. The gradual process of heating over time, when it reaches a threshold, finds a conversion from the liquid state to the gas state (Mukherji 2014a; Goldstone 1991; Taleb and Blyth 2001; Finnemore and Sikkink 1998).

Scholars think that many social phenomena have a tipping characteristic as well. Both India's globalization and its embarking on the rights-based approach largely adhered to the tipping model. If class and vested interests revealed why change was difficult in India, the tipping model demonstrated how economic transformation was enacted gradually because of the strong will of the state. We detail this dynamic through the evolution of Indian growth and welfare policies.

Economic Growth and Industrialization

India's growth and industrialization trajectory can be divided into three phases. The first is the period of slow growth between 1956 and 1974, famously called the Hindu rate of growth. The economy grew at a snail's pace of 3.4 percent annually at a time when the economies of South Korea, Japan, Taiwan, and Singapore had taken off. This was when India embraced import substitution, or the closed economy model of development, with substantial government intervention (Bhagwati and Desai 1970). The second period, between 1975 and 1990, was when India began to analyze critically its old policies and accord the private sector and trade a bigger role. Here economic change favoring entrepreneurship was gradual. It resembled the situation when water is supplied with heat but does not begin to boil. Gradual deregulation, however, led to a surge in the rate of growth (4.8 percent). Finally, in 1991, came the tipping point. Even though globalization was aided by a balance-of-payments crisis, the deregulation momentum of the 1980s led India to herald substantial policy change favoring deregulation. India had faced a similar crisis in 1966. But then policymakers were convinced about the closed economy model and, notwithstanding pressure from the United States, the country turned even more inward after 1967 (Frankel 2005: 434–490; Panagariya 2008: 59–71). The dominant economic ideas within the Indian state were important both in 1966, when the closed economy model was at its height, and in 1991, when the state had reached a tipping point favoring globalization.

State Control and Economic Independence, 1956–1974

There is substantial evidence to demonstrate that it was the dominant view within the state that led to the health and long life of the import substitution or closed economy model. During this period trade and foreign investment were considered exploitative and Indian industrialists were not considered significant for propelling growth. As mentioned earlier, this is the classic period that can be characterized as the Hindu rate of growth.

During the period 1956–1974, economic planning with a dominant role of the state was consolidated. Nehru's chairmanship of the Planning Commission ensured influence. The prime minister invited eminent statistician and economist Prasanta Chandra Mahalanobis to head the commission as its deputy chairman. Mahalanobis was not just the deputy chairman of the Planning Commission; he also established the world-renowned Indian Statistical Institute. This institute became a mecca for scholarship on economics and statistics. Mahalanobis worked very closely with the prime minister to give economic direction to the country. Soviet planning impressed both, even though they were not willing to give up India's liberal democratic framework.

Consequently, the Indian Statistical Institute and later the Planning Commission became the venue for debates on the trajectory of the Indian economy. Indian policymakers heard arguments ranging from left-oriented scholars, such as Maurice Dobb, to free market liberals, like Milton Friedman, and such varied perspectives allowed them to judge the pros and cons of economic models and their suitability for the times.

When the Planning Commission formulated India's famous second five-year plan in 1956, it was clear that economic thinking had moved in the direction of centralization and state control. Powerful industrialists such as Ghanshyamdas Birla became less influential and were not allowed to construct a steel plant. Likewise, the Tata Group, another powerful industrial conglomerate, was not permitted to manufacture cars. Such was the power of the Planning Commission that India's first finance minister, John Mathai, resigned from his position in 1950. He was unhappy that the Planning Commission was usurping the job of the Ministry of Finance (Hanson 1966: 122–145; Frankel 2005; Dhar 2003: 230–233).

Capital-intensive industries such as iron and steel, which were too important to be made the purview of private companies, were expected to propel India toward economic modernity, and they could not be left to the initiatives of profit-making private companies. The financial demands of capital-intensive industrialization even led India toward a balance-of-payments crisis in 1957, just a year after the ambitious plan

The Ambassador, the definitive Indian automobile before liberalization of the economy and still the standard vehicle of choice for India's ministers and top bureaucrats, pictured here in the mid-Himalayas. Photo by Neil DeVotta.

was initiated. India's capital-intensive import substitution produced poor-quality consumer items like the famous Ambassador car that could have contributed to the overall inefficiencies that dodged the economy.

The second five-year plan neglected agriculture for the same reason. There were very few resources left for investment in agriculture after all the spending on heavy industrialization. The planners tried to compensate for low investment levels with land reforms and cooperative farming. Land reforms distributed plots to landless peasants so as to make agriculture more intensive, while cooperative farming allowed farmers to pool their lands and introduce modern methods to increase yields. But such organizational changes failed to produce the desired effect (Varshney 1998: 28–47).

India consequently became heavily dependent on food-grains imports from the United States. The United States was concerned that India's democratic experiment should not fail as a result of an agricultural crisis. Thus the cheap wheat imports from the United States served as a bulwark against communism and revolution in India (Muirhead 2005).

The extent to which import substitution was entrenched in the state's thinking was on display during the balance-of-payments crisis of

1966 following wars with China (1962) and Pakistan (1965) and droughts during 1965 and 1966. Indeed, India could have experienced famine-like conditions if not for the subsidized US food-grains exports. The United States had considerable leverage over Indian policymakers at this time and sought to use it.

What did the United States demand from India? President Lyndon Johnson and World Bank president George Woods both wanted India to move toward an export-oriented system with greater importance given to private enterprise. They also desired India to become self-sufficient in food grains and invite foreign technology and investment. They felt the Indian rupee needed to be devalued to more realistic levels. These were the main conditions placed on policymakers. Devaluation by making exports cheaper and imports more expensive would have moved the economy toward globalization.

The Indian response was to pretend acquiescence by devaluing the currency in June 1966. This, however, was just a pretense, and most of the policy conditions were reversed by 1967. Not only did India reverse the devaluation decision after the shipments of wheat arrived, but the government even distanced itself from the export model (Mukherji 2014a: 38–62; Ganguly and Mukherji 2011: 67–68; Bjorkman 1980: 232–233).

The most stringent policies associated with the closed economy, or import substitution, model took place between 1969 and 1974. For instance, the Monopolies and Restrictive Trade Practices Act (1969) regulated large Indian private enterprises to a greater degree, while the Foreign Exchange Regulation Act (1974) reduced the maximum foreign equity in an Indian subsidiary from 51 percent to 40 percent, which drove many foreign enterprises out of India. Additionally, many companies that were hitherto allowed to operate privately were nationalized. Only the government was allowed to invest in sectors such as wheat production, copper production, banking, and insurance.

When it came to attaining self-sufficiency in food grains, India did take advice from the United States, consistent with import substitution. The Mexican wheat variety enabled India to double wheat production between 1965 and 1970. Dependence on US-supplied food grains may have driven India to bow to US conditions on agriculture (Lewis 1995: 135), but it ensured India would not face a similar food crisis.

Puzzling over Policies, 1975–1990

The period after 1975 witnessed a growing disenchantment regarding the slow pace of economic growth in India. India's import substitution was supposed to engender growth and reduce poverty. But growth at a level below 3.5 percent annually was accompanied by a stagnant poverty rate. The government responded in two ways. First, various committees began criticizing old policies. Second, gradual but discrete measures were taken to deregulate the economy. There was emphasis on according a greater role to private companies than on attracting foreign investment or competing with the global economy.

It is these policy experiments that brought India to a tipping point in 1991. The first stage had witnessed the rise of the closed economy model. The second stage found the government criticizing the closed economy model and implementing policies that gave the private sector greater powers in running the economy. These experiments created a threshold in policy experience that emboldened the state to break from the past by embracing globalization in 1991.

One of the greatest impediments to investment was the state dictating which company could produce what and how much. It was a bizarre situation where the state was telling industrialists to curb production. These government controls retarded investments.

The first schemes for increasing investment capacity without the government's permission were announced in 1975 and 1976. Prime Minister Indira Gandhi (1966–1977), who had authored the most stringent version of the closed economy model, would now become the initiator of these policy changes. This trend continued during the Industrial Policy Resolution of 1980 under her premiership (1980–1984) and beyond.

Indeed, there was bipartisan support for deregulation after 1975. From here until 1991 all parties supported critical reforms within the state. The idea of deregulation and the need to engage the world was becoming hegemonic over time. Various reports of the government of India criticized the import substitution model. These influential reports were chaired by eminent economists and public servants such as Padinjarethakal Cherian Alexander (1978), Vadilal Dagli (1979), Abid Hussain (1984), Arjun Sengupta (1984), and Maidavolu Narasimham (1985).

These reports stressed the need for exports in order to promote India's development. The closed economy had negatively impacted India's economic health. Moreover, physical and financial controls on industry and entrepreneurship throttled manufacturing productivity. Industrialists were mired in a plethora of controls such as who would produce where, and how much.

Some of the founding fathers and consolidators of Indian planning now began to express themselves against planning. For instance, Lakshmi Kant Jha, a former finance secretary and governor of the Reserve

Bank, opined that the Indian economy was running not with one or two but sixteen brakes. By just releasing a few brakes the economy would automatically take off (Mukherji 2014a: 68). Another economic czar, Indradas Gordhanbhai Patel, argued that the Indian economy had turned into a rent-seeking racket (Patel 1987: 216–218), referring to how industrialists invested in maintaining contacts with politicians to keep their business privileges. Patel had drafted the second five-year plan under the tutelage of Mahalanobis.

The government paid heed to its own self-criticism and gradually deregulated Indian industry. Prime Minister Rajiv Gandhi delicensed thirty industries and eighty-two pharmaceutical products. The Monopolies and Restrictive Trade Practices Act was diluted as well. All companies worth less than 200 million rupees were freed from government controls. Sectors such as information technology, pharmaceuticals, and auto components, which were delicensed in the 1980s, became the very sectors where India subsequently became globally competitive in the 1990s. Companies in these industrial sectors could open production without seeking the government's permission. To spur India's information technology, the prime minister established the Department of Electronics under the direct supervision of the prime minister's office. India's information technology and services sector later became the poster child of the country's globalization drive when leading companies outsourced their work within and beyond India.

Private companies were empowered in two other ways as well. First, income and corporate tax rates were reduced. Second, there was some import liberalization—especially for promoting exports. Liberalization of computer imports, for example, helped private companies engage with software exports.

Another significant area of deregulation was Indian telecommunications. Two events are notable in this area. The government created the Department of Telecommunications (1985) within the Ministry of Communications to spearhead the development of telecommunications. The department helped create the Mahanagar Telephone Nigam Limited (MTNL) in Delhi and Mumbai (1986). Prime Minister Rajiv Gandhi had envisioned the MTNL operating in six Indian cities, but with the telecom work force opposing the government-owned MTNL being run like a private enterprise freed from political interference, he settled for just Delhi and Mumbai.

Another major development in the area of Indian telecommunications was the establishment of the Center for the Development of Telematics (CDOT) in 1984, directly under the supervision of Prime

Minister Rajiv Gandhi. The CDOT turned out to be so successful in creating innovative technology that its telephone exchange switches were superior to those manufactured by the Indian Telephone Industries (in collaboration with the French multinational Alcatel), which led to CDOT technology being licensed to private companies (Athreya 1996; Mukherji 2014a: 112–114).

Prime Minister Rajiv Gandhi was also instrumental in encouraging those associated with the Association of Indian Engineering Industry (AIEI), which eventually became the Confederation of Indian Industry (CII), to help the economy take off, and the organization played an important role in India's globalization beyond 1991 (Mukherji 2014a: 89–92; Sinha 2005: 1–27).

This was also a period when India's agriculture boomed in relative terms, fueled by farmers' movements. The state became generous with prices given to farmers for producing food grains such as wheat and rice. It ensured generous prices no matter what the international fluctuations were. Agriculture growth at 3.4 percent annually was higher than ever before but still lower than industrial growth, which nearly reached the 5 percent level (Ganguly and Mukherji 2011: 77–78; Dev 2010: 28; Omvedt 2005: 185–190).

India's growth engine, which was based on industrialization, took off during this period. This is why the period from 1975 to 1990 can be considered the second phase leading to the 1991 tipping point. This tipping point was reached only because politicians and bureaucrats experimented with industrial deregulation that yielded results. By 1990, the year before India sought assistance from the International Monetary Fund, the special secretary to Prime Minister Montek Singh Ahluwalia circulated a memo regarding the drastic nature of reforms required to make a clear break from the past. This memo became the basis for India's economic reforms.

Tipping Point: Deregulation and Globalization, 1991–2014

The year 1991 was a tipping point for two reasons: it culminated in new ideas being enacted, and led to drastic change. To give one example, the drastic devaluation of the rupee in July 1991 was carried out after the Reserve Bank of India had tried the effects of gradual devaluation in the 1980s. Overall, India's economic policies were substantially transformed to promote private and foreign investment. India became far more dependent on international trade and investment after 1991. India's growth rate beyond 1991 at 6.3 percent annually rendered it among the fastest-growing economies in the world.

In this regard, the proximate cause was the balance-of-payments crisis that erupted in early 1991 in the aftermath of the 1990 Gulf War. This war drastically raised the price of oil, which increased India's import bill. Foreign commercial banks were unwilling to lend to India at a time when the country's budget deficit had shot up to 10 percent of gross domestic product. Credit-rating agencies such as Moody's likewise signaled commercial lenders to not lend to India. Under these circumstances, India devalued the rupee in early July 1991 and the historic industrial policy resolution and budget were announced on July 24. These are the big measures that constituted a tipping point in India's economic journey.

There was certainly an external shock to the economy at this time, but at 1 percent of GDP it was no greater than the two earlier oil shocks in 1973 and 1979. India had weathered those shocks with greater ease when its budget was rather more balanced. In 1991, on the other hand, India was spending beyond its means and the lending agencies did not deem India to be creditworthy. It is important to take note of the fact that India's woes had more to do with internal spending than with the oil shock after the Gulf War (Joshi and Little 1994: 180–189; Bhaduri and Nayyar 1996: 22–30; Mukherji 2014a: 74–76).

Were the reforms homegrown or imposed due to foreign pressure? There are important reasons to claim the reforms were spurred by largely indigenous factors. First, crises have made only a temporary impact on India. As noted earlier, the balance-of-payments crisis of 1966 led to a short and halfhearted retreat to devaluation, only to be overtaken by the most stringent version of the closed economy model. The crisis of 1966 and consequent foreign pressure did not spur globalization when India was thoroughly convinced about the closed economy model.

The second reason supporting an indigenous impetus for reforms has to do with the manner in which the recovery package was negotiated with the IMF and World Bank. Classic adjustment demands that countries drastically reduce expenditure, bring down the power of trade unions, lower farm subsidies, and sell government-owned enterprises. India reduced its fiscal deficit for only one year, kept farm subsidies, and did not reduce the power of trade unions. There was no selling of public sector assets.

What then were the tumultuous changes that marked 1991 as a tipping point? The changes of 1991 were rather discontinuous from the past. First, there was drastic currency depreciation that immediately made Indian exports more competitive. Second, the policy of controlling industrial investment by the central or federal government was reversed. Most industries could now invest in products without prior permission of the central government. Third, the consequences of the

Foreign Exchange Regulation Act were reversed. Most sectors could invite foreign investment up to the 51 percent level, and in some sectors the level was even raised to 74 and 100 percent. Tariffs, especially those on intermediate goods, were also drastically reduced.

Powerful Indian industrialists, especially those grouped as the Federation of Indian Chambers of Commerce and Industry, had opposed the reforms of 1991. The crisis helped to deal with these powerful groups because the state was convinced that deregulation and globalization was in industry's long-term interest. That decision has catapulted Indian business to a higher level (Mukherji 2014a: 89–92).

These changes cemented India's reputation as an investment destination. Sectors such as telecommunications, which were entirely serviced by state-owned enterprises, are now served predominantly by private and foreign players. Indeed, India today enjoys one of the lowest telecom tariffs in the world. Companies such as the Tata Group became substantial multinational companies, buying up automobile brands such as the Land Rover and Jaguar. Today these cars, manufactured in Britain, come under the rubric of Tata Motors. Likewise, Bharat Forge became the third largest metal-forging company in the world, just behind Thyssen Krupp and Sumitomo Metal.

Artifacts for export manufactured in Faridabad at Adhya Design. Photo by Ayon Mukherji.

These developments have also transformed the dynamics of relations between the center and the states. Before the 1990s, the union government and Planning and Finance Commissions were responsible for making decisions associated with the allocation of resources. As a result, subnational states had little direct influence on economic planning and investment decisions. The Planning Commission was earlier the main actor when it came to economic planning (five-years plan) and financial transfers.

All this changed after 1991. The role of the subnational states in investment decisionmaking increased substantially. This new investment process has led to the heightened role of subnational state governments in economic planning. This phenomenon is popularly known as the emergence of a federal market economy, with subnational states now playing the dominant role in investment (Rudolph and Rudolph 2007; Zarhani 2019).

In this new environment, state governments compete to attract investments from domestic and multinational companies and international financial organizations such as the World Bank. This earlier confrontation between the center and state governments has now transformed itself into interstate competition for financial resources. In this new federal market economy model, the prime minister and union government may determine economic planning and financial allocation, but the subnational, state-level chief ministers also play important roles (Wyatt 2017; Zarhani 2019).

India's globalization story is driven more by its prowess in the software sector than in manufacturing. Software multinationals such as Tata Consultancy Services, Wipro, and Infosys have earned India a valuable global reputation, besides foreign exchange. For example, Infosys began with a startup capital of $250 in 1981 and had earned a market capitalization of $46.5 billion by 2019.

Substantial challenges remain for India's economic growth. First, the country needs to develop its manufacturing sector. Second, India's growth has not produced jobs. The National Sample Survey data suggested that unemployment stood at an all-time high of 6.1 percent in 2017–2018 (National Statistical Office: 82). While infrastructure sectors such as telecoms, airlines, and airports have taken off, other provisions such as power, roads, and ports are in dismal shape. India has to address these problems to ensure that growth is more robust and equitable.

Third, India is not one but a diversity of many different types of economies that produce divergent standards of living. If one were living in Tamil Nadu, Karnataka, or Gujarat, it would be like residing in an upper-middle-income country; in Rajasthan or West Bengal, it would be like living in a lower-middle-income country; but in Bihar or Uttar Pradesh, India would resemble sub-Saharan Africa. India's economic growth has exacerbated inequalities, and there are so many Indias within one country that it is difficult to draw conclusions about the entire country's living standards from any one location. This economic diversity poses a significant challenge for India.

Trends After Prime Minister Narendra Modi, 2014–2019

This section discusses the recent trends in India's political economy under Prime Minister Modi's first government (2014–2019). It describes India's growth story after 2014 and other significant developments like the establishment of the National Institution for Transforming India (NITI) Aayog (Agency); implementation of the goods and services tax; and the controversy over demonetization. Most of these current developments represent the incremental experimentation and cogitation embedded within Indian technocracy and its political class. The 2016 demonetization decision, however, can be attributed to the sudden fancy of the prime minister's office, which was rather abrupt and chaotic.

The Modi government came to power with the promise of good governance and a determination to fight corruption. Consistent with Prime Minister Modi's reputation as the former can-do chief minister of the subnational state of Gujarat, international competitiveness in manufacturing was emphasized (Jaffrelot 2015b). Moreover, the National Democratic Alliance (NDA) manifesto admitted the importance of rapid economic growth.

The country clocked an impressive annual average rate of growth rate of 7.35 percent between 2014 and 2018.[6] But the government has spurred unprecedented controversy over the new methodology used by the National Sample Survey Organization (NSSO) to calculate employment and economic growth.[7] The methodological alterations make it difficult to compare the new and old data. Former government economic adviser Arvind Subramanian (2019) has argued that India's growth between 2011–2012 and 2016–2017 has been about 4.5 percent rather than 7.35 percent. It does not bode well that India's economic growth, using the new methodology, has plunged to a six-year low of 5 percent during the three months leading up to June 2019.

Moreover, the government refused to release unemployment figures on the eve of the 2019 elections because the statistics portrayed a dismal picture for the year 2017–2018. Two members of the National Statistical Commission resigned owing to the delayed release of the National Sample Survey's December 2018 report. They claimed that

132 Rahul Mukherji and Seyed Hossein Zarhani

the NSSO was being unfairly challenged by the deputy chairman of the NITI Aayog.

The abolition of the Planning Commission and its replacement by NITI Aayog was touted as another major change by the Modi government. While the previous United Progressive Alliance governments had overseen the destruction of the planned economy, and Prime Minister Manmohan Singh had argued for a transformation of the Planning Commission from a "money allocator" that coerced economic reforms to an organization that "persuaded" stakeholders, the actual structural reconfiguration took place under the Modi administration (2014–2019).

It is difficult to assess the impact of the NITI Aayog given that it has been around for only half a decade. Its function is substantially different from that of the old Planning Commission. For example, NITI Aayog, unlike the Planning Commission, does not enjoy financial powers and therefore cannot allocate funds to ministries and state governments. NITI Aayog is designed to resemble a think tank rather than an implementing agency. That authority has been transferred to the prime minister's office and the Ministry of Finance (Swenden and Saxena 2017).

Implementing the historic goods and services tax at the pan-Indian level is another important development under the NDA regime. This is a comprehensive tax system that subsumes all indirect taxes levied and collected by the center and state governments and aims at integrating various sections of the economy to create a unified and comprehensive tax system and seamless national market. This is a significant milestone in the history of taxation in contemporary India. The goods and services tax was to be implemented during Prime Minister Manmohan Singh's second term, but various stakeholders delayed its implementation. Notwithstanding complaints about the implementation of the tax, the NDA government has displayed remarkable political will by amending the constitution and the goods and services tax bill to institute tax reform.

The goods and services tax, like other government efforts, is not a sudden policy innovation of the Modi regime. The saga began in the 1980s when Finance Minister V. P. Singh announced the modified value-added tax under Prime Minister Rajiv Gandhi. And successive governments under Prime Ministers Atal Bihari Vajpayee and Manmohan Singh had worked on the tax to make the idea part of the government's reform discourse.

Finally, the infamous Indian demonetization of 2016, unlike the efforts described earlier, was purely a product of Prime Minister Modi's calling. It was a sudden and unexpected move, decided and planned by the prime minister and his close circle of advisers. Demonetization ordained that certain currency notes cease to be legal tender. It took effect when the Modi government declared all 500 and 1,000 rupee banknotes invalid in November 2016. The government also announced the issuance of new 500 and 2,000 rupee banknotes in exchange for the demonetized banknotes. The government justified demonetization to fight the untaxed black economy. Moreover, the prime minister believed that it would target the cash deployed to fund insurgencies and terrorism. The government opined that several separatist groups in Jammu and Kashmir and Maoist outfits deployed fake bank notes to finance terrorist activities.

Despite early optimism both within and outside India, the economic impact of demonetization was largely negative. In the short term, demonetization engendered a cash famine that hit the middle and the poorer sections of Indian society. The agricultural and informal sectors that rely on the cash economy were severely hit by this move. Indeed, demonetization may have led to the substantial job losses described earlier (Ghosh, Chandrasekhar, and Patnaik 2017). The Reserve Bank of India even reported that demonetized currency worth 15 trillion rupees had found its way back into banks by June 2017.

Citizen Well-Being

This section details how India attempted to deal with the poverty problem after independence. It delineates different phases of poverty alleviation in India. The phases include land reforms, direct redistribution to the poor, and the rights-based approach stressing that every Indian has a right to certain minimum human needs like government information dealing with citizen well-being, work, education, and forest resources.

One of the first responses to substantial rural poverty was the redistribution of lands among farmers. These measures were land reforms or land-ceiling initiatives at the national and subnational levels. The logic of land reform was mostly based on the idea of fair distribution of the means of production among farmers to uplift their life and create capital surplus at the village level (Burgess and Besley 2000). Nevertheless, the results of land reform in the first decades after independence were mixed. In some states, such as West Bengal, leftist parties supported and executed land reform (Bandyopadhyay 2003); on the other hand, in other states, like Bihar and Andhra Pradesh, the dominant-caste groups either hindered the process of reform or used it to garner superior quality lands for themselves (Reddy 1989; Indu 1992).

Land reforms, economic planning, and import substitution, however, did not reduce poverty. Between 1951 and 1974, the total number of people below the poverty line did not vary significantly.[8] The poverty ratio remained in the range of 45 percent to 50 percent during this period. The trend was only reversed in the 1990s. The partial success of antipoverty schemes meant to directly benefit the poor from the mid-1970s and during the 1980s contributed to this effort (Panagariya 2008: 133–136). This was the time when the economy was undergoing the domestic deregulation described earlier (Ganguly and Mukherji 2011: 80).

The proportion of people living below the poverty line declined more sharply after 1991. The national poverty headcount ratio[9] in 1993–1994 was 45.3 percent, and this ratio declined steadily to 37.2 percent, 29.8 percent, and 21.9 percent in 2004–2005, 2009–2010, and 2011–2012 respectively.

More comprehensive indicators like the Multidimensional Poverty Index (MPI)[10] reiterate this decline. Alkire and Seth analyzed the change in India's poverty level between 1999 and 2006. Their findings show that there was considerable reduction in the national MPI from 0.300 to 0.251, by 2.6 percent per annum between 1999 and 2006 (2015: 91). However, this reduction was not uniform across different regional states. For example, Andhra Pradesh had the best performance in the absolute reduction of MPI, while Bihar reduced MPI to the lowest extent. There is a scholarly opinion that while rapid economic growth can be viewed as an important poverty reduction tool, the implementation of a new rights-based approach and redistributive schemes played a significant part in dealing with immiserization (Mukherji and Jha 2017; Mukherji, Zarhani, and Raju 2018).

Rights-Based Approach

The rights-based approach to development has evolved over a large number of policies that India adopted to fulfill the "Directive Principles of State Policy" enshrined in the Indian constitution, giving every citizen certain basic amenities to lead their lives. These principles were not justiciable under the directive principles, even though liberal courts could use them for furthering citizen well-being. These principles had evolved largely endogenously, and the demonstration of certain norms in the global arena often proved useful. Moreover, rapid economic growth, with rising inequalities and unsubstantial impact on well-being, had rendered these rights even more vital for citizens. To give just one example, the story of the right to education began with the National Literacy Mission under Prime Minister Rajiv Gandhi (1988); this became the Education for All Program (2001) under Prime Minister Atal Bihari Vajpayee. The right to education was finally legislated as a right in 2009.

India adopted a rights-based approach to development after 2005 when the Congress-led United Progressive Alliance (UPA) government came to power. Government expenditures for welfare expanded considerably during this period. India could tax its economic growth, especially corporate growth, toward improving the quality of life of its citizens. The rights-based approach included basics such as the right to access privileged government information, the right to become literate, the right to work, and the right to forest resources.

Statutory recognition of citizens' rights to work, basic education, information, food, and livelihood protection (against alienation of land and rights to commons) was brought in via a series of landmark bills during the first (2004–2009) and second (2009–2014) UPA regimes.

The Right to Information Act

The Right to Information Act (RTIA) of 2005 provides a practical administrative framework for seeking and accessing information from public authorities across the country at various levels. While accessing and disseminating governmental information was illegal before this act, it is now a fundamental right of every Indian citizen to seek information from the government. The RTIA makes it justiciable and legal to request

Villagers seeking information about their rights in rural Rajasthan. Photo by Ayon Mukherji.

government information, and expands the constitutionally defined nature of fundamental rights (see Roberts 2010; Jha 2018a, 2018b).

The act was conceived in the run-up to India's 2004 general elections. While it is widely known that this enactment was due to citizen movements for transparency in public services spearheaded by NGOs, movement toward the legislation was a more gradual process. The Mazdoor Kisan Shakti Sangathan (MKSS), a nongovernmental organization based in Rajasthan, was at the helm of a widely discussed need for greater transparency in state activities (Roy and the MKSS Collective 2018). It was also a leader of the National Campaign for People's Right to Information (NCPRI), which spearheaded the demand for an act such as the RTIA. The NCPRI was instrumental in creating pressure on progressive political parties during the first UPA regime in 2004. However, Jha (2018a, 2018b) explains that ideas on "openness" emerged as part of opposition politics within the state after independence in 1947. Such politics, upholding the need for greater accountability in governance, incrementally brought the idea of openness into mainstream politics, so much so that all mainstream, national political parties came to a general consensus regarding the necessity of such a right. This eventually led to the RTIA at an opportune political moment. This institutional change, wherein the norms of secrecy built into the very structure of state institutions tipped toward the norm of openness, is a testament to the gradualist story of reforms and welfare regime in India.

Clearly, the RTIA is a symbol of a new kind of politics around openness in India. It has created new channels of accountability between state and society, linked deeply to national as well as local politics. Jha (2018a), for example, describes an emergent class of right-to-information activists and practitioners whom he terms "agents of accountability." They take up filling out right-to-information applications as an entrepreneurial activity as well as a political assertion, in the process enhancing their local status and agency. A look at right-to-information usage data shows how the act has changed the way people obtain government information today in India. In 2017–2018, over 1.3 million right-to-information applications were filed, an increase of over 26 percent from 2016 to 2017.[11] A total of 96 percent of them were responded to by public authorities, the highest volume and response rate since the act came into being in 2005.

The Right to Work

The right to work was granted to all Indians residing in rural areas in 2005 under what is called the Mahatma Gandhi Rural Employment Guarantee Scheme. It provides every citizen living in villages an ensured 100 days of work. Work needed to be provided on demand. The right was based on the realization that India's economic growth had not generated a substantial number of jobs and that rural India and Indian agriculture had grown slower than Indian industry.

The impact of the right to work was rather uneven. The most poverty-stricken states, like Bihar and Jharkhand, did not implement the right meaningfully. This led to a paradox where dire human misery through economic deprivation did not create any substantial demand for jobs. This was, however, not true for all states. Poverty-stricken states such as Chattisgarh and Rajasthan, on the other hand, created a substantial number of jobs to service this right. Moreover, the right was most successfully implemented in Andhra Pradesh and Rajasthan.

Andhra Pradesh partly succeeded because the state was able to deal meaningfully with the opponents of the right to work (who were large farmers with landholdings and construction companies). These employers worried that implementing this right would lead to an increase in wages and hurt their profitability. They formed a powerful lobby that artificially found ways to suppress the demand for work in rural areas. Such class conflict between the landed class and the landless and marginal peasants is the reason why the right-to-work policy has had limited success in certain states.

How then could Andhra Pradesh empower the landless and the less-well-off sections? First, the state decided that all payments should go to workers rather than be channelized via local, village-level governments. Village-level governments are known for corruption. Wages were therefore paid directly to workers through local post offices and banks. Second, India's leading software company, Tata Consultancy Services, provided a software program that would track the movement of funds from the state to the worker. Third, and perhaps most important, the Society for Social Audit Accountability and Transparency (SSAAT) was established by the state's Department of Rural Development in collaboration with some nongovernmental organizations. The SSAAT administered village-to-village checks for corruption by engaging the beneficiaries. It made such a deep impact on governance in Andhra Pradesh that this social audit was later incorporated as a best practice in other states as well (Mukherji and Jha 2017).

It was the combination of direct wage payments, tracking funds, and social auditing that enabled the state to successfully target the poor in Andhra Pradesh. The Department of Rural Development had learned how to deliver over time, given its experience with poverty alleviation programs and the creation of women's self-help groups.

The Forest Rights Act

Over one-fifth (22 percent) of India's landmass is covered with forests and administered directly by the Department of Forests, located within the Ministry of Environment, Forests, and Climate Change (Forest Survey of India 2017). The ministry has governance powers over 150 million forest-dwelling citizen-inhabitants who belong to the socially oppressed Scheduled Castes, Scheduled Tribes, and Other Backward Classes. They are among the most vulnerable segments of the population. These communities have been residing in forests for generations, and a majority of them rely on access to forests for livelihood, water, wage, fodder, fuel, building materials, medicinal herbs, and food.

The forest dwellers' rights to inhabitation and forest resource use, however, were never properly recorded by a state-dominated forest governance regime (Guha 1983; Gadgil and Guha 1992). Forest dwellers were at the mercy of lower-level forest bureaucracy in their daily experience with the state. They were also rendered defenseless against national enterprises that regularly diverted forested land for developmental and extractive-industrial needs— such as mining, dams, railways, and industrial zones—without appropriate consent or compensation (Radhakrishna 2016). These diversions led to large-scale displacement and dispossession, loss of livelihood, and destruction of lives and cultures throughout India's postcolonial history. It is estimated that over 50 percent of India's tribes have migrated out of their original inhabitation in a state of dispossession.

The Forest Rights Act of 2006 (implemented from 2008 and amended in 2012) is a landmark legislation in favor of forest-dwelling tribes. A recent study by the Rights and Resources Initiative estimates that the act has the potential to redistribute over 40 million hectares of forestland to over 150 million forest dwellers (Community Forest Rights—Learning and Advocacy 2016).

Implementation of the Forest Rights Act at the subnational state level, however, is marred by several problems. Only 3 percent of the potential forestland was formally transferred to forest communities. There is lack of awareness about the act (Community Forest Rights—Learning and Advocacy 2016). Forest officials want to preserve their old rights to the forests rather than grant them to forest dwellers. Moreover, agencies of the state that wish to grant land rights are often at odds with other agencies that wish to protect the status quo.

There is substantial subnational variation in implementation of the Forest Rights Act. Even so, 4.2 million claims were filed up to April 2019, of which just under 2 million were approved (Ministry of Tribal

Affairs 2019). Besides protection from eviction and harassment at the hands of forest officials, the families and communities now have greater say in forest-land diversion projects, and enjoy better access to irrigation, housing, education, rural credit, and agricultural extension schemes. The transformative impact of the Forest Rights Act is gradually becoming visible (Lele and Menon 2014).

There have also been setbacks in the recent past. Forest Rights Act provisions have often been ignored and bypassed using legal loopholes in India's antiquated and labyrinthine local and subnational land laws. State-supported private enterprises in mining and metal industries have emerged as the most visible players in this matter. In February 2019, the Supreme Court of India ordered the eviction of over a million tribal citizens whose Forest Rights Act claims had been rejected due to a case filed against the Forest Rights Act by a group of exclusivist conservationists. While civil society action and support from the Ministry of Tribal Affairs helped stay this order, the state could weaken Forest Rights Act implementation in its true spirit by awarding more powers to the forestry department in the name of wildlife conservation and exclusive afforestation. Creating legislation that makes forest-land diversion for industrial usage easier by bypassing people's self-governance groups (made mandatory by the Forest Rights Act and other progressive land acts) could be on the anvil (see Rajalakshmi 2019). How this story unfolds will decide the future of social justice for India's forest dwellers.

The Predicament of Covid-19

In September 2020, India was adding the largest number of daily Covid-19 infections in the world (approximately 80,000).[12] At the number two position in the world, India overtook Brazil in September 2020. Its economy had contracted by almost 24 percent in the second quarter of 2020.[13] Both these figures reveal that economic and health management in India had been dealt a severe blow by the government headed by Prime Minister Modi. The poor implementation of the goods and services tax described earlier enabled the state to collect much less revenue than originally predicted. Consequently, state governments that were starved for funds could not be paid their dues at the very moment when they needed more finance. Health, after all, is a state-level subject in India. Second, there were also substantial policy failures. Migrant laborers who come to metropolitan cities from villages and small towns were forcibly restrained by a curfew-like lockdown in Covid-infested metropolises. They were left in the lurch without work and without much economic support from the end of March 2020 until mid-May 2020. When they were allowed to return in mid-May, they carried with them infections, and left behind the productive capacities that they had nurtured (see Mukherji, Prasad, and Zarhani 2020).

Conclusion

The Indian economy is not just a matter of economic data. Its movement and transition have much to do with social and political processes. While the industrial classes can retard the move toward globalization when powerful companies benefit from a closed economy model, ideas within the state can alter this over time—be it for embracing globalization or implementing the right to work. Unless the state is firm in its resolve, it will be difficult to deal with powerful social adversaries of reform.

India represents a gradual model that evolves after issues are debated deeply and widely; it is not dictated by the whims and fancies of a prime minister. Both the embrace of globalization and the rights-based approach were debated before they were taken from drawing board to implementation. On the other hand, when the country sought to manage the economy without such deliberation—demonetization under Prime Minister Modi—it resulted in unnecessary disruption and substantial unemployment.

Economic ideas often follow a tipping logic. For example, the policy formulations associated with economic growth under a closed economy model are different from those associated with the globalization model. These ideas evolve over time and, after they have reached a threshold, tip to produce discontinuous change. This is how economic change favoring globalization occurred in India.

Going forward, India faces challenges on both the growth and welfare fronts. The rights-based approach needs strengthening at a time when lower growth is having a dismal impact on citizen well-being. In this context, the government's attempt to weaken citizens' right to information does not bode well. For information is key to government accountability in India. The manner in which the country's thinking process evolves even while combining politicking with citizens' necessities will determine how India's economy continues to develop.

Notes

1. World Bank, "World Development Indicators 2019," https://data.worldbank.org/indicator/NY.GDP.MKTP.KD.ZG?locations=IN.

2. India is the third largest economy in the world in terms of purchasing power parity (PPP). The PPP figure, which is more realistic than nominal GDP, tells the US dollar value of the goods and services produced in India, if they were valued in the United States. World Bank, "World Development Indicators 2019," https://databank.worldbank.org/data/download/GDP_PPP.pdf.

3. United Nations Development Programme, *Human Development Report 2018,* http://hdr.undp.org/en/countries/profiles/IND.

4. It was 40.7 percent in 2017.

5. A state does develop some dominant ideas about how to run various spheres of economic activity. The closed economy policy model, for example, will produce an industrial policy that is quite a contrast from the globalization model.

6. This calculation is based on World Bank, "World Development Indicators 2019," https://data.worldbank.org/indicator/NY.GDP.MKTP.KD.ZG?locations=IN.

7. The new methodology measures the GDP by market prices instead of factor costs, to consider gross value addition in goods and services as well as indirect taxes. Moreover, in the new methodology, the base year was shifted to 2011–2012 from the earlier 2004–2005 base year.

8. The poverty line in these calculations is defined as 57 rupees ($7.36) per capita per month for urban areas and 49 rupees ($6.33) per capita per month using 1973–1974 as the base year.

9. National poverty headcount ratio is the percentage of the population living below the national poverty line. National estimates are based on population-weighted subgroup estimates from household surveys.

10. The Multidimensional Poverty Index identifies multiple deprivations at the household and individual level in health, education, and standard of living.

11. Press Information Bureau, Ministry of Personnel, Public Grievances, and Pensions, January 3, 2019, https://pib.gov.in/newsite/PrintRelease.aspx?relid=187141.

12. This calculation is based on data provided by the Johns Hopkins Coronavirus Resource Center, https://coronavirus.jhu.edu/region/india.

13. "GDP Contracts by Record 23.9% in Q1," *The Hindu,* August 31, 2020, https://www.thehindu.com/business/Economy/indias-gdp-contracts-by-record-239-in-q1/article32489345.ece.

6

International Relations

Sumit Ganguly

What have been the key drivers of India's foreign policy since its emergence as an independent state from the collapse of the British Indian Empire in 1947? How have these underlying determinants of its foreign policy evolved over time? What are its likely directions in the foreseeable future? This chapter discusses the sources of India's foreign policy, highlights key turning points, and focuses on the country's likely future course.

The roots of India's foreign policy must be traced to its nationalist movement in general and to a specific nationalist leader, Jawaharlal Nehru, in particular. The nationalist movement was, for the most part, secular, anticolonial, and anti-imperialist. Consequently, these ideas were to manifest themselves in postindependence India's foreign policy. Without question, the most important exponent of these views was India's first prime minister, Jawaharlal Nehru. He had long evinced a deep interest in international affairs, had traveled widely during the interwar years, and had a subtle grasp of both Indian and world history. His understanding of international affairs was more than evident in his writings on critical global issues of the day (Nehru 2018).

Not surprisingly, though some of his other nationalist colleagues had had some interest in global affairs, he emerged as someone who was first among equals. Consequently, he faced no real challenge when he not only assumed the mantle of the office of the prime minister after independence but was also his own minister for external affairs (foreign minister).

From the outset Nehru's foreign policy priorities were clear. He was determined to maintain India's hard-won independence in foreign affairs, promote decolonization, hobble the use of force in international affairs, and reduce global inequalities. To that end, quite early in the day, Nehru forged the doctrine of nonalignment along with Gamal Abdul Nasser of Egypt, Marshall Josef Broz Tito of Yugoslavia, and President Sukarno of Indonesia (Abraham 2008). The doctrine, as is well known, was designed to steer India away from the emergent struggle between the two principal ideological blocs that the United States and the Soviet Union were spearheading. Nehru was genuinely fearful that aligning with either bloc would distort India's fundamental developmental priorities, lead to wasteful defense spending, and above all curb India's freedom of action in the realm of foreign policy (Rana 1969). Furthermore, he was also concerned about the dangers of Bonapartism in a nascent nation if scarce funds were lavished on the military (Ganguly 1991).

Nehru's aversion to the use of force faced an early test. This came about in the wake of a Pakistan-based tribal invasion of the princely state of Jammu and Kashmir designed to seize the territory through the use of force (Whitehead 2007). When the ruler of the state, Maharaja Hari Singh, appealed to Nehru for assistance, he promptly allowed the airlifting of Indian forces to stop the tribal onslaught (Sen 1994). While the Indian forces successfully stopped the onslaught of the tribal invaders along with their Pakistan army, supporters managed to seize a third of the state. On the advice of Lord Mountbatten, the last viceroy, Nehru referred the issue to the United Nations Security Council. While the Security Council successfully secured a ceasefire, the issue quickly became embroiled in the politics of the Cold War (Dasgupta 2001). Despite two subsequent wars (in 1965 and 1999) over the status of the state, the issue is no closer to a resolution.

Despite this resort to force to protect what he deemed to be India's legitimate security interests, Nehru proved to be a relentless campaigner for global peace. In this context it appears appropriate to discuss three of his principal initiatives: international peacekeeping operations, global nuclear disarmament, and decolonialization. The first two endeavors reflected his conviction in the power of what American scholar Andrew Kennedy (2011) has referred to as the role of "moral efficacy" in the transformation of international politics.

India took an early lead in United Nations peacekeeping operations. As early as 1950, it had contributed a medical contingent during the Korean War and also provided a custodian force for the Neutral Nations Repatriation Commission at the cessation of active hostilities (Ramesh 2018). Later it was a member (and chair) of the International Control Commission and contributed a substantial number of troops to support its operations in Vietnam. The purpose of this organization was to implement the Geneva Accords, which had called for the partition of Vietnam following the defeat of the French at Dien Bien Phu (Thakur 1984). In subsequent years, India was also a major contributor to the United Nations Emergency Force in the Gaza Strip and the Sinai in the wake of the 1956 Arab-Israeli conflict.

Nehru was also an ardent proponent of multilateral nuclear disarmament. To that end, as early as 1954 Nehru proposed a "standstill agreement" on all further nuclear testing. Later this proposal was forwarded to the United Nations Disarmament Commission (Johnson 2009). Though the quest for a comprehensive nuclear test ban proved to be mostly fruitless, it nevertheless paved the way for the Partial Test Ban Treaty of 1964.

Finally, Nehru was also a staunch advocate of decolonization. He spoke out vigorously about the need for decolonization and played a significant role in its delegitimation, especially at the United Nations (Kochanek 1980). Accordingly, when faced with strident criticism from a number of African leaders who were seeking independence from various colonial powers, Nehru authorized the Indian military to oust the Portuguese from their colonial possessions on the west coast of India in 1960. It is important, however, to underscore that Nehru saw the use of force against the Portuguese as a last resort: it was allowed only when negotiations with the Salazar dictatorship to dismantle the colonial enclaves had reached an impasse (Rubinoff 1971).

The Challenge to Nonalignment

The Nehruvian project, however, suffered a major setback in 1962 when the Chinese People's Liberation Army (PLA) launched a well-planned and carefully orchestrated attack on India's Himalayan borders. The Indian army was grossly unprepared for this onslaught. Consequently, despite valiant attempts to stop the intruders, Indian resistance virtually collapsed. The war came to a close with the People's Republic of China (PRC) declaring a ceasefire, but not before it had seized at least 14,000 square miles of what India deemed to be its own territory (Garver 2006).

The impact of the war on Indian foreign and security policy was dramatic. Among other matters, an important debate ensued with the country on the viability of nonalignment. A number of parliamentarians argued quite vociferously that the doctrine had failed to protect India at its hour of need and should therefore be abandoned. However, even in his waning days, few within the Congress Party could challenge Nehru and his legacy. Consequently, the doctrine, at least nominally, remained as the guiding principle of the country's foreign policy.

India did, however, embark on a substantial program of defense modernization in the wake of this war. To that end it chose to place a million men under arms, to raise ten new mountain divisions equipped and trained for high-altitude warfare, and to create a forty-five-squadron air force. These capabilities, though far from being fully realized, nevertheless enabled India to acquit itself well when faced with a second Pakistani attack on its western borders in 1965. Nehru's immediate successor, Lal Bahadur Shastri (1964–1966), although he had had little or no experience in foreign affairs, deftly coped with the consequences of the September 1965 Pakistani attack on India. Among other matters, to relive pressure in Kashmir, he allowed the Indian army to open a second front in Punjab. After the war, Shastri, with Soviet intercession, successfully negotiated a peace accord with his Pakistani counterpart, Mohammed Ayub Khan.

Within six years, India became embroiled in another war with Pakistan. This war stemmed from internal discord within Pakistan, leading to a military crackdown in East Pakistan and the subsequent flight of close to 10 million refugees into India. Indian decisionmakers quickly decided that they could ill afford to absorb this refugee burden and drew up plans for an invasion of East Pakistan. Simultaneously, India started to train and arm an indigenous guerrilla organization, the Mukti Bahini (Liberation Force) to attack and harass Pakistani forces within East Pakistan. In early December, Pakistan, frustrated with India's covert involvement in East Pakistan, launched an air attack on India's northern air bases. With a clear casus belli, India launched a coordinated, full-scale ground, air, and sea-borne attack on East Pakistan and defeated the Pakistani forces in a short, sharp war, leading to the creation of the independent state of Bangladesh.

India's ability to prosecute this war with a free hand in considerable part stemmed from a treaty that it had signed with the Soviet Union in August 1971. This treaty, for all practical purposes, had granted India a virtual security guarantee (Donaldson 1974). In considerable part, India had forged this strategic partnership with the Soviet Union because of US overtures toward the PRC. Pakistan, one of India's principal adversaries, had played a critical role in facilitating this process. Fearing the emergence of a United States–PRC–Pakistan nexus, India felt compelled to guarantee its security interests, leading to the Indo-Soviet treaty. After the 1971 war, India moved even closer to the Soviet Union, distancing itself from the United States.

The bilateral relationship with the Soviet Union, though highly beneficial to India, did entail some diplomatic costs. India's closeness to the Soviet Union kept its relations with the United States both frosty and distant. Its relations with the PRC also remained in limbo, apart from a fitful attempt to improve relations in 1978. This attempt, made during the coalition government led by the Janata Dal (People's Party), floundered when the PRC attacked Vietnam during the visit of the Indian minister for external affairs, Atal Behari Vajpayee, to China. The Chinese stated that they were teaching Vietnam a "lesson" just as they had done with India in 1962. Not surprisingly, Vajpayee cut his visit short, ending any prospect of a rapprochement.

The robust Indo-Soviet relationship was disturbed in the wake of the latter's invasion of Afghanistan in December 1979. At the time of the invasion, India had an interim government under Prime Minister Chaudhuri Charan Singh. It is a little-known fact that the Charan Singh government, despite its shaky status, upbraided the Soviets for their invasion of Afghanistan. When Indira Gandhi returned to office in January 1980, she publicly reversed course. Under her instructions, India's permanent representative to the United Nations, Brajesh Mishra, simply echoed the Soviet position that the regime in Afghanistan had invited the Soviets in. This proved costly for India in both symbolic and material terms. At the level of political symbolism, India's international image was tarnished because it was the only democratic country that appeared to uncritically accept the Soviet explanation for its actions in Afghanistan. It also proved costly in material terms as the Association of Southeast Asian Nations (ASEAN) became wary of India's overtures in that direction.

Despite the bonds that India had forged with the Soviet Union, Indira Gandhi and her advisers realized that they could not indefinitely afford to alienate the United States. Accordingly, in 1981 she met with President Ronald Reagan in Jamaica at a North-South Summit. She also visited the United States at President Reagan's invitation in 1982. The changes that took place in Indo-US relations nevertheless proved to be mostly cosmetic. They did, however, provide a basis for an improvement in relations under her son and political successor, Rajiv Gandhi.

India's dependence on the Soviet Union continued during Rajiv Gandhi's term in office. (1984–1989). However, his fitful attempts to reform the hidebound and near-stagnant Indian economy contributed to some improvement in Indo-US relations. As India moved to slowly dismantle the complex regulatory apparatus that had governed trade and investment regimes, US firms took an interest in the Indian economy. With the growth of commercial ties, some government-to-government contacts also widened. When Rajiv Gandhi visited the United States, a major memorandum of understanding was signed that enabled India to purchase various high-technology items that had previously been unavailable because of US export restrictions.

Closer to home, India's relations with most of its neighbors suffered. India became embroiled in the civil war that had wracked Sri lanka, helping to negotiate a peace accord between the Sri Lankan government of Junius Jayawardene and the principal Tamil insurgent group, the Liberation Tigers of Tamil Eelam (LTTE). India sent a peacekeeping mission, the Indian Peace Keeping Force (IPKF), to monitor a peace that it had brokered between the Sri Lankan regime and the LTTE. The LTTE, however, failed to adhere to the terms of the accord and very quickly the IPKF's role metamorphosed into one of military enforcement. It was ill-suited for this new mission and, after a bloody experience of nearly two years, it withdrew at the request of the next president, Ranasinghe Premadasa.

Relations with India's long-standing adversary, Pakistan, also deteriorated during Rajiv Gandhi's tenure in office. Undeniable evidence emerged about Pakistan's support for the Sikh insurgents in the Punjab and, despite repeated warnings to Pakistan, that support continued unabated. Although many Indians were in favor of some form of similar retaliation, India did not offer aid to insurgents in Pakistan's Sind province. However, the Brasstacks exercise of 1986–1987 may have, in part, been a response to the Pakistani actions.

In late 1986 and early 1987, India carried out its largest peacetime military exercise Brasstacks. It involved tests of some newly developed battlefield tactics and the coordination of some rapid-movement armored formations. Though firm evidence remains unavailable, it is reasonable to conclude that one of the goals of the exercise was to send a message to Pakistan. To the dismay of General Krishnaswmi Sundarji, chief of staff of the Indian army and the architect of the exercise, the Pakistani response proved to be unexpectedly vigorous. Fearful of being trapped in an escalatory spiral, Prime Minister Rajiv Gandhi and the minister of state for defense, Arun Singh, sought US and Soviet intercession. Primarily as a consequence of US help, the crisis was brought to a close (Bajpai et al. 1997).

The End of the Cold War

In the 1990s, India faced several critical foreign policy choices. One involved a response to Saddam Hussein's invasion of Kuwait. India, which had long enjoyed good relations with Iraq, found itself in a quandary. It could hardly endorse the invasion of a sovereign state. At the same time, it did not wish to alienate a major supporter in the Arab world and a critical oil supplier. More to the point, it had several thousand expatriate workers in Iraq. In the end, Indian leaders adopted a cautiously supportive policy toward the US-led coalition forces in the Gulf. In a remarkable departure from past practices, it even allowed US aircraft to refuel in Bombay (Mumbai); this decision, however, was overturned once the matter became public, and several political leaders, most prominently Rajiv Gandhi, sought to embarrass the ruling regime.

Relations with the United States, which had shown some signs of improvement in recent years, again became contentious as the decade drew to a close. In large part because of a more robust relationship with the United States in such areas as trade, investment, and security, the ties fell victim to a single and nettlesome issue, that of nonproliferation. In the mid-1990s, India and the United States found themselves at loggerheads over the US decision to pursue an unconditional and indefinite extension of the Nuclear Nonproliferation Treaty (NPT). From its very inception in 1968, India had been opposed to it.

When the NPT review conference started in New York, India did not attend the formal proceedings but nevertheless sought to informally forge a third world coalition to forestall its unconditional extension. The Indian effort proved futile, and the US initiative prevailed. Subsequently, India took a far more active stance at the UN Conference on Disarmament in Geneva, which was attempting to draft the Comprehensive Test Ban Treaty (CTBT). India, which had proposed an incipient version of the treaty as early as 1954, now emerged as one of its most vocal critics on the basis of a number of technical reasons. In particular, India objected to the unwillingness of the nuclear weapons states to make some firm commitment toward the elimination of nuclear weapons; it also questioned the loopholes that allowed the nuclear states to test the reliability of their stockpiles through the use of laboratory experiments. In the end, India's objections were overruled, and the treaty was sent to the United Nations General Assembly for a vote.

It has been argued in some quarters that India's decision to test a set of five nuclear weapons in May 1998 stemmed in considerable part from the relentless pressure that was being applied to it to renounce its nuclear weapons program (Ganguly 1999). The tests were carried out under the auspices of the right-of-center Bharatiya Janata Party (BJP) without significant consultation or much public debate. Nevertheless, apart from some self-aggrandizing opposition from the Congress Party, they were mostly popular with the Indian electorate.

Closer to home, the test spurred the Pakistani political leadership to test their own nuclear weapons. In the aftermath of these tests, following several months of acrimony, India and Pakistan appeared to embark on a path of rapprochement. The high point of this process involved Prime Minister Vajpayee's visit to Lahore, Pakistan, in February 1999 to inaugurate a bus service between Lahore and New Delhi. However, the bonhomie that the Lahore visit had generated proved to be rather short-lived. In early May 1999, Indian army patrols discovered that several Pakistani army units of the Northern Light Infantry had made significant incursions across the line of control in the disputed state of Jammu and Kashmir near Kargil (Kargil Review Committee 2000). Faced with this colossal intelligence failure, the Indian politico-military leadership acted with considerable alacrity and within two months the intruders were dislodged. In the aftermath of this conflict, Indo-Pakistani relations remained deeply strained.

In a renewed effort to improve relations with Pakistan, Prime Minister Vajpayee invited General Pervez Musharraf to the historic city of Agra (the home of the Taj Mahal) for a summit in July 2001. Despite a promising start, the summit failed to accomplish much. Many mutual recriminations followed in the aftermath of the summit and India-Pakistan relations continued down a desultory course.

In the aftermath of the terrorist attacks on the United States on September 11, 2001, relations between the two countries worsened. India sought to link its own troubles with Pakistan over terrorism in the disputed state of Jammu and Kashmir to the US-led effort against global terror. Pakistan quite understandably sought to distinguish its support for the Kashmiri insurgents from support for terror, insisting that it was merely aiding a freedom struggle in the state. Pakistan's insistence on maintaining this distinction suffered an important blow in the wake of a terrorist attack on India's parliament on December 13, 2001. Two Pakistan-based terrorist organizations, the Jaish-e-Mohammed (JeM) and the Lashkar-e-Taiba (LeT), claimed responsibility for the attack.

Under substantial pressure from India and the United States, General Musharraf made various pledges to cut off support to these two radical groups. Despite his public commitment to end support for these organizations, terrorist attacks on India continued, leading to a steady worsening of Indo-Pakistani relations. Another terror attack on an Indian military base at Kaluchak in Jammu on May 30, 2002, deepened the ongoing crisis. As India moved substantial numbers of troops to the Pakistan border, Pakistan retaliated in kind. Many Western powers raised the prospect of a nuclear war between the two countries. In an effort to defuse tensions, the United States, along with a number of allies, under-took a series of diplomatic initiatives. Toward mid-July 2002, tensions abated as General Musharraf reiterated his pledges to end support for the insurgency in Kashmir. Indian officials, while willing to reduce some force deployments, nevertheless expressed skepticism about Musharraf's willingness to abide by his professed commitments.

However, owing to US diplomatic prodding, the two parties did embark on what was referred to as a "composite dialogue." This process made fitful progress over the course of the next several years. However, in 2007 it all but collapsed as internal discord within Pakistan led to General Musharraf's ouster from office. It was all but on its last legs when in November 2008 the LeT launched a bold and brazen attack on a number of sites including the iconic Taj Mahal Hotel in the city of Mumbai (Bombay). Indian security personnel were caught completely flat-footed in the wake of this attack and it took them close to three days to bring it to a close. In its aftermath the dialogue lost all momentum despite some halfhearted attempts on the part of the second Congress-led United Progressive Alliance government to revive it.

The new BJP government that came to power in 2014 made an initial attempt to revive a dialogue with Pakistan. This came in the form of an invitation to Prime Minister Nawaz Sharif (along with the elected heads of the other members of the South Asian Association for Regional Cooperation) to attend the initial inauguration of Prime Minister Narendra Modi in May 2014. Any hopes of the revival of a dialogue, however, were quickly dashed when the Pakistani high commissioner (ambassador) to New Delhi invited the members of a secessionist Kashmiri organization, the All-Party Hurriyat Conference (APHC), to his residence on the eve of an India-Pakistan meeting. Previous governments had expressed their reservations about similar invitations but had eventually overlooked them. The BJP regime, however, took exception to his actions and called off the talks.

Subsequently, relations with Pakistan mostly deteriorated largely because of two factors. First, the BJP regime faced growing disaffection among a new generation of Kashmiris in the portion of the state under Indian control. Its response, which was mostly a harsh, unyielding strategy, only exacerbated matters significantly. Second, seeing an opportunity to sow further discord, Pakistan ramped up its support for terror in the region. Indeed, in February 2019 Indian intelligence sources traced a major terrorist attack to a Pakistan-based terrorist organization, the Jaish-e-Mohammed. Within weeks India retaliated using airpower to cross the international border for the first time since the 1971 war striking at what it deemed to be a terrorist training camp at Balakot within Pakistan. Pakistan, in turn, retaliated with its air force, carrying out a sortie and shooting down an aging Indian MiG-21 in the process. In the wake of these incidents, Indo-Pakistani relations reached a particularly low ebb. For the foreseeable future it is hard to envisage any meaningful improvement in the relationship (Ganguly 2019).

India's relations with the PRC remained fraught in the first two decades of the new century, despite efforts on the part of both Congress and BJP regimes to improve relations. During this period the People's Liberation Army continued to make small incursions across the line of actual control, mostly in efforts to probe the readiness and responsiveness of Indian forces deployed along this working border. One episode, early in Modi's first term in 2014, proved to be especially troubling. This intrusion took place during President Xi Jinping's visit to India, which had been accompanied with considerable fanfare (Press Trust of India 2014). The incident demonstrated that the growth in trade and investment could not serve as a solvent for fundamental strategic differences. Though the two sides reached a modus vivendi of sorts at a meeting in Wuhan in April 2018, it was at best a tactical understanding that did not address underlying differences.

Matters worsened in the waning days of the first Modi regime. In the summer of 2017, Chinese construction workers in conjunction with PLA units began a road-building project through disputed territory in the region of Doklam near the Bhutan-China-India trijunction. Bhutan, which lacked the military wherewithal to challenge the PLA forces, appealed to India for assistance. India responded with alacrity, sending in troops to prevent the construction of the road. This led to a military standoff that lasted almost two months. Eventually, the construction process was halted, but it is far from clear that the PRC has abandoned its claims (Ganguly 2017).

Worse still, in May 2020, contingents of the People's Liberation Army made what India claimed were significant incursions across the line of actual control in the region of Ladakh. As Indian forces deployed in the area responded to the PLA's actions, skirmishes ensued in June. These clashes, though, with a resort to arms, nevertheless resulted in the deaths of at least twenty Indian military personnel and an unknown number of PLA soldiers. In July, following extensive discussions between senior military commanders on both sides, a process of de-escalation started. However, the likelihood of further clashes in this or other disputed areas along the border simply cannot be ruled out (Goldman 2020).

Apart from these three episodes, New Delhi remains acutely concerned with the PRC's pursuit of the Belt and Road initiative. This massive infrastructural enterprise in South Asia and beyond that the PRC is boosting impinges on at least two of India's interests. First, it is enabling the PRC to make significant inroads into virtually all of India's neighbors and thereby expand its political influence. Second, part of this project passes through disputed territory in the state of Jammu and Kashmir. Not surprisingly, India has expressed its misgivings about the entire endeavor.

The security challenge that New Delhi faces from the PRC will be its principal foreign and security policy dilemma for the foreseeable future. It clearly lacks the domestic resources to meet this challenge. The PRC's gross domestic product is at least five times that of India's, and its defense spending is three times that of India. Other, comparable indicators also suggest a growing gap between the two parties. It is hard to visualize how India can, within a reasonable time horizon, catch up with the PRC. The only viable strategy available to India to balance the power of its major adversary is to forge a set of strategic partnerships with key states. The linchpin in any such strategy should logically be the United States. To that end, New Delhi has fitfully sought to improve relations with Washington, D.C. Fortunately, in this endeavor, it has found support from the United States since the waning days of the second Clinton administration. Remarkably, regardless of administration, to varying degrees New Delhi has found support in Washington, D.C.

The turning point in the relationship, it can be argued, came with the United States–India civilian nuclear agreement of 2008 under the George W. Bush administration, as it removed a major stumbling block in Indo-US relations (Ganguly and Mistry 2006). Since then, despite changes in regimes in both states, US-Indian relations have improved significantly, albeit fitfully. Since the last days of the Obama administration, India has assumed considerable significance largely because the United States has become increasingly concerned about the challenge that the PRC poses to its interests in Asia. To that end, a range of administrations have courted India despite disagreements in particular issue areas ranging from trade to investment. The importance that the United States came to attach to India can be discerned from the decision of the Department of Defense to designate the former Pacific Command as the Indo-Pacific Command during the Trump administration in 2018 (Press Trust of India 2018).

In the early 1990s, after decades of neglect, India under Prime Minister Narasimha Rao embarked upon its "Look East" policy with a view toward engaging the vibrant economies of Southeast Asia. In considerable part this process was tied to India's own fitful embrace of policies of domestic liberalization. This policy, though belated, did enable India to establish a substantial economic presence in Southeast Asia. Under Narendra Modi, this policy was renamed as the "Act East" policy. The emphasis on enhancing economic ties remained in place, as the new policy also sought to boost transportation links with the region from India's northeast. Finally, though unstated, it clearly had a security component included in its ambit, focused on coping with China's substantial presence in the region (Farrell and Ganguly 2016).

In this context, India has also sought to enhance its ties with Japan. Two factors helped this relationship flourish in recent years. First, both Prime Minister Modi and his main Japanese counterpart, Shinzo Abe, are ardent nationalists and keen on asserting the prerogatives of their respective states in Asia. Second, both states realize that they face an uncertain strategic future in Asia because of the rise and increased assertiveness of the PRC. These two factors, in considerable part, have led to a strategic convergence (Joshi and Pant 2015).

Finally, a country that may assume greater important in India's foreign policy is Australia. The significance of Australia is also likely to increase for strategic reasons having to do with a shared interest in ensuring the security of sea lanes across the Indian Ocean. Despite a common interest in this vital maritime issue, India has been hesitant about openly forging strategic bonds with the country. This disinclination, in considerable part, stems from its misgivings about possibly incurring the wrath of the PRC. India's indecisiveness is evident from India's uncertain attitude in including Australia in the naval exercises under the aegis of the Quadrilateral, a four-power consultative security arrangement between Australia, India, Japan, and the United States (Roy-Chaudhury and Sullivan de Estrada 2018).

Institutional and Societal Factors in the Policymaking Process

The making of India's foreign policy (except for relations with its immediate neighbors and most notably Pakistan) for the most part has been and remains the concern of only an elite. During the long years of his tenure in office, Prime Minister Nehru had held the foreign policy portfolio. Subsequent prime ministers, on various occasions, had had a minister for external affairs.

Key foreign policy decisions generally reflect the ruling party's political and ideological orientation and are mostly the product of cabinet-level deliberations. In this context, it may be pertinent to mention that at least two prime ministers, Indira Gandhi and Narendra Modi, appear to have relied more on key, trusted advisers rather than on the advice of cabinet colleagues in the formulation and implementation of their foreign policy agendas.

Immediately below the level of ministers is the highest-ranking bureaucrat, the foreign secretary, drawn from the ranks of the elite Indian Foreign Service (IFS). Entry into the IFS, in turn, is through a highly competitive national examination. Currently, the IFS has approximately 700 serving officers. In recent years there has been an effort to expand the service, but it has been met with considerable resistance from within. In an effort to augment its capabilities, the Ministry of External Affairs has developed the practice of hiring consultants on short-term contracts. Beyond the IFS cadre and the temporary appointees, the IFS also has a second tier of officers who are drawn from other national services; they mostly tend to perform clerical, administrative, and security functions.

The Role of Parliament, the Cabinet, and Other Institutions

In parliamentary systems, legislators, whether they belong to the ruling party or the opposition, are expected to oversee foreign policy formulation and implementation. India's parliamentarians, with marked exceptions, have not performed this task with any degree of competence or skill.

During the Nehru era, some members of parliament did demonstrate and interest in and an understanding of India's foreign policy. Minoo Masani, for example, an ardent critic of the Congress Party governments and a member of the pro-US (and now long defunct) Swatantra Party, was known for his parliamentary eloquence on matters pertaining to foreign policy. Frank Anthony, a member of parliament from the Anglo-Indian community, had also evinced considerable interest in foreign affairs. Later, George Fernandes, a trade union leader and subsequently defense minister, also took an interest in foreign affairs. With the possible exception of Shashi Tharoor, a trained political scientist and a former senior United Nations official, few recent entrants to parliament have shown any great interest in matters of foreign policy.

The relative lack of interest and expertise in foreign affairs should not obscure the fact that parliament can wield significant power in certain areas pertaining to foreign policy. For example, it has the power to ratify both bilateral and multilateral treaties. In 2015 it ratified a major land-boundary agreement with Bangladesh—a subject that had been languishing for years.

The record of the cabinet in foreign policy making has also been quite uneven. Under Nehru, it hardly played any significant role. The prime minister simply made major decisions and informed the cabinet. In effect, it was for the most part an ineffectual entity in the realm of foreign policy. A similar trend continued under Nehru's daughter, Indira Gandhi. During her tenure in office the various cabinet committees, including that of external affairs, were folded into the unified Political Affairs Committee (PAC). The PAC, then, is the primary body for the formulation and conduct of foreign affairs. Except in its earliest years, the PAC routinely deferred to Indira Gandhi. In subsequent years, to varying degrees, depending on who has held the office of the prime minister, it has shown greater independence.

Finally, since 1998, when the Bharatiya Janata Party–led coalition came to power, it created the National Security Council (NSC). The NSC is mostly an advisory and consultative body and is composed of the secretaries of defense, external affairs, home, and finance, and the vice chair of the NITI Aayog. The national security adviser chairs this entity. Beneath this apex body are the Strategic Policy Group (SPG) and the National Security Advisory Board (NSAB). Under the second Narendra Modi regime, the national security adviser, Ajit Doval, was granted cabinet-level rank, signifying his importance in the realms of both foreign and security policy making.

The Mass Media and Other Institutions

Apart from the individuals who have institutional responsibilities for the formulation and conduct of the country's foreign relations, a small handful of influential journalists in the English-language press, some research analysts based in think tanks, and a handful of academics who are also public intellectuals seek to influence the direction of foreign policy.

In recent years there has been a proliferation of think tanks mostly based in New Delhi. Several of these hold seminars on topical subjects, release research reports, and also consult for the government. Some of them, such as the Institute for Defense Studies and Analysis, the Center for Land Warfare Studies, the Center for Airpower Studies, and the National Maritime Foundation, rely wholly on government funding. Others, such as the Vivekananda Foundation, while mostly privately funded, are widely believed to be close to the Bharatiya Janata Party. On the other hand, the Rajiv Gandhi Foundation serves as the think tank for the Congress Party. Still others, such as the Center for Policy Research, one of the older think tanks, while it houses individual researchers with an explicit political agenda, maintains a degree of political independence as an organization. The same could be argued for the Observer Research Foundation. More recently, at least two US-based think tanks, the Brookings Institution and the Carnegie Endowment for International Peace, have also opened offices in New Delhi.

The role of private think tanks on policymaking varies with which government happens to be in office as well as their own ideological leanings. However, it is difficult to ascertain with any degree of certainty the precise influence that these organizations wield on the foreign policy formulation process. Some reflect the ruling regime's preferences and seek to generate public support for policies; others proffer what they deem to be sound, policy-relevant advice; and finally some attempt to generate debate on topical issues.

Within the elite English-language press, three or possibly four news magazines stand out for their coverage of foreign affairs: *India Today, Outlook, Frontline,* and on occasion a more recent entrant, *Caravan,* a pioneer of long-form journalism in India. All four have a generally independent political stance, though *Frontline* has a left-wing bias on most issues having to do with economics or foreign affairs. In recent years, several of the major English-language dailies such as *The Hindu,* the *Hindustan Times,* the *Times of India,* and the *Indian Express,* have employed full-time foreign and strategic affairs correspondents. Some of them, it may be surmised, probably wield a degree of influence in the corridors of South Block, the home of the Ministry of External Affairs. Determining their ability to influence specific issues on particular decisions, however, is all but impossible. Suffice it to say that they play a consultative role and, on occasion, serve as channels for the ruling regime to use in building support for existing policies.

Since the 1990s, with the advent of various forms of economic deregulation, television has become an important means for the dissemination of news about foreign affairs, and access to television has become emblematic even for aspirants into the middle class. The state-run television network, *Doordarshan,* which for decades had a monopoly in television news, now competes with a dizzying array of private news networks in terms of current news coverage. It is pertinent to mention, however, that the quality of news coverage across television channels varies widely and some are notorious for mingling opinion with basic news coverage. Despite the uneven quality of reportage, it seems reasonable to assume that the dramatic growth in the number of television viewers has contributed to a more informed populace, and that in the future this knowledge may well have important consequences for India's foreign and defense policies.

There is at least some anecdotal evidence that television coverage of foreign and security issues is assuming some significance for both foreign and security policies. Two episodes in particular appear worthy of some discussion. The first involved the coverage of the 1999 Kargil War. Since the ruling BJP was facing an election, it deemed it vital to bring the war to a quick close with limited casualties, because of the extensive coverage of the war. The second episode where television almost certainly played a critical role was in the wake of a Pakistan-based terrorist attack on an Indian military convoy in February 2019 in the state of Jammu and Kashmir. In its aftermath, there was widespread television coverage of an Indian retaliatory air strike on Pakistan. A number of observers and some polling data suggest that jingoistic television coverage played a not inconsequential role in influencing the outcome of the 2019 general (national) elections.

Despite the growth of television and print coverage of foreign and security policy issues, the mass electorate in India, though increasingly politically sophisticated, has yet to demonstrate a sustained interest in the nation's foreign policy. There are, of course, important exceptions to this proposition. In northern India, the physical proximity to Pakistan and the presence of a significant, if increasingly dwindling, number of post-Partition immigrants from Pakistan helps sustain an interest in India-Pakistan relations. In the state of Tamil Nadu, there is concern about the plight of fellow Tamils in Sri Lanka. Similarly, illegal immigration from Bangladesh has long been an electoral issue and was politically exploited, once again in 2019, in India's northeastern states, particularly West Bengal and Assam.

The Future of India's Foreign Policy

The tasks that face India's current foreign policy decisionmakers remain challenging. At a procedural level, India urgently needs to strengthen its institutional capacity for the formulation and conduct of its foreign relations. Doing so will require improving the recruitment processes and training of its foreign service personnel, significantly expanding the size of its foreign service, and designing institutional mechanisms for obtaining policy-relevant advice from external sources.

At a substantive level it confronts the task of managing relations with its fractious neighbor and adversary, Pakistan. It also needs to devote more energy and effort toward improving its relations with its smaller neighbors, especially in the aftermath of the Covid-19 global pandemic, which has ravaged South Asia (Siddiqui 2020). Most important, it also needs to devise a long-term strategy to cope with the rise and assertiveness of the People's Republic of China.

In dealing with the PRC, India has two possible choices. First, it can resort to a strategy of self-help and build up its domestic capabilities. This, however, may be a daunting task, as India is well behind the PRC on a range of economic and military indicators. It is hard to visualize how it could rapidly close these gaps. The alternative strategy would be to knit together a series of strategic partnerships with key states ranging from the United States, Japan, and Australia to balance the power of the PRC. In this context, the future of the strategic partnership with the United States may prove to be the most crucial. As argued earlier, India has taken fitful steps in that direction. However, to adequately deal with the challenge that the PRC poses, a more concerted strategy that builds on the strategic partnership with the United States seems in order.

Finally, India needs to consider what role it wishes to play in a range of global regimes ranging from nonproliferation to trade liberalization. It cannot aspire to be a great power while shirking the responsibilities that also accompany such a status. To that end it has to demonstrate a capacity for leadership and innovation in these regimes and not merely dwell on their extant shortcomings. How it addresses these challenges at both regional and global levels will, in considerable part, determine its standing in the global order in the years and decades ahead.

7

The Politics of Caste

Christophe Jaffrelot

The caste system is inseparable from Hinduism, although it is not limited to this religion; in India, its logic is also present in Sikhism, Islam, and Christianity. The first indication of this social system appears in the *Rig Veda*—the oldest text among Sanskrit literature—which dates back to approximately 2000 B.C.E. One of the stanzas in this text (90.X) relates a myth of origin in which the world is said to derive from the sacrificial dismemberment of a primordial man—the Virat Purush—whose mouth gave rise to the Brahmans; his arms, the Kshatriyas; his thighs, the Vaishyas; and his feet, the Shudras. This fourfold division of society is hierarchical: the mouth is naturally higher than the arms, which in turn are higher than the thighs and the feet. Similarly, under the Shudras is a group called the Untouchables, which is not mentioned in the *Vedas* but noted in the *Dharmashastra*—which also dates back to Indian antiquity. The very name of this fifth category reflects a cardinal principle of caste hierarchy, which is the relationship between the pure and the impure (Dumont 1966; Gould 1987).

The Brahman personifies purity par excellence, while the Untouchable embodies impurity and causes repulsion, as contact with him is polluting (Sarukkai 2009). Between these two, there is a whole range of "grades" of relative (im)purity divided by two thresholds: Brahmans, Kshatriyas, and Vaishyas form a higher group, the "twice-born" or *dvijas;* Shudras are clearly lower, but still well above Untouchables, and these two categories cannot be bracketed together. In an Indian village, this social segmentation traditionally results in a separation of spaces, with each caste living in a distinct neighborhood, and the Untouchables sometimes even confined to a separate hamlet, with their own temple and well (lest they should pollute the water of the rest of the village).

The castes are not only defined by their relative purity, but also by socioeconomic functions, which go hand in hand with status. Brahmans specialize in the work of the spirit, as priests who serve in temples (although priests are far from being the most prestigious among the Brahmans), astrologers, or literati serving the state administration (Brahmans more or less monopolized higher public office in Hindu kingdoms over centuries).

The Kshatriya is the quintessential warrior. His avocation is to defend society and to conquer territories. Kings were drawn from the Kshatriya class and depended on local chieftains also derived from the same caste. Their descendants—whether maharajahs or minor landowning village leaders—developed their fiefs to become regional satraps or local notables, and then landowners after the British introduced the concept of land as private property. Among the Kshatriyas, the Rajputs are the most famous all over north India.

The Vaishyas were originally craftsmen and tradesmen, but over time this first function passed over to the Shudras, and they retained only the second occupation. These merchants handle money without any inhibition. The emergence of India as a capitalist power, following colonization, caused many Vaishyas, such as the Marwaris, to go into industry, and even today a significant number of companies listed on the Bombay Stock Exchange are in the hands of members of castes belonging to this category.

The Shudras are therefore the craftsmen—ranging from blacksmith to jeweler to weaver—but more of them are farmers and stockbreeders. This is the caste whose demographic weight is by far the most important. When Shudras possess more land and are more numerous than any other subcastes, they form what M. N. Srinivas (1995) called a "dominant caste." In that case they, in fact, exert local authority—including over the upper castes in some respects.

As for the Untouchables, who call themselves Dalits, their economic functions are even more closely related to their status. They are, therefore, in charge of the most degrading tasks, such as scavenging, meat-cutting, tanning, and shoe-making, as leatherworking is particularly stigmatized in Hindu society, which reveres the cow as the preeminent sacred animal.

In addition to (im)purity and occupation, there is a third structuring principle of caste to consider, and that is endogamy, which logically completes this social system, as the mixing of castes must naturally be banned for this pattern of inequality to be perpetuated. The boundaries of endogamy define the perimeters of castes, which are routinely called *jatis,* a word that, significantly, derives from the verb *jana,* meaning "to be born."

While Brahmans, Kshatriyas, Vaishyas, and Shudras form what is known as the *varna* system, these *varnas* are subdivided into *jatis,* which are in many ways the "real" castes. The Jats of Rajasthan, Haryana, and Punjab; the Marathas of Maharashtra; the Lingayats and Vokkaligas of Karnataka; and the Reddys and Kammas of Andhra Pradesh represent major examples of *jatis. Jatis* are usually defined by their occupation—as evident from the references made before to Rajputs, Marwaris, or dominant castes—and by endogamous rules. Traditionally, one gets married within one's *jati.* Matrimonial unions are arranged by the parents, who generally commit their children, while very young, to socially legitimate weddings, taking into account their astrological birth charts. To this day endogamy remains the rule in villages and, in a looser form, in the city, except among a small cosmopolitan elite, which is evident from the structure of the "matrimonials" section of most newspapers. Indeed, every daily publishes a supplement on Sundays wherein brides and grooms are classified by caste (and increasingly by region and occupation), and websites are doing likewise on an even larger scale.

From the Caste System to Caste-Based Competition

This social hierarchy forms a caste system because the dominant—Brahmanical—values are regarded by the whole society as providing universal references and role models. Hence the notion of Sanskritization, which M. N. Srinivas defined as "the process in which a 'low' Hindu caste, or tribal or other group, changes its customs, ritual, ideology and way of life in the direction of a high, and frequently, 'twice-born caste' that is the Brahmans, but also the Kshatriyas or even the Vaishyas" (1995: 6). Low castes may, for instance, adopt the most prestigious features of the Brahmans' diet and emulate vegetarianism. Such a process reflects a special coherence in society, with all groups admitting the values of the upper castes as *the* legitimate value system. For Srinivas, "the mobility associated with Sanskritization results only in *positional changes* in the system and does not lead to any *structural change.* That is, a caste moves up above its neighbours and another comes down, but all this takes place in an essentially stable hierarchical order. The system itself does not change" (1995: 6; emphasis in original). Indeed, the values sustaining the social system remain the same. Members of low castes adopted, for example, the most prestigious features of the Brahman food regimen and thus became vegetarians. Such a process highlighted the enactment of social coherence, since all groups looked upon the values of the high castes—and especially of the Brahman—as the legitimate values of society. Still, coherence did not equal cohesion. In fact, Sanskritization in itself testified to the aspiration of low castes to rise socially, but for centuries they did not have any alternative choices available—except conversion to Islam or Christianity, a strategy that did not make much of a difference, since both religions had developed their own caste system.

Among the Muslims, the key element is not so much purity and impurity as geographical origin. The Muslim upper castes, the Ashrafs, claim that they descend from outsiders who came from Saudi Arabia, Central Asia, and the Turkish world. In contrast, the Ashlafs are Indians who converted to Islam from the eighth century onward and who often were Hindu Shudras by caste—weavers, for instance. In their case, conversion to a supposedly equalitarian religion made little difference, because while they could more or less mix with others in the mosque during prayer, the rest of their lives hardly changed. This was also the case for the Dalits who converted to Islam and became Arzals. Similarly, those who converted to Christianity—mostly Dalits—were kept at arm's length even in the church by so-called old Christians who claimed that they had come from the Middle East (hence their name Syro-Malabar Christians) with Saint Thomas or that they had been converted by him before his death in India in 52 C.E.

Alternative, egalitarian repertoires crystallized during the British Raj when individualistic values were taught to lower-caste children who were allowed to go to school for the first time (Rao 2009). The British also suggested that the lower-caste people may well be from a different non-Aryan ethnic stock—like Dravidians, for instance—and even be "sons of the Indian soil." Lower-caste leaders built up a reformatory, even revolutionary, zeal based on these ideas, as illustrated by E. W. Ramaswami Naicker, popularly known as Periyar (in Tamil Nadu), and Jotirao Phule and Bhimrao Ambedkar (in Maharashtra). The latter was the first leader of Untouchables, whom he preferred to call Dalits ("broken men") for the first time within a pan-Indian context.

While the caste system began to change significantly under the British thanks to the spread of more egalitarian ideas, it was also affected by more concrete transformations. The modernization of the bureaucracy implied the making of a new class of functionaries, the industrialization process relied on a new working class, and the development of new means of transportation resulted in the building of national railways. These three phenomena transformed castes (Bayly 1999: 263), which until then were confined to reduced territories and delimited by matrimonial relations. Geographical mobility due to the changing job market—and made possible by the new means of transportation—fostered the territorial extension of the frontiers of caste and the emergence of horizontal solidarities. This mobility not only generated feelings of anomie, but also made locating suitable matches for endogamous marriages more complicated—hence the idea to create associations that could link members of the same caste. However, these associations were also stirred up by the census, which from 1871 onward was a key element in the formation of the colonial state. The census raised among several castes the sentiment of having common interests, since the British, not content merely with enumerating people, also classified them. Caste associations were therefore also created as pressure groups whose aim was to improve their rank in the census tables. This process was especially prominent among the lower castes, but it was also obvious among not-so-low castes such as the Kayasths, the scribes who had been so prominent in the administration of most of the princely states, be they Hindus or Muslims, though they were Shudras by caste. Each census provided castes with an opportunity to petition the government for getting a higher place in the order of precedence and for being recorded under new, Sanskritized names.

Caste associations were transforming themselves into interest groups and lobbying not only for symbolic concessions, such as their ranking in the census, but also for more concrete conquests. They gradually acquired features of mutual aid structures. They founded cooperative movements and schools for children in their caste groups. In that sense, they were modern institutions (Rudolph and Rudolph 1966: 448).

Quota Policies and Quota Politics

During the colonial era, the British initiated a policy of positive discrimination favoring the Untouchables, who gradually came to be known as the Scheduled Castes. As early as 1892, a network of schools reserved for the Untouchables was established. The British policy was not that precocious so far as the state bureaucracy was concerned, but it became more and more ambitious. In 1934, the government decided to reserve 25 percent of vacancies in the administration for Muslims and 8.3 percent for other minorities, including the Scheduled Castes, who at the time represented 12.5 percent of the population. In June 1946, the quota for Scheduled Castes was increased to 12.5 percent, which means that the notion of proportionality was introduced under the British.

Quotas in the Bureaucracy

This measure was extended by the first government of independent India, and the proportionality principle has continued to apply since then. When the 1951 census indicated that the Scheduled Castes were 15 percent of the population, the quota for the Scheduled Castes was increased to 15 percent and this same quota was implemented in educational institutions.

However, most of these quotas remained unfulfilled, allegedly because of a lack of good candidates, but also because of a lack of goodwill among those in charge of recruiting them. For instance, in 1961 the Untouchables represented between 1 and 2 percent of the graduates of one age class, and only 6 percent of them really benefited from the redistribution effect of quotas (Galanter 1991: 61, 94, 108). In fact, the quotas were only fulfilled in the lower categories of the administration, which meant that the Scheduled Castes continued to accomplish some of their traditional tasks, but with a uniform. For instance, sweepers come mostly from the Untouchable Bhangi caste. This is evident from Table 7.1, which shows the proportion of the Scheduled Caste employees in the central government services.

In 1967, twenty years after independence, the Indian state was far from satisfactorily implementing the positive discrimination programs. By contrast, the quotas in the assemblies were strictly implemented, although they contributed to the Scheduled Castes being dependent on an upper-caste-dominated Congress, something Ambedkar, following years of conflict with Gandhi, had unsuccessfully tried to avoid.

Table 7.1   Classwise Distribution of Scheduled Castes in the Central Government Services, 1953–1987 (percentages)

Class of the Indian Administration	1953	1961	1963	1967	1974	1980	1987
Class 1	0.53	1.2	1.78	2.08	3.2	4.95	8.23
Class 2	1.29	2.5	2.98	3.1	4.6	8.54	10.47
Class 3	4.52	7.2	9.24	9.33	10.3	13.44	14.46
Class 4	20.52	17.2	17.15	18.18	18.6	19.46	20.09

Sources: The Commissioner for Scheduled Castes and Scheduled Tribes, vol. 1 (New Delhi: Udyogshala, 1969), cited in S. N. Dubey and Usha Mathur, "Welfare Programmes for Scheduled Castes: Content and Administration"; Economic and Political Weekly, January 22, 1972, p. 167 (for 1961 and 1967); and O. Mendelsohn and M. Vicziany, *The Untouchables: Subordination, Poverty, and the State in Modern India* (Cambridge: Cambridge University Press, 1998), p. 135 (for all the other years).

Reservations in the Political Domain

The 1932 conflict between Gandhi and Dalit leader Bhimrao Ambedkar was eventually settled by the Poona Pact, which favored Gandhi's position. In contrast to separate electorates, the new reservation system disallowed the Scheduled Castes' designating of their representatives. The Poona Pact did establish a Scheduled Castes electoral college that designated in each constituency the four Scheduled Caste candidates who were then allowed to contest the elections. But the Scheduled Castes exerted an exclusive influence during the primary elections only. Thereafter, they were not in a majority in any constituency, and it was the other castes that, in the main, elected the successful Scheduled Caste candidate. The system based on the Poona Pact not only ruled out Ambedkar's demand regarding separate electorates, but also disallowed the Scheduled Castes from gaining representation proportional to their number. The 1935 Government of India Act gave them only 7 seats out of 156 in the Council of State, 19 out of 250 in the Central Assembly, and 151 out of 1,585 in the different provincial legislative assemblies.

Naturally, the Constituent Assembly examined closely this question—especially after Ambedkar, Nehru's law minister, was appointed chairman of the Drafting Committee. The Congress leaders wanted to continue the reservation system, but in a diluted fashion. One of Ambedkar's disciples, S. Nagappa, proposed an alternative to it. According to this schema, in the constituencies reserved for Scheduled Castes, the candidates winning more than 35 percent of the Untouchables' votes could be declared victorious. But the Congress Party opposed this and eventually the constitution established a system of reserved seats on a population basis for ten years. It was extended ten years later, and has continued to be extended to this day. The primary elections system was abolished, which deprived the Scheduled Castes of a crucial leverage. Article 330 of the constitution simply established quotas for the Scheduled Castes and the Scheduled Tribes in proportion to their population, through double constituencies that were located in the places where the Scheduled Castes and Scheduled Tribes people resided in large numbers. There, two members of the legislative assembly, or members of parliament, were returned: one from the non–Scheduled Castes/non–Scheduled Tribes candidates, the other from the Scheduled Castes/Scheduled Tribes candidates. Thus as far as the Scheduled Castes were concerned, in 15 percent of the constituencies, in areas where they were in large numbers, two seats were contested (in a very small number of constituencies, a third seat was reserved for Tribals), and each voter was provided two ballots (exceptionally, three). Even if none of the Scheduled Caste candidates received the largest or the second largest number of votes, the one who came first among them won the reserved seat. However, if two Scheduled Castes (or Scheduled Tribes) candidates came first, they both won seats.

That's what happened in 1957 in a constituency of Andhra Pradesh in which one of the seats was reserved for the Scheduled Tribes. Two tribal candidates came first and were elected, whereas the third was V. V. Giri, an influential—Brahman—Congress Party leader who became president of India in 1969. He brought the case before the Supreme Court, which upheld the election results as pronounced by the electoral commission. But the system was modified before the 1962 elections, allegedly because the double constituencies were too big, but obviously because the defeat of Giri had shown that Scheduled Castes or Scheduled Tribes candidates could win both seats.

This means that only single constituencies have been in place since 1961. In 15 percent of them, where the Scheduled Castes are in the largest numbers, the candidates can only be from their community. But the Scheduled Castes are everywhere in a minority. Under the 1961 delimitation of parliamentary constituencies, seventy-five seats were reserved for representation by the Scheduled Castes. The proportion of the population made up by these castes in these constituencies varied considerably, but they were never in a majority—in thirteen out of seventy-five they were more than 30 percent of the voters. Besides, 75 percent of the Scheduled Castes were in nonreserved constituencies (Galanter 1979:

Ambedkar poster in the Dharavi, Mumbai. Photo by Christophe Jaffrelot.

438–439). A coalition of high and intermediate castes could very well have their Scheduled Caste candidate returned, even if the Scheduled Castes did not vote for him. Congress thus became adept at co-opting Scheduled Caste leaders by mobilizing non–Scheduled Caste voters (Galanter 1991: 549). One of the Scheduled Caste leaders co-opted by the Congress, Jagjivan Ram, admitted that "since one had to depend on the non–Scheduled Caste vote, one went along with the fortunes of the party" (quoted in Frankel 1989: 83).

What Party for the Scheduled Castes?

Ambedkar launched his first political party, the Independent Labor Party (ILP), in 1936. As evident from its name, this party did not confine its appeal to the Scheduled Castes. The ILP focused on labor laws for protecting factory workers and obtaining better educational facilities in technical institutions. The party even tried to project itself as a virtual spokesperson for the "lower middle class," which contained few Untouchables. These efforts notwithstanding, the party remained a marginal force, and this led to the formation of the Scheduled Castes Federation (SCF, or Dalit Federation in Marathi) in July 1942. Ambedkar had given up the idea of broadening his base to encompass the working class and put stress, instead, on the need to unify the Scheduled Castes on a pan-Indian scale. The party enjoyed little success, and just prior to his death in December 1956, Ambedkar suggested that the SCF should be dissolved and a new party formed instead. He invited party workers to join hands with leaders from non-Dalit communities.

Thus the Republican Party of India (RPI) was launched in October 1957 with the goal of representing all of India's poor. But the RPI was badly affected by factionalism and enjoyed only meager success in the state of Maharashtra. It was not until the Bahujan Samaj Party (BSP) was formed that a Dalit party was able to command clout on the Indian political scene, but it is first necessary to discuss the rise of the lower castes before noting the success of the BSP.

The Lower Castes Take Power

When Nehru moved the Objectives Resolution before the Constituent Assembly on December 13, 1946, he used the term "Other Backward Classes" and announced that special measures were to be taken to favor "minorities, backward and tribal areas and depressed and other backward classes." However, he did not elaborate further. Clarifying the definition of Other Backward Classes thus became the first task of the Backward Classes Commission, which was appointed on January 29, 1953, under the chairmanship of Kakasaheb Kalelkar. Caste was not the only criterion that the commission identified, but it was a key element; and the commission therefore established a list of 2,399 castes representing about 32 percent of the Indian population as forming the bulk of the "socially and educationally backward classes." In order to redress the backwardness of the Other Backward Classes, the commission recommended that quotas should be reserved for these castes in central and state administrations, which were divided in four classes: 40 percent of the vacancies in the third and fourth classes, 33.3 percent in the second class, and 25 percent in the first class. The Nehru government refused, officially because it was dedicated to a socialist system in which caste differences would be dissolved, and semi-officially because the higher-caste elites feared being dislodged from power by peasants who were already politically significant because of their economic and demographic importance.

Some states in the south of the country had early on applied social programs favoring groups described as Other Backward Classes, but they had to wait until 1990 to know whether the federal government would implement the recommendations of a commission that dated back to 1978. This was the Mandal Commission (named after its president), which had identified 3,743 castes as Other Backward Classes, accounting for 52 percent of the national population. Their report noted that these Other Backward Classes occupied only 12.5 percent of civil service posts, and it recommended that this figure be raised to 27 percent. When this quota was announced in 1990, members of higher castes, especially students, protested vehemently about the reduction of their job prospects, and this calling into question of the sociopolitical order that they still dominated. The Supreme Court suspended its decision before validating the recommendations of the Mandal Commission in 1992 with a slight twist: the children of the Other Backward Classes elite (the so-called creamy layer) could not profit from the quotas. Still, higher-caste resistance had provoked a countermovement among the Other Backward Classes to defend against the higher castes depriving them of the quota. New political parties claiming large Other Backward Classes membership turned the tide and nominated greater numbers of candidates from lower castes starting in the elections of 1991 (Jaffrelot 2003). This was an increasingly successful strategy, because the Other Backward Classes—who constitute at least a relative majority throughout India—voted more from that point on for candidates from their own castes, rather than from higher castes. They thus seized power in the large states of northern India, such as Bihar and Uttar Pradesh.

The most recent episode in the rise of the Other Backward Classes to power occurred in April 2008 in the domain of higher education. The lower-caste leaders desired to extend the quota policy for Other Backward Classes to universities, in their eyes a necessary measure to prepare these castes for the responsibilities that awaited them in the civil service. The Congress Party–led government had agreed to this demand in 2007, but the Supreme Court had immediately suspended this decision under the pretext that no statistics supported the theory that Other Backward Classes were underrepresented in higher education. It cleared the 27 percent reservation for the Other Backward Classes in the universities and other public higher education institutions the following year, but kept to its argument specifying that elites of the Other Backward Classes could not benefit from quotas and that the establishments concerned should increase their capacity by 54 percent so as not to reduce the number of places open to those without positive discrimination support.

The BSP's Rise to Power:
Kanshi Ram and the Bahujan Samaj

Kanshi Ram was born in 1932 into a Sikh Dalit family in rural Punjab.[1] His family, like Ambedkar's, had benefited from the military jobs that the British reserved for Untouchables. He was consequently able to study until he graduated with a bachelor of science degree, after which he went to work for a laboratory as an assistant chemist. The laboratory was associated with the Ministry of Defense and the job in turn was thanks to the reservation system.

He resigned from his job in 1971, however, to devote time to social work among Dalits and others. Kanshi Ram strongly felt that the RPI had betrayed Ambedkar by focusing too much on Dalits. He wanted to promote the cause of the *bahujan samaj*—the "great numbers"—and he included in this group religious minorities as well. In 1971, Kanshi Ram created the Scheduled Castes and Scheduled Tribes, Other Backward Classes, and Minority Communities Employees Association, since he believed that the most urgent need of the *bahujan samaj* was to organize its elite, which in the case of the Dalits was thanks to the reservations mandated in the education system and administration. But Kanshi Ram wanted to include other components of the *bahujan samaj,* namely lower castes and religious minorities. In 1974, he transformed his organization into a new one, called the Backward and Minority Communities

Employees Federation (BAMCEF) (with "Backward" comprising the Scheduled Castes, Scheduled Tribes, and Other Backward Classes), which was officially launched on December 6, 1978, the anniversary of Ambedkar's death. The organization made rapid headway and reached a degree of critical mass because of the growing number of educated Scheduled Caste civil servants. BAMCEF reached 200,000 members and included 500 PhD recipients, 15,000 scientists, 3,000 medical graduates and 7,000 other graduate and postgraduate degree holders—most from Uttar Pradesh and Maharashtra (Omvedt 1994: 163). After BAMCEF endowed Kanshi Ram with a core group of followers, he shifted to party politics in 1981 and launched the Dalit Shoshit Samaj Sangharsh Samiti (DS-4), a committee for fighting for the community of the Dalits and the oppressed. The terms used in the name of this organization departed from the official euphemisms ("backward castes," "Scheduled Castes," etc.). Today "Dalit" and "Shoshit" are the words that politicized Untouchables use more frequently when referring to themselves. However, "Dalit" does not refer here to the Untouchables only, but also to lower castes. In addition, the DS-4 also tried to attract Muslims, especially in Uttar Pradesh.

In 1984, the DS-4 was replaced by the Bahujan Samaj Party, whose name reflected the sociopolitical ambitions of Kanshi. The BSP made rapid progress on the electoral front. During the general elections of 1984, it received more than a million votes. This number was multiplied by six in 1989 when the party won 6.2 million votes, or 2.07 percent of the recorded votes, and obtained three seats in the Lok Sabha. In 1991, the party won only two seats, capturing 1.61 percent of the votes, but five years later it gained eleven seats with 3.64 percent of the votes.

The growth of the BSP following the 1996 elections allowed the electoral commission to grant it national party status. This growth chiefly resulted from Kanshi Ram's continuous efforts since the 1960s to get the *bahujan samaj* organized. However, the rise of the BSP has also much to do with the party's implantation and mobilization techniques and his actions while in office.

Kanshi Ram tried to emerge as a spokesman for the *bahujan samaj* by advocating the interests of all its components against the upper castes, including the Other Backward Classes. Even before the Mandal affair, when the debate (in the Lok Sabha and outside) on the Mandal Commission report pertaining to reservations for Other Backward Classes was gaining momentum, Kanshi Ram emphasized the claims of the Other Backward Classes. Kanshi Ram thus admitted that in some respects the conditions of the Scheduled Castes were better than those of the

A Bahujan Samaj Party campaign advertisement with its party symbol (the elephant) and the name of its local candidate in Shivpuri District, Madhya Pradesh. Photo by Christophe Jaffrelot.

Other Backward Classes. He thus recognized that thanks to reservation, the Scheduled Castes and Scheduled Tribes had a larger presence in the bureaucracy than the Other Backward Classes.

Similarly, he noted in 1994 that of some 500 Indian Administrative Services officers in Uttar Pradesh, 137 were from the Scheduled Castes whereas only 7 were Other Backward Classes, 6 of whom were from the prominent Yadav caste (Mendelsohn and Vicziany 1998: 224). Kanshi Ram was very much in favor of reservations that could help the Other Backward Classes, which he regarded as unprivileged. One of the BSP's slogans has been *mandal ayog lâgû karo, kursî khâli karo* ("implement Mandal Commission [report] or vacate the seat [of power]"). This was part of his strategy of constituting the *bahujan samaj* into a political force. The BSP undoubtedly benefited from the atmosphere created by the "Mandal affair" and tried to tap the Other Backward Classes vote at the time of elections. While the BSP has done well in the Punjab, Uttar Pradesh is the only state where it has made real inroads in the past two decades.

From the 1980s onward, Kanshi Ram considered capturing power to be his chief priority; hence his strategy of coalition-making. The ground for his alliance with Mulayam Singh Yadav in 1993 was certainly prepared by the so-called Mandal affair. The mobilization of the upper castes against the implementation of the Mandal Commission report had triggered a countermobilization cutting across the (lower) caste cleavages. At this point, the Other Backward Classes and Dalits discovered the need for more solidarity and increased activism, especially when some upper-caste movements began to question the validity of reservations—including reservation for the Scheduled Castes. The BSP was clearly a potential ally of the Other Backward Classes, since Kanshi Ram had advocated the need for Other Backward Classes quotas in the administration. The context created by the Mandal affair was therefore conducive to the alliance between the BSP and the Samajwadi Party (or Socialist Party), which was the legatee of the strong Uttar Pradesh socialist movement in the 1960s and 1970s, and enjoyed solid support among Yadavs (a caste of cattle breeders), from among whom came its leader, Mulayam Singh Yadav. However, this alliance responded primarily to tactical considerations.

In the 1993 Assembly Elections, the Samajwadi Party won 109 seats out of 425 and the BSP won 67. Both parties formed the government thanks to the Congress Party's support. Mulayam Singh Yadav became chief minister and the BSP obtained 11 ministerial portfolios in a government of 27. During the first month of this coalition, the BSP and the Samajwadi Party showed great solidarity, standing firm against the Bharatiya Janata Party (BJP) and some members of the Congress who protested vehemently against the implementation of quotas for Other Backward Classes in Uttarakhand (at the time a subregion of Uttar Pradesh, where the Other Backward Classes represented only 2 percent of the population).

Relations between the two partners, however, soon deteriorated. First, the BSP was getting worried about the "Yadavization" of the state with the appointment of a large number of Yadavs in the state apparatus. Second, the backward castes, who were anxious to improve their social status and keep the Untouchables in their place, reacted violently to the Dalits' efforts to achieve social mobility. The class interests of the Other Backward Classes and the Dalits are clearly antagonistic in some regions of Uttar Pradesh, where Untouchables are often landless laborers. Conflicts about the wages of agricultural laborers and disputes regarding landownership have always been acute, but became more frequent since both groups—the Dalits and the Other Backward Classes—had become more assertive after the 1993 elections.[2] But the dominance of the Samajwadi Party in the 1995 panchayat elections and Mulayam Singh Yadav's willingness to accommodate BSP dissidents in his party also influenced the demise of the coalition.

This led to the BSP becoming actively involved in an alliance with the BJP, which led to Kumari Mayawati becoming chief minister of the

Uttar Pradesh government on June 3, 1995. This alliance was even more tactical than the one with the Samajwadi Party. It was primarily directed against Mulayam Singh Yadav, whom the BSP and the BJP wanted to keep in check because of his increasing political influence, which was reflected in the growing assertiveness of the Other Backward Classes (and especially the Yadavs). The alliance of the BSP with the BJP epitomized the convergence between Dalit and upper-caste leaders against the Other Backward Classes; but it was also directed against the Yadavs, who were now posing a threat to the Scheduled Castes and elite landowners and civil servants as well, due to the new OBC reservation policy.

Mayawati is a Chamar from Uttar Pradesh (her native village, Badalpur, is located in the district of Ghaziabad). At the time of her birth in 1956, her father was employed in the telephone department. Mayawati was successful in her studies in Meerut, where her family settled when she was two years old. She became a school teacher in 1977. She was preparing herself for the Indian Administrative Services examination in 1980 when she met Kanshi Ram, who persuaded her to enter politics. In 1984, she left her job to devote herself to the BSP. Apparently Kanshi Ram had been impressed by her rhetorical skills, and indeed Mayawati made a name for herself through deliberately aggressive and even provocative speeches.

With Mayawati as chief minister, Uttar Pradesh, India's largest state, was for the first time governed by a member of the Scheduled Castes who forcefully advocated the cause of the *bahujan samaj*.[3] For most Dalits, she became a source of pride. Mayawati's accession to the top post in Uttar Pradesh therefore played a major part in the consolidation of the BSP's Dalit vote bank.

Such a consolidation also resulted from the special treatment Mayawati granted to members of the lower castes. The Dalits were the first to benefit from it. The Ambedkar Villages Scheme, which had been started by Mulayam Singh Yadav for allotting special funds for socioeconomic development for two years for villages with 50 percent Scheduled Caste populations, was revised so as to enable villages with more than 30 percent (and even 22 percent in certain areas) Scheduled Caste members to qualify.

The BSP decided to contest alone during the 1996 Lok Sabha elections, and the party doubled its share of valid votes in Uttar Pradesh—going from about 10 percent during the 1989, 1991, and 1993 elections to 20.6 percent. The BSP was especially successful in consolidating the Scheduled Castes behind its candidates. The electoral dividends the BSP drew from the Mayawati government confirmed Kanshi Ram's belief that any coalition was worth considering provided it allowed the BSP to come to power.

When the Uttar Pradesh Assembly elections approached in September 1996, several parties sought to tie up with the BSP. The party eventually reached an agreement with Congress. On June 25, at a highly symbolic press conference, P. V. Narasimha Rao, as Congress president, and Kanshi Ram presented the details of their agreement: for the first time, the Congress accepted the role of a junior partner in a coalition, and in this case with a party representing the *bahujan samaj*. The BSP repeated its score of the Lok Sabha elections (with about 20 percent of the votes; the alliance winning 27.8 percent) and obtained the same number of members of the legislative assembly (sixty-seven) as in 1993 (when it was associated with a stronger partner, the Samajwadi Party). None of the political parties captured a majority of seats and New Delhi imposed president's rule once more upon the state.

The BSP leaders announced straightaway that they would form a coalition with any political force willing and able to allocate the chief ministership to Mayawati. After six months of president's rule, the BJP accepted their conditions. This decision could be once again explained by the apprehensions that Mulayam Singh Yadav generated in the BJP and the BSP. According to the BJP-BSP agreement, Mayawati would be chief minister for six months, followed by a BJP leader, and they would then function in rotation. As for the government, it was to be made up with equal numbers of BJP and BSP ministers. The BSP thus returned to power due to a new reversal of alliances.

The Ambedkar Villages Scheme was revived in a big way to cover 11,000 villages under the direct supervision of the chief minister, who admitted that she was focusing her attention on the Dalits. After six months in office, she left the post of chief minister to the BJP's Kalyan Singh. But the BSP soon thereafter criticized the Kalyan Singh government for questioning the need of the Scheduled Castes and Scheduled Tribes Prevention of Atrocities Act (1989), which is supposed to protect the Dalits and tribals, and withdrew its support. Indeed, Mayawati had implemented this act in more drastic ways than any of her predecessors, so the complaint and withdrawal of support from the government was clearly opportunistic.

The BSP contested the 1998 Lok Sabha elections on its own in Uttar Pradesh, and it polled almost the same number of votes as in 1996. It continued its steady growth during the following years, as can be seen in Table 7.2. The BSP peaked in the 2009 elections when it crossed the 6 percent mark (see Table 7.2) and was recognized as a national party.

Table 7.2   **Votes Polled by the BSP in Nine General Elections, 1989–2019**

	Winning Candidates	Percentage of Candidates	Percentage of Valid Votes
1989	246	3	2.07
1991	231	2	1.61
1996	117	11	3.64
1998	251	5	4.70
1999	225	14	4.20
2004	435	19	5.33
2009	500	21	6.17
2014	503	0	4.19
2019	351	10	3.63

Source: Election Commission of India.

It crossed the 5 percent mark in seven states (see Table 7.3) and made significant inroads among Dalits in almost all states (see Table 7.4). Uttar Pradesh remains the party's stronghold, where it continues to make progress (going from capturing 24.6 percent of the valid votes in 2004 to 27.4 percent in 2009). Over the past decade, the BSP has been declining, partly because of the leadership vacuum left by Kanshi Ram's demise, partly because of Mayawati's strategy of going alone to electoral battles, partly because of the co-option of BSP cadres by other parties, and partly because of the divisions among Dalits.

This last factor badly affected the prospects of the BSP during the 2019 elections, while the party had, at last, forged an alliance with the Samajwadi Party in Uttar Pradesh. This decision enabled the BSP to jump from zero to ten members of parliament in the Lok Sabha, but the party would have been even more successful if Dalits had supported it as a bloc. In fact, only the Jatavs voted en masse for the BSP, and other

Table 7.3   **Valid BSP Votes by State, 2004 and 2009 (percentages)**

State	2004	2009
Uttarakhand	6.8	15.3
Uttar Pradesh	24.6	27.4
Punjab	7.7	5.8
Haryana	4.9	15.7
Delhi	2.4	5.3
Maharashtra	3.1	4.8
Madhya Pradesh	4.8	5.9

Source: Election Commission of India.

Table 7.4   The Dalit Vote for the BSP in Seven States, 2009 (percentages)

State	Dalit Votes
Chhattisgarh	27
Delhi	23
Haryana	57
Madhya Pradesh	Jatavs: 27
	Other Dalits: 6
Maharashtra	Mahars: 15
	Buddhist Dalits: 37
	Dalits: 9
Punjab	21
Uttar Pradesh	Jatavs: 85
	Pasis: 64
	Other Dalits: 61

Source: Adapted from Rahul Verma, "Dalit Voting Patterns," *Economic and Political Weekly* 44, no. 39 (September 26, 2009): 95–96.

Dalit *jatis* turning to the BJP. This party, in Uttar Pradesh, became the rallying point of the non-Jatav voters by cashing in on the resentment of small Dalit groups accusing the Jatavs—who are indeed better off than other Dalits (Jaffrelot and Kalaiyarasan 2019)—of monopolizing access to reservations. In Uttar Pradesh, the BSP has given more than 20 percent of its tickets to Jatavs, whereas the BJP has nominated only 5 percent of Jatavs, 7.7 percent of Pasis, and 9 percent of Other Scheduled Castes (Verniers 2019). Certainly, the BSP–Samajwadi Party won 75 percent of the Jatav vote, but it received only 42 percent of the Other Scheduled Castes vote, against the 48 percent that went to the BJP. Interestingly, at an all-India level, the BSP can only win more supporters than the BJP among the "poor" Jatavs; all the other Jatavs prefer the BJP over the BJP, which suggests that class considerations are gaining momentum, even if *jati* identity continues to prevail in Uttar Pradesh (see Table 7.5).

Voting One's Caste While Casting One's Vote

If caste has lost the kind of importance it had in terms of ritual hierarchy, it remains a key institution so far as the matrimonial market and electoral politics are concerned. Many Indians vote their caste while casting their vote, because they feel a natural inclination toward the candidates who belong to their group and because they want to have their people in the corridors of power—if not at the helm. This is so they could benefit in a clientelist fashion: the members of a caste group

Statues of Mayawati and Dalit leaders in Lucknow. Photo by Christophe Jaffrelot.

will vote for an individual or party that represents them not merely for atavistic reasons but because of some material benefit. Beyond primordial ties, the transformation of castes into interest groups plays a major role here. This brand of realpolitik has much to do with reservation policies, since these positive discrimination programs are caste-based. As a result, political parties have had to articulate caste-oriented discourses, either because they were in favor of reservations for Dalits and then Other Backward Classes or against. In fact, no party could afford to be openly against schemes that concern almost 50 percent of society. But the Bharatiya Janata Party and the Congress have traditionally tried to dilute the impact of caste-based reservations by suggesting class-based reservations that would have benefited the poor from the upper castes. Narasimha Rao, when he became prime minister of India after the 1991 general elections, tried to introduce a 10 percent quota for these poor people in the public sector. But the Supreme Court ruled it out in its 1992 decision, which sanctioned the implementation of the Mandal Commission report, claiming for the first time that castes could be considered as classes—something the judiciary had refused to do for decades. The Congress has been able to remain a rather convincing "catch-all party" in terms of castes (see Table 7.6), whereas the BJP has tended to become the refuge of the upper castes (partly having to do with its opposition to the Mandal reforms).

Table 7.5   The 2009, 2014, and 2019 Lok Sabha Elections—Jatav/Chamar Vote by Class (percentages)

Class	Congress +			BJP +			BSP		
	2019	2014	2009	2019	2014	2009	2019	2014	2009
Poor	16	17	26	21	29	10	36	28	41
Lower	23	14	37	26	26	11	21	31	32
Middle	25	16	35	28	34	12	19	32	25
Rich	22	14	33	26	23	21	25	44	29

Source: Lokniti-CSDS, National Election Surveys.
Note: Row percentages do not sum to 100 because "Others" are not included.

Ethnic voting is especially obvious at the state level given the regional dimension of castes—most of them (especially the dominant castes) do not expand beyond a linguistic area, which is often coterminous with one state. A few examples will suffice to make this point, given the fact that when more than 50 percent of a caste group, tribe, or religious community vote for one party, we can speak of "ethnic voting," all the more so as a rival party will nominate candidates of the same caste in order to cut into its vote. In Andhra Pradesh, each of the three most important parties continue to identify themselves with one of the three dominant castes. According to an exit poll (Center for Developing Societies 2009) in the 2009 general elections, 65.9 percent of the Reddys have voted for the Congress, 63.7 percent of the Kammas have voted for the Telugu Desam Party and its allies, and 53.1 percent of the Kapus have voted for the Praja Rajyam Party. In Uttar Pradesh, 53 percent of the Brahmans, 53 percent of the Rajputs, and 54 percent of the other upper castes have voted for the BJP, whereas 84 percent of the Jatavs—the most important Dalit caste—and 64 percent of the other Dalits have voted for the BSP. So far as the Muslims are concerned, 58 percent of them have voted for the Congress-Trinamool Congress alliance in West Bengal, and 69 percent of them have supported the Congress in Maharashtra. Such figures do not mean that the Congress is not a catch-all party, because it does attract voters from different segments, but it shows that many groups continue to vote as a bloc.

Caste and Politics in the Age of Hindutva

Interestingly, the rise to power of the BJP has not sealed the fate of caste politics. Certainly, Narendra Modi and his party claim that they are above caste and have, indeed, used religion in order to polarize soci-

Table 7.6 Votes of Castes, Tribes, and Religious Communities in the 2009 General Elections (percentages)

Parties	Congress		BJP				
	Congress	Allies	BJP	Allies	Left	BSP	Others
Upper castes	26	7	38	6	10	3	12
Peasant proprietors	25	13	15	9	3	2	33
Upper Other Backward Classes	22	9	22	5	2	3	37
Lower Other Backward Classes	27	4	22	7	9	4	27
Schedules Castes	27	7	12	3	11	21	20
Scheduled Tribes	39	8	23	3	7	1	19
Muslims	38	9	4	2	12	6	29
Christians	38	9	6	4	11	1	32
Sikhs	41	2	10	36	2	3	7
Others	26	10	21	5	12	9	21
Total	29	8	19	5	8	6	26

Source: Yogendra Yadav and Suhas Palshikar, "Between Fortuna and Virtu: Explaining the Congress' Ambiguous Victory in 2009," *Economic and Political Weekly* 44, no. 39 (September 26–October 2, 2009): 41.

ety along sectarian lines (on the Hindus vs. Muslims mode), but they have also polarized society along caste lines. This strategy does not operate at the level of aggregates like Other Backward Classes and Scheduled Castes, but rather at the *jati* level, and therefore at the level of the Indian states—where *jatis* are relevant identities in the political arena. If one goes by the aggregates just mentioned, the BJP seems to make overall progress among Other Backward Classes and Scheduled Castes. This is evident from Table 7.7, which indicates how the percentage of BJP voters among the Other Backward Classes jumped from 22 percent in 2009 to 34 percent in 2014 and 44 percent in 2019. The popularity of the BJP among Dalits is even more dramatic: the Scheduled Castes vote for the BJP has increased from 12 percent in 2009, to 24 percent in 2014 and 33.5 percent in 2019.

But Other Backward Classes and Dalits have not voted together for BJP. In fact, only certain *jatis* rallied around the party. In Uttar Pradesh, for instance, the BJP has emerged as the rallying point of non-Jatav Dalit *jatis,* who resented the way Jatavs have cornered reservations for Scheduled Castes and gained so much power under BSP rule. The BJP has won its votes by nominating candidates of these Dalits' caste groups, as evident from the Centre National de la Recherche Scientifique (CNRS)–sponsored dataset that Ashoka University and Sciences Po have built together, SPINPER (Social Profile of Indian National and

Table 7.7   The 2009, 2014, and 2019 Lok Sabha Elections—Votes by Caste, Tribe, and Religion (percentages)

	BJP			BJP Allies			BSP		
Parties	2019	2014	2009	2019	2014	2009	2019	2014	2009
Upper castes	52	48	28	7	9	7	2	1	3
Other Backward Classes	44	34	22	10	8	6	5	2	3
Scheduled castes	33.5	24	12	7	6	3	11	14	20
Scheduled tribes	44	38	24.5	2	3	2	2	2.5	1
Muslims	8	8.5	4	1	1	2	17	4	5.5
Others	12	15.5	12.5	3	3	5			

	Congress			Congress Allies		
Parties	2019	2014	2009	2019	2014	2009
Upper castes	12	13	25	5.5	3	9
Other Backward Classes	15	15	24.5	7	4	7
Scheduled castes	20	19	27	5.5	1	6.5
Scheduled tribes	31	28	39	6	3	8
Muslims	33	38	38	12	8	9
Others	39	23	35	4	4	8

Source: Lokniti-CSDS, National Election Surveys.

Provincial Elected Representatives). While the BSP has given more than 20 percent of its tickets to Jatavs, the BJP has nominated 5 percent of Jatavs, 7.7 percent of Pasis, and 9 percent of Other Scheduled Castes (http://liaspinper.com; Jaffrelot 2019a). As mentioned earlier, the BSP–Samajwadi Party won 75 percent of the Jatav vote, but it received only 42 percent of the Other Scheduled Castes vote, against the 48 percent that went to the BJP.

The BJP has operated in the same manner vis-à-vis the Yadavs. As the non-Yadavs Other Backward Classes, who often belong to poorer strata of society, usually resent the Yadav domination, and the way they corner most of the reservations in particular, the BJP has successfully wooed them by nominating many candidates from this milieu. Whereas 27 percent of the Samajwadi Party candidates were Yadavs in 2019, Yadavs represented only 1.3 percent of the candidates of the BJP, which, on the contrary, gave 7.7 percent of tickets to Kurmis and 16.7 percent to Other Backward Classes, who often came from small caste groups (Verniers 2019). This strategy translated into votes: while 60 percent of the Yadavs voted for the BSP–Samajwadi Party alliance, 72 percent of the Other Backward Classes supported the BJP (Beg, Pandey, and Kare 2019), showing that the Other Backward Classes milieu was now polarized along *jati* lines, irrespective of class. Indeed, "poor" Yadavs and "rich" Yadavs voted for the BSP–Samajwadi Party alliance in the same proportions (see Table 7.8).

Table 7.8   The 2009, 2014, and 2019 Lok Sabha Elections—The Yadav Vote by Class in Uttar Pradesh (percentages)

Class	Congress			BJP			BSP + Samajwadi Party	BSP		Samajwadi Party	
	2019	2014	2009	2019	2014	2009	2019	2014	2009	2014	2009
Poor	1.5	4	12	27.5	11	7.6	68	0	3	82	76
Lower	4	6	19	24	32	6.3	58	6	3	49	70
Middle	15	10	8	22	29	5.6	59	3	8	49	78
Upper	7	11	5	18	26	5.4	66	2	5	47	77

Source: Lokniti-CSDS, National Election Surveys.
Note: Row percentages do not sum to 100 because "Others" are not included.

Conclusion

Caste in India is transformed from what it was 150 years ago. No longer merely the component of a hierarchical social system, caste today operates as an interest group that is sometimes identified with a political party at the *jati* level. While caste still exists, the caste system is undergoing significant change, at least in urban areas where the lower orders refuse to accept that the upper castes embody superior values. This kind of hierarchical mindset, however, continues to remain strongly internalized in different parts of society, especially in rural India.

In the 1990s, the rise of the BJP was not only due to the growing popularity of political Hinduism, but also to the fact that most of the high castes and dominant castes, irrespective of class, turned to the BJP—an upper-caste-dominated party that had never promoted caste-based reservations—in order to resist the rise of the Other Backward Classes and Dalits, not only via quota politics, but also in terms of status as evident from Mayawati's decision to strictly enforce the Scheduled Castes and Scheduled Tribes Prevention of Atrocities Act of 1989 when she was chief minister of Uttar Pradesh in from 2007 to 2012. The subtext of Hindutva, then, was upper-caste revenge, as the comeback of

Brahmins and Rajputs in the Lok Sabha and many state assemblies shows (Jaffrelot and Verniers 2015; Verniers 2019).

But the rise of BJP does not mean the end of caste politics for other reasons pertaining to their attitude vis-à-vis Dalits and Other Backward Classes. Despite the party's claim that the party's ideology was not compatible with any caste-based approach that may divide the nation, its strategists have meticulously studied the caste equation at the local level in order to select the right candidates. They have especially nominated representatives of small Other Backward Classes and Dalit *jatis,* who resented the domination of other caste groups of their categories— whose quotas they cornered. Yadavs and Jatavs of Uttar Pradesh are two cases in point: in this state, in 2014 and even more in 2019, the BJP could consolidate the anti–Samajwadi Party and anti-BSP voters among Other Backward Classes and Dalits. This tactic reconfirms that the role of caste in politics must be analyzed at the state level and at the *jati* level (Jaffrelot 2015a, 2019a).

Not only is the BJP playing the caste card at the time of selecting its candidates, but it is also increasingly instrumentalizing caste-based reservations at the state level. In Maharashtra, the Fadnavis government granted a 16 percent quota to Marathas (a dominant caste) three months before the 2019 state elections. In Uttar Pradesh, the government of Yogi Adityanath has included seventeen Other Backward Classes castes in the Scheduled Castes list where they will escape the competition of Yadavs and other strong Other Backward Classes castes. This caste logic is promoted at the state level even as the Modi government introduced a new 10 percent quota at the national level for the poor of all castes, claiming it represented a non-casteist approach.

Notes

1. Author interview with Kanshi Ram, November 12, 1996, New Delhi.

2. Ambedkar statues became a cause of disagreement between Dalits and Yadavs in this context. In March 1994, in Meerut, Dalits demonstrated against the removal of one of these statues from a public park. The police dispersed them and killed two demonstrators. In Fatehullapur (Barabanki District), Yadavs protested against the installation of a bust of Ambedkar on a plot they had been occupying for a long time. Over a period of four months, about sixty incidents linked with the installation of Ambedkar statues caused twenty-one casualties among Dalits. The BSP insisted that Mulayam Singh Yadav should take all necessary measures to ensure the Yadavs halted their protests, which he failed to do. For Kanshi Ram, the rising graph of atrocities was the main reason for the divorce between the BSP and the Samajwadi Party.

3. Before Mayawati, there had been only three Dalit chief ministers, none of them a woman: D. Sanjiviah in Andhra Pradesh, Ram Sunder Das in Bihar, and Jagannath Pahadiya in Rajasthan.

8

Religion

Chad M. Bauman and Ainslie T. Embree

As Mark Twain entered Bombay harbor on his round-the-world trip in the 1890s, he was aware, he wrote, that he had come at last to India, the land that everyone desires to see "and having seen once, by even a glimpse, would not give up that glimpse for all the shows of the world combined." India was so intriguing, he wrote, because it was "the home of a thousand religions and two million gods" (Twain 1989: 347–348). Twain saw no need to move beyond bemused irony, but the title of this chapter requires us to attempt a definition of what it means when we use the word *religion* in the context of contemporary India.

Toward a Definition of Religion

Scholars have endeavored endlessly to define the term *religion,* but all attempts have been contested as misleading or incomplete, and all definitions seem limited and local, such that some scholars have argued the term should be abandoned altogether. For that reason, we offer only a provisional definition for religion as we understand it within the context of this chapter: religions are social institutions that create and perpetuate rituals and beliefs oriented around objects, humans, or gods/goddesses believed to possess powers that transcend the mundane and ordinary. Utilizing processes of socialization and influenced by those with power within the community, religions construct relatively coherent life systems in which adherents' conceptions about the nature of the cosmos and the supernatural, on the one hand, and their practices and prescribed behaviors, on the other, reinforce one another, and "in so doing sustain each with the borrowed authority of the other" (Geertz 1973: 89).

Religion is clearly one aspect of culture—that is, the full range of patterns of behavior and thought that are transmitted from one generation to another. Religion also helps structure and is structured by society. Religion is, finally, also embedded within historical and political processes. For these reasons, the nature and shape of religion differs from time to time, and from place to place. For these same reasons, it is difficult to succinctly describe contemporary Indian religion in all its bewildering diversity. However, the task is greatly simplified if we may assume that readers encounter this chapter in the context of those that precede and follow it because, as will be frequently stressed in this chapter, it is impossible to understand contemporary Indian religion without reference to Indian history and politics, and elements of Indian society like caste and gender.

Religious Demographics

India is a religiously pluralistic society, not just in terms of the many religious communities represented (which is true of most large modern nations), but also in the very large numbers of people adhering to different religious groups. For example, in the most recent census (2011), Muslims constituted a mere 14.2 percent of the population. However, 14.2 percent of 1.21 billion is more than 170 million people, which means that India's Muslim population is roughly similar in size to Pakistan's, which is second, globally, only to that of Indonesia. The most dominant religion in India, of course, is Hinduism (79.8 percent). In addition to Islam, Christians (2.3 percent) and Sikhs (1.7 percent) are the largest religious minorities, with Buddhists, Jains, Zoroastrians (called Parsis in India), Baha'is, and other religions all constituting less than 1 percent of the population. Although each of these smaller groups is interesting in terms of its beliefs, location within Indian history, and contemporary status, Hinduism and Islam will command the most attention in this chapter, as they do in social and political discourse in contemporary India.

India's Four Major Indigenous Religions: Hinduism, Buddhism, Jainism, and Sikhism

Four major religions—Hinduism, Buddhism, Jainism, and Sikhism— were born in South Asia. While these four indigenous religions comprise many sects and factions, each with their distinctive characteristics, they nevertheless share certain common beliefs and practices. One commonality is an acceptance of the idea of reincarnation, or samsara—that is, the idea that all living things, after death, will be reborn again in some form. A second common belief is karma, the notion that all intended actions—mental, emotional, and physical—have consequences that alter our current experiences and have the potential to propel us into additional lives and determine the circumstances of our (re)birth. A third common notion is dharma. Dharma can mean something like "essence" or "duty," as in, "it is the dharma of students to learn." But it can also convey the meaning of "law," "morality," or "teachings" (the primary meaning of the term in Buddhist contexts). Dharma is often used by Indians to refer to what Westerners would call "religion," though in Indian usage, dharma includes a more expansive array of phenomena (including, for example, elements of what Westerners might call "custom") than the term *religion* implies to most Westerners who use it. In any case, dharma is one's duty, what one does and should do. Good people are those who fulfill their dharma. Fourth, Indian religions generally agree that a primary goal of the spiritual life is to escape the suffering of samsara—that is the endless round of rebirths, into a heavenly paradise or an existence of bliss or nothingness. Hindus and Sikhs tend to call this goal *moksha* ("liberation"), while Buddhists tend to call it *nirvana* ("to be blown out," as in a candle), but these terms, and several others, are often used interchangeably. While commonly embraced across India's indigenous religions, these concepts are not universal, nor is belief in them generally considered a prerequisite for inclusion in the groups that commonly espouse them.

Hinduism

Some Westerners and Indians argue that Hinduism is not a single religion but many forms of belief and practice with differing cultural and historical origins that have come to be amalgamated over time. Hinduism has no single authoritative scripture, but rather a multitude of sacred texts. It has no identifiable historical figure as a founder, no creedal statements to summarize its beliefs, and no institutional structure to guarantee conformity. Moreover, instead of insistence on one god, as in Christianity, Judaism, and Islam, it permits belief in the existence of many, one, or none.

Despite this, in contemporary discourse in India, "Hindu," "Hinduism," and "Hindu dharma" are used by Hindus themselves, not only in English but also in Indian languages, to differentiate themselves from adherents of other religions. So too, however, are terms like *sanatana* ("eternal") dharma, which implies the belief that Hinduism is the first, most basic, and most perfect religion.

Many cultural streams contributed to the complex mosaic of the indigenous religious systems of contemporary India. What we now call Hinduism is a result of the slow amalgamation of many distinct regional and even local religious practices from not only the Indo-Aryan and Dravidian peoples, but many other smaller ethno-linguistic groups as well (e.g., the Mongoloid peoples of northeastern India). From this amalgamation, in the period from roughly 2000 to 600 B.C.E., a vast array of religious texts were produced on the Indian subcontinent. We call the earliest of these the "Vedic" texts, though the term is somewhat confusing, since there are four main genres of scripture that scholars consider Vedic, and the Vedas constitute only one of them. (In addition to the Vedas, the Brahmanas, the Aranyakas, and the Upanishads constitute the genre of Vedic literature.) The Vedas, written in Sanskrit in the earliest years of this era, contain, among other things, hymns of praise and invocations addressed to various gods and goddesses. They emphasize the role of priests, or Brahmans, who are portrayed as absolutely indispensable because they alone possess knowledge of the correct performance of rituals (e.g., sacrifice of various substances to the gods) that, according to the Vedas, are responsible for maintaining the cosmic order, and even sustaining the cosmos itself.

Between the time of the Vedas and that of the Upanishads, which were produced toward the end of this period, we can observe a remarkable development of religious and philosophical ideas. The Upanishads pay a great deal of attention to the goal of finding release from the unending cycle of birth and death, that is, to *moksha*. While the Upanishads contain many competing views, one of the most typical is that *moksha* is most easily obtained through the accumulation of spiritual knowledge, and in particular through knowledge of the unity, or nondual (*advaita*) nature of all reality. In such a view, which remains popular today, we are all ultimately nondistinct from each other, just as we are all ultimately nondistinct from the divine. All indications to the contrary are illusory. In this abstruse speculation, the gods play little role; the emphasis is on the spiritual seeker who develops spiritual knowledge with the help of spiritual disciplines (*yogas*), like meditation. *Advaita* thinking also leads to a blurring of the distinction between divine and human that Christians and Muslims who have encountered Indian religions have often found objectionable.

The centrality of this Vedic literature and, within it, the role of Brahman priests, differentiates this form of Hinduism (what scholars have sometimes called Brahmanical Hinduism) from the other great movements that emerged in the era of the Upanishads: Buddhism and Jainism. These distinctive Brahmanical Hindu ideas survived over the millennia, and remain central to contemporary expressions of Hinduism. In part, that is because of the fact that the two great Indian epics that came into their final form around the third or fourth century C.E., the *Mahabharata* and the *Ramayana,* both center on dharma and articulate Brahmanical conceptions of the good life. Both epics also remain immensely influential in the lives of contemporary Indians. In recent years, both the *Mahabharata* and the *Ramayana* have been modernized and reimagined in immensely popular television serials, Bollywood films, theatrical performances, graphic novels, and video games. It is difficult to walk more than a few yards in many parts of India without seeing images of the epics' primary characters (e.g., Rama, Sita, Lakshman, Hanuman, and Krishna), many of whom have been deified and appear in domestic, roadside, and temple shrines.

One short section of the *Mahabharata,* the *Bhagavad Gita,* has achieved a popularity during the past two centuries that it had not enjoyed before. Primarily a conversation between a reticent warrior, Arjuna, and the god Krishna, who convinces him it is his duty (dharma) to fight because he comes from a warrior caste, the Gita is now perceived by many Hindus and non-Hindus alike as a kind of summary of Hindu beliefs. The text is given diverse and often contradictory interpretations, but one reason for its recent popularity is surely the fact that it acknowledges and attempts to legitimize and harmonize multiple modes of religious life within Hinduism, particularly karma yoga (the discipline of action, or of advancing spiritually by doing one's dharma without attachment to results), bhakti yoga (the discipline of passionate devotion to the gods), and jnana yoga (the discipline of spiritual advance through the accumulation of spiritual knowledge).

Two kinds of religious specialists—both complementary and competing—were integral to Brahmanical Hinduism, and remain so today. One is the priest, who knows the sacred formulas used for approaching the deities in the great Vedic ceremonies. In everyday life, he (for it is almost always a he) is the individual with the special qualifications required to perform temple rituals as well as rites of passage surrounding birth, initiation, marriage, and death. Brahmans are also called upon by individuals, families, or communities for a variety of other functions, like reciting mantras to bring success and ward off evil, blessing the building of a house or other significant endeavor, and providing horoscopes to ensure the astrological compatibility of couples in marriage.

A magnificent temple in south India, which had pools for bathing, emphasizing the importance of ritual cleansing in Hindu worship. Photo by Ainslie T. Embree.

The other type of religious specialist is the guru. Gurus, who, unlike Brahman priests, may be male or female, are spiritual guides who have found the way to truth and are able to lead others to it. Gurus are numerous throughout all levels of Indian society, ministering to the spiritual needs of ordinary folk in their own localities or at pilgrimage sites. New gurus regularly emerge and gather followers, with most operating only locally. However, since the 1960s, several Indian gurus have achieved a large global following, like Maharishi Mahesh Yogi, Satya Sai Baba, Rajneesh, and Mata (Mother) Amritanandamayi, the so-called hugging saint. Many of these gurus are considered divine by their devotees, and what one scholar said of Sai Baba before his death could be said of these global gurus: "He does the things a deity should: he receives the homage and the devotion of his devotees, and he reciprocates with love and boons. And, above all, he performs miracles" (Babb 1986: 160–161).

In modern India, those who advocate a return to "Hindu values" generally have in mind the way of life that was articulated by Brahmanical Hinduism. The ideal of the good society that emerges in this literature can be summarized under two grand concepts. The first of these is of society divided into four great divisions, or *varnas* (generally translated in English

*Father and son devotees in front of
the Hindu Sree Padmanabhaswamy
Temple, Thiruvananthapuram. Photo
by Neil DeVotta.*

as "castes"), with each being bound to the others by reciprocal duties, creating a harmonious society. There is no historical evidence that such a society ever existed in reality, but the idea has had immense appeal through the ages, with Mohandas Gandhi being an influential exponent of a modernized version. The other, closely related concept is dharma—that is, that the good person is one who follows the social and spiritual duties appropriate to his or her *varna* and stage in life. In the Gita, for example, Krishna convinces Arjuna to fight by reminding him that he was from the warrior and ruler *varna,* a Kshatriya whose duty it was to fight for justice and against evil. While one's *varna* and stage in life might affect one's dharma—for example, a student ought to be celibate while a householder ought to be fruitful and multiply—there are also aspects of dharma that are universal, such as kindness, devotion, truthfulness, and charity.

Despite the interaction and amalgamation just described, regional Hindu beliefs and practices continued to retain their distinctive flavor. Nevertheless, two historical developments cut across geographical, linguistic, and cultural boundaries. One was the development of what has been called Puranic religion, in reference to the Puranas, religious texts produced beginning around the third century C.E. The Puranas include wildly popular stories about prominent local, regional, and national gods and goddesses. Aside from their appeal as engaging stories, the

Images of gods, goddesses, and other spiritual figures depicted on one of the towers (gopurams) of the famous Sri Meenakshi Temple in Madurai. Photo by Chad M. Bauman.

Puranas have also influenced Hindu iconography and worship in significant ways. Want to know why the god Ganesha is depicted with an elephant head and a broken trunk? The Shiva Purana will give you the backstory. Why is the god Shiva called *neelakanth* ("blue-throated")? Consult the Vishnu Purana. Want to know how and why one should show devotion to Krishna? Read the Bhagavata Purana.

The Puranas are woven into the everyday life of India, for although they were written in Sanskrit, the myths and legends they contain are known everywhere in all languages. Three major forms of deity are celebrated in the Puranic literature—Vishnu, Shiva, and the Goddess—but all have many manifestations and families (Ganesha is part of Shiva's, for example). The feminine divine power alone is given 1,008 names in one of the Puranas. Vishnu is worshiped through his avatars or incarnations, of which the most widely known and worshiped are Rama and Krishna, who has been especially celebrated in poetry and painting. Shiva is worshiped in various forms, but most commonly in the form of the *lingam,* an ancient columnal symbol of fertility that possibly dates back to the prehistorical Indus Valley civilization. The third form of the deity widely worshiped throughout India is some form of the Mother Goddess.

The second important, transregional historical development was the bhakti movement. Bhakti—intense, emotional devotion to a particular deity that is characterized as a relationship of love—is what many Hindus, both now and in the past, understand to be the essence of the Hindu religion. Bhakti found its most notable expression in the songs of poets in regional languages, those spoken by the masses, celebrating the local deity they loved and worshiped, and from whom they received the joy of personal communion (Hawley and Juergensmeyer 1988). Many of these poet-saints, as they are often called, were women (like Mirabai) and members of the lowest castes who, in their poetry, flouted stultifying social hierarchies of caste and gender as they claimed the right to develop a passionate relationship of devotion directly with the divine. The Ramcaritmanas, the story of Rama's life, composed in the sixteenth century in Hindi by Tulsidas (c. 1532–1623), is perhaps the most influential of all the bhakti works. Mohandas Gandhi called it "the greatest book of all devotional literature," and in northern India every year, thousands of performances are given of plays celebrating Rama's story as told by Tulsidas.

Bhakti by its very nature is constantly changing, and new forms of devotion appear continually. Because of this, new gods and goddesses can appear to answer new human needs in new circumstances, or old ones can take on new functions. A fascinating example of this is the goddess Shitala Mata, who protected against smallpox. With the disappearance of

Shiva in a Bangalore temple. Photo by Neil DeVotta.

The influence of the Puranas in the bhakti movement can be perceived in the ubiquity of devotional displays in everyday Indian practice. Here, the god Venkateshwara, worshipped as an incarnation (avatar) of the god Vishnu, appears on a taxi's dashboard shrine. Photo by Chad M. Bauman.

that disease, she has come to be associated instead with the current spread of HIV/AIDS in India. Then, in early 2020, shrines to the Goddess of Coronavirus emerged around India, with worship conducted in her presence in hopes of limiting the virus's devastation.

Similarly, Rama has become extraordinarily important in recent times through his use as a potent symbol of the assertive (or bellicose, depending on one's perspective) defense of "Hindu" ideals and traditions against the putative threat of religious minorities and secularization, as demonstrated by the fervor aroused in the 1990s by events leading to the destruction of the mosque known as the Babri Masjid (more on this later), which, it was asserted, had been constructed at the location of a destroyed Rama temple.

Tribal Religion

We lack the space to engage fully in contemporary debates about India's various tribal religions, but the chapter would be incomplete without some mention of them. The religions of India's tribal peoples have historically differed somewhat from the Hinduism described earlier. They have been less scripturally oriented, for one, and less oriented around the ritual superiority and direction of Brahmans. They have also more prominently featured shamanistic forms of religion (e.g., exorcism, possession, and contact with the dead) than has Brahmanical Hinduism. Scholars sometimes label tribal religion "animistic," and in so doing are consciously making a connection between the religions of India's tribal peoples and those of tribal peoples in Africa, Australia, and elsewhere. The status of tribal religion—as "Hindu" or not—has been a matter of great debate in India. Hindu nationalists are particularly inclined to describe it as "Hindu," in part because it serves the goal of constructing a large, unified "Hindu" voting bloc, in the pursuit of which Hindutva-inspired activists have established educational facilities among tribal communities aimed at further Hinduizing them. Often, their local competitors are Christians, who have gained many converts from among tribal peoples, and who sometimes seek to portray them as not "Hindu," in order to drive a wedge between tribal peoples and nontribal Hindus. What we can say without controversy is that India's tribal religions have participated in the long process of amalgamation described in the preceding paragraphs, such that the religions of tribal peoples have come, over time, more and more to resemble the religion of nontribal Hindus across the nation. At the same time, the religions of tribal peoples have influenced all-Indian Hinduism as they have been drawn up into it.

Jainism and Buddhism

Throughout history, the religious and social dominance of Brahmanical Hinduism was challenged by other systems, of which Jainism and Buddhism were the most influential. Both played significant roles in Indian history, with Buddhism becoming one of the three great world religions, along with Christianity and Islam, as it spread throughout Asia and then into many other parts of the world, while virtually disappearing from India itself.

Buddhism and Jainism both differ from Brahmanical Hinduism on three important points: they reject the authority of the Vedas, they assign Brahmans no preordained hierarchical spiritual role, and they deny the spiritual significance of distinct social obligations that separate castes have within society. Jainism stresses nonviolence/noninjury (*ahimsa*) and the refusal to take life in any form as a requirement in the quest for *moksha*. Although believing in great spiritual leaders named *tirthankaras* (the most important of whom is Mahavira) who offer guidance and inspiration, Jainism rejects belief in deities.

Buddhism's disappearance from India itself can probably be explained by its absorption into the mainstream of Hindu culture as well as by aggressive attempts by exponents of Brahmanical Hinduism to stamp it out. A curious reversal has taken place in modern India, however. Since

Buddhist temple at Sarnath. Photo by Neil DeVotta

1954, census figures show a thousandfold increase in the number of Buddhists in India. This is due to the social reform movement initiated in the 1930s by Bhimrao Ramji Ambedkar (1891–1956), who was a leader of the Untouchables, or Dalits, the most socially oppressed of all classes in India. Believing that Hinduism was the cause of their condition, he decided to convert his followers to Buddhism, a religion that he regarded as older than Hinduism and free, in his view, from the degrading oppression of caste. These new Buddhists now number over 4 million and are a very important element in the increasing refusal of the lowest groups to follow the political leadership of the Hindu upper castes and classes.

Sikhism

Sikhism developed in the fifteenth century. The origins of Sikhism can be found within the Indian tradition of bhakti as transformed by Guru Nanak (1469–1539). Out of his teachings came one of the most distinctive of religious communities. Although relatively small in number, Sikhs have had a memorable impact on India, as well as on other countries to which they have migrated, including Great Britain, the United States, and Canada.

Three elements define Sikhism as a faith and a community. One is the teachings of Guru Nanak and other spiritual teachers, as preserved in the Sikh scripture, the *Adi Granth*. These teachings recommend worship of the divine as Satnam ("True Name"). Another is the institution

The Golden Temple in Amritsar, the holiest site for Sikhs. Photo by Neil DeVotta.

of the guru, or teacher, who is in some sense the voice of God. Historically, there were ten gurus, beginning with Nanak and ending with Gobind Singh (1675–1708), who transferred the authority of guruship to the *Adi Granth* itself. The third distinctive element of Sikhism is the *khalsa,* which according to Sikh tradition was formed by Gobind Singh to defend the faith. Members of the *khalsa* were instructed to mark their membership with visible symbols, one of the most distinctive of which is the uncut beards and hair of men (which is why observant Sikh men often wear turbans).

Two Nonindigenous Indian Religions: Islam and Christianity

The wording of this heading asserts the theme of this section: that Islam and Christianity are firmly rooted in Indian civilization, despite their foreign origins, and despite the frequent assertion by Hindu nationalists that they are alien to Indian society.

Islam is a religion founded by the Prophet Muhammad in the early seventh century, in what is now Saudi Arabia. While Muslims trace their spiritual lineage back to the Hebrew prophet Abraham just as Jews and Christians also do, Muslims conceive of their faith as a return to the simple and unspoiled monotheism of Abraham prior to the unnecessary complications, innovations, and falsehoods later introduced by Judaism and Christianity (e.g., the Christian claim that Jesus is God). This simple monotheism, Muslims believe, was effectively revealed to Muhammad, over time, by the angel Gabriel (Jibril in Arabic), in and around the city of Mecca. The Quran records Muhammad's recitations of these revelations to others. Beyond humble submission to God—the meaning of the term *Islam*—Muslims demonstrate their devotion by participating in the five central rituals: bearing witness to their belief that there is no God but God and that Muhammad is his messenger, praying five times a day, paying a charitable tax, fasting during the lunar month of Ramadan, and (if possible) making a pilgrimage to the city of Mecca at least once in their lifetime.

Chapter 3 contains far more detail, but suffice it to note here that Muslim warlords and rulers began making inroads into north India by the eighth century, and achieved dominance over much of South Asia under the Delhi sultanate (c. 1192–1526) and then the Mughal Empire (1526–1857) in the twelfth to nineteenth centuries. During these centuries, everyday Indian life remained relatively unchanged. The majority of people remained Hindu, agricultural life went on as before, and patterns of trade and taxation seem not to have been altered significantly (except at the top). But something new had certainly been added: Islam, as the well-defined, articulate creed of the ruling class, was henceforth a profoundly important element in Indian social and cultural life.

There are no reliable statistics, but by the middle of the eighteenth century, about one-fifth of the population of the subcontinent was probably Muslim. The Muslim population of South Asia has composite origins. Members of the upper classes proudly claim descent from immigrants from the older Islamic regions—Central Asia, Iran, Iraq, Arabia—who came as soldiers, scholars, and refugees seeking opportunities under the new Muslim rulers. In the urban areas, traders, artisans, officials, and service providers in the lower castes might have seen advantages in adopting the religion of the rulers, and the same was probably true in the rural areas, where most Muslims lived. Communities such as these may have converted to Islam in hopes of securing powerful patrons in their struggle with exploitative landlords. Another very important reason for the attraction to Islam was the work of Sufis, members of mystic Muslim orders who migrated to India in sizable numbers. The Sufis made Islam accessible to the people of India by using regional languages to express their fervent devotional poetry, which had much in common with Hindu bhakti. Within this Muslim population were found all the schools and sects of Islam, including the two great divisions of Sunni and Shia.

A Muslim rests in the spacious halls of the Jama Masjid in Delhi, built by Mughal emperor Shah Jahan in the seventeenth century. Photo by Chad M. Bauman.

By the end of the eighteenth century, the political presence of Islam in India had undergone a dramatic change, for everywhere Muslim rulers were being replaced by non-Muslims. Their challengers included indigenous political powers, like the (largely Hindu) Marathas and regional Sikh dynasties, but in this era the British East India Company was rapidly becoming the major actor on the Indian scene, bringing with it elements of a new and competing religion and civilization. Islam had always been a minority religion in India, but now the rulers of the subcontinent's Muslims were increasingly adherents of an alien religion that was historically unsympathetic to Islam.

Three major historical distortions have negatively affected the perception and treatment of Muslims in India. One that often finds expression in popular writing by both Indians and foreigners is that there is a legacy of a thousand years of hatred between Hinduism and Islam. Hatred does not endure for a thousand years; it must be nurtured in specific contexts—and that is what one sees in modern India. Another error, egregiously common even in scholarly writing, is that Muslim conquerors of India offered their defeated peoples the choice of conversion or the sword. There is little evidence for large-scale forced conversions, and the continuing presence of an immense Hindu population suggests that such a policy was never systematic. Like early East India Company officials, Muslim rulers were interested in profiting from the people, not alienating them. Another frequent assertion is that there was widespread destruction of Hindu temples by Muslim rulers. Certainly there was some such destruction, but it was not wholesale, as witnessed by the many Hindu temples that survived the conquests of Muslim rulers. The reading of history that sees Hindus and Muslims in a state of perpetual enmity throughout history assumes that "Hindu" and "Muslim" have always been dominant forms of self-identity, with the two groups self-conscious of themselves in broad religious categories. Until the late eighteenth century, however, it seems clear that the signs or symbols by which Indian groups identified themselves had more to do rather with castes, religious sects (whether Hindu or Muslim), and geographic regions. It is therefore anachronistic to read "Hindu-Muslim" conflict back into Indian history, though it is certainly a feature of modern India.

Although Christians remained a small minority in comparison with Hindus and Muslims, they played a special role in relating India to the new rulers and to Western society and culture. There are three quite distinct phases of the history of Christianity in India. The first one dates from very ancient times, for according to the traditions of the Saint Thomas or Syrian churches of South India, Saint Thomas, one of the twelve apostles of Jesus, came to India and founded the church in 52 C.E., before he was martyred near what is now Chennai. Although historical evidence for this tradition is lacking, it is fairly certain that there were churches in India by the fourth century, making Indian Christian-

Muslim women in Hyderabad. Photo by Neil DeVotta.

ity older than that in most of northern Europe. Cut off from Western Christianity but in contact with the churches of the Middle East, the Christians in South India, principally in what is now Kerala and Tamil Nadu, were integrated into the wider Indian society as a community with relatively high status, and they seem to have made no attempt to seek converts outside their own community.

The second phase of Christian history began with the establishment of Portuguese power at the beginning of the sixteenth century. The splendors of the great churches at Goa, the capital of the Portuguese Empire in the East, bear witness to the Portuguese activity in spreading Christianity, often by force and compulsion. The large Roman Catholic population in Goa and elsewhere is also the result, however, of the work of missionaries, the most famous of whom was Saint Francis Xavier (1506–1552). The Roman Catholic missionaries traveled throughout India and were active in the courts of Mughal rulers. They seem to have made little lasting impression there, although their letters to their superiors in Europe provide valuable information about Indian conditions.

The third phase of Christianity in India, which began with the establishment of British power by the British East India Company at the end of the eighteenth century, was marked by contradictions and ambiguities. In contrast to the Portuguese, the British East India Company forbade missionary activity in the territories it acquired in India until 1813, on the grounds that Christian proselytizing would cause resentment among the people and threaten British power. This attitude remained quite widespread among British officials throughout the modern period, although some of them in both civil and military branches felt compelled by their faith to support missionary activity (Embree 1992: 151–165).

By the middle of the nineteenth century, representatives of the major European and North American churches became active in the founding of Western-style institutions such as schools, colleges, hospitals, orphanages, and printing presses without government support. The story of the missionary enterprise in India in the period of British rule is complicated, however, by the inevitable association of Christian missionaries, because of racial similarity and the special privileges they received, with the imperial ruling power. The relationship was double-edged, because Indians saw the missionaries as sharing in the power and the prestige of the ruling class, while many missionaries, captive of their time and place, adopted the attitudes of the rulers toward the ruled. It is fair to note that the number of converts made was small in proportion to the expenditure of human and material resources, but Christian activity was important in spreading Western ideas, especially in higher education.

Christians in India often express their devotion through conspicuous and dramatic use of images of various kinds, like adherents of other Indian religions. Here, Jesus and the Virgin Mary appear at an intersection in the Nilgiri Hills. Photo by Chad M. Bauman.

Religions in Interaction and Reinterpretation

Obviously, no date can be set for the beginning of modern India, but it is conventional to assign to it the period toward the middle of the eighteenth century, when the Mughal Empire, based in northern India, lost effective control over the subcontinent. Partly because of these political changes but also, importantly, because of internal forces long present in Indian religion itself, Indian religions began at this time to transform themselves in a variety of important ways. Some of the most socially significant of these changes came about as a result of interactions with European Christian communities that on occasion prompted adherents of other Indian religions to reconsider and reinterpret their religious beliefs and practices. Others were no doubt a response to significant advances in communication and transport (e.g., the telegraph, postal system, railways, and steamships) and the globally disorienting diffusion of the economic, technological, and political ideas, practices, and institutions we have come to associate with modernity: bureaucratic organization of the modern state (with its control of all military power), capitalism, industrialization, a global trading system, and Western scientific explanations of nature. Most of these aspects of modernity, it should be kept in mind, were not only new to India but new to the rest of the world as well, and in a very real sense Britain was itself modernizing as it took control of and contributed to the modernization of India. And so, while some of the changes that took place within Indian religions during this period were certainly provoked by external factors, the nature and trajectory of these changes were informed and often propelled by indigenous patterns of thought and behavior that far preceded their arrival.

For good or ill, one of the prominent features of Christian activity in India after the sixteenth century was its bitter and forceful denunciation of Hinduism and Islam. The reaction of both Hindu and Muslim leaders and intellectuals to the verbal assaults from the West had important ramifications for the intellectual history of India. Christians compiled and distributed long lists of what they considered "barbarous" practices and degrading "superstitions" that were, in their view, directly related to the prevalence of Hinduism, including animal worship, human sacrifice, polygamy, female infanticide, child marriage, widow-burnings, and "idolatry" (a term scholars avoid because of its pejorative connotations, but that Protestant Christians in this era used liberally to demonize the use of images in worship). More priggish and prudish critics also objected to the sometimes ribald and salacious behavior of Hindu gods and goddesses, as depicted in the Puranas, in other texts, and in temple art. Similarly, Islam was excoriated for its treatment of women, the cruelty of Muslim rulers, and Muslim rulers' commitment to waging holy war against non-Muslims.

One common response among Hindus and Muslims was an apologetic and defensive one ("apologetic," in the religious sense, means to justify or defend one's beliefs). But there can be no doubt that criticisms such as these encouraged introspection, and may have occasionally hastened movements of reform. It should be acknowledged that interaction with Hindus and Muslims had a similar effect on Christianity. Among other reforms, many Christian communities in India came by midway through the twentieth century to abandon or at least soften their polemical treatment of Hinduism and Islam, coming to consider it possible that divine truth could be possible outside of Christianity, though the rapid rise of evangelical and Pentecostal forms of Indian Christianity in the past few decades has reversed the trend.

Another challenge from the forces of Christianity was somewhat different: Christian mission societies introduced institutional patterns that were part of nineteenth-century Western society. They included educational institutions of all kinds, orphanages, hospitals, and social service centers. The churches in the West were persuaded to support

204 Chad M. Bauman and Ainslie T. Embree

these institutions on the grounds that they would facilitate conversion through example and precept. They were, at the same time, expressions of the humanitarian and philanthropic impulse characteristic of the nineteenth-century Western world, particularly of Great Britain and North America. Colleges for women were a special innovation and were largely the work of US churches. Though there were remarkably few conversions in any of the many colleges and schools founded by the Western churches, Christian educational institutions did provoke many intellectual "conversions" to Western science, philosophy, and literature, and have at times also intentionally or unintentionally inculcated disdain for Indian religions, philosophies, and traditional Indian social mores and norms. Similarly, while Christians and non-Christians have often lauded the contribution that the missionary schools, colleges, and hospitals made to India, some have criticized Christian social service endeavors for mixing up service with evangelistic efforts, thereby luring Indians to Christianity through demonstrations of superior wealth and technological power.

Movements Within Hinduism

Scholars of Indian religions sometimes denominate the various reform movements that originated within Hinduism in the nineteenth and twentieth centuries as "neo-Hinduism." There is some justification for the term, but it also misleadingly obscures how much the core beliefs and practices of Hinduism remained consistent even in the most radically innovative movements.

One of the most prominent reformers of the nineteenth century was Rammohun Roy (c. 1772–1833), who enunciated positions in regard to religion that have become an important part of the intellectual inheritance of India. Personal experience had made him bitterly critical of certain aspects of his society, especially the use of images of gods and goddesses in worship, child marriage, polygamy, dowry, and the poor treatment of women. Roy was especially incensed by the practice of sati, in which widows in certain areas of Bengal and Rajasthan had occasionally immolated themselves on their husbands' funeral pyres (as discussed by Lisa Trivedi in Chapter 9). While there was little scriptural basis for the practice, those who went through with it were considered particularly pious and virtuous women—the term *sati* can be translated as "the true one"—and often came to be venerated or worshipped themselves (posthumously, of course). Roy's criticism of this and other social practices was likely encouraged at least in part by contemporary Western criticism of Indian society (though there is also some historical evidence suggesting that colonial-era economic transformations may have encouraged such practices, on which see Oldenburg 2002).

Roy's method was not to deny the existence of such practices nor to defend them, but to declare them perversions of the true essence of Hinduism, which he believed was to be found in the Vedic texts. The use of images in worship, for example, derived not from the Vedas or Upanishads but from the much later Puranic texts. Corruptions such as these had crept into the religious tradition through Hindus' ignorance of their foundational texts. If these corruptions were swept away, he insisted, only a pure monotheism would remain.

In fact, according to Roy, monotheism constituted the original core of all religions, including Christianity and Islam. This conclusion led Roy to what was perhaps his most influential argument: because a simple monotheism lay at the original core of all religions, and because this monotheism was articulated just as well within Hinduism as it was in other monotheistic faiths, Indians should be willing to adopt whatever was useful to them in Western civilization, without positioning Christianity or the aspects of modernity associated with it (e.g., science, education, bureaucratic governance) as an existential threat to Hinduism. Accordingly, he made a passionate plea for the introduction of education in English so that Indians could learn the best of Western philosophical and scientific thought. Roy's reading of the ancient texts caught the imagination of a generation of young Indians, particularly those in the northeastern state of Bengal, who were anxious to reconcile themselves with modernity without denying the validity of their own culture. For many, this reconciliation was facilitated by the remarkable society Roy helped to found: the Brahmo Samaj. Although frowned upon by the orthodox, the Brahmo Samaj provided a spiritual center for many Bengali Hindu intellectuals, and from its membership came an astonishing array of scholars, scientists, artists, and writers.

Reinterpretation and reform could take varied forms, as can be seen in the work of another remarkable religious reformer, Dayananda Saraswati (1824–1883). Like Roy, Dayananda condemned many Hindu practices, but the reforms he proposed were somewhat different, as was his stance vis-à-vis Christianity and the West. After a long spiritual pilgrimage in search of truth, he determined, like Roy, that truth was to be found in the Vedas, and that the Puranas and the bhakti movement had introduced corruptions. However, because *all* truth was to be found in the Vedas, there was no need to accept anything from the West. He mounted a strenuous attack on what he considered false religions, among which he included many forms of Hinduism, as well as Sikhism, Christianity, and Islam. He also founded an organization, the Arya Samaj, which won a wide following, probably partly because its declaration that India did not need to look outside itself for truth was appealing to those espousing nationalist ideals (but also because of his vigorous defense of Hinduism in the face of Christian and Muslim criticism).

The Arya Samaj's polemics undoubtedly increased tension between Hindus and Muslims, especially in northwestern India, where it was the strongest. However, at the same time it also provided Indians with greater self-confidence and a new sense of pride in being Indian. Not surprisingly, many of the best-known leaders in the nationalist movement in northwestern India came from within its ranks. Whereas the Brahmo Samaj had appealed to upper-class intellectuals, especially Brahmans, the Arya Samaj attracted many of its members from the urban middle castes and classes.

Another important reformer was Swami Vivekananda (1863–1902), who concluded that all religions, in all forms, were true. This meant that reformers like Rammohun Roy and Dayananda were wrong to denounce the use of images in worship. One should worship the form of the divine and in the manner that best suited one's own personal needs. Furthermore, while Western materialism had conquered India, India's tolerant and generous spirituality was superior, and therefore should and would conquer the world. This positive conquest could only be achieved, however, if India had a vigorous, robust national life. Vivekananda was a great orator in both English and Bengali. Making use of modern means of communication and a modern vocabulary, Vivekananda carried his message throughout India, Europe, and the United States, with a particularly sensational appearance at the World's Parliament of Religions in Chicago in 1893.

Through reformers like these, various forms of Hinduism were being fused with national pride in ways that would have a significant impact on India's struggle for independence from the British. Moreover, to a remarkable degree, and though they are sometimes not aware of it, contemporary Hindus, in their understanding of Hinduism, have been influenced in important ways by these neo-Hindu reformers. This is also true to a considerable extent of the views of a far more famous thinker and activist, Mohandas Gandhi (1869–1948), who brought religion to the center of Indian political and social discourse. A political leader of consummate skill who personified the Indian national movement from 1920 to 1947, Gandhi always insisted that his religion informed his political activities. Although admittedly influenced quite a bit by Jainism and reinterpreting many aspects of traditional Hinduism in somewhat novel ways, he insisted that his beliefs were consonant with true Hinduism. He summarized his religious and political philosophy in words such as *ahimsa* ("noninjury," or nonviolence) and *satyagraha* ("truth-force," or insisting upon the truth), and frequently asserted, "Truth is God." Gandhi was fond of referring to the New Testament and famous authors such as Henry David Thoreau, Leo Tolstoy, and John Ruskin, but the appeal he made to the people of India was successful because it resonated deeply with their own religious beliefs. Although some Indians, both Hindu and Muslim, regretted Gandhi giving religion a central role in defining Indian nationalism, it is possible that there was no other way to appeal to the Hindu masses.

Movements Within Islam

The reinterpretations of Hinduism throughout the nineteenth and twentieth centuries had counterparts within Islam, but Muslims' social and political position in this era altered the shape of their reform movements in significant ways. If Hindu leaders quickly saw in the British conquest of India an opportunity to reclaim the social and political position they had lost under Muslim rule, Muslim leaders perceived that very same conquest as a threat to the political power they had enjoyed during 700 years of Muslim rule. Muslims felt further threatened by the newly assertive spirit within Hinduism.

Some Muslim leaders talked of a jihad, a holy war against the British, but they lacked the resources and support from fellow Muslims necessary for such a response. Other leaders, notably those associated with the Islamic seminary at Deoband in north India, determined instead to withdraw from the politics of their time in order to preserve the traditional teachings and institutions of Islam. Through their network of schools, these scholars sought to rediscover and reassess the essential and authentic core of their religion. Unlike some of the Hindu movements discussed earlier, however, their reforms did not involve intentional acculturation to Western patterns (Metcalf 1982: 348).

There were, however, Muslims who advocated accommodation with Western learning and science. Among them, the most effective was Sayyid Ahmad Khan (1817–1898). In a move similar to that of Roy and Dayananda, Khan insisted that the Quran alone was the authority for Muslim belief and practices, and disparaged as unessential a variety of social customs that had attached themselves to Islam through the centuries. Khan argued that the findings of modern science should be accepted by Muslims. According to him, the role of science is to discover the laws of nature, which are also a revelation of God's word and law. There could therefore be no conflict between science and the Quran. Where they seemed to conflict with the Quran, the quranic passages should be interpreted allegorically. Furthermore, Khan insisted,

the authority of the Quran was established not by the miracles it contained but by its inherent truth and accordance with reason. The college
Khan founded at Aligarh in North India, now Aligarh Muslim University, became the most important center for Muslims wanting to come to
terms with British power and Western learning.

In contrast to the modernism of Sayyid Ahmad Khan and his followers, the most powerful defenders of traditional Islam in India came from
two movements, the Jama'at-i-Islami and the Tablighi Jama'at, whose
leaders went to the masses, calling for a revival of Islam. The founder of
the Jama'at-i-Islami was Maulana Maududi (1903–1979). For Maududi,
there could be no distinction between Islam as a religious faith and politics, and more than anyone else he provided Islam in India (and Pakistan)
with a political vocabulary. Terms and phrases first used by Maududi, such
as the "Islamic system of life," the "Islamic constitution," the "economic
system of Islam," and the "political system of Islam," remain in wide
usage by Muslim writers and political activists throughout South Asia,
especially in Pakistan and Bangladesh (Ahmed 1991: 464).

Founded in 1927, the Tablighi Jama'at does not, by way of contrast,
seek political power but stresses the necessity of the individual's acceptance of the basic teachings and practices of Islam. It is in essence a
revivalist and missionary organization, and proceeds by isolating individuals from their family and everyday life, forming them into small
temporary communities for religious teaching and devotions, and then
sending them out to win over others.

Communal Tensions and Secularism: The Politicization of Religion

No discussion of contemporary Indian religion can avoid consideration
of the growth of tensions between Muslims and Hindus from the 1920s
onward, which led to frequent, deadly riots in the first half of the twentieth century, and violence on a massive scale after the partition of the
Indian subcontinent into two nation-states, India and Pakistan, at independence in 1947. In the months after partition, as millions of Muslims
migrated from India to Pakistan, crossing paths with millions of Hindus
and Sikhs moving in the opposite direction, riots broke out on both
sides of the new border, resulting in hundreds of thousands, perhaps
even more than a million, deaths.

In this era, the term "communalism" came to be used to denote the
privileging of narrow religion or caste community identities, loyalties,
and political interests over broader, more national ones, in ways that

lead to conflict among communities. Those thinking communally often deploy a kind of zero-sum political logic that prevents peaceful negotiations or coexistence. Only a decisive and complete victory over the other is satisfactory to those who think in this way.

Not surprisingly, then, violence is always a risk of communal thought and action, particularly if and when communities believe they can effectively and safely advance their political agenda through its use. In such cases, they may be tempted to engage directly in violence, or to produce it by knowingly engaging in provocative action, such as when one community organizes a loud, intimidating procession past another's place of worship (Brass 2003). Many Hindu-Muslim riots in India have begun with provocative acts such as this, or with an act of intentional desecration (e.g., Hindus throwing pork—considered particularly unclean by Muslims—into a mosque). Just as frequently, participants in communal violence justify their participation with reference to what turns out to be pure rumor (e.g., that members of one community had kidnapped or sexually assaulted a woman from another, that members of one community had tried to poison the food or wells of another, etc.).

The communal riots that have been such a common feature of Indian life since the 1920s are obviously the result of more complex and systemic causes than the real or imagined acts of provocation described earlier. One factor that has contributed to the regularity of interreligious conflict in India is the introduction of modern politics. Just as politicians in democratic systems everywhere exploit economic, ethnic, linguistic, or religious alliances for political gain, Indian politicians have frequently appealed to their own and closely aligned religious and caste groups for electoral support. One of the best ways to create unity and loyalty among one's own community is of course to create an "other," a scapegoat, an enemy. And one of the most effective ways to do that is to provoke or produce violence between one's own community and another.

Yet modern politics do not always lead to interreligious violence. One of the reasons that they have in India is because even before Indians began to participate in modern democratic elections their body politic had been dissected, in various ways, along religious lines. It is frequently said that the British controlled India through a policy of "divide and rule." While such a statement oversimplifies reality, it is certainly the case that many British officials considered Indians inherently communal and predisposed toward interreligious conflict and violence. The presumption that Indians were predisposed toward interreligious conflict led British officials to govern in ways that attempted to preserve interreligious (and particularly Hindu-Muslim) harmony by keeping members of various religious communities separate in various social and political institutions. Unfortunately, this separation impeded the development of national unity and integration, both in colonial and independent India, which enshrined as law many British practices with regard to religion.

For example, in the nineteenth century, British officials began balancing the proportion of Hindus and Muslims in city police forces. Then, toward the end of the nineteenth century, colonial officials implemented the decennial censuses, which inquired about religious identity and then politicized it by having Hindus, Muslims, and a few other groups vote in separate electorates for their representatives in colonial legislatures, and apportioning the number of representatives allotted to each separate electorate according to the size of their community. The British also allowed religious communities to develop their own, distinctive personal law (governing things like marriage, divorce, and inheritance), a practice independent India has continued.

The revivalist and reform movements discussed earlier were also a very important factor in making religious identity a visible and consequential element of India's social and political life, thus leading to communal tension. Within Hinduism, there were many such movements, but three were especially significant in creating a sense of Hindu identity and provoking concern among Muslims. One was the *shuddhi* (purification) movement led by a dynamic Arya Samaj figure, Swami Shraddhanand (1856–1926). The *shuddhi* movement aimed to reconvert Muslims to Hinduism on the grounds that they had once been Hindus. This aim aroused intense opposition among Muslims, especially from the Tablighi Jama'at movement, and the bitterness caused by the *shuddhi* movement culminated in the murder of Shraddhanand, in 1926, by a Muslim.

Two other movements that date from the 1920s illustrate the difficulty in separating religion from politics. One was the Hindu Mahasabha. While the Mahasabha was a political party, it also had as a central goal the strengthening of Hindu self-confidence. Leaders within the Mahasabha always denied that they were anti-Muslim, but the organization was formed in 1909 in response to the formation of the All India Muslim League in 1906, and, by the 1920s, the Mahasabha had come under the influence of V. D. Savarkar (1883–1966), who had coined the term *Hindutva* ("Hindu-ness") to assert the essential and inherent connection between Indian and Hindu identity. The Mahasabha positioned itself as a properly Hindu party vis-à-vis the at least somewhat less sectarian Indian National Congress (INC), that attempted at times to work with the All India Muslim League. The Mahasabha did not attract a large formal membership, but its positions became well known and were widely accepted among Hindus, even by many leaders of the competing and less ostentatiously Hindu INC. Muslims perceived the Mahasabha as an exclusionary group, and feared that nationalism was being equated with Hinduism.

Another organization, the Rashtriya Swayamsevak Sangh (RSS; National Volunteer Organization), was founded in 1925 by K. B. Hedgewar (1889–1940). Hedgewar had been inspired by Savarkar's writings, though the RSS denied that it was a religious or political organization like the Mahasabha. Nevertheless, its stated function, as eventually described in its constitution, had significant political implications: "To eradicate difference among Hindus; to make them realize the greatness of their past; to inculcate in them a spirit of self-sacrifice and selfless devotion to Hindu society as a whole; to build up an organized and well-disciplined corporate life; and to bring about the regeneration of Hindu society" (Embree 1994: 619).

Since independence, the RSS has emerged as the most vocal proponent of the ideology of *Hindutva,* and of the notion that "foreign" religions like Hinduism and Christianity, with their expansionistic tendencies, represent a threat to the tolerance inherent in Hindu religion and culture. The electoral successes of the Bharatiya Janata Party (BJP) since the mid-1990s, with its leadership, including the most recent prime minister, Narendra Modi, drawn to a significant degree from RSS cadres, exemplifies the continuing and perhaps even growing appeal of these ideas, as noted in the discussion on Indian electoral politics in Chapter 4.

In the postindependence period, Indian Hindus continued to exploit their numerical dominance for political advantage, while for Indian Muslims, independence from the British brought with it a number of significant challenges. Many of the best-known Islamic leaders, both in politics and religion, had remained in or migrated to the lands that became Pakistan at Partition. Indian Muslim leadership was weakened as a result, leaving Muslims in India in a vulnerable position. Moreover, the Muslims who remained in India constituted one of the poorest and least-educated communities in India, and also carried the stigma of belonging to the community whose leaders, in the view of many Hindus, were responsible for the partition of what they considered the unified nation of India into India and Pakistan. In addition, India's Muslims were justifiably anxious about how they might be treated in post-Partition India, where Hindus held a numerical majority far greater than they had in British India.

Despite such fears and the strident anti-Muslim campaigns of organizations like the RSS, the Indian constitution has protected Indian Muslims' freedom of religion. The constitution places no legal restraints on religious practices in the hundreds of mosques throughout the country, and Muslim personal law governing marriage, inheritance, divorce, and adoption, as codified by the British in the nineteenth century, was retained by the new Indian government.

Despite formal freedom, contemporary Indian Muslims continue to deal with social stigmatization and prejudice, as well as acts of intimidation or violence perpetrated by their opponents, and particularly by those who espouse the ideology of Hindutva. One issue that continues to plague contemporary Muslim communities in India, and that restricts their (and others') culinary and vocational freedom, is cow protection. Because of their iconographic and mythological association with the god Krishna, and as a symbol of abundance, plenty, and prosperity associated with Aditi, the Vedic mother of all goddesses, cows are sacred to many Hindus. For more than a century, various Hindu organizations and individuals (including Swami Dayanand Saraswati and Mohandas Gandhi) have therefore promoted a ban on the slaughter and consumption of beef in India. The constitution of India recommends the prohibition of cow slaughter, and in 2005 the Supreme Court upheld the constitutionality of the various cow-slaughter bans now enacted in the majority of Indian states. Hindutva organizations have periodically used these bans as a pretense for vigilante violence and lynchings targeting those, usually Muslims, who consumed or were rumored to have consumed beef. Such lynchings have also targeted Dalit communities, some of whom had as their traditional occupation scavenging and then tanning or eating meat from the carcasses of deceased cows. The frequency of such lynchings has increased exponentially since the 2014 elections brought the BJP to power at the center. According to Wilkes and Srivastava (2017), for example, 28 Indians (24 of them Muslim) were killed by cow vigilantes between 2010 and 2017, while 124 were injured, with the majority of these attacks taking place since the election of the BJP.

Although India's various religious communities maintain continuity with their respective religious pasts, a new political role became possible for them in India's contemporary liberal democratic society. The issue raised by this new possibility was, in broad terms, similar to that in other similar societies elsewhere: What role should religion have in society, and what should be the relationship of the state to religion? Before independence, there had been persistent demands from groups like the Mahasabha and the RSS that Hinduism be given a privileged place in the new nation's constitution (as was done for Buddhism just off the southern coast of India in Sri Lanka). Such groups justified their demands on the grounds that India's major minorities, Islam and Christianity, were alien ideologies that threatened to undermine the essence and genius of India (which, in their view, was inextricably tied to Hinduism). Such attitudes had been rigorously denounced by the leaders of the INC, most notably by Jawaharlal Nehru. Nevertheless, despite the fact that secularism prevailed in India, the desirability and nature of secular governance (or at least secular governance on prevailing Western models) remains a matter of great public debate and contestation.

Challenging Secularism

One of the most pressing questions that confronted India in the months and years after independence was how to heal the wounds caused by the partition's interreligious bloodletting while ensuring harmonious interreligious interactions in the future. In 1947 the majority of opinion makers in India—journalists, academics, politicians, and businesspeople—would probably have given assent to Nehru's proposition that "the cardinal doctrine of modern democratic practice is the separation of the state from religion" and that the idea of a religious state "has no place in the mind of the modern man" (Smith 1963: 155). This emphatic rejection of the role of religion in national governance, however, contrasts significantly with the perception of India, by both Indians and non-Indians, as a particularly religious place. For Nehru and those who agreed with him, however, it was precisely the religiosity of Indians that made the secular state necessary. Secular governance seemed, for Nehru, to be the only possible bulwark against religious communalism and violence.

Nevertheless, the meaning of secularism in India differs from that in the West (where, it should be acknowledged, it is also diversely understood), for in India "secularism" does not imply any hostility to religion, or a denial of its importance. Nor does it mean what is implied by the phrase "separation of church and state." Rather, in India, secularism is most commonly understood to mean the equal treatment of all religions. Sorting out precisely what that means in theory and practice, however, is no easy task.

The debates surrounding the drafting of India's constitution in 1948–1949 illuminate this difficulty. The advocates of a secular state found themselves in a dilemma that has remained central for India. As a secular state, the government could not in any way favor Hinduism, but as a nation-state it had the right and duty to promote unity around shared visions of Indian culture. Historically, however, the culture of India—its art, literature, music—had been saturated with and colored by Hinduism, just as that of European lands in the Middle Ages were by Christianity.

What, then, was to be the place of other religions with different and, at times, conflicting cultures (a question that was particularly pressing with regard to Islam, Christianity, and other religions that had origi- nated outside of India, which were perceived with some justification to bear within their beliefs and practices the vestiges of cultural mores and norms developed elsewhere)?

In a study whose title implies its thesis, *The New Cold War? Religious Nationalism Confronts the Secular State* (1993), Mark Juergensmeyer argues that what we are witnessing in India and around the world in sec- ular nations is a challenge by indigenous religious forces to constructions of modern liberal democracy that attempt to ignore, demote, or margin- alize religion and religious people. While religious minorities occasion- ally challenge the marginalization of religion in secular democracies, they often rely on secular governance to ensure their own religious freedoms. Religious majorities therefore have far more to lose, politically speaking, from the secular insistence that all religions be treated equally. While all religious communities may resist the most anti-religious elements of sec- ularism, then, it is generally from within the religious majority (e.g., Christianity in the United States, Buddhism in Sri Lanka, and Hinduism in India) that the most vociferous resistance emerges. At times, this resist- ance proceeds through democratic processes, but if religious majorities encounter legal impediments to their self-assertion, they may turn to vio- lence, as has periodically been the case in India.

Perhaps the most illuminating example of how debates over the role of religion in India can turn violent is the destruction of the Babri Masjid (Babur's Mosque), and the violence that followed it, in 1992. While controversy surrounding the Babri Masjid in Ayodhya was noth- ing new, in the 1980s, Hindu nationalists began more forcefully and with broader support to demand the destruction of the Babri Masjid. According to Hindu nationalists, the mosque, which bears inscriptions suggesting it had been built on the orders of the Mughal emperor Babur (thus its name), was made possible by the destruction of a temple on the same spot that Hindus believed marked the birthplace of the god Rama. Eminent Indian historians, many of them Hindus, pointed out that there was no real evidence for any of this story and that, in any case, Rama was a mythical character. Attempts to settle the matter with archaeology on the site were inconclusive. In any case, as one scholar remarked, it is not possible to dispose so easily of religious belief. "We cannot counter- poise history to myth as truth to falsehood. These are different modes of knowledge, varying ways of understanding the world, ordering one's life and defining one's actions" (Gopal 1991: 122).

For many Hindus, the mosque was a galling symbol of the defeat of "Hindu" India by Muslim Turks; for Muslims, calls to destroy a centuries-old mosque were a reminder of their precarious position in a nation dominated by Hindus, some of whom desired the eradication of religious minorities. In December 1992, thousands descended upon and destroyed the mosque with light tools and their bare hands. While most were men, in the days leading up to and during the destruction they were urged on by prominent female Hindutva firebrands like Uma Bharati and Sadhvi Rithambara, who raised chants like, "If a Hindu's blood does not boil, then it's water, not blood in their veins." As the 400-year-old building collapsed, a Hindu holy man exclaimed, "The sun sets on Babur at last. The taint has been removed forever" (Embree 1994: 647–648).

In the days after the destruction of the mosque, a wave of violence swept north India, with at least a thousand people killed, mostly Muslims. Some supporters of secularism feared the violence marked the beginning of an unstoppable slide toward the redefinition of India as a Hindu nation. At the very least, the destruction of Babri Masjid, which had the support of prominent leaders of Hindutva organizations (like the RSS and the BJP, and including a future prime minister, Atal Bihari Vajpayee), signaled the growing power of Hindu nationalist elements within India. The BJP has been in power, nationally, for roughly half of the years between 1998 and the publication of this volume, after enjoying power for only thirteen days before that. More than twenty-five years of litigation involving what to do with the site of the destroyed mosque finally came to an end in late 2019, when India's Supreme Court ordered that it be turned over to Hindus (with the government supplying land nearby to relocate and rebuild the mosque). On August 3, 2020, Prime Minister Modi himself laid the foundation stone for a Rama temple to be built on the site.

While the most illuminating example of anti-minority communal violence, perhaps, the anti-Muslim riots that took place after the destruction of the Babri Masjid were not unique. Even before Ayodhya, in 1984, after Prime Minister Indira Gandhi (of the more secular Congress Party) was assassinated by Sikh bodyguards in revenge for her ordering the Indian military into Sikhism's holiest shrine, the Golden Temple, where Sikh separatists had barricaded themselves, the prime minister's enraged supporters, mostly Hindu, went on a killing spree, murdering thousands of Sikhs.

In 2002, Muslims were again victims of riots, this time in Gujarat, a state then ruled by future BJP prime minister, Narendra Modi. The Gujarat riots began after dozens of pilgrims on their way home from a pro-Hindu religious ceremony at the contested Babri Masjid site were killed by a train fire for which Hindu nationalists immediately blamed Muslims. After several days of rioting, more than a thousand Gujaratis had lost their lives. Again, the vast majority of them were Muslims. Similar though less deadly riots and attacks have led to more lost life (primarily Muslim) in places like Muzaffarnagar, Uttar Pradesh (in 2013), and Narsingbari, Assam (in 2014).

Since the late 1990s, there has also be a marked increase in Hindu nationalist violence targeting India's Christians. In 1998, there were anti-Christian riots in the Dangs region of Gujarat. None were killed, but many Christian homes and places of worship were destroyed. Atal Bihari Vajpayee, who had by that time become prime minister, placed blame for the attacks on Christian evangelizing. Then, just a month after the Dangs riots, Australian missionary Graham Staines and his two young boys were immolated in their own jeep by an anti-Christian mob in the state of Odisha. In the new millennium, attacks on Christian churches, converts, catechists, evangelists, and preachers have increased dramatically, and now number in the hundreds annually. Most of these attacks are relatively local and isolated affairs, but in the state of Odisha, in 2007 and 2008, leading up to and after the assassination of a prominent, Hindutva-inspired cleric, Swami Lakshmanananda Saraswati (which was, following the pattern in Gujarat, immediately blamed on Christians), Hindu nationalist-supported mobs rioted, killing around fifty Christians and displacing as many as 30,000, some of them permanently. Several Hindus were also killed or displaced in the violence, including, of course, the Swami and several of his supporters (Bauman 2010).

These attacks represented a new and puzzling phenomenon, distressing to many Hindus as well as to Christians in India and abroad. Those who attack Christians generally justify their violence as a response to Christian proselytization efforts, which, it is asserted, proceed with great success through the use of "force, fraud, and allurement," to lure gullible and impecunious Indians to the fold. In theory, the growth of Christianity would represent a threat to Hindu political power, and particularly to upper-caste Hindu political power (since most converts to Christianity come from Dalit and tribal communities). Yet the Christian share of the population has remained relatively steady since independence at a little over 2 percent. Hindu nationalists therefore radically overstate or overestimate the demographic threat of Christianity.

The view that religious proselytization is undesirable or inappropriate for religious people is a view held not only by hardline Hindu nationalists but also by many Indians who would normally support secular, liberal positions. To Westerners who have grown accustomed to people changing their religion in much the same way as they do their political allegiances, this attitude may seem in contradiction to secularism. It is, however, congruent with deeply embedded Indian cultural and religious values. Opposition to conversion and evangelism is related to the common Indian religious view that all religions offer equally adequate routes to spiritual enlightenment, such that conversion from one religion to another is unnecessary, and conversion away from the religion of one's family or community is disruptive and therefore undesirable. Moreover, deeply embedded structures of Indian society assert the primacy of the family and the community over the individual. In such a context, individuals who convert away from the religion of their families or caste communities are often considered disrespectful, even traitors. In fact, the very concept of conversion from one faith to another presumes a degree of individual autonomy that many Indian traditionalists finding troubling in and of itself.

In addition to the issues noted earlier, opposition to conversion derives from three primary sources. The first is the notion that religions are and should be ethnic and tied to particular places and peoples, rather than universal and expansionist. Closely related to this idea is a second: that conversion to another religion is socially disruptive and destructive because it introduces novel and alien customs, beliefs, and practices. It was for this reason that Mohandas Gandhi frequently alleged that Christian converts tended to become denationalized, having given up not only their ancestral faith but also their national culture (Smith 1963: 165).

The third source of Hindu opposition to conversion involves that most difficult of modern social and political concepts: toleration. Hindus correctly stress that Hindu society has been and remains remarkably tolerant of a wide variety of belief patterns and practices. This tolerance derives from the insistence by Hindu intellectuals and spiritual leaders that all religions are potentially true and spiritually efficacious. While such sentiments produce respect for most other religions, those who espouse them reject as illegitimate forms of religion that do not in the same way consider all religions equally true. They are therefore inclined to condemn proselytizing religions, like Islam and Christianity, as forms of bigotry because they make universal claims for the truths they assert while declaring the practices and beliefs of other religions inadequate or even demonic.

Through the years, the RSS and other Hindu nationalist groups have used arguments like these to effectively marginalize and produce enmity toward "foreign" faiths like Islam and Christianity. The target of Hindu nationalist groups, however, is not merely religious minorities. Violence targeting religious minorities may in some cases manifest a boiling frustration about the particular nature of India's secularism. In governance and law, India's brand of secularism evinces the influence of both Western and more indigenous religious and political ideals. Many Hindu nationalists complain that the balance of the two is inappropriately tilted in favor of the former, or, to put it another way, that Indian secularism favors and coddles religious minorities while infringing more regularly upon the religious rights of the religious majority, thereby failing to recognize and utilize valuable Hindu (as opposed to Western) conceptions and practices of tolerance, and—even worse—facilitating their defeat at the hands of expansionistic and putatively intolerant religions like Christianity and Islam.

Despite protests from those hoping to ban religious conversion, Article 25 of the Indian Constitution, which guarantees individual religious freedom, states that "all persons are equally entitled to the freedom of conscience and the right freely to profess, practise and propagate religion." Christians and Muslims fought hard for the inclusion of the right to proselytize, and the fact that the right to "propagate" was included, then, must be seen as a kind of concession to these and other proselytizing faiths. However, state laws passed beginning in the 1950s forbid conversion by "force, fraud, and allurement," and have been used to limit religious proselytization. At issue is the fact that threats of damnation or promises of greater equality and respect can be construed as "allurement," such that the laws can and have frequently been invoked simply to harass Christian evangelists. Nevertheless, the constitutionality of these laws was upheld by India's Supreme Court in a 1977 ruling (*Rev. Stanislas vs. Madhya Pradesh*) that considerably narrowed the right to propagate one's faith by interpreting the term to refer to the *dissemination* of religious ideas and beliefs only, not to an *intentional attempt to convert* others to one's faith.

The last two parliamentary elections in India have been won by the BJP. The party's victory in 2014 was decisive, and the 2019 victory was practically a landslide. Given the Hindu nationalist orientation of the BJP and its regional allies, and the increase in anti-minority rhetoric and violence after 2014, religious minorities and supporters of secularism in India are justifiably concerned about what appears to be the mainstreaming of pro-Hindu, anti-minority sentiment in contemporary Indian politics.

Nevertheless, there are additional factors at play. A Muslim terrorist attack just before the election, which provoked a military response that BJP leaders managed to frame as strong and effective (despite evidence otherwise) boosted the BJP's electoral prospects. Moreover, despite the fact that the BJP failed to deliver meaningfully on 2014 campaign promises to promote development and economic growth, and despite rising and outrageously high unemployment, many in India continue to perceive Modi as an incorruptible political leader who has conscientiously and courageously tried to tackle India's many challenging problems. Even if he hasn't been terribly successful, his perceived integrity and energetic, decisive action is preferred by many in the electorate to the corruption and incompetence that are widely perceived to have characterized Congress rule. In a surprisingly self-critical tweet, longtime supporter of Hindutva politics and BJP member of parliament Subramanian Swamy expressed happiness that placing "Hindutva and anti corruption" at the center of the BJP's electoral campaign had kept the electorate's attention there, rather than on what he acknowledged was his party's "incompetent macro economic performance."

Another factor, widely acknowledged, even internally, is that the opposition Congress Party is in organizational disarray. Moreover, the party is currently led by Rahul Gandhi, who in the 2019 elections simply could not compete with Modi's charisma and savvy use of social media. Given the recent "presidentialization" of Indian politics—meaning the electorate's increasing focus on parties' candidates for prime minister rather than on the parties' respective platforms—Gandhi's charisma deficit was consequential. For all of these reasons, then, it is perhaps best to interpret these strong BJP victories as an indication that the Indian electorate either approved of or was willing to accept Hindu nationalist rhetoric and action as the new normal in exchange for what they perceived (despite the struggling economy) to be stronger, more competent, more business-friendly, and more effective leadership. Whatever the reason for the BJP's electoral success, the party's rising power will certainly have a significant impact on religion and interreligious dynamics in India for many years to come, in ways both major and minor. To give just one recent example, many BJP politicians politicized the early spread of the novel coronavirus

Subramanian Swamy ✓ @Swamy39 · May 22   ⌄
I am happy that I was right that economy   is not an overpowering factor if Hindutva and anti corruption are the campaign issues. So we escaped incompetent macro economic performance. But if economy collapses then it will become an issue

○ 845   ⟲ 3.8K   ♡ 20K   ✉

in India by focusing nearly exclusively on infections related to a large meeting of the Muslim Tablighi Jama'at that was held in Delhi in April 2020 (i.e., after Delhi authorities had warned against large gatherings, but before any ban was being broadly enforced).

Conclusion

To conclude a survey of "lived religion" in India on a note of tension and violence may seem pessimistic, but it is done deliberately as a reminder that religion, as it was defined at the beginning of this chapter, is woven inextricably into the tapestry of Indian history. Mohandas Gandhi used to say that when people argued that religion should be kept out of politics, it only showed that they knew nothing of either religion or politics. All religions have political implications, and all political ideals are informed by the ideals (religious or otherwise) of those who strive after them.

Jawaharlal Nehru was often critical of contemporary religion, yet few have spoken more movingly of the enduring gift of religion to India's historical consciousness. Brought up in a family of wealth and educated in England's most famous schools, he traveled throughout India as a young man and was depressed by the poverty and misery of the people. Then he discovered that India possessed a vitality that had, impressively, allowed it to periodically renew itself throughout the ages: India, he said, "was like some ancient palimpsest on which layer upon layer of thought and reverie had been inscribed. . . . All these [layers] existed in our conscious or subconscious self . . . and they have gone to build up the complex and mysterious personality of India. [Yet India's] essential unity had been so powerful that no political division, no disaster or catastrophe, had been able to overcome it" (Nehru 1946: 42–47). Nehru refused to give the name of *religion* to that source of vitality, and yet at the end, it is hard to escape the claim of religion as the vitalizing force, for good or ill, in contemporary India, as it has been in the past.

9

The Status of Women

Lisa Trivedi

Understanding the status of women in contemporary India may at first seem quite straightforward. Most international press coverage of Indian women appears when "traditional" social practices, including dowry, dowry death, enforced widowhood, and widow immolation (sati), are featured, all of which are portrayed with little explanation and rendered emblematic of India's "traditional" society and unchanging culture (Manji 2009; Shrine 2009; Schott 2009). Others emphasize women's inequitable access to education and economic opportunities without considering the constraints under which women labor or the extent to which multinational corporations have reinforced historic economic and social inequities that have disadvantaged women. Since 2012, the press has regularly featured stories about rape, sexual assault, and molestation of women (Mandhana and Trivedi 2012). The conclusions most often drawn from the media are that Indian women are exploited, helpless, and abused. In short, women in India are understood to need humanitarian relief and international intervention. This perspective obscures the circumstances in which women in India struggle today against the forces of both "tradition" and "modernity."

For nearly twenty years, India's gross domestic product has grown at between 6 and 7 percent annually (United Nations Development Programme 2009; International Monetary Fund 2018; John 2019). Between 2005–2006 and 2015–2016, some 271 million Indians were lifted out of poverty according to the United Nations. Yet today India ranks only 130th among 189 nations in the United Nation's Human Development Index (United Nations Development Programme 2018). Still, there is no denying that the lives of Indian women can be improved. With the second-fastest-growing economy in the world (Government of India 2016–2017), it is hard to accept that so many millions of Indian women earn no more than 100 rupees ($1.41) per day. Although the United Nations cannot estimate the number of Indian women who remain in poverty, many indicators suggest that women and girls continue to fare far worse than men and boys even after India's sustained economic boom. Indian women's continued poverty in the face of economic growth confirms their marginal place within the economy, a position that has not been substantially reversed since India's independence in 1947.

Yet women's place within Indian society amounts to far more than this troubling information suggests. In terms of political representation, India was among the first countries to be led by a woman prime minister; it has had a woman serve as its president, and it fields a number of strong female leaders prominent in its major political parties. Women also occupy 33 percent of the seats in panchayats, or village councils, nationwide. Furthermore, women's representation in the Lok Sabha (lower house of parliament) grew from 4.4 to 14.3 percent between 1952 and 2019 (Radhakrishnan 2019; Menon-Sen and Shiva Kumar 2001: 66; Rai 1998). Seventy years after independence, women hold more than three times the number of seats in the Lok Sabha as they did at independence, seventy-eight in 2019 compared to twenty-two in 1947 (Government of India 2019a; Raju 2006: 90–91; Sen 2008).

As impressive as these political gains may be, the record is mixed when it comes to education and employment. While women's literacy was estimated at only 8 percent in 1947 and is now estimated at roughly 65 percent, rates for women's literacy remain a little more than 10 percent lower than those of men (Central Intelligence Agency 2019). More troubling is the fact that a literacy gap has widened as parents in urban areas provide daughters with a lower-quality education than they do their sons, who are also more likely to be educated in English. While the final effects of such disparities are not fully understood, the double-gap in literacy and language of education is cause for concern as India increasingly competes in the global economy.

Considering women's place in the globalized economy, *Forbes Magazine* tells us that Indian women today are leaders in banking and business, and we can also identify women as national leaders in the fields of education, science, and medicine (Bharee 2006). Indeed, more Indian women hold graduate degrees than do men. Furthermore, Indian women are the backbone of a world-renowned microcredit system (Bhatt 2006: 12). At the other end of the economic spectrum, women's

Schoolgirls in Hyderabad. Photo by Neil DeVotta.

disproportionate participation in the informal sector of the economy has ensured their earning capacity remains limited. Women generally find fewer formal sector jobs, are paid less than men, work in poor conditions, and have worse health as a result. Whereas one can point to successful women leading India's economy, these women are few and far between. How do we reconcile these conflicting realities when assessing women's status in contemporary India?

The Indian constitution, ratified in 1949, is remarkable in its attention to women. Among many constitutional measures for women is a provision that guarantees equality (Article 14) and another that restricts the state from discriminating on the basis of sex (Article 15). Further, the Indian constitution guarantees equality of opportunity (Article 16) and equal pay for equal work (Article 39) for all its citizens. In this constitutional framework, it is hardly surprising that Indian women have served as heads of state, led major political parties, and held key bureaucratic positions across government. Thus, to view women in contemporary India as victims of a "traditional society" belittles their advancement to the highest levels of power in society.

The basic issue is that even as Indian women have gained rights, improvements in their welfare have not kept pace with those of men. This

Woman selling roasted corn. Photo by Neil DeVotta.

chapter begins with a couple of conceptual pointers to thinking about women's status in contemporary India. It continues by exploring how women emerged first as subjects of social reform in colonial India and how they took up struggles for equality on their own behalf in the twentieth century. It concludes with a consideration of women in postindependence India, focusing on civil rights, education, employment, and safety.

Thinking About "Indian Women"

There are two points of caution to observe when exploring the status of women in India. First, while some struggles by Indian women may seem familiar, one should not assume that the concerns and priorities of Indian women are the same as women elsewhere (Mohanty 1988). Indian women have articulated and pursued priorities that reflect their own particular circumstances. It is only by understanding the context in which Indian women lived and the possibilities they wished to create that one can adequately assess women's status in contemporary India.

A second point of caution is that while it may seem natural to think and write about "Indian women," this term and the identities that it presupposes are quite recent. Indeed, the identities of both "Indian" and "women" were products of the nineteenth and twentieth centuries, during which colonialism and the rise of nationalism shaped how the state identified people and the ways in which individuals located themselves in relationship to others. Prior to the nineteenth century, female members of an Indian family did not subscribe to an identity as "women." Instead, they thought of themselves largely through their relationships to those in their family—be it their parents, husbands, in-laws, or children—and other social groups.

For Indian women, as well as men, the family unit has significantly shaped opportunity and status. Women's relationships to their families were not so different from men's in that decisions typically demanded conformity in the interest of the extended kin group. Ultimately, family beliefs and customs determined how a child matured to adulthood, the type of education the child received, and who the child married, regardless of whether the child was male or female. Scholars of women in colonial India associate the rise of an identity as "women" with the nineteenth century, when British reformers and administrators, as well as native modernizers and orthodox religious leaders, debated the condition of women and defined what has become "Indian" culture (Sangari and Vaid 1989).

Women in Colonial India

The nineteenth century, as Radha Kumar has written, could be considered the "age of women" (1993: 7). What marked this period apart from others, whether one was in India or any part of the Western world, was that the status of women emerged as a central subject of political and social debate. In the case of India, discussions about women also occurred within a peculiar colonial context, which shaped the particular forms it took. The British East India Company had been doing business in India for more than a century before transitioning from a trading company and revenue collector into an administrator. By the early nineteenth century, a company-state had emerged as a powerful military, economic, and administrative force (Metcalf and Metcalf 2008). As the British East India Company's trade interests grew, so too did the need to protect its preferences. This saw the company extending its authority over a foreign population and intervening increasingly in native lives.

Debates about the condition of Indian women developed in this specific context (Sangari and Vaid 1989). They were in part motivated by the humanitarian initiatives of evangelical Christians that were popular in Britain and among British East India Company officials. The poor status of Indian women conveniently served to legitimize the company's project of modernizing Indian society, even while the company also claimed to be protecting "true" native customs that had been allegedly corrupted over time. Indian women's condition emerged as an important point of contestation between British and Indian elites, who asserted their own authority, while debating over who would define Indian "tradition" (Mani 1989).

For instance, the British abolition of sati, or widow immolation, in 1829 demonstrates how women first emerged as the focus of debate in the colonial context (Mani 1989; Yang 1989). In addition to a British administrative discourse, two kinds of native responses emerged from debates over the practice of sati. On the one hand, there were those natives, often connected with the British East India Company's activities, who sought to modernize their society and viewed sati as emblematic of Indian weaknesses that would have to be addressed in order to do so. Rammohan Roy (1772–1833) was a Brahman religious social reformer best known for his attack on the practice of sati. His Brahmo movement also sought to reform Hinduism more broadly by adopting a new interpretation of ancient scriptures. Like other nineteenth-century modernizers, Roy accepted that the status of Indian women was poor and needed to improve if his society was to progress. Demonstrating that the practice of sati was illegitimate in scriptural terms—although there was a scriptural basis for sati if practiced in a different manner—Roy supported British efforts to outlaw its practice in 1829 while claiming to preserve a sense of spiritual authority for Hinduism.

Traditional religious elites also agreed that women's status was the key to a vigorous and moral defense of society. Like British officials and native modernizers, the orthodox religious officials, who in contrast protested against the abolition of sati, made their case through a close examination of "Hindu scriptures." However, they privileged those scriptures that were confirmed by observable customary practice. British administrators, native reformers, and religious elites all sought to enhance their own authority vis-à-vis one another through a debate about women.

As critical as we may be today about the ideological justifications for British imperialism that were made in the name of women, it is important to keep in mind that this circumstance also produced "women" as the topics of debate for both Europeans and, critically, "native" communities in India. Debates over child marriage, widow immolation, and enforced widowhood, to mention only a few nineteenth-century social reform causes, were important not only because they were used to establish Indian society as inferior, even barbaric, in relation to British society, but also because they made the condition of "women" and the status of "Indian tradition" visible. Both the new and traditional elites of Indian society vied for the authority to speak on behalf of women, and by extension to define Indian tradition. As we will see, India today continues to be embroiled in this struggle.

Indian Women and the "Nation": From Objects of Reform to Subjects

By the second half of the nineteenth century, two significant changes with regard to the status of Indian women emerged. First, nationalists saw women as vital to the moral upliftment and progress of the nation as a whole. Indian nationalists focused on preserving the spiritual authority of Indian women, as well as protecting them from the potentially degrading effects of Western reform. The "nationalist resolution to the women's question," according to Chatterjee (1993), was premised upon the claim that Indian women were superior to their British counterparts. For that very reason, women's reform should be postponed until the threat of colonial intervention had been stayed. This claim wrestled from the British some of the force of their ideological argument for domination and also transformed Indian women from being nearly invisible and a subject around which power was negotiated to being objects of nationalist reform.

The second major change was that women themselves became participants in debates about women. By the late nineteenth and early twentieth century, elite Indian women, including Pandita Ramabai (1865–1922), participated in movements to reform women's educational opportunities. As Uma Chakravarti has shown, Ramabai's remarkable contributions to social reform and women's education were made possible in large part by the exemplary education she received from her learned father (Kosambi 1988, 1993; Chakravarti 2005), thus demonstrating the critical importance of the family in making her extraordinary life possible. Elite women became advocates for new educational opportunities for women more broadly, founding schools as well as carrying on campaigns within their communities for girls' education.

By the turn of the twentieth century, elite Indian women joined political organizations, including the Indian National Congress, calling for national regeneration and self-rule. In this way they took political advantage of their special role in the nation as mothers of a modern community. Beginning with the Women's Indian Association in 1917 and the All India Women's Conference in 1926, Indian women created all-India organizations, albeit elite in membership, that were aimed at bettering the lives of women (Basu and Ray 1990). When women found little sympathy among government officials or their local communities, they turned to these new, national organizations to publish articles, file petitions, hold lectures, and convene conferences. The creation of these organizations enabled them to effectively identify problems for public debate and communicate their proposed solutions to others.

Women and the Franchise

The struggle for enfranchisement was arguably Indian women's single most impressive accomplishment in the colonial period. Indian women won the vote under the Government of India Act (1935), more than a decade before independence and sixteen years before the ratification of the Indian constitution. It is noteworthy that this accomplishment was driven by Indian women and men, rather than by a Western suffrage movement or the British government. Following the announcement by British authorities in 1917 that their policy was to bring "responsible government" to India, the Southborough Committee—led by the viceroy of India, Lord Chelmsford, and the secretary of state for India, Edwin Montagu—was established and charged with identifying the desires of their Indian subjects and recommending reforms that would be passed in 1919. Over the course of a year, the committee interviewed thousands of people, including mill owners and workers, peasants and landlords, princes and religious leaders. A prominent Congress worker and poet, Sarojini Naidu, led a delegation of leading women to meet with Chelmsford and Montagu on December 17, 1917 (Forbes 1996).[1] In their meeting, the women's delegation made a case for women to have both political and civil rights within the reformed colonial state (Forbes 1996: 92). So began the struggle for the enfranchisement of Indian women. Elite Indian women and their European allies demanded enfranchisement on the same terms as men.

At the end of its year-long study, the committee did not recommend that forthcoming reforms include the extension of political rights to women. The committee set aside the issue claiming that Indian men would never stand for the enfranchisement of women. In the face of disappointment, women and their allies regrouped and pursued a sustained campaign in provincial bodies. Between 1921 and 1930 they won the vote in multiple provinces: Bombay and Madras in 1921; United Provinces in 1923; Punjab and Bengal in 1926; and finally Assam, the Central Provinces, Bihar, and Orissa in 1930 (Forbes 1996: 101). But enfranchisement under the government of India remained elusive. The fruits of their efforts nonetheless provided the momentum for women's subsequent enfranchisement in the Government of India Act in 1935 (Forbes 1996: 110).

The enfranchisement of Indian women, built upon earlier provincial victories that women had won over the previous decade and nineteenth-century social reforms, created a space for women to become agents of their own futures. This remarkable change in status was the preference neither of British colonial officials nor British suffragists, who might have been expected to champion the extension of women's democratic political rights in the empire, but did not (Ramusack 1992; Sinha 1992). Instead, Indian women's political equality followed nearly two decades of concerted and unrelenting organization and coalition between like-minded Indian women and men (Forbes 1996: 92–120).

Although few women became leaders of nationalist bodies before independence, many women gained important political experience that prepared them to assume new roles in public life after independence. Jawaharlal Nehru (1889–1864), India's first prime minister, appointed Kamaladevi Chattopadhyay, a Congress Party member and socialist leader, to be the first head of the Ministry of Culture. He appointed his sister, Vijayalakshmi Pandit, to be India's first ambassador to the United Nations. He tapped Mridula Sarabhai, the daughter of a prominent industrialist and niece of a labor leader, to oversee the process of repatriating Hindu women and children from Pakistan following Partition. Thus, women's prominence in India's political landscape today, whether as heads of major political parties, members of parliament, president, chief minister, or prime minister, owes much to the changes that occurred in the status and position of Indian women in the first half of the twentieth century.

Women and the Republic of India

Prime Minister Indira Gandhi (1917–1984) succeeded her father, Jawaharlal Nehru, as India's prime minister between 1967 and 1977 and served again as prime minister from 1980 to 1984. Gandhi remains one of India's most important national figures and one of the world's most recognizable female leaders. Although Prime Minister Gandhi continued social welfare policies that were initiated by her father and introduced aggressive reproductive policies aimed at reducing the size of India's families, her leadership is known more for the authoritarian exercise of power than for the positive effects it had on the lives of Indian women. Yet women's regular and sustained participation in public debate and policy reform continued to increase during her tenure as prime minister.

Since independence, Indian women have organized around a wide range of issues, including the abolition of dowry and bride-price, the establishment of effective laws against rape and sexual harassment, and the preservation of the rights to livelihood in the face of a liberalized economy (Basu 2008; Krishnan 2008; Lateef 2008; Palit 2008). They have organized to improve working and living conditions, affordability of fuel, and access to clean water. Indian women have also been at the forefront of various environmental movements, including those that seek to protect the forests and jungles, protect access to water, and protect communities from industrial disaster. While the most recognizable Indian women activists hail from elite women's organizations, most women participants do not. A larger number of women activists participate without the benefit of elementary education or even literacy. Most are not associated with a particular kind of feminism, a national women's organization, or even a political party. Still, they have been successful in organizing in defense of their communities.

Civil Rights

There exists no uniform civil code for India's citizens; women's civil rights depend, as do those of men, on a body of customary religious practices that are treated as law and applied according to religious community, be it Hindu, Muslim, Sikh, Christian, or so forth. Although the framers of the Indian constitution assumed that a uniform civil code would eventually come into being, this particular issue has never been resolved (Vatuk 2009: 353). Indeed, the passage of time and communal politicking have fostered increasing discord over the very idea of a uniform civil code. Because the circumstances of marriage, divorce, and inheritance remain central to women's poverty and marginality in society, this subject has remained at the center of women's activism in India. However, the issue is also one that has divided women's organizations and different communities of women. Some have vigorously supported efforts to fulfill the intention of the framers of the constitution by providing a universal legal structure for all of India's citizens, while others have sought to ensure that the constitution continues to preserve the rights of women within religious communities.

Tensions erupted in the 1980s when the Indian Supreme Court ruled on a dispute over maintenance for a divorced Muslim woman, Shah Bano, who had sued for support following her divorce in 1978 (Agnes 2001; Carroll 1988; Engineer 1987; Hasan 1999; Khory 2005; Kishwar 1986; Parashar 1992; Pathak and Rajan 1989; Vatuk 2009). What made this case so significant was both what it exposed about Muslim women's position under existing customary law related to divorce and how the courts interjected and claimed authority to arbitrate between customary law and the constitution. As we will see, many of the issues at stake remain alive in contemporary India.

The Shah Bano Case

Shah Bano was sixty-two-years old when her husband, Mohammed Ahmed Khan, divorced her. Under Muslim customary law in India, a husband may divorce his wife without explanation, and this is what Khan did. Without any means of supporting herself, Shah Bano sought the maximum maintenance from her husband allowed under law, which amounted to 500 rupees (just over $10 at the time) per month. Shah Bano's claim did not place an undue burden on Khan, given that he was a successful lawyer whose monthly income was estimated at 5,000 rupees per month (Vatuk 2009: 355). Under Muslim customary law, a divorced wife is entitled to maintenance for only three months follow-ing her divorce, as well as the payment of the *mahr,* a fixed sum agreed upon at the time of the marriage. The local Indore court ruled in favor of Shah Bano, but granted maintenance of only 25 rupees (or a little more than 50 cents at the time) per month. Khan approached the court to reconsider its ruling on the grounds that under customary law he was not required to pay maintenance beyond the three-month period. In the meantime, Shah Bano's lawyer successfully persuaded the Madhya Pradesh High Court to raise her maintenance to 179 rupees per month.

The Supreme Court of India then received a petition from Khan, whose appeal took four and a half years to be resolved. Khan's petition requested that the court preserve Muslim personal law by reversing the rulings of both lower courts. Ultimately, the Supreme Court upheld Shah Bano's right to maintenance by sidestepping customary law and instead turning to a vagrancy provision of the Criminal Procedure Code. The Supreme Court's ruling did not favorably reaffirm the authority of religious customary law without qualification. The opinion, authored by Chief Justice Yashwant Vishnu Chandrachud on April 23, 1985, dis-agreed with Khan's claim that a husband under Indian law is not obli-gated to maintain his former wife. Although Chandrachud acknowl-edged that Muslim customary law required a husband to pay maintenance for three months following a divorce, he pointed out that customary law did not *restrict* maintenance from being paid for a longer period. Chandrachud's reading of the Quran may have been question-able, but there was recent precedent to support Shah Bano's claim to additional maintenance if the *mahr* agreed upon at the time of marriage and the *iddat* (maintenance granted for a period of three months follow-ing divorce) was not sufficient to sustain her survival. Moreover, Chan-drachud argued that Shah Bano could not be denied further provision from her husband because under the Criminal Procedure Code of India, men, regardless of community, are required to keep their wives, includ-ing divorced wives, from becoming vagrants.

Some in the Muslim community voiced outrage over the Supreme Court ruling, which they saw as violating their religious beliefs, prac-tices, and rights under the Indian constitution. Particularly irate were the orthodox elite and the ulema (clerics). They were deeply troubled by a ruling that chipped away at religious customary law. They were just as troubled that a Hindu judge would dare interpret the Quran. Eventually, public agitation by the All India Muslim League Personal Law Board led to calls for new legislation. Liberals, conservative Hindus, and some feminists were no less angry about the emerging controversy. They denounced the Muslim community for their treatment of women and argued that Muslim women should not be excluded from the same civil rights as other Indian women. An unusual coalition of these groups reasserted their support for a uniform civil code in India. For her part, Shah Bano found herself in an untenable position, eventually apologiz-ing to her community for having contributed to a situation in which Muslim customary law was scrutinized and limited.

In a stunning move, Prime Minister Rajiv Gandhi's government, with an eye to Muslim votes, challenged the controversial Supreme Court ruling by supporting the passage of the Muslim Women's Protec-tion of Rights in Divorce Act (1986). Contrary to the bill's name, the legislation outlined the specific provisions to which Muslim women were entitled in the case of divorce. In other words, the legislation sought to remove the ambiguity under which the case had been brought and upon which Justice Chandachud had ruled. The law reaffirmed the right of a divorced Muslim woman to her *mahr* and a reasonable main-tenance during the *iddat* period. It also included a provision for the care of children from the marriage until they reached two years of age. Should a divorced woman need further maintenance, a magistrate would be given the option of appealing to adult children or natal relatives for support. The legislation also explicitly denied Muslim women any future redress under the Criminal Procedure Code (Kishwar 1986). Many women's groups protested against the bill, finding themselves in the uncomfortable position of allying with the Hindu right, which had applauded the Supreme Court's decision (Hasan 1993, 1999).

The Sabarimala Dispute

The Sabarimala Controversy is another instance where the Indian state's responsibility to uphold both equality and religious freedom has reemerged as a flashpoint with implications for the status of women. In September 2018, the Supreme Court of India issued a ruling, twenty-eight years in the making, over what had come to be known as the Sabarimala Controversy (Tripathi 2018). At stake in the case was whether or not female devotees of the Hindu temple between the ages of ten and fifty could be denied access on the grounds that they were of menstruating age and therefore impure. This exclusion was legally formalized by a Kerala High Court ruling of 1990.[2] While proponents characterized women's exclusion as founded in religious custom for centuries, those who challenged the ban demonstrated that the ban both lacked historical roots and violated Article 15 of the Indian constitution.[3] Interestingly, there had appeared no controversy over the Kerala High Court's ruling for six years after it formalized the ban. It was only in 1995, when the shrine's devotees petitioned the court about poor facilities at the temple, that a conflict began to unfold.

Sympathetic to the need for sanitary facilities, the Court directed the local district collector to investigate the conditions at the temple and ameliorate them as required. As it happened, the district collector at the time was a forty-two-year-old woman. Recognizing the ban in place, the district collector explained to the Court that she would be unable to gather firsthand information because she was prohibited from entering the temple because of her sex and age. The Court had no choice but to grant special permission to the district collector to enter the temple in order to complete her work as a civil servant. Officially, the district collector was the first woman to enter the Sabarimala Temple since the 1990 ban had been formalized.[4] Shortly after her visit, the district collector shared her personal opinion that other devotees, like herself, should be allowed to visit the temple: "If women are bodily and mentally pure, they should not be denied access to the Lord" (Radhakrishnan 1995). Although the Travancore Devaswom Board, which oversaw the temple, had fought the district collector's entry, the board's President, N. Bhaskaran Nair, acknowledged the precariousness of their position, stating that "a change is inevitable. Once the lower caste people were denied entry into temples. The ban on women may also change" (Radhakrishnan 1995).

For a decade after the district collector's entry to Sabarimala Temple there was no conflict with the ban on women of menstruating age. It was a full decade later, in July 2006, that six female members of the Young Lawyers Association filed a petition with the Supreme Court challenging the ban (Anand 2006 and 2012). It would take an additional ten years before their case was finally heard by the Supreme Court in New Delhi. In the intervening years between the formalization of women's ban from the temple in 1990 and its challenge before the Supreme Court in 2016, a lot had changed in the political landscape in India. In addition to the revitalization and extension of a gender equality movement connected to the 2012 Delhi rape case, India had also elected an unabashedly pro-Hindu and religiously sympathetic government. As M. A. Deviah explained, "Sabarimala isn't the only place of worship that has restrictions on women entering. Mosques, temples and other places of worship fully or partially ban women, non-adherents, foreigners, the improperly dressed. . . . The court can be expected to do its duty by the Constitution, but will this open a door to a flood of similar litigation" (2016). This observation proved prescient.

Faced with the challenge in the Supreme Court, the Kerala state government had to weigh in on the case. This time it took a new position, filing an affidavit in the Supreme Court that supported the entry of female devotees without restriction (Deviah 2016). In doing so, the state government found itself on a collision course with the temple's governing board, with millions of devotees, and with both the Bharatiya Janata and Congress Parties. Both national parties would go on to support widespread strikes in reaction to the Supreme Court's ruling. The conflict produced several months of protest, some violent. Others undertook hunger strikes[5] and in one case a devotee died after self-immolation (Nair 2018). Despite repeated attempts under police escort, women seeking to exercise the right conferred by the Supreme Court in September were unable to enter the temple even under the cover of darkness.

Three months after the Supreme Court had struck down the ban, no women had succeeded in entering the Sabarimala Temple. A turning point in the conflict was reached suddenly on January 1, 2019, when counter-protesters favoring women's right to enter the temple staged a protest in the form of a human chain 390 miles long.[6] Between 3 and 5 million women protesters locked arms to proclaim their support for the Supreme Court's decision. Pictures of the protests captured by the press and ordinary citizens and circulated on social media brought attention to the issue. The very next day two women under police escort entered the temple without incident. The temple, however, was immediately closed for "purification" rituals before being reopened (BBC News 2019; Saikiran 2019). Protests against women's entry to the temple continue.

BJP Harthal activists protesting against women's entry into Sabarimala Temple at Angamaly, in January 2019. Photo by Kannan, VM0.

The Haji Ali Dargah Controversy

At approximately the same time the Supreme Court issued the Sabari-mala ruling, the Bombay High Court was considering a challenge to a ban on women entering the gravesite at the center of Mumbai's Haji Ali dargah, or shrine (Subramanian 2016). Noorjehan Nias, a co-founder of the Bharatiya Muslim Mahila Andolan (BMMA; Indian Muslim Women's Movement), was among those challenging a decision to close the inner chamber of the Haji Ali Dargha to women. Trustees of the Sufi Dargha, like those of the Sabarimala Temple, had instituted the change affecting women recently. That is, Nias herself had known a time when female devotees were allowed to approach the saint's final resting place to pay their respects and make their prayers. Trustees of Haji Ali pro-vided at least a couple explanations for the restrictions that were in place. One was that the restriction was a means by which women devo-tees would be "protected" from unwanted sexual attention (Dhillon 2016). While another, which largely echoed the claims of Sabarimala's temple authorities, was that it was sinful for menstruating women to go near the saint's grave (Dhillon 2016). The BMMA was aware that its own struggle to open the shrine and mosques to women would have implications for restrictions that applied in Hindu temples.

In the month before the Supreme Court's decision on the Sabari-mala Temple, the Bombay High Court issued the ruling over women's exclusion at the Haji Ali Dargha. The high court concluded that the ban on women's entry to the inner sanctum of the dargah violated numerous articles of the Indian constitution and rejected the claims of the trustees that Islam prohibited women from darghas and mosques. The high court made clear that the Haji Ali Trust must treat "women at par with men." The decisions about the Sabarimala Temple and the Haji Ali Dargha continue to reverberate in other parts of India.

In previous decades, India's courts had been careful to protect the rights of India's religious communities, sometimes at the expense of gender equality. As was the case in the Shah Bano controversy, the relationship between the rights of religious communities to live according to their beliefs and the responsibility of the Indian state to uphold equality of all citizens, regardless of their sex, remain in tension. In the past few years, however, the courts seem inclined to strike a balance between religious freedom and equality, both of which are protected under the constitution (Dhillon 2016). In the absence of a uniform civil code, Indian courts will most certainly be asked to determine whether particular practices, although treating individuals unequally, can continue within the context of religion. The question that remains is whether religious communities themselves will engage in self-reform much as nineteenth-century reformers of sati, in an effort to avoid court intervention that might otherwise chip away at religious freedom and open the door further to a uniform civil code.

The Muslim Women's Protection of Rights on Marriage Bill

The status of customary religious law and gender equality under the Indian constitution has remained ambiguous, as seen in controversies related to women's entry at religious sites. This ambiguity has also persisted with regard to women's rights in marriage, divorce, and inheritance. The Shah Bano case discussed earlier offered only a limited compromise over a conflict that was too challenging to resolve entirely in the 1980s. Recently both Indian courts and the legislature have acted to further clarify the rights of women to be treated equally regardless of their religious community and customary law.

Sharya Bano, a mother of two whose husband divorced her in 2015, brought a case to the Supreme Court that resulted in a decision that struck down the practice of triple talaq, a form of divorce in which a Muslim husband may divorce his wife simply by pronouncing the word *talaq* (meaning "divorce") three times. This decision amounted to the first significant challenge to a Muslim personal law application act of 1937 that had remained in place following independence. The All India

Muslim Personal Law Board (AIMPLB) fought to maintain its autonomy from the state over religious matters as stated in Article 371 of the constitution. They defended the practice by presenting evidence that the practice was not as widespread as claimed by the case and that they had the widespread support of the Muslim community in general and Muslim women in particular. The AIMPLB also clarified the practice of triple talaq, issuing a warning that violation of its perimeters would be rebuked with social boycott (Shaurya 2017). Nonetheless, the Supreme Court's decision characterized the practice of triple talaq as the "worst form of marriage dissolution" and confirmed that its practice violated Article 14 of the constitution (Soni 2017). The decision also noted that the practice was not justified by the Quran and had been outlawed in a range of Muslim-majority countries, including Afghanistan, Bangladesh, and Pakistan. Finally, the Court issued a temporary injunction against the practice and appealed to the legislature to address the matter once and for all.

The ruling Bharatiya Janata Party introduced the first of three bills on the matter to parliament in August 2017. This bill was easily passed by the Lok Sabha a few months later. The original bill outlawed triple talaq in any form and prescribed up to three months' imprisonment for a husband found guilty of the practice. Without a majority in the Raja Sabha, the bill expired in 2018 without passage. In 2018 the government again introduced a bill, the Muslim Women's Protection of Rights of Marriage Ordinance. It further expanded upon the initial legislation by clarifying the parties eligible to bring a complaint, authority over bail for those accused, child custody, and spousal maintenance. These new provisions answered some of the concerns expressed in the previous year. A slightly revised version of the ordinance was replaced with a new bill and passed by the Lok Sabha, but again failed to clear the Raja Sabha. Following the 2019 election, the Bhartiya Janata Party again reintroduced the bill. With the additional seats gained in the upper body of parliament and the Congress's decision that it would no longer oppose the measure, the bill was passed both chambers of parliament at the end of July 2019 and successfully presented to President Ram Nath Kovid for approval.[7]

The Muslim Women's Protection of Rights on Marriage Bill became law in August 2019. This outcome was only possible because of the unprecedented alliance between Muslim groups and the ruling party and its allies. While many women's groups, including the Bharatiya Muslim Mahila Andolan, which played a critical role in the Haji Ali case as well, have welcomed the new law, many other supporters remain wary of the government's motives behind the law and its prospective long-term implications. There are real dangers to politicization of a delicate and complex balance between religious customary law and equality as demanded by the constitution.

Panchayats and Reservation for Women

Perhaps the most important constitutional change since India's independence relating to women's political status was the passage of Amendments 73 (1991) and 75 (1993) to the Indian constitution, guaranteeing that 33 percent of all seats in village councils, or panchayats, be reserved for female candidates. The question of legislating seats for women's representation was first raised as early as 1957, only ten years after independence. This early discussion was set aside, however, and it was not until 1974 that the issue emerged again for public debate in India. Many officials and civil society questioned whether women, because of their low literacy rates and poor education, were capable of assuming the responsibilities of panchayat membership. One outcome of the debate in 1974 was the creation of a structure to facilitate women's representation in the state of Maharashtra as an experiment. Although the experiment in Maharashtra was met with skepticism, it eventually demonstrated that even illiterate women, when trusted with panchayat funds, led their communities responsibly, bringing water taps, biogas plants, schools, and other improvements to their communities (Omvedt 1990). With the issue of illiteracy discounted as an argument against women's political participation, women's groups organized to gain reservations for women. The direct catalyst for the constitutional amendments in the early 1990s, however, appears to have been the World Conference on Women held in Nairobi in 1985, which ceremonially concluded the UN's Decade for Women. After that international meeting, India established the National Perspective Plan for Women, which eventually recommended 33 percent reservation for women in 1988.

Soon thereafter, the Indian parliament adopted the measure during the premiership of P. V. Narasimha Rao (Sengupta 2005). Thus, Indian women—like Dalits, tribal, and low-caste groups—became the beneficiaries of special electorates at the local level. The reservation of 33 percent of panchayat council seats for women is viewed today with ambivalence. There were a number of studies done in the years immediately following the adoption of Rao's measures suggesting that women's panchayats acted primarily as proxies for their husbands. Only one study, conducted by Jawaharlal Nehru University's Women's Studies Program, demonstrated that women's status as proxy voters diminished over time. While reelection of women is limited by the rotation of seats reserved for women, political experience seems to have changed women's relationship to those in their local communities. As one woman elected to her panchayat explained, "I was the one who was elected. But I was not allowed to go out, never to speak. I have learnt to speak, to use the microphone. Now that the mike has come into my hand, it will remain with me for my entire life—nobody can take it away" (Sengupta 2005).

While there has been mixed reaction to women's increased power at the local level, the effects of the changes that have accompanied the greater participation of women is not in dispute (Patel 1993). India's experiment with reservations as a means of empowering women's leadership was so successful that the government of Prime Minister Manmohan Singh introduced a bill to amend the constitution and reserve 50 percent of seats in panchayats for women. Given the entrenched nature of gender inequality in India, legislative reform has become an important precondition for ensuring that women command a degree of political power and have formal political means of redressing the inequities that shape their lives.

Education

In addition to transforming working women's lives, India recognizes that women's low literacy rates impact not only their own well-being but also that of society as a whole. Closing the gap between male and female literacy has been seen as a key to addressing a number of social development goals, including reducing the birthrate, ameliorating poverty, improving infant mortality rates, and raising life expectancy. Women's literacy is an integral component to creating an economy that in years to come will support economic development and enable India to maintain an edge in the global economy.

Since the colonial period, educational policy in India has been aimed primarily at university education. Elites who find their way to the doors of India's universities have reaped the greatest rewards in securing employment. Because university-level educational investment has limited effects upon the broader population, the government pursued constitutional measures to prioritize primary education. In 2002, the constitution was amended to make education a right of all citizens. This measure was followed by a 2009 amendment that secured the right to an education for children ages six to fourteen. Both measures were an acknowledgment that the average Indian needs not simply a free

Young girls obtaining a few hours of schooling after completing their work in the fields as part of a program sponsored by a nongovernmental organization. For the vast majority, this may be the only schooling they receive in their lives. Photo by Neil DeVotta.

education, but rather a quality primary education if the society as a whole is to advance. Government budgets after 2009 doubled the resources available for primary education. The government also began prioritizing women's literacy, which significantly lagged behind that of men. A decade after those programs were initiated, the gap between male and female literacy has significantly improved.

The Modi government has promised a new education policy since 2014 and has delivered a draft that underwent public comment through the summer of 2019. In the wake of the Covid-19 pandemic, the government refocused the new policy for the purpose of "making job creators" by emphasizing instruction in one's native tongue through year five of primary education, limiting state board examinations on admissions, proposing common entrance exams, and standardizing requirements across public and private institutions (Press Trust of India 2020). With the literacy goals of the previous government largely met, the new government appears focused on reforming higher education and building research capacity. Limited resources for education are in danger again of being diverted disproportionately to India's universities, which alone cannot solve the economic plight of India's women (or the majority of India's men, for that matter). The extent to which the government succeeds in its broader economic agenda depends upon not only educating women at equal rates as men, but also India's ability to facilitate higher rates of women's employment in the formal sector of the economy.

Employment

Indian women are not new to the work force. Indeed, Indian women made up approximately one-quarter of the labor in India's textile factories in the early twentieth century. Women's opportunities in the industrial factories plummeted during the worldwide financial crisis in the 1920s and 1930s. Their current rates of employment remain almost unchanged since that time. Women's groups have advocated for greater employment opportunities, albeit with mixed results. But with only 27.2 percent of women in the work force (World Economic Forum 2017) today, India ranks 114th out of 131 countries in terms of female labor force participation (Bahal 2015).

Indians expected that the economic reforms introduced in 1991 would significantly improve economic conditions for everyone. Because the majority of Indian women who are employed work in the agricultural or unorganized sectors of the economy, women have been largely passed by in India's recent economic gains. While new wealth has most certainly been created, the majority of growth in employment has taken place in the service sector of the economy, where India's largely male, English-speaking work force has found new opportunities. Some urban and college-educated young women have also seen new opportunities in the service sector, where jobs more than doubled for women in the first decade of the millennium (Manji 2009).

The development of call centers in the early 2000s certainly contributed to new employment opportunities for some women (Pradhan and Abraham 2005). Today an estimated half of the 350,000 workers answering calls in India are women, although the call centers employ upward of 3.1 million workers (White 2015). While these opportunities may suggest that India's new economy is empowering women, the realities are quite mixed. While young, educated women employed in call centers may be able to leverage their incomes for greater autonomy, this in turn has been seen as a threat to gender roles in an Indian society that continues to see itself, and particularly its women, through a "traditional" prism.

On the one hand, there is no denying that the women employed in the service sector are redefining the role of Indian women in urban India. Newspapers, for instance, regularly carry stories about how women employed in call centers prefer to delay marriage, live independently of their in-laws, and have purchasing power independent of their husbands.

On the other hand, the increased financial autonomy that women in the new service industries enjoy has been linked to marital discord and is commonly portrayed as a threat to the traditional Indian joint family. Thus, even as young, urban, English-educated women find new employment opportunities, economic autonomy comes at a personal cost.

New employment opportunities have also led to a backlash against what is seen as too much autonomy for young urban women. There have been calls for women to stop working night shifts, even though this is when international corporations require their labor. Consequently, some employers have increasingly becoming gender-segregated workplaces even as women's financial independence has also been associated with low respectability. For some, a woman's employment raises a suspicion that she is sexually active and hence "impure." Ironically, the Indian women who have most directly benefited from jobs in the globalized economy find themselves criticized for working both outside the family and in places and at times that raise questions about their morality.

Working women's position has been rendered all the more precarious by incidents of sexual assault, often as they commute for work. Although legislation has been enacted to require employers to provide safe and reliable transportation for female workers who travel to work in the early hours of the morning or late at night, there have been thousands of reported attacks. Notwithstanding the contribution they are making to India's economic transformation, Indian women's physical mobility and financial independence continue to challenge traditional notions of women's mobility and to find a backlash among some in society.

The Nirbhaya Rape Case, 2012

In 2012, 706 cases of rape were reported in the nation's capital, New Delhi. With New Delhi having a population of nearly 19 million residents, this figure most certainly reflects the stigma attached to the crime more than the frequency of sexual violence, which largely goes unreported.[8] One of the 706 cases in 2012 fundamentally changed the conversation around rape, assault, and molestation of women in India, precipitating widespread public demonstration and significant legal reform. The brutal assault and gang rape of a twenty-three-year-old physiotherapy student, Jyoti Singh Pandey,[9] on December 16 in New Delhi awakened public attention to sexual assault and violence against women like never before.[10] To be clear, women's and feminist groups in India had been organizing for decades around these and closely related issues, but had previously been successful in making only incremental changes to a legal framework largely inherited from the colonial period (Kumar 1993: 127–142). The so-called Nirbhaya ("fearless one") case precipitated significant legal changes and drove an important shift in public discourse around sexual violence against women before the advent of either #MeToo or #TimesUp movements. Consequently, India now leads the global South in terms of legal frameworks on sexual violence, including molestation, trafficking, and rape.

As in many other parts of the world, feminist and women's organizations in India had taken up the issue of rape because of its brutality and its long-term effects upon women (Kumar 1993: 128). In the postindependence era, according to Radha Kumar, much of the focus had been on organizing around accountability for "police rape," which was perpetrated not only by police, but also by members of the army and security services. The other major focus of work had been directed at curtailing so-called landlord rape associated with the "right of first night" in both agricultural and industrial contexts. Most efforts in the 1970s and 1980s involved individual cases that while powerful in local contexts, failed to garner widespread, sustained national attention. This changed in 1980 when demonstrations in Bombay, Delhi, Nagpur, Pune, Ahmedabad, Bangalore, and Hyderabad successfully coordinated a protest of the Mathura rape case.[11] Even if legal changes did not immediately materialize, the national coordination caught the attention of the Indian press, which began reporting sexual violence cases with greater regularity. Perhaps the single most important advancement, before the Nirbhaya case had been won, occurred in 1983 when a law was passed against custodial rape. In addition to holding state designates accountable, the legislation also sought to distinguish mass and gang rapes as crimes more serious and therefore worthy of mandatory ten-year sentences. An attempt to place the burden of proof on the accused rather than the victim was nearly won, but turned back by courts that determined the approach was inconsistent with legal protections for the accused.

Although the police quickly identified the suspects in the Nirbhaya case and arrested four of the six accused within two days of the assault, the government was overwhelmed by protesters in the nation's capital.[12] Unprepared for the scale of public outrage, the government first focused on maintaining law and order. Initially, the government closed nine metro stations in the center of the city, blocked off roads, and suspended bus routes that brought citizens to the seat of government. Eventually, it established a curfew in the city and invoked section 144 of the Criminal Procedure Code that restricted assemblies of four or more persons. Women's and students' organizations, as well as thousands of individual citizens,

Students protesting the rising violence against women in Delhi in December 2012. Photo by Nilanjana Roy.

nonetheless took to Delhi's streets more than a week after the assault and rape, demanding action from law enforcement and local officials.

The government regrouped and redirected its efforts on December 23, 2012, when it announced the formation of a three-member committee of jurists charged with the task of surveying the situation and recommending reforms. In addition to collecting public opinion on the subject, the commission was to consult with eminent jurists, legal professionals, nongovernmental organizations, and women's groups. The commission was given a thirty-day period in which to provide a report to the government suggesting amendments to the criminal and other relevant laws to provide for quicker investigation, prosecution, and trial, as well as enhanced punishment for those convicted of sexual assaults of an extreme nature.

While the Verma Commission began its work to understand the larger context of the attack and considered possible action, the victim succumbed to her injuries on December 29, 2012, in a Singapore hospital to which she had been taken for treatment. Delhi, Mumbai, Hyderabad, Thiruvanathapuram, and Bangalore again witnessed major public demonstrations. This time demonstrators were broader-based according to news reports; men as well as women across age groups and social strata appeared in public protests across the country.[13] In Delhi, where protests were more peaceful than they had been earlier, students from Jawaharlal Nehru University marched to the bus stop where the victim had boarded the bus in which she was attacked, demanding that New Year's celebrations be used to honor the victim. The second wave of protests precipitated further government response. This time the local government established a thirteen-member joint task force to coordinate efforts to improve women's safety across the city.[14] Delhi's New Year's celebrations were canceled or curtailed for the year.

Although there was growing public outcry both for the death penalty for convicted rapists and for charging teens as adults when they were involved in heinous crimes, the Verma Commission recommended neither course when its 630-page report was submitted.[15] Praising the youth of the country for agitating for stronger anti-rape laws, the report criticized the police, government, and public at large for failures that contributed to an environment in which such crimes against women occur. The report recommended criminalizing a series of activities that were inadequately addressed under Indian law, including voyeurism, stalking, and trafficking of women and children. Women's and feminist advocates welcomed the commission's recommendation. The commission also sought a thorough review of the Armed Forces Special Powers Act, which it identified as an obstacle to both deterrence and justice. It recommended that security forces personnel accused of rape be tried under criminal, not military, law. It also proposed that the mandatory minimum sentence for those convicted of rape be increased from seven to ten years and that sentences of life be defined as "the entire natural life" of the convict. And they suggested that the death penalty be considered in cases where rape led to death. Upon receipt of the Verma Commission's report, the cabinet and the president of India moved quickly on the recommendations, backing an amendment to the law on February 3, 2013, less than two months after the assault had galvanized public attention.

Not all were satisfied by the government's proposed course of action. Some characterized the proposed ordinance as "piecemeal and fragmented." The All India Democratic Women's Association (AIDWA) advocated that parliamentary action should be taken because they believed a more comprehensive solution would be produced with greater public debate.[16] These constituents had also sought the criminalization of marital rape, the review of the Armed Services Special Powers Act, barring politicians accused of sexual assault from standing for election, and moving all rape cases to criminal courts, measures the proposed ordinance did not address. Even with these significant omissions, the proposed changes necessitated alterations to the Indian penal code, the Criminal Procedure Code, and the Evidence Act. In other words, there was an attempt on the part of government to address the matter in a comprehensive manner, if not on every subject recommended by the Verma Commission.

The juvenile defendant accused of Jyoti Singh Pandey's assault, rape, and murder was found guilty and sentenced to a maximum of three years in a youth facility; he is currently out of prison and living under a new identity. One of the accused, Ram Singh, committed suicide before the case was concluded. Mukesh Singh, Vinay Sharma, Akshay Thakur, and Pawan Gupta were found guilty on all counts in September 2013, roughly nine months after their heinous assault (Hills 2013). Each was subsequently sentenced to death by hanging, with these punishments confirmed by Indian courts in the years following the convictions. Although the public was pleased by the convictions, many human rights and feminist organizations voiced dissatisfaction with the sentences, which did not provide a sufficient deterrent to end violence against women. Having exhausted the appeals process and six years after their conviction, the four men convicted of Jyoti Singh Pandey's brutal assault, rape, and murder were executed by hanging on March 20, 2020.

The effects of the Nirbhaya case continue to this day. In 2016 there were 40,000 rapes reported in India, a 60 percent increase from 2012. Understanding how to interpret this data is important. Undoubtedly, the increase is an indication of an environment that is gradually improving such that women and their families are willing to report rape to the police, even if conviction rates for reported cases have improved only incrementally. Police officials are eager to argue that reforms they have put into place, including all-women police stations and improved training, have encouraged reporting at new levels. Activists across the political landscape agree that there is a need to increase the number of public prosecutors dedicated to adjudicating these cases, to enhance further police sensitivity through better training. But to date, very little additional funding has materialized for these purposes. While India is far from eradicating sexual violence, the 2012 Nirbhaya case demonstrates that norms in India are undoubtedly changing. In 2018, over 33,000 cases of rape were reported in India, 30 percent more than reported in 2012 (Statista Research Department 2018). Many more women and their families are willing to report types of crime that had previously been unchallenged. This is the necessary first step in coming to terms with the systemic violence that women in India have faced. With India having some of the strongest legal frameworks to curtail sexual crimes in the world, its challenge remains reporting and conviction. The question for India, like so many countries, remains: How long will it take to achieve an end to violence against women?[17]

Conclusion

It is difficult to overstate the extent to which a woman's status in India has been shaped historically by her family and how much this remains the case today. As Kalpana Mehta (2008), a thirty-year veteran of India's women's movement explains: "The last few decades have witnessed substantial economic and political changes in India. Yet women remain controlled by families, communities, the state and increasing corporate power. Our labour is controlled through strict sexual division of labour at home and the workplace." More so than any other single factor, the family continues to define the contexts into which women are born, grow up, marry, work, and die. Even today, a woman, whether she lives in a village or in one of India's megacities, grows up expecting that her marriage will be arranged by her family. While greater numbers of young people are experiencing "love marriages," in that they select their life partner, this number remains comparatively low and confined largely to the urban middle class. For most young women, including middle- and upper-class women, the family continues to determine the conditions of their lives. Even with internet dating, greater mobility, and newfound financial independence, young Indian women do not organize their lives according to priorities of Western individualism. On the contrary, Indian women appear to seek their own mode of being modern women.[18]

Aside from the legal status of women under religious customary law, women's poor economic position in India today remains a target of political effort. Partly as a result of being excluded from recent economic growth, women have been unable to realize the promises of India's constitution and unable to participate fully in India's economic development. While new areas of employment have opened up in urban India for middle-class, educated women, changes to women's broader status can only be achieved by addressing the needs of those who, with only rudimentary education, continue to labor in the context of family and rural communities. Key to improving women's status in India is the expansion of educational and employment opportunities. Indeed, women's greater participation in the formal economy promises rewards for society as a whole.

While India rightly boasts of the many women who have achieved political prominence and made important contributions in business and education in the modern era, it will need the success of millions of

Daily wage earners in Meghalaya. Photo by Neil DeVotta.

additional Indian women to attend to the enormous challenges posed by the impoverishment of millions of its citizens ("Quick Take" 2018). Indian women remain at a distance from being granted their full rights as equal citizens, but their aspirations are increasingly within reach. Having established themselves as a significant voice in a wide range of issues of public concern for over a century, women in contemporary India can be expected to maintain, if not exceed, the momentum they have built and to chart a bright course not only for themselves, but also for their country as a whole.

Notes

1. Sarojini Naidu was a prominent poet and member of the Indian National Congress, a body she led as president in 1925. She was the only Indian woman to lead the Congress prior to independence and among the Indian women who offered testimony before the Southborough Committee on behalf of women, discussing the progress they had made and their aspirations.

2. A restriction on women entering the temple goes back further to Rule 3(b) of the Kerala Hindu Places of Public Worship Authorization of Entry Rules of 1965. This rule was formalized decades later.

3. Article 15 of the constitution reads: "The State shall not discriminate against any citizen on grounds only of religion, race, caste, sex, place of birth or any of them." Article 15 also makes the state responsible for checking and eliminating any such discrimination perpetuated by any section of the society (Tripathi 2018).

4. Other women between the ages of ten and fifty had visited the Sabarimala Temple over the course of the twentieth century. Most recently was a visit by a film star

turned politician, M. L. C. Jayamala, who set foot in the temple in 1986 at the age of twenty-seven (Shreyas 2016).

5. "Rahul Easwar, Face of 'Save Sabarimala' Campaign, on Fast in Prison." *The Hindu,* October 20, 2018.

6. "Women's Wall Highlights: Massive Turnout in Kerala for Equal Rights." *Times of India,* January 1, 2019.

7. "History Made, Triple Talaq Bill Passed by Parliament." *India Today,* July 30, 2019, https://www.indiatoday.in/india/story/triple-talaq-bill-passed-in-rajya-sabha-1575309-2019-07-30.

8. There were 24,923 reported cases of rape in India in 2012 according to the National Crime Records Bureau of India.

9. Although under Indian law a victim is not named publicly, I do so here because the victim's father wanted her name to be known both so that she was associated with fearlessness and so that she would serve to help other victims of this crime. Both her brother and mother also spoke publicly using her name (Hills 2013).

10. The particulars of the rape are well reported by the Indian and international press and need not be revisited here.

11. The Mathura rape case involved a seventeen- or eighteen-year-old girl who was taken to the police station and raped by police. The case was registered, but the accused were acquitted by the sessions court. The accused were subsequently convicted by the High Court, but this was overturned on appeal by the Supreme Court. The defense successfully argued that because the victim had a boyfriend, she was thus "loose" and could not be raped. This position was not supported by the legal definitions of rape at the time (Kumar 1993: 129–135).

12. "Delhi Gang Rape Case: Chronology of Events," *The Hindu,* August 3, 2013.

13. "Delhi Gang Rape: Protests Go Viral," *Economic Times,* December 29, 2012.

14. "Special Task Force to Look Into Safety Issues of Women," *Zee News,* January 2, 2013. Included in the task force were Delhi's chief secretary; police commissioner; special commissioners of traffic, law, and order; the chair of the Commission for Women; the chair of the Municipal Council; the transport commissioner; the commissioners of east, north, and south of the corporation (Government of National Capital Territory Delhi); and the joint secretary in the Ministry of Home Affairs.

15. Sandeep Joshi, "Verma Panel No to Death Penalty," *The Hindu,* January 23, 2013.

16. Surabhi Mallik, ed., "We Have Accepted 90% of Justice Verma Panel's Recommendations: Law Minister to NDTV," *NDTV,* February 3, 2013.

17. Sexual violence against women is one of several major crises facing Indian women. Inequitable health and educational opportunities is also very significant. Amartya Sen has written about the millions of "missing" Asian women. He has estimated that there are approximately 60 million missing women in India, whose sex ratio declined since independence from 983 per 1,000 men in 1951 to 914 per 1,000 men in 2011. Amartya Sen, "More Than 100 Million Women Are Missing," *New York Review of Books,* December 20, 1990; Amartya Sen, "Missing Women—Revisited: Reduction in Female Mortality Has Been Counterbalanced by Sex Selective Abortions," *British Medical Journal,* 327 no. 7427 (2003): 1297–1299; Annie Gowen, "India Has 63 Million 'Missing' Women and 21 Million Unwanted Girls, Government Says," *Washington Post,* January 29, 2018.

18. To get a broad sense of the range of particular concerns facing women in India, see the April 2008 special issue of *Seminar,* titled "Unequal Status." The internet edition can be accessed at http://www.india-seminar.com/semframe.html.

10

Population, Urbanization, and Environmental Challenges

Kelly D. Alley

India is one of the fastest-growing democracies in the world, and its urban centers are busting at the seams with middle- and upper-income housing complexes and corporate parks that consume more water and energy than the urban slums they are displacing. The growing population and rapid urbanization are producing environmental strains and stresses that affect all residents and every sector of society. The urban poor shoulder a disproportionate share of the burden in terms of air, water, and soil pollution as well as toxic exposures. The Indian subcontinent is rich with resources, but these resources are stretched thin across a billion people. This makes for big challenges and risks in urbanization, planning for long-term resource sustainability, and public health.

This chapter introduces key trends and problems in urban sprawl, environmental and resource degradation, and population and health. It sketches out areas of crisis as well as rejuvenation and innovation, taking topical direction from hearings produced in the National Green Tribunal. This new environmental tribunal hears all the resource conflicts of the country in a real-time way, so the daily cause lists in the National Green Tribunal (the list of cases heard on a given day) offer insight into the critical matters of the day. These and other legal cases direct attention to the most acute problems, and this chapter contextualizes these problems with descriptions of current trends. Before reviewing these trends, this chapter introduces some institutional background and explains the role of the judiciary in shaping responses to rapid urbanization, environmental strain, and public health risks.

Environmental Regulations
and the Activist Judiciary

This section lays out the reality of governance in India for the sectors encompassing energy, water, public health, and climate change, drawing attention to the various interventions carried out by the courts in the regulation of highly sought-after resources. The formal regulatory agencies are housed in the state and central governments of India, specifically in the state and central pollution control boards; the Central Groundwater Authority; the Union Ministry of Environment, Forests, and Climate Change; and the Ministries of Jal Shakti, Power, Renewable Energy, and Health and Family Welfare. Unlike other environmental regulations that have longer gestations, the health standards set by a central government agency are in an emerging stage of development. In this institutional interplay, it is important to know that a good portion of the regulatory push comes not from government departments and agencies but from judicial bodies, the high courts, the Supreme Court, and now the National Green Tribunal.

The role played by these judicial bodies was established during the early years of independent India, when activist judges shaped the first procedural codes and fundamental rights lodged in the Indian constitution. The first judges of the Supreme Court were generous to petitioners while elaborating fundamental rights and what they should stand for. Justice S. P. Bharucha explained the opening of legal debate in the early years of the Indian union in this way: "There was then the age of expanding the scope and ambit [extent] of fundamental rights using, particularly, the wide language of Article 21. 'Due process' deliberately eschewed by the founding fathers was judicially brought into play by holding that a 'procedure established by law' had to be just and fair" (Alley 2009: 793; Bharucha 1998: 797). Over time, public interest or social-action litigation developed alongside investigative journalism. This litigation spawned advocacy for human and animal rights and supported broad-based environmental activism. These litigations have been rooted in advocacy for the poor, the marginalized, and the dispossessed, and now the environment. These liberties and the general approach to public interest litigation have allowed citizens to engage directly with the state and regulatory agencies on energy, water, and environmental matters. Public interest cases aim to hold government and private sector officials and industrialists accountable to their jobs and to the policies and laws of the state at all levels. While this kind of litigation enables the citizen and transforms the citizen into a potentially powerful petitioner, it also courts the charisma of judges. Charismatic justices and petitioners have been central to the direction of public interest litigation over the past three decades (Bhuwania 2017: 157). The Supreme Court became the primary site for contesting resources in a wide variety of cases ranging from water pollution, deforestation, and mining, to the impacts of extractive industries.

After the turn of the century, discussions emerged on the need for a specific environmental court. Eventually, these discussions led to the establishment of the National Green Tribunal (NGT) in 2010. The tribunal was set up as a three- to five-member bench composed of a leading judge, called the chairperson, at least one additional judge, and one to three expert members with knowledge of science and environment. The expert members are supposed to have a background in environmental assessment or ecological or another environmental science (Amirante 2012). Since the majority of the tribunal's cases deal with pollution (31 percent) and environmental clearances (35 percent), the chairperson and expert members adjudicate issues involved with these areas and need to have an understanding of what a developer or project proponent's environmental impact assessments should include. The NGT is empowered by the law to investigate environmental harm and issue punishments and penalties. The NGT can also issue, to petitioners, compensation for damages.

As Gill (2018: 15) notes, the establishment of the NGT encouraged the Supreme Court to review its own environmental caseload and consider its limited expertise. In 2012, the Supreme Court began ceding most of its environmental decisionmaking to the National Green Tribunal. By 2015, the Supreme Court had transferred more than 300 cases to the NGT. In 1,130 cases between July 2011 and September 2015, the majority of plaintiffs were nongovernmental organizations, social activists, and public-spirited citizens (Gill 2017, 2018: 17). Gill explains the approach of this new adjudicating body as follows:

> The stakeholder consultative adjudicatory process is the most recent of the NGT's problem-solving procedures. Major issues having a public impact either on public health, environment, or ecology can be better handled and resolved when stakeholders are brought together alongside the tribunal's scientific judges to elicit the views of those concerned—government, scientists, NGOs, the public, and the NGT. Stakeholder process evokes a greater element of consent rather than subsequent opposition to a judgment. The ongoing Ganga river, Yamuna river, and air pollution cases are illustrations of the new stakeholder consultative adjudicatory process involving open dialogue with interested parties. (2018: 19)

In 2016, the Supreme Court passed one of the most important environmental cases, commonly known as the Ganga pollution case, to the National Green Tribunal. The river Ganga is a sacred river for Hindus and millions bathe and perform rituals in river waters and along the riverbank. However, the Ganga's flow is heavily burdened with municipal and industrial sewage, and extractions for irrigation and urban water reduce these stressed flows further. In 1985, M. C. Mehta filed a writ petition in the Supreme Court charging that, despite the strides made in the legal code, government authorities had not taken effective steps to prevent water pollution. While the Ganga pollution case was under way, the government of India initiated the first environmental scheme, named the Ganga Action Plan (GAP). Under the GAP, sewage diversion and treatment systems were constructed to clean up polluted waterways. The hope was that they would be turned over to city municipalities for operation and maintenance in due time.

By the mid-1990s, problems with industrial compliance to pollution laws had come to the fore. The new or upgraded sewage treatment facilities were failing to operate effectively in most locations. These facilities were proving inadequate as the pollution load increased, and the small amount of treated water was reabsorbed by the wastewaters running into canals, streams, and rivers. To address these pollution problems, the Supreme Court stepped up its monitoring of the malfeasance of government and industry. In its orders, the Supreme Court fined over 200 industries in the basin, penalized the state pollution control boards for false reporting, and pressed the Ministry of Environment to streamline its proposals through a less wieldy set of supervisory committees (Alley 2009). In these Supreme Court cases, monitoring of compliance was considered necessary for the functioning of government and the effective use of its assets. In this monitoring, the judges' concerns and ideas on standards grew central to the directions and orders they issued. Judges grew eager to hear cases and follow up on their orders regularly. As cases remain active for an extended period of time, the judges can participate in monitoring and regulation as they assume the work that should be done by the government regulatory agencies. In this way, the well-known environmental cases focusing on rivers, the Taj Mahal, dams, and forests became omnibus cases over time, absorbing ongoing questions, issues, and problems into their purview.

When the NGT took over, it took the approach of creating discussion during hearings. This was more dialogic and produced collaborative solutions (Gill 2018). When the Ganga case was transferred to the NGT, the chairperson and others on the bench addressed the pollution and flow problems by separating the river into four stretches: from Gangotri to Hardwar; from Hardwar to Unnao; from Unnao to the border of Uttar Pradesh and Bihar; and from the border of Bihar to Kolkata port.

The bench pressed the government departments to update their data on water quality and quantity and put the data in the public domain. The chairperson was also astonished that the government held so little information on the number of polluting industries along the Ganga and their volume of effluents. So the NGT chairperson asked the primary government departments in charge of pollution prevention—the Ministry of Environment, Forests, and Climate Change; the Ministry of Water Resources (now the Ministry of Jal Shakti); the Central Pollution Control Board; and the state pollution control boards—to form a joint committee and go out, locate, document, and measure the flow of all the effluent drains entering the river. The agencies were bound to comply at least in performance. But beyond appearances, there have been many actions of noncompliance in pollution prevention. The NGT is forced to follow up and monitor these activities and noncompliances. By 2018, the NGT had issued over a hundred orders and judgments in the Ganga case. The orders and judgments doled out punishments to polluters; closed industries operating without pollution control facilities; and required hotels, ashrams, and housing complexes to install their own wastewater treatment plants.

These interactions between government departments and judicial branches produce a complicated picture of governance, and in this picture, everyday realities are veiled by appearances. The formal state actors appear as weak regulators unwilling to carry out national policies evenly. The main policy institution—the Ministry of Environment, Forests, and Climate Change—is also mandated to involve input from various experts in the field of environment in order to strengthen its perspectives, yet it is often defensive in the face of scientific input. The ministry's experts are appointed to two key committees, the Expert Appraisal Committee (EAC), which assists in making decisions on the environment clearance for projects, and the Forest Advisory Committee, which issues the forest clearance if forest land is impacted. Experts on the Indian Board for Wildlife also decide whether wildlife is impacted by a project and are empowered to issue the wildlife clearance. At the state level, there are other "no-objection certificates" that must be collected from state irrigation and public health departments, the public works, and the revenue and fisheries departments. Some of these clearances are being eliminated to open the way for rapid development of projects. Recently, the chief minister of Himachal Pradesh removed the no-objection clearances from the regulatory process in that state (Narain 2014; Rajshekhar and Sukumar 2013).[1] On many occasions, the NGT criticizes the Ministry of Environment, Forests, and Climate Change for failing to observe its own procedural rules and responsibilities—for example, by improperly granting permits and clearances without environment impact assessments.

Recently, government agencies and committees have attempted to dilute original environmental protections to open the path for development and industrialization. In 2014, a high-level governmental committee, named the Subramanian Committee, was set up to review and suggest amendments to environment-related acts and procedures. It targeted the Environment Protection Act (1986), the Forest Conservation Act (1980), the Wildlife Protection Act (1972), the Water Prevention and Control of Pollution Act (1974), the Air Prevention and Control of Pollution Act (1981), and the Indian Forest Act (1927) (Subramanian et al. 2014). Its report proposed a streamlining of environmental permits and clearances through a "single window" and recommended that the clearance powers be removed from the Ministry of Environment, Forests, and Climate Change and vested in two agencies, the national-level National Environmental Management Agency and the state-level State Environmental Management Agency.[2] The committee argued in its report that this would enable "expeditious clearances," especially in projects of national importance. Environmentalists and others concerned with the integrity of public interest protections saw the committee's proposals as an attempt to reduce the monitoring role of the judiciary and reduce the steps required to clear projects with government agencies.[3] Eventually, after much protest and discontent with the report, a standing parliamentary committee shelved it.

Despite these attempts to dilute standards and laws, the courts and tribunal have issued a number of strong, pro-environment judgments. One example is the decision regarding the Ministry of Environment, Forests, and Climate Change's notification dated November 9, 2016, exempting real estate projects from environmental impact assessments and environmental clearances. The notification included a self-declaration clause that would have ensured permission from urban local bodies. The notification also stated that residential buildings would not require consent to establish and operate from state pollution control boards, which is mandated under the air and water acts. After the discussion, the tribunal barred any new constructions under this notification, essentially quashing it. The bench, headed by NGT chairperson Swatanter Kumar, told advocates representing the ministry, "You can't do legal blunders and get away with it." The tribunal also canceled the clearance given to coal blocks in the Hasdeo-Arand forests of Chhattisgarh, which had been issued by the union minister for environment, forests, and climate change. In November 2016, the Kolkata bench of the NGT banned all noise pollution and solid waste dumping in the Sunderbans to protect wildlife. It also prohibited construction activity in eco-sensitive areas. These cases show that the tribunal intends to deliver good judgments legally and scientifically, as it ploughs through dozens of cases every day. Yet at times, the bench passes some extremely unconvincing decisions that are indicative of succumbing to pressure from interest groups.

Peri-Urban Growth and Intensification of the Urban Cores

With this general understanding of the institutional setting and its governance dynamics, a discussion of the key trends in urbanization, environment, and population can proceed. According to the Indian branch of the World Resources Institute, a research think tank, India is amid an urban transformation. The population growth in cities is outpacing growth in rural areas by far. From 1981 to 2011, the urban population increased from 23 to 31 percent of total population.[4] In 2015, India's urban population reached 420 million, and accounted for 33 percent of the total population (Shastry et al. 2018). It is hard to imagine that this number is projected to double to about 800 million by 2050, when one in every two citizens will live in a town or city (Shastry et al. 2018: 2). In addition to the megacities of Mumbai, Delhi, Chennai, Bangalore, and Kolkata, large towns are establishing the second tier of urbanization. Constituting this large-town category are cities with populations of around a million or more. Between 2001 and 2015, the number of cities with a population over a million increased from thirty-five to fifty-three.

In addition to population growth, the liberalization of the economy in terms of business deals and trade pushes the pace of urbanization (Dupont and Sridharan 2007). Favorable environments in terms of services and tax breaks have been created for the private sector and for speculative investments in real estate. Corporate parks for information technology and other industries are expanding in the peri-urban fringes, where land is cheaper than in the urban core. These activities create a pattern of growth through the expansion of peripheral areas and the intensification of urban cores (Bhattacharyya 2019; Mehta and Karpouzoglou 2015; Sood 2019; Vij, Narain, Karpouzoglou, and Mishra 2018). With rapid development of residential housing and office buildings, the installation of basic infrastructure cannot keep up. Peripheral zones of growing cities—the peri-urban areas—lie outside the city's grids for water and sewerage. In these off-grid conditions, residents and workers must find their own water sources and create their own sewerage facilities. The Indian branch of the World Resources Institute notes that in the current pattern there is no guarantee that cities will evolve in ways that maximize net agglomeration effects and productivity. Instead, market failures, weak institutions, and ineffective policies may impede the ability of cities to provide critical public goods, ensure planned and serviced urban growth, or manage industrial growth. This could spawn an increase in informal settlements, more excessive congestion, and decreased productivity (Shastry et al. 2018: 2).

Bangalore's (or now Bengaluru's) predicaments provide a prime example. In 1970, Bangalore had 1.6 million people. Within a decade, the public sector institutions such as the Indian Space Research Organization, Bharat Electrical Limited, and Hindustan Machine Tools pushed growth. Information technology companies added corporate parks and facilities for workers. In the 1980s, the population was growing at a rate of 45 percent. By 2011, the city limits spanned 710 square kilometers. Today, economic reforms and growing employment opportunities continue to accelerate the pace of urbanization. Bengaluru adds about 500 families and 80,000 square meters of built up area per day within its limits, and this trend is expected to continue well into the next decade (Pai and Dhindaw 2017).

Urban vehicular transportation is also on the upswing as more residents are able to afford cars. This creates traffic congestion but also forces more investment in the upgrading of mass transport infrastructure. In the largest cities, authorities are expanding metros and public transportation as well as airports. Road-widening projects are advancing connectivity between cities. In this cluttered growth, buses and taxis in all the large metros are required to run on compressed natural gas, which is cleaner than diesel or gasoline. Private car owners are also turning to compressed natural gas, which is cheaper than gasoline. The Indian car companies Maruti Suzuki and Hyundai Motor India Ltd. are now producing natural gas vehicles that are powered by compressed natural gas. These vehicles require filling stations, compressed natural gas storage facilities, and investments in supporting businesses. To meet these new needs, the union government has proposed a natural gas infrastructure development plan to build 10,000 compressed natural gas stations over the next decade. There is no doubt that greater reliance on natural gas could reduce the need for oil. According to one estimate, this shift could yield savings to the tune of $153 billion by 2030 (Vaidya 2019). A shift to compressed natural gas–powered vehicles can also help bring down the amount of particulate matter in the air and reduce carbon dioxide emissions.

Stressed Water Resources

As mentioned, water problems are severe in urban centers. In some regions, water-related problems threaten the viability of everyday life (Sengupta 2018). In the peri-urban areas of Delhi, Mumbai, Chennai, Kolkata, and Bangalore, there are limited piped water services, and almost no sewer lines to functioning sewage treatment plants. At least 2.2 million residents of Bangalore's population of 12.3 million do not have access to piped water (Biswas and Jamwal 2017). In south Delhi, high-end apartment buildings are coming up in areas where the courts and government have banned pumping up groundwater. There is also limited piped water supply in Gurgaon, now Gurugram. When residents of these neighborhoods and towns obtain potable water from tanker trucks rather than from municipal pipes or hand pumps, they are especially squeezed by escalating costs (Ranganathan 2014). Residents in peri-urban areas, which include "unauthorized" areas, pay more for a kiloliter of water from a tanker or a water automatic teller machine. The prices are much higher than what the city water boards charge for piped water (Anand 2017; Bjorkman 2015; Narain 2018; Niti Aayog 2018). This is especially stressful for low-income families. Those who are water-stressed meet their daily needs by combining small amounts from different sources: from low-quality piped water, if available; from

Collecting water from a government pipe. Photo by Kelly D. Alley.

reverse-osmosis water produced in the home or by vendors; from groundwater; and from water supplied by city and private water tankers (Maurya et al. 2017).

The recent limits and bans on groundwater push households and businesses to find other sources, and some are now turning to treated wastewater. Court orders and state government policies now require new residential buildings over twenty units to have on-site wastewater treatment facilities. Some residential communities are using this treated water for their on-site needs. When a new building is constructed, the builder must install the sewage treatment system, and housing welfare associations inherit the facilities when they move in. After a year, the housing welfare associations must raise the funds for ongoing operation and maintenance from their annual fees. The residents must then learn how to run their own on-site sewage treatment plants or hire a maintenance person. They are also able to decide whether to reuse the water. The buildings that have a dual piping system can facilitate reuse inside their homes as well, for toilet flushing, cleaning, and air-conditioning cooling towers (Alley, Maurya, and Das 2018).

Business buildings are following suit. A large office and conference compound in New Delhi, the India Habitat Center, treats its own wastewater on-site and recycles it for use in its gardens. The Marriott Hotel

A state-of-the-art sewage treatment plant on the campus of IIT-Chennai. Photo by Kelly D. Alley.

Treated water from the IIT-Chennai sewage treatment plant. Photo by Kelly D. Alley.

and Conference Center in Mumbai treats its own wastewater and reuses it for gardening, toilet flushing, and air-conditioning cooling towers. Institutions such as the Indian Institutes of Technology have set up or are setting up their own sewage treatment plants to reuse the water on campus.

These projects are experiments in decentralization that parallel experiments with modular systems in electricity generation (Cross 2016; Gupta 2015; Ulsrude et al. 2011). While public acceptability for reuse varies across the world, in India there is a growing interest in using the water for nonpotable purposes. The disinterest in using this water for potable needs has not turned people off to the idea or experience of using it for nonpotable purposes.

On the problem of depleting groundwater tables, the NGT is taking action. The tribunal is instructing the Central Groundwater Authority to set strict limits and bans on groundwater extraction, especially in zones where depletion has reached critical levels. Debates on groundwater depletion began in the NGT in 2013 as citizens filed legal petitions on the subject. In eight different cases, the NGT ruled that industries or other large-quantity users must curb their use of groundwater. The NGT ordered that large-quantity groundwater users must obtain a no-objection certificate from the Central Groundwater

Authority. Households in Delhi were also forbidden to use bore well water for gardening and horticulture, but this rule has been harder to enforce and monitor. New permits are now harder to obtain. The draft guidelines of the groundwater bill strengthen the powers of gram sabhas, panchayats, and municipal bodies in the regulation of groundwater, which sounds positive for conservation. However, some have argued that these guidelines are trying to "make a system wherein state or district level authorities will have the ability to issue [no-objection certificates] without having the understanding to do so" (South Asia Network for Dams, Rivers, and People 2017).

In critical zones marked by the Central Groundwater Authority, groundwater tables are dramatically lower and businesses and residents in critical zones must constantly probe for new water. In the process, a great deal of electricity is used to pump water to the surface. In Bangalore, the water table lies at a depth of 800 feet below the surface. According to Goldman and Narayan (2019), in 2015 there were 105,500 private bore wells registered with the Bangalore Water Supply and Sewerage Board, with over 200,000 bore wells unregistered. Across Karnataka, 5,000 new bore wells are sunk every month, in many cases to replace other ones that have dried up.

Other cities have groundwater tables lurking at 200–300 feet below the surface. In some places, groundwater is contaminated by industrial activities and rendered unusable. Groundwater in the peri-urban areas of Kanpur is severely contaminated by tanneries and other small industries. Residents of the largest resettlement village outside Delhi are not able to use their groundwater for potable and bathing uses and must limit use to washing clothes. They rely upon water tankers from the Delhi Water Board for their drinking-water supply. These are just a few of the many examples of the stresses related to groundwater accessibility and usability.

Urban governments are always on the lookout for new sources of water. While wastewater recycling can meet some of these demands for new water supplies, it is a common first desire of political leaders to find ways to transfer water from a larger bulk source such as a reservoir or river. When new water is captured and diverted to the city through these water transfer projects, city growth is promoted. Generally, urban centers are the biggest guzzlers of water from long-distance water transfer projects, and they get a good deal more than small towns and villages do. The building of the Tehri dam in the Uttarakhand Himalayas has directed more water to Delhi to enable the city's growth. The water stored behind the Tehri dam provides Delhi with 470 cubic feet per second through the Upper Ganga Canal. That is 27 percent of Delhi's total water supply. However, big dams have consequences for populations living in the catchment areas. Dams affect flows of water and sediment within riverbeds and they reduce biodiversity (Grumbine and Pandit 2013). By the time it was completed in 2006, the Tehri dam had diverted a massive amount of water away from the main tributary, the Bhagirathi river, to cause many location and downstream problems. The dam's reservoir pushed thousands of people from their ancestral homes, bringing on human misery.

This pattern is being repeated in Bangalore, where urban dwellers and industrialists are trying to guzzle more water from the Cauvery river. This is reducing flows to farmers downstream in Tamil Nadu. The tensions over water diversions and the increasing water demands in urban cores and peri-urban zones are leading to conflicts within and between states. The judicial bodies generally mediate these conflicts (Ghosh, Bandyopadhyay, and Thakur 2018; Iyer 2003). Regarding the Cauvery river, the Supreme Court is regulating the water disputes between Karnataka and Tamil Nadu. Ghosh, Bandyopadhyay, and Thakur argue that the recent ruling of the Supreme Court of India on the allocation of water of the Cauvery, between the states of Karnataka and Tamil Nadu, is historic on two counts.[5] They write: "First, it marks the culmination of an old inter-state water dispute that has been an epitome of hostile hydropolitics in India; second, it sent a signal to the agricultural economy to practice demand management of water for attaining higher water-use efficiency, and crop-choice consistent with natural water endowment" (2018: 1). As they put it, the ruling is a case of "robbing Peter to pay Paul"—reducing water for Tamil Nadu by nearly 15 billion cubic feet and providing the same to Karnataka. It also recognizes a bigger global phenomenon of intersectoral water conflicts: agriculture versus urban-industrial water demand. Such water conflicts and transfers may also be responsible for the rise in farmer suicides in Tamil Nadu and the other states of Maharashtra, Karnataka, and Andhra Pradesh. These calamities are tied to declining access to irrigation water and to the stresses produced by rising temperatures and climate change (Carleton 2017).

Climate Change, Floods, and Drought

This discussion of water problems leads to the larger problem of climate change. One way to understand the dangers of climate change is to consider change in Earth's planetary boundaries. Planetary boundaries are parameters that scientists have identified to explain the limits of the safe realm for life on the planet. The designated boundaries are the possible tipping points into nonsustainable conditions for humans and other species. According to recent reports, the Earth system has reached the limits of several of the nine planetary boundaries, signaling that humans are entering the danger zone for life on the planet (Steffen et al. 2015). The intensive and aggregated uses of fertilizers and fossil fuels put more nitrogen, phosphorous, and carbon dioxide on land and into water and the atmosphere, and these activities change the climate system. The overproduction of nitrogen and phosphorus from the use of fertilizers and industrial products is contaminating soil and water bodies and changing the nitrogen cycle in ways that may produce harmful system feedbacks. Carbon dioxide concentrations in the atmosphere are blocking more of the longwave radiation bouncing off the earth, and the carbon dioxide is absorbing this energy and creating a warming effect. This warming triggers other planetary processes such as the intensification of the hydrological cycle. This intensification brings more intense storms and precipitation events and affects the circulation of the Indian monsoon (Barua, Narain, and Vij 2018).

The Indian government has argued that, as a country of the global South, the subcontinent is forced to bear the burden of the atmospheric greenhouse gases created by the advanced industrial countries over the past century. Yet today India produces the fourth largest concentrations of carbon dioxide worldwide. India's representatives to the United Nations Framework Convention on Climate Change have been vocal in pointing out the role of advanced industrial nations in creating the current concentrations of atmospheric gases. Prime Minister Modi spoke passionately at the Conference of the Parties in 2015, when the Paris Accord was debated and eventually signed. He argued that India should not have to limit its development before it has achieved the progress enjoyed by other nations. The view of the leadership is that the government should not be instructed by international coalitions on how to limit its own carbon emissions. The country's representatives to the framework convention argued that carbon reduction schemes are policies the country must decide for itself.

Interestingly, after the strong pronouncements on the international stage, the government moved forward with the rhetoric of climate change at home. One now sees climate change framing the discussions on many topics related to water, energy, and health. Public awareness of climate change appears substantially higher among the educated elite in urban centers; this indicates that public-awareness programs have had some effect (Thaker 2017). Horrible floods such as those occurring regularly in the Himalayan region are also raising concern and fear among residents (Adam, Mehta, and Srivasta 2018). These fears and concerns are building interest in renewable energy, water conservation, and wastewater reuse. For example, urban residents are debating initiatives in sanitation, and farmers are looking for ways to decrease biomass-burning across northern agricultural land. The latter involve critical behavior changes, as biomass-burning in north India contributes high concentrations of aerosols to the atmosphere that threaten public health.[6] These higher aerosol loads also bring changes in precipitation and in the circulation of the monsoon.

The flood of 2013 in Uttarakhand was a result of the combination of anthropogenic and climatic forces. The giant cloudbursts and extreme rainfall occurred at a time when scores of people were practicing their cultural rituals in Kedarnath and surrounding areas. The satellite image from the Indian meteorological department taken on June 17, 2013, showed the convergence of the southwestern monsoon and westerly disturbances above the northwestern Himalayas. This convergence produced gigantic clouds that dumped up to 325 millimeters of rain over the Kedarnath area within forty-eight hours (Dobhal, Gupta, Mehta, and Khandelwal 2013: 171). This heavy rain led to a rapid rise in river flows. The pressure from this intense rainfall also created glacial lake outbursts higher up in the Himalayas. Glacial lake outbursts are the result of warming trends like the one that occurred the previous month. In May, temperatures rose 4 to 5 degrees Celsius above normal and this spike in warming accelerated seasonal glacial melting. This melting created small glacial lakes in the unstable spaces between glacial snouts and rock moraines. During the intense rain event, the lakes were inundated with millions of gallons of water within two days (Dobhal, Gupta, Mehta, and Khandelwal 2013: 174). The pressure proved too great and the water of one glacial lake, Chorabari, forced open the moraine dam. A surge of water tumbled down the riverbed to drown the town of Kedarnath. Thousands of pilgrims who were visiting the Shiva shrine in Kedarnath at the time were caught in the tsunami wave and lost their lives. The massive flood caused catastrophic loss of life and property across the region.

Under the United Nations Framework Convention on Climate Change, Indian officials are developing a national climate adaptation plan that gives special attention to the Himalayan region and to the drought-prone areas of the plains (Barua, Narain, and Vij 2018). Government agencies may seek funds from the National Adaptation Fund for Climate Change under the framework convention to support adaptation projects. For instance, Phayeng, a scheduled caste village in the Imphal West district of Manipur, may be India's first declared carbon-positive settlement if it can meet the goal of sequestering more carbon than it creates (Nandi 2019). Its conservation efforts revolve around the belief that the forest is a sacred grove.

Energy and Pollution

The planetary boundary of carbon dioxide in the atmosphere, which should stay below 350 parts per million for safe life on Earth, is directly related to activities in the energy sector, especially to the burning of fossil fuels. The energy sector in India is blessed with coal, but the country lacks domestic sources of oil and natural gas. The fact that there is no domestic supply of oil and gas in the country means that imports are critical. These imports, being expensive, have strained the exchequer since the 1960s (Madan 2006). On the other hand, coal that is sourced domestically has steadily provided for 50 percent of the country's needs for energy over this half-century. Eighty-four percent of India's coal is mined in the states of Madhya Pradesh, Chhattisgarh, Jharkhand, Orissa, Maharashtra, and Andhra Pradesh (Lahiri-Dutt 2014). However, it is predicted that India's overall energy consumption will rise from 724 million tons of oil equivalent in 2016 to 1,921 in 2040, with an average per annum growth rate of 4.2 percent. The increase in India's energy consumption will push the country's share of global energy demand to 11 percent by 2040, at which time it will account for the second largest share of the BRIC (Brazil, Russia, India, China) countries (British Petroleum 2018).

Given the increasing demand, it is expected that environmental and human impacts will be compounded. Open-pit coal mining started in the 1950s and then surged in the 1990s. Environmental destruction from coal mining has been pervasive across the Chotanagpur and Orissa plateaus that connect Jharkhand, Chhattisgarh, and Orissa. Over the years, with interest in pollution control rather lax, fly ash and other residuals from mining have been dumped on vacant land near the mine sites and power plants. Fly ash is soupy and when it is deposited on the ground, it creates large gray lakes that are highly toxic. All freshwater supplies in the mining regions have been contaminated by fly-ash lakes. The health impacts of mining and dumping are noticeable among Adivasi or Dalit communities living and working near the mines.

Other forms of mining are causing havoc as well. Sand mining, or removing sand from riverbeds and flood plains, is a contentious issue.

In some states, the sand mafia pushes government departments to issue them permits to mine. There have been fierce oppositions to these practices. The bans on sand mining in riverbeds, created by the NGT and many high courts, were enforced for four years, until the Supreme Court overturned them in a recent order.

This kind of reversal in regulations has also occurred in iron-ore mining. In 2010, the Shah Commission found that iron-ore mining companies were mining in Goa with expired leases. Some were mining outside the permissive mining area and some had failed to maintain a required distance between overburden, or the rock and soil that lies above a coal seam, and irrigation canals. After a government-led investigation into the environmental impacts of industry operations, the state government shut down all ninety iron-ore mines in 2012. A similar move had occurred in Karnataka in 2011. In 2018, the Supreme Court lifted the ban on iron-ore mining in the western state of Goa but limited the permitted extractions to 20 million tons a year.

The government will cite its achievements in renewable energy, especially with regard to solar energy, as a way to appease climate activists. But the reliance on domestic coal is unshakable. Even with renewed interest in nuclear power, coal is expected to constitute 50 percent of the energy budget for the next two decades. Coal burning puts a concentrated amount of carbon dioxide and particulate matter into the atmosphere, and this augments the pollution loads created by industries and urban centers. The air quality index for all the major urban metropolises is in the severe to hazardous range, with some pockets experiencing extremely hazardous levels. The rising incidence of asthma in all cities and towns is the strongest indicator that atmospheric concentrations of carbon dioxide and particulate matter caused by the burning of fossil fuels severely affect public health and the quality of life.

Renewable Energy

Amid these complicated energy and pollution scenarios lies the growth of renewable energy. New government policies are offering tax and financial incentives for investors to develop solar and wind power (India Briefing 2018). The beginning of the push for solar renewables appears to have been during India's involvement in the Paris climate accords in 2015. A window into the negotiations is provided in the new film *An Inconvenient Sequel: Truth to Power,* wherein government officials of India, the United States, and other countries are filmed during their negotiation sessions. The film covers some of the discussions and arrangements that occurred as the member nations in the United Nations

Solar panels for water heating in a housing complex in peri-urban Bangalore. Photo by Kelly D. Alley.

Framework Convention on Climate Change were trying to set targets for reducing greenhouse gases. The scenes show that Indian leaders were more interested in going along with a climate agreement after they were offered critical solar photovoltaic property specifications from the SolarCity Corporation (a subsidiary of Tesla) in the United States. The transfer of intellectual property provided the incentive to join the climate agreement. Following this deal on intellectual property, the World Bank promised funding for the technology build-out across India, to the tune of billions of dollars. This has jump-started the construction of solar parks around the country, which officials say will bring 40 gigawatts of solar power by 2022.[7] Beinecke (2017) writes: "The overall growth of renewable energy in India has been remarkable. India has added 9 gigawatts (GW) of solar power in just the past two years—the equivalent of 4.5 Hoover Dams—for a total of 12 GW of total solar power capacity."

The growth in solar power has helped slow contracts for new thermal power plants. The replacement of coal with solar can also reduce the total greenhouse gas emissions in the country. Reports predict that demand for renewables will see the highest growth, of 1,409 percent, or up to 256 million tons of oil equivalent, in 2040, as the sector moves up

A dam in the state of Sikkim, in northeast India. Photo by Kelly D. Alley.

from 17 million tons recorded in 2016. This means an annual growth of 12 percent. The government's aim is to increase the renewable-energy share in India's energy mix to 13 percent by 2040.

In other fields of renewable energy, the picture is more conflictual. In hydropower, for instance, a start-and-stop approach has characterized projects over the past several decades. Early in this century, government officials and developers started pushing for investment in hydropower projects as gas reserves were dwindling and coal block development was delayed by corruption allegations (Alley 2012, 2014; Menon and Kohli 2005; Vagholikar and Das 2010). Hydropower is generated by many small run-of-the-river projects and by the large dams such as the Tehri dam in Uttarakhand (Baviskar and Singh 2008; Drew 2017).

However, there has been strong opposition to hydropower develop-ment across the Himalayas (Lord, Drew, and Gergan 2020). Citizens have blocked roads and dam sites and have shut down parts of the gov-ernment's hydropower agenda through direct action and litigation. From time to time, the power lobby manages to overcome citizen protests, and regulations protecting river flows and forest areas are reversed at the highest levels. In the northeastern states, hydropower development solidifies claims to sovereign territory in a one-upmanship with China. India aims to match China's dam developments along the Yarlung Tsangpo in Tibet. Meanwhile, Chinese agencies remain minimalist in the sharing of hydrological data and when disclosing information on upstream constructions (Alley 2016, 2017). The Indian government also funds hydropower projects and buys back the power from Bhutan, Nepal, and Myanmar.

It is understandable that proposals and actual activities involved with dam-building across the Himalayas have worried citizen groups and drawn the attention of the courts and the National Green Tribunal. Judges have appointed numerous committees to document and regulate construction activities and avoid or mitigate the impacts of tangled infrastructures made up of barrages, tunnels, and debris. Scientists have wondered about the amount of methane produced by the dam reservoirs, which would add to climate complexities. When climate conjunctions (e.g., the collision of two weather systems) produce extreme floods, they become "wicked" flows able to destroy dam infrastructure, farmland, houses, lives, and livelihoods overnight (Khan et al. 2010). In the Himalayan region, this hydro-complexity is magnified by glacial lake outbursts that are increasing with the warming climate (Jain et al. 2012; Richardson and Reynolds 2000).

Pollution and Public Health

There are a myriad of health effects emerging from urbanization, environmental degradation, and climate change. It is a huge achievement that a few communicable diseases are now under control and many diseases, such as polio, guinea worm disease, yaws, and tetanus, have been eradicated (Narain 2016). However, noncommunicable diseases, especially cardiovascular diseases, are major killers in the country, and now novel viruses such as the one causing Covid-19 are wreaking havoc on health and the economy. In 2006, the prime minister established the Public Health Foundation of India to incorporate more public health policies and diverse professionals into the healthcare sphere. This foundation is collaborating with international public health organizations to gather public health knowledge as it directs discussion around needs and improvements. Endemic diseases such as HIV/AIDS, tuberculosis, malaria, and tropical diseases continue. As Covid-19 enters the list of new communicable diseases, outbreaks are challenging public health authorities and scientists in ways they have never seen before. The rapid spread of infection is overwhelming medical facilities and causing human tragedy as people succumb to the disease. High levels of readiness in terms of early detection and rapid response will be ongoing priorities (Bush et al. 2011). Vector-borne diseases, such as dengue, chikungunya, and acute encephalitis syndrome, are still on the rise (Narain 2016). Occurrences of vector-borne diseases may be linked to climate change, since temperature and humidity determine where vectors proliferate and pathogens survive. While other communicable diseases have stressed urban systems, the Covid-19 pandemic may spur transformative effects on urbanization and the economy across all scales, as residents search for safer housing and work environments. The Covid-19 pandemic is making urban life less attractive and more dangerous and limiting the consumptive and religious practices of residents. The need to focus on safer ways to protect human life through the pandemic can also reduce the amount of time and energy spent on the stewardship of the environment.

While the past decade has seen gross domestic product increase, this progress is accompanied by growing disparities between the rich and the poor. This income inequality or disparity between socioeconomic classes worsens health outcomes and affects the survivability of citizens during pandemics such as Covid-19 (Narain 2016). In just five years, there has been a 30 percent increase in acute respiratory infections brought on by severe air pollution in cities, which makes citizens more vulnerable to covid-19.[8] Levels of particulate matter in the air are at dangerous levels throughout the year, from the emissions of industries, trucks, and other forms of transport, and from the burning of coal and biomass. In Delhi, the particulate load in the air increases exponentially at the end of rabi season, when farmers must burn the harvest refuse and turn their fields for another crop within a matter of weeks. Schools in Delhi and the surrounding areas are closed during these periods of hazardous air quality. This dangerous air condition occurs around the time of Diwali, when firecrackers add even more smoke into the air.

In the area of sanitation, there has been a great deal of activity recently. In October 2014, Prime Minister Modi launched the Swatchh Bharat Abhiyan, or Clean India Campaign, to align the country's policies and practices with the UN's Sustainable Development Goals of sanitation and clean water for all (Alley, Barr, and Mehta 2018). Prior to 2014, 65 percent of the population had been defecating in the open. The first objective of the Swatchh Bharat Abhiyan was to eliminate open defecation. In recent tallies, government authorities have claimed that open defecation is now limited to 20 percent of the population. However, programs to build toilets in urban and rural areas have had mixed success (Coffey and Spears 2017). There is no doubt that sanitation facilities will help to eliminate conditions where residents are exposed to fecal coliform and pathogens in the soil and water around them. But infrastructures for total sanitation must be made more effective by creating functional treatment systems for fecal sludge and wastewater. As wastewater runs untreated through villages, antibiotic-resistant bacteria multiply. Recent studies in microbiology have found that these bacteria multiply in the tanks of sewage treatment plants when digestion of wastewater is activated (Lamba and Ahammad 2017). The presence of deadly bacteria in canals and sewage tanks is alarming public health authorities to the extent that global health surveillance programs are also scrambling to identify and keep track of the spreading of these bacteria. However, health and science budgets are severely stretched, and regulatory power is virtually zero. According to one estimate, superbugs kill around 60,000 newborns in India every year (Altstedter 2018).

Conclusion

This chapter has aimed to show the direct connections between urbanization and the environment, as human growth and development push ecological, hydrological, and planetary cycles into danger zones for human and other species life. Water resources are severely stressed by demand, and people are stressed by temporary and permanent scarcity and pollution. Energy demands are running high and are projected to run higher, feeding the expectation that near-future energy sources must be more diverse. Renewables are projected for continued growth, and this shift in energy sources may bring down total greenhouse gas emissions. Indian citizens are facing the brunt of climate change as the hydrological cycle intensifies and causes dangerous flooding in the Himalayas and drought and water conflicts on the plains. The public health consequences from each of these crosscutting trends are borne out in rising cases of asthma, communicable and vector-borne diseases, and infections caused by antibiotic-resistant bacteria.

At the same time, the judicial organs of environmental consciousness continue to be as vital and vigilant as they were in early postindependence India. The cases taken up by the high courts, the Supreme Court, and the National Green Tribunal are addressing the spectrum of challenges and guiding critical negotiations over resource uses. In this context, regulation and enforcement appear to work best when there are multiple players checking each other's powers and vetting each other's behaviors. The judicial bodies have established this state of affairs in India, where citizens are able to check the powers and behaviors of government ministries, departments, and projects through their writ petitions.

While citizens are able to submit their input into decisionmaking through the courts and the NGT, the judiciary remains fundamentally dependent upon executive will. The central government has a role to play in the appointment, removal, and resignation of NGT judges, judicial members, and expert members.[9] Under Section 10 of the NGT Act, the central government can remove the chairperson and judicial and expert members in consultation with the chief justice of India. The Ministry of Environment, Forests, and Climate Change also provides financial support to the tribunal. The central government exerts influence and control over many key aspects, and this becomes important given the fact that many environmental cases are against the government. After retirement, judges and members can be absorbed into positions in various commissions. In fact, this is a problem across the judiciary in India. For example, former chief justice of India P. Sathasivam was appointed governor of Kerala by the central government. The excessive influence of the central government and the interest of judicial members to maintain relations with the government for the sake of future appointments can shape the actions of judges while on the bench.

Along with the NGT, the high courts play an important role in environmental decisionmaking. In 2019, the NGT's regional benches were not operational because retiring judges had not been replaced and the chairperson handled cases by Skype from the main bench in Delhi. This caused a backlog of cases and reignited activity within the high courts.

The tribunal can be credited with filling the gap in environmental governance and requiring, under the threat of punishment, some coordination among the government units in charge of pollution prevention. This adds a level of third-party monitoring that is critically needed. However, the NGT is far from independent and judges may use delay to appear to follow the law as they avoid the harshest punishments for powerful leaders and interest groups. Meanwhile, the government agencies responsible for regulation and monitoring as well as public health assurances may remain nearsighted, preferring to act quickly for economic gain but avoiding long-term planning for the next generation.

Notes

1. Gill documents that regulatory agencies (comprising the Ministry of Environment, Forests, and Climate Change; state government; local authorities; and pollution control boards) constituted 942 defendants (83.4 percent) of 1,130 reported judgments between 2011 and 2015. The ministry was the defendant in 284 cases (25.1 percent); state government appeared as the defendant in 341 cases (30.2 percent); a local authority was listed in 78 cases (6.9 percent);

and pollution control boards were listed in 239 cases (21.2 percent). The data suggest a repeated failure on the part of regulatory authorities to undertake their statutory environmental protection duties and social responsibilities regarding environmental matters.

2. The Subramanian Committee's report noted: "The Committee finds uneven application of the principle of separation of powers as established by the Constitution of India, in the administration of environmental laws. The state—arbitrary, opaque, suspiciously tardy or in-express-mode at different times, along with insensitivity—has failed to perform, inviting the intervention of the judiciary. Judicial pronouncements frequently have supplanted legislative powers, and are occupying the main executive space. The administrative machineries in the Government in the domain of Environment & Forests at all the levels, authorized to administer by Parliament's statutory mandate, appear to have abdicated their responsibilities. The doctrine of proportionality, principles of sustainable development and inter-generational equity, doctrine of margin of appreciation—these have been the basis of judicial orders in the matters of environment and forests laws. However, the perceived role of ad-hoc committees in decision-making and implementation appears to have reduced the [Ministry of Environment, Forests, and Climate Change] to a passive spectator, with little initiative except waiting for the Court to say what next. The Committee's aim is to restore to the Executive the will and tools to do what it is expected to do by the statutes" (Subramanian et al. 2014: 8).

3. The South Asia Network for Dams, Rivers, and People (2015) notes: "In the name of reducing and eliminating the 'inspector raj,' the Committee reposes complete trust on the Industry and views people's voice with suspicion." Dharmadhikary (2013) notes with regard to the Subramanian report's position on exceptions: "Further, the Report says that public hearings can be dispensed with 'in the matters of projects of strategic importance and national importance.' This offers a very easy escape route for exempting projects, particularly since national importance is not defined, and virtually every major project could be considered nationally important. For example, the Polavaram dam and irrigation project has been declared a national project; this could well mean that it is of national importance. Then, even such a controversial project, facing serious challenge from local people, could be exempt from public hearings."

4. Census of India 2001, 2014.

5. Civil Appeal no. 2453 of 2007 with Civil Appeal no. 2456 of 2007.

6. The development agenda is strong, and the "Make in India" framework along with smart-city schemes and special economic zones are frustrating efforts to set up protections and conservation programs for the eco-fragile watersheds of the upper Himalayas and for drought-prone regions in need of groundwater recharge. Deforestation and cropland expansion have taken a toll on India's forest cover over the past century (Tian et al. 2014), but new research argues that a green wave is occurring from cropland expansion (Chen et al. 2019).

7. Press Information Bureau, Ministry of New and Renewable Energy, July 19, 2018.

8. Air pollution can significantly aggravate asthma. *Down to Earth,* September 17, 2018.

9. National Green Tribunal Act, Act no. 19 of 2010, sec. 6.

11

Looking Ahead

Neil DeVotta

It is likely that the world will discuss future events using pre–Covid-19 and post–Covid-19 prisms given the harm done by the coronavirus. In India's case, Covid-19 has laid waste to millions of livelihoods even as the country was struggling to grow economically. At the time of writing, over 20 million people in India have been infected with the coronavirus, leading to over 220,000 deaths. Some estimates suggest that around 25 percent of Indians may have lost jobs in March and April 2020 due to the pandemic. The coronavirus crisis, however, has also highlighted the Modi government's authoritarian proclivities, even though it has not dented the prime minister's popularity thus far. The reasons for this include the strongman image Modi has cultivated, the success with which the Bharatiya Janata Party has been able to combine loyalty toward Modi with pro-Hindu sentiment, and the weakness of the Congress Party.

In the run-up to the 2014 elections, pundits predicted Narendra Modi was bound to become prime minister as part of a coalition because his BJP would not win a majority of seats in parliament. The BJP, however, won 282 seats and thereby upended nearly a quarter century of national politics wherein no party had won a majority. Modi was expected to win reelection in 2019, but once more analysts predicted the BJP would not win with a majority. This time, the party won 303 seats. Pollsters in the past decade have proven to be wrong when predicting various outcomes, including Brexit and Donald Trump's victory in 2016. Whatever the reasons for this, Narendra Modi today is a more powerful and emboldened leader than he was in his first term. However,

275

it is debatable as to whether this is a good or bad thing for India in the long term given the numerous challenges the country faces on multiple fronts, challenges that have been compounded due to Covid-19.

Economic Challenges

As per the International Monetary Fund, India's economy was set to shrink by over 10 percent in 2020, with the International Labour Organization estimating that the downturn would force 400 million people into deeper poverty. India's economy will bounce back once the coronavirus is tackled, but the country must grow by at least 8 percent yearly for a number of years if people's modest aspirations are to be met. However, it does not appear that the Modi government is capable of instituting reforms that will allow India to reach such heights.

The 1991 economic reforms that India pursued stemmed from a balance-of-payments crisis, and not because India's leaders were eager to pursue open market policies. Indeed, those at the top remained exceedingly unenthusiastic about any reforms being implemented notwithstanding the crisis (Ahluwalia 2020). This aversion toward more open market policies remains among politicians associated with the BJP, Congress, and other leading parties. It is therefore not surprising that successive governments have avoided instituting further reforms even as state-owned banks have made numerous bad loans to those with links to prominent politicians, loans that are most unlikely to be fully paid. Modi too has harped on the concept of a self-reliant India, with thinking rooted more in autarky than the open market reforms of 1991. All this means that despite promises to develop India like the state of Gujarat, which was ahead of most Indian states before Modi became its chief minister, most Indians have seen little positive economic change since the BJP under Modi came to power in 2014. Ultimately, "Modinomics" is rooted more in protectionism and favoritism, as opposed to bold structural changes designed to better integrate India with the global economy (Sharma 2019).

Modinomics also appears to be impulsive. As discussed in Chapter 5, Prime Minister Modi's decision in 2016 to summarily demonetize 500 and 1,000 rupee banknotes caused widespread difficulties especially for India's rural poor, but the justifications used for doing so—eliminating corruption and tackling terrorism—allowed him to build on his reputation as a decisive and strong leader and maintain his popularity. On March 24, 2020, the prime minister acted likewise when he declared that the country would go into lockdown within four hours for

Young employees at a hotel in Assam. Photo by Neil DeVotta.

three weeks to stop the spread of Covid-19. It appears that how India's estimated 120 million migrant workers would adjust to the decree was not considered. In subsequent days, the world read of people walking hundreds of miles to rural villages, with some dying along the way.

India will soon overtake China as the world's most populous country. Today over 50 percent of India's population is under age twenty-five, with the country's average age being twenty-nine. Economists and demographers use the term "dependency ratio" to refer to the difference between workers and retirees. With India comprising so many young people, going forward it will have more workers than retirees (a low dependency ratio). Hypothetically, this will allow for a more productive work force with increased savings to fund everything from welfare programs to defense at an easier rate than countries that will have more retirees than workers (a high dependency ratio).

A youth bulge, however, provides both opportunities and dangers. Countries that have experienced a youth bulge and failed to accommodate the aspirations of their young citizens have seen insurgencies and other violent movements. In India's case, such an outcome can easily undermine the country's democratic gains made since independence. Disenchanted youth are fodder for radical organizations, and this is already evident in some parts of India.

When Narendra Modi became prime minister, India needed to create a million jobs every month to accommodate youth entering the job market. This did not happen, with the country averaging under 6 percent unemployment throughout Modi's years as leader. Consequently, how India leverages its youth bulge is going to be very important to the country's future success. Whether it does so as a vibrant pluralist democracy or an illiberal majoritarian Hindu policy will also affect its fortunes.

Illiberalism amid Rising Authoritarianism

Narendra Modi wants to outdo the legacy of Jawaharlal Nehru. Nehru, however, promoted pluralism and democracy. Modi seeks to build a legacy as a Hindutva strongman. What is troubling is how quickly democratic India has caved in to this majoritarian message, because Modi won reelection not by transforming India's economy as promised, but by fanning Hindu nationalism and compromising democratic institutions (Jaffrelot 2019b; Mukherji 2020).

A democracy as diverse as India is best governed amid consensus politics. Modi, however, is the most divisive leader in India's postindependence history. In line with his long-standing Hindutva leanings, he has fanned Islamophobia for both ideological and politicking reasons. India's Muslims number around 200 million and constitute the largest minority of any country. While there exist some extremely wealthy and prominent Muslims in the country, most who are part of the community live marginalized and poverty-stricken lives. In the main, the community's status is now second to the country's Dalits. There is no way for India to develop appreciably while a 200 million–strong community is consigned to the margins of society. Consequently, while Narendra Modi and his Hindu right brigades may succeed in terrorizing and humiliating the country's Muslims, they will not simultaneously make India a great power.

Many leaders around the world have used the Covid-19 crisis to force through illiberal practices undermining democracy (Repucci and Slipowitz 2020). Prime Minister Narendra Modi and his Hindu nationalist government have done likewise, given how they went about making decisions without parliamentary approval and input from states that ultimately had to bear the brunt of the costs associated with their decisions. The brusque decisionmaking is consistent with Modi's authoritarian proclivities, which is hardly conducive to transforming India's fortunes. If anything, the evidence thus far is that Modi's authoritarianism has compounded the woes facing India.

As noted in Chapter 4, Indira Gandhi's rule was famous for an authoritarian streak that undermined independent institutions that her father, Jawaharlal Nehru, worked hard to set up. It is to India's credit that bodies like the Supreme Court and electoral commission were able to reassert themselves in the years since Indira Gandhi departed the political scene. The assault that Modi and the BJP are currently carrying out on India's institutions appear to go beyond anything Indira Gandhi attempted. Not only are vaunted institutions like the Supreme Court and electoral commission becoming politicized, but pro-BJP mobs and student unions now threaten academic independence and civil liberties. Increasingly, individuals today are appointed to high academic positions and government bodies not because they have the requisite credentials, but because they promote the right-wing Hindutva agenda.

According to Freedom House's *Freedom in the World 2020* report (Repucci 2021: 3), India experienced the worst democratic regression when compared to the world's twenty-five largest democracies. This despite the crackdown in Kashmir left out of the analysis, since Freedom House evaluates the region as a separate territory. The BJP and Modi's anti-Muslim politics and their attempts to undermine the country's independent institutions are a big reason for this.

Malgovernance amid Greater Unity

A striking paradox of India is the incongruous relationship between democracy and governance, and the Modi government is exacerbating this. On the one hand, India is an awe-inspiring democracy, and the introduction in this volume highlighted why this is so. On the other hand, the haphazard and unaccountable governance signals dysfunction and abuse of power. Indeed, for millions of Indians, there appear to be two systems of governance in the country: one for those who are affluent or connected to the corridors of power, and another for those who are poor and marginalized. Often, politicians, judicial authorities, and the police collude to cover each other's criminal activity, which especially hampers India's poor from seeking justice. The situation is so rotten that in many instances the police simply refuse to take down a complaint if it happens to be against fellow police officers, politicians, or well-known individuals. Such dysfunction may be branded "political decay," which refers to a situation in which the individuals and institutions representing the state function in a corrupt, partial, and violent manner, whereby they jettison the norms, values, and practices that ensure liberal democracy, operate with impunity, engender anomie, and undermine citizens' confidence in the state.

This notwithstanding, the Indian union is more robust today than at any time in its past. For years after independence, many—especially in the country's south and east—identified more with their regional identities than an Indian identity. For instance, few southerners used to care about what transpired in Kashmir and instead focused on regional dominance by emphasizing their languages and cultures. The north-south divide in India can still resonate with racist overtones, but such occasional contestation takes place amid a sense of being Indian. Jawaharlal Nehru's willingness to accommodate regional demands is a major reason for this pan-Indian milieu. Hindi cinema also helped bridge the linguistic divide between and among regions, as has cricket, which is akin to a religion in India. The Indian cricket team hails from across the country and their camaraderie has helped advertise India's unity amid diversity.

The 1991 open market reforms not only expanded economic interaction with the rest of the world, but also led to increased trade among Indians and migration within states. This too has helped Indians cultivate a national consciousness even while taking pride in their regional identities. In recent times, the terror attacks that have originated mainly in Pakistan and targeted major Indian cities have further contributed to a sense of Indian solidarity, partly because Indian cities today are full of people from across the country, and they think of these adopted cities as their new homes.

In this regard, the 1999 Kargil crisis, which was India's first war featured live on television, further fostered pan-Indian solidarity (Verma 2002). Indeed, from a television standpoint, the Kargil War was to India what the Vietnam War was to the United States. The difference was that while the accounts from Vietnam beamed into US living rooms helped build opposition to the war, the accounts about troops from across India fighting and dying together to reclaim a portion of the country solidified Indian identity. The nationalist emotions that were unleashed following the June 2020 confrontation between Indian and Chinese troops in the Galwan Valley further evidenced this. Yet the identity politics that Hindutva manipulates stands to undermine such unity.

In India, the term "identity politics" refers to how groups mobilize to vote and make demands on the state along the lines of language, region, religion, and caste, with the latter two categories being most salient. The success of caste-based and regional parties is due to identity politics. This means that religion and caste will continue to play a major role in Indian politics amid the more stable governance emanating from the center. The rise of the Dalits and the lower castes has radically changed the electoral dynamics in India, because politicians have no choice but to take into consideration the preferences of people who vote in large numbers. It also represents a social revolution, if only because what we are now seeing is the upending of an all-encompassing social, political, and economic system that has held sway for more than 2,000 years—a social revolution that is rooted in particularistic politics even as it strengthens Indian identity.

Going forward, the northern-southern divide noted above stands to test this sense of Indian identity as politicians within the BJP who mainly represent northern states dictate the national agenda in ways unfavorable to southern states. For instance, higher literacy rates combined with successful family planning programs in the south saw the region register lower fertility rates, a development the national government sought. But lower population would lead to lower representation at the national level and also a smaller share of central government funding that is distributed based on state population figures. In order not to punish states that succeeded in lowering fertility rates, the Indian government has since 1976 used its 1971 population statistics for representation and funding allocations purposes. The Modi government, however, has decided to use the 2011 census statistics when allocating resources across states. It will also use the 2011 statistics for redistricting purposes in 2026, which will see the five southern states have fewer representatives and lower financial resources. As noted in Chapter 1, Prime Minister Nehru's tact and predilection to accommodate and compromise ended the Dravidian Movement that threatened southern secession over the Hindi language being made the national language (Hardgrave 1965). Prime Minister Modi, on the other hand, appears to associate compromise with weakness. He and the BJP, which does not enjoy much support in the south except in the state of Karnataka, may consequently end up unleashing a second Dravidian Movement that undermines Indian unity.

Security and Foreign Relations

Going forward, three types of security issues will affect India. The first pertains to terrorism. Some terrorist groups based in Pakistan not only want to see India-administered Kashmir divested from India, but also consider Hindus, Christians, and Jews to represent an anti-Islamic triumvirate. India's growing links with the United States and Israel have encouraged such thinking, and many of these groups' cadres have crossed into India and committed numerous terrorist acts in the past three decades. The November 2008 killings in Mumbai (that killed over 170 people over four days) and the February 2019 suicide attack in Pulwama in Jammu and Kashmir (that killed 40 soldiers) evidence how vulnerable India is to such cross-border terrorism. Poor intelligence-sharing among various central government and state agencies (a situation that also contributed to the attacks of September 11, 2001, on the United States), lax enforcement in security, and low morale stemming from internal divisions within the intelligence community have all contributed to India's vulnerability. Only a few Indian Muslims are hitherto implicated in such cross-border terrorism, but this could change unless the Indian state deals appropriately with the community's legitimate grievances.

Domestic terrorism in the form of separatist movements and Naxalite violence is a second security issue India faces. The country has dealt forcefully with separatist movements, but the guerrilla-style violence the Naxalites have waged over decades has destabilized large tracts of the country.

The communist revolution Karl Marx predicted required the working class to rise against the bourgeoisie, but Chinese leader Mao Zedong claimed peasants would do just as well. This notion of peasants creating revolution against the state is a fundamental feature of Maoism. India's Maoists are also called "Naxalites," the term stemming from a West Bengal village called Naxalbari where divisions within the Communist Party of India (Marxist) influenced an uprising against landlords in 1967. Naxalites (or Maoists) claim that India is ruled by the upper classes, who are merely interested in exploiting the lower classes, and that the state therefore needs to be overthrown.

The disregard with which successive Indian governments have treated India's peasants and tribal groups has contributed immensely to the Maoist movement. For often those accused of being Naxalites are also among India's poorest, living in areas without schools, few jobs, and little healthcare. These regions are among the most inaccessible and neglected, with around 300,000 villages in the so-called Red Corridor or Sickle Corridor having no road access. Feudalism and corruption are rampant, and law and order in these areas hardly exist, so that many among the police, military, and paramilitary forces operate with impunity by extorting, beating, raping, disappearing, and murdering civilians. Those killed are often conveniently branded Naxalites who had engaged the police in an "encounter." In India the term "encounter" typically refers to instances where the police assassinate someone in self-defense. Many are the encounters associated with Naxalites or Maoists, and the numerous bogus incidents have merely radicalized innocent peasants and prompted many to join with the Maoists.

Foreign relations will especially play a major role in determining India's security going forward. As noted, India today enjoys close military ties with the United States and most Western democracies, and a big reason for this is China's expanding influence throughout Asia and the globe. China's expanding tentacles in South Asia have especially roiled India. While the United States would like to see India play a more assertive role countering China, the latter's economy is five times that of India, so there are limits to what India can do to counter the Chinese in South Asia. This is amply clear when one considers Chinese investments in South Asian states vis-à-vis Indian investments.

India dislikes alliances and it has avoided drawing too close to Western powers in ways that would upset China. India-China tensions over the border, however, have recently escalated, and the deadly confrontation in June 2020 that killed twenty Indian soldiers (and an unknown number of Chinese soldiers) has especially rattled Indians. There is growing agreement in Indian circles that China cannot be trusted, and most Indian analysts now agree with US analysts that China is a revisionist power. For India, this means that China would gradually seek to take over contested territory even as it seeks to constrain India in its own South Asian neighborhood. These concerns appear to be drawing India closer to the United States. While India is unlikely to be part of an official alliance, it will likely end up being in a closer security relationship with the United States and other states (Japan, Australia, and France) that also harbor serious concerns over China's increasingly destabilizing geostrategic ambitions especially in the Indo-Pacific.

Whither Rising India?

India is most certainly on the rise, both domestically and globally, and it has caused hyper-enthusiastic Indians to get carried away and talk about India becoming a superpower. A country that is still a long way from providing its citizens basic services in education, health, sanitation, and the environment has no business pursuing such status. For instance, ten of the fifteen most polluted cities are in India (Bernard and

Kazmin 2018: 7) and Indians and foreigners were making decisions on when to avoid cities like New Delhi a long while before Covid-19 and its deadly links to pollution were clear. Nearly seventy-five years after achieving independence, around 270 million Indians live in poverty with about 25 percent of the country's population (over 325 million) illiterate—although at independence in 1947 only 15 percent of Indians were literate.

These figures related to poverty will be obsolete by the time India overcomes its Covid-19 crisis. So will all numbers noted in this volume associated with the coronavirus. As this book went to press in May 2021, New Delhi and other big cities in India were generating harrowing images of people lining up outside hospitals seeking treatment for the coronavirus. This as Indians were begging for oxygen to treat ailing relatives and cremating their dead on sidewalks and in backyards, since crematoria were unable to deal with the high number of Covid-19 victims. Prime Minister Narendra Modi and the BJP government were pilloried for being incompetent, with many claiming that Modi's arrogance, vanity, and authoritarianism failed to prepare the country to deal with a new Covid wave that epidemiologists had predicted. The excoriation is deserved, since Modi bragged about how India under his leadership had defeated the coronavirus and encouraged mass gatherings associated with state elections and religious festivals even as a new virus wave was evident. While the prime minister's popularity has been severely dented, he need not seek reelection until May 2024, by which time Modi may successfully rebrand himself. Irrespective of how Modi fares as a result of the Covid-19 debacle, there is no gainsaying that India's image is severely compromised. Indeed, the crises stemming from Covid-19 has starkly proved how behind India is in meeting citizens' basic needs.

The point is that it is not in India's interest or its postindependence ethos to aspire to superpower status. The country's main interest lies in pursuing a development trajectory that improves the living conditions of its teeming population even while ensuring its territorial integrity. India is likely to become a great power in a twenty-first-century multipolar world. How its political leaders deal with the country's economic, communal, and security challenges will especially determine whether and how soon it gets there.

Glossary

ahimsa nonviolence: Originating from the Jain sect, *ahimsa* was popularized in the twentieth century by Mohandas K. Gandhi.

antibiotic-resistant bacteria: Antibiotic-resistant bacteria are bacteria that are not controlled or killed by antibiotics. They are able to survive and even multiply in the presence of an antibiotic. Most infection-causing bacteria can become resistant to at least some antibiotics.

arya: "Noble," related to the ancient Aryan migrants into India.

ashvameda horse sacrifice: A Vedic ritual associated with increased settlement of the Aryan peoples in the Gangetic plains.

bhakti: Devotional practices associated with the veneration of a deity commonly associated with Hinduism.

carbon dioxide emissions: Carbon dioxide emissions are emissions stemming from the burning of fossil fuels and the manufacture of cement. They include carbon dioxide produced during consumption of solid, liquid, and gas fuels as well as gas flaring.

caste: A European term that refers generally to endogamous, occupational status groups who associated with a specific position in South Asian communities. A form of hierarchical social differentiation in South Asian communities.

communalism: Creation of exclusionary communities based on ethnicity or religion.

compressed natural gas: Methane stored at high pressure. It is a fuel that can be used in place of gasoline, diesel fuel, and liquefied petroleum gas. Combustion of compressed natural gas produces fewer undesirable gases than these other fuels. It is made by compressing natural gas, which is mainly composed of methane, to less than 1 percent of the volume it occupies at standard atmospheric pressure. It is stored and distributed in hard containers at a pressure of 20–25 megapascals (2,900–3,600 pounds per square inch), usually in cylindrical or spherical shapes.

Dalit: Literally "ground under," coined by B. R. Ambedkar to express the position of those in South Asian communities not associated with a caste. Known as Untouchables in the colonial period and renamed *harijan* ("beloved of god") by Mohandas K. Gandhi.

dasa: Slave.

Delhi sultanate: A political regime of North Central India, 1206–1526.

dharma: Duty.

dharma-chakra: Wheel of law associated with early Buddhism.

doctrine of lapse: A policy under which the East India Company assumed direct administrative control over territories in which "native" rulers were found either guilty of "misrule" or without an heir deemed legitimate by the company.

dowry: Property or money brought by a bride to her husband at the time of, and often as a condition of, marriage.

dvijas: "Twice born," referring to those of the first three *varnas* (Brahmin, Kshatriya, and Vaishya).

dyarchy: A division of responsibilities between central and provincial governments in which subjects including education, health, and agriculture were devolved to provincial bodies, in which Indians found greater participation after the Government of India Act of 1919. Responsibilities such as revenue and law enforcement were reserved responsibilities for the central government, overseen by the viceroy.

fly ash: A coal combustion product composed of the particulates driven out of coal-fired boilers together with the flue gases in electric power–generating plants.

gross domestic product: Total dollar value of all goods and services produced in a country.

gross national product: Total dollar value of all goods and services produced by a country's population within and outside its borders. The measure was used for US production between 1941 and 1991 until it was replaced by gross domestic product.

Gupta Empire: A political formation from 320 to about 497 C.E. associated with the emergence of bhakti.

harijan: "Beloved of God," Mohandas K. Gandhi's term for those previously known as Untouchables.

Hinduism: A term generally associated with bhakti practices. The term has no equivalent in any South Asian language, although the Persians used "Sindu" and Europeans in turn used the term as a descriptor of religious practices. In the nineteenth century, "native" communities began adopting the term *Hinduism*, hence its wide use today.

Hindutva: "Hinduness," typically advocated by extremist Hindu groups as part of an ideology that claims all Indians, irrespective of their religion, should subscribe to a Hindu ethos.

Islam: "Submission" (to God) in Arabic. Refers to the religion founded by the Prophet Muhammad.

Jain: An adherent of an ancient sect of renouncers associated from at least the sixth century B.C.E. with Mahavira. In addition to ascetisicm, Jains pursue nonviolence in their lives with dietary restrictions. In contemporary society, Jains are well known as bankers and merchants because these professions are regarded as nonviolent.

jajmani relations: Intercaste exchanges by which groups of different social status conducted services for each other in varied ways depending on where the services took place.

jati: The group (subcaste) one is born into and the one people identify with as part of their caste identity.

jharoka: Viewing of a king, used by the Mughal rulers.

jizya: A tax levied on non-Muslims in many Islamic polities, including the Mughal Empire.

joint family: An extended, usually cohabitaing family consisting of a husband and wife, their sons and daughters-in-law, their unmarried daughters, and surviving parents of the husband.

karma: The effects resulting from one's actions.

khadi: Homespun, homewoven cloth; associated especially with Gandhi's *swadeshi* movement—a boycott of goods manufactured in Britain with an emphasis on indigenous production.

khalsa: "The pure," the order instituted for Sikhs by their guru, Gobind Singh, about 1699, requiring its members to identify themselves to both friends and enemies as true Sikhs, devoted to the protection of the faith, by always having five symbols—leaving their beards and hair uncut, carrying a comb, wearing a sword, wearing a steel bracelet, and wearing knee-length shorts. Originally, the *khalsa* was a military group, under strict discipline.

Lok Sabha: House of the People, the popularly elected lower house of the Indian parliament.

maharajadhiraja: "King of kings" or "king upon kings."

Maratha Empire: An empire that challenged Mughal authority and dominated large stretches of the Indian subcontinent from 1674 with the coronation of Shivaji until the defeat of his successors by the British East India Company in 1818.

Mauryan Empire: The subcontinent's first empire associated with the spread of Buddhism, c. 300s to 185 B.C.E.

moksha: Release from the cycle of rebirth, associated with both Buddhism and Hinduism.

Mukti Bahini: Liberation Force, comprising East Pakistani guerrilla fighters whom India supported in the lead-up to the 1971 war with Pakistan that led to the creation of Bangladesh.

nabob: A European who adopted the lavish lifestyles of native local rulers, known as nawabs.

National Green Tribunal: A specialized body set up in 2010 for the effective and expeditious hearing of cases related to environmental protection and conservation of forests and other natural resources. The tribunal has five branches, in New Delhi (the principal bench), Bhopal, Pune, Kolkata, and Chennai.

Naxalites: Another term for Maoist forces in India that seek to overthrow the state.

Other Backward Classes: An open-ended category of affirmative action to accommodate those belonging to the Shudra *varna,* or lowest caste.

panchayat: Council of five village elders responsible for village governance.

panchayati raj: A three-tier model of local government instituted by the central government in 1959.

Partition: The division of British India into the independent states of India and Pakistan in 1947.

peri-urban: Peri-urban areas are the periphery zones of an urban center, the landscape interface between town and country, or the rural-urban transition zone.

peshwas: Brahman prime ministers within the Maratha Empire.

planetary boundary: In 2009, Johan Rockström led a group of twenty-eight internationally renowned scientists to identify the nine processes that regulate the stability and resilience of the Earth system. The scientists proposed quantitative planetary boundaries to mark the zone within which humanity can continue to develop and thrive for generations to come. Crossing these boundaries increases the risk of generating large-scale abrupt or irreversible environmental changes.

pollution control boards: The Central Pollution Control Board (CPCB) of India is a statutory organization under the Ministry of Environment, Forests, and Climate Change. It was established in 1974 under the Water Prevention and Control of pollution Act. The CPCB is also entrusted with the powers and functions under the Air Prevention and Control of Pollution Act of 1981. It coordinates the activities of the state pollution control boards by providing technical assistance and guidance and resolving disputes among them. The CPCB conducts environmental assessments and research and is responsible for maintaining national standards under a variety of environmental laws, in consultation with zonal offices, and tribal and local governments. It has responsibilities to conduct monitoring of water and air quality and maintains monitoring data. The CPCB and state boards work with industries and government in pollution prevention programs and energy conservation efforts.

public interest litigation: Litigation undertaken to secure the public interest and provide justice to socially or financially disadvantaged parties.

Rajya Sabha: Council of the States, the upper house of the Indian parliament, whose members are mostly elected by state legislatures, or Vidhan Sabhas.

reverse osmosis: A water purification process that uses a partially permeable membrane to remove ions, unwanted molecules, and larger particles from drinking water.

Rig Veda: The oldest text associated with the Vedic, or Aryan, peoples; later deemed as a source of Bhakti or Hindu practice.

Rowlatt Bills: A series of laws passed in 1919 that enabled the suspension of various civil liberties in peacetime, including the right to hold subjects without trial.

ryot: Farmer or laborer.

Sabha: A community, association, or organization.

sati: The practice of burning a widow on her husband's funeral pyre; outlawed in its territories by the East India Company in 1829.

satrap: A regional governor deployed by Greeks in India.

satyagraha: "Truth-force" or "soul-force."

Scheduled Castes: Term used to denote Dalits after the Indian constitution abolished untouchability.

sepoy: An Indian soldier.

sewage treatment plant: A sewage treatment plant removes contaminants from municipal and industrial wastewater. Physical, chemical, and biological processes are used to remove contaminants and produce treated wastewater that is safe enough for release into the environment or for reuse.

shuddhi: A movement aimed at reclaiming Hindus who had converted to Islam.

Sikh: An adherent of the religious community that originated with Nanak (1469–1539) in Punjab who preached a message of devotion to the divine name and of obedience to his teaching and his successors, known as gurus. Their followers became famous as warriors, farmers, and entrepreneurs.

soma: A drink consumed by Vedic society, likely a form of mushroom.

Sufi: A Muslim mystic.

swaraj: Self-rule.

Swatchh Bharat Abhiyan: Clean India Campaign, a country-wide campaign initiated by the government of India in 2014 to eliminate open defecation and improve solid waste management.

thugi: A criminal.

triple talaq: A formal repudiation of a wife, which when repeated three times results in divorce in Islamic societies.

ulema: Muslim community of scholars.

Untouchables: A European colonial term previously used for those in South Asia who were not associated with a particular *varna.* Today "Untouchable" has been replaced with "Dalit."

varnas: "Colors" in Sanskrit, which over time morphed into a system of social stratification associated with caste.

Vedas: The most ancient and most sacred collection of the religious texts regarded as of fundamental truth. In its narrower sense, the term *Vedas* refers to the four collections, some of which may date from 1800 B.C.E., the Rig Veda, Sama Veda, Yajur Veda, and Atharva Veda, but the term *Vedic literature* is used for an immense body of writings that trace their origin to one of these texts.

zamindar: A landholder or landlord.

References

Abraham, Itty. 2008. "From Bandung to NAM: Non-Alignment and India's Foreign Policy, 1947–65." *Commonwealth and Comparative Politics* 46, no. 2: 195–219.

Adam, Hans Nicolai, Lyla Mehta, and Shilpi Srivasta. 2018. "Uncertainty in Climate Science Extreme Weather Events in India." *Economic and Political Weekly* 53, no. 31 (August 4): 16–18.

Adeney, Katharine. 2007. *Federalism and Ethnic Conflict Regulation in India and Pakistan.* New York: Palgrave Macmillan.

Agnes, Flavia. 2001. *Judgement Call: An Insight into Muslim Women's Right to Maintenance.* Mumbai: Majlis.

Ahluwalia, Montek Singh. 2020. *Backstage: The Story Behind India's High Growth Years.* New Delhi: Rupa Publications India Pvt.

Ahmed, Rafiuddin. 1991. "Islamic Fundamentalism in South Asia." In *Fundamentalisms Observed,* Martin E. Marty and R. Scott Appleby, eds. Chicago: University of Chicago Press.

Aiyar, Mani Shankar. 2004. *Confessions of a Secular Fundamentalist.* New Delhi: Viking.

Aldrich, John W. 1995. *Why Parties? The Origin and Transformation of Political Parties in America.* Chicago: University of Chicago Press.

Alexander, Padinjarethakal Cherian. 1978. *Report of the Committee on Import-Export Policies and Procedures.* New Delhi: Ministry of Commerce.

Alkire, Sabina, and Suman Seth. 2008. "Measuring Multidimensional Poverty in India: A New Proposal." OPHI Working Paper no. 15. Oxford: University of Oxford Press.

———. 2015. "Multidimensional Poverty Reduction in India Between 1999 and 2006: Where and How?" *World Development* 72: 93–108.

Alley, Kelly D. 2002. *On the Banks of the Ganga: When Wastewater Meets a Sacred River.* Ann Arbor: University of Michigan Press.

———. 2009. "Legal Activism and River Pollution in India." *Georgetown International Environmental Law Review* 21: 793–819.

———. 2012. "Water Wealth and Energy in the Indian Himalayas." *Silk Road* 10: 136–145.

———. 2014. "The Developments, Policies and Assessments of Hydropower in the Ganga River Basin." In *Our National River Ganga: Lifeline of Millions*, Rashmi Sanghi, ed. Cham, Switzerland: Springer.

———. 2015. "Rejuvenating the Ganga." *Global Water Forum,* July 13.

———. 2016. "Governance, Connectivity, and Knowledge Transparency in the Brahmaputra Basin." In *Heading East: Security, Trade, and Environment Between India and Southeast Asia,* K. Farrell and S. Ganguly, eds. Delhi: Oxford University Press.

———. 2017. "Modes of Governance in India's Hydropower Development." *WIREs Water* 4: e1198.

Alley, Kelly D., Jennifer Barr, and Tarini Mehta. 2018. "Infrastructure Disarray in the Clean Ganga and Clean India Campaigns." *WIREs Water* 5: e1310.

Alley, K. D., N. Maurya, and S. Das. 2018. "Parameters of Successful Wastewater Reuse in Urban India." *Indian Politics and Policy* 1, no. 2: 91–122.

Altstedter, Ari. 2018. "The Startups Waging War Against Superbugs." *Bloomberg,* June 25.

Amarasinghe, Upali, Tushaar Shah, Hugh Turral, and B. K. Anand. 2007. "India's Water Future to 2025–2050: Business-as-Usual Scenario and Deviations." Research Report no. 123. Colombo: International Water Management Institute.

Amirante, Domenico. 2012. "Environmental Courts in Comparative Perspective: Preliminary Reflections on the National Green Tribunal of India." *Pace Environmental Law Review* 29, no. 2 (Winter): 441–469.

Anand, Geeta. 2006 and 2012. "Sabarimala Controversy: Women Lawyers Move Supreme Court." *The Hindu,* July 31 and March 22.

———. 2016. "Forging a Path for Women Deep into India's Sacred Shrines." *New York Times,* April 29.

Anand, Nikhil. 2017. *Hydraulic City: Water and the Infrastructures of Citizenship in Mumbai.* Durham: Duke University Press.

Andersen, Walter K., and Shridhar D. Damle. 2018. *The RSS: A View to the Inside.* Haryana: Penguin Random House.

Asher, Catherine B., and Cynthia Talbot. 2006. *India Before Europe.* Cambridge: Cambridge University Press.

Athreya, M. B. 1996. "India's Telecommunications Policy." *Telecommunications Policy* 20, no. 1: 11–17.

Athreya, Venkatesh B., R. Rukmani, R. V. Bhavani, G. Anuradha, R. Gopinath, and A. Sakthi Velan. 2010. *Report on the State of Food Insecurity in Urban India.* Chennai: M. S. Swaminathan Foundation.

Austin, Granville. 1999 [1966]. *The Indian Constitution: Cornerstone of a Nation.* New Delhi: Oxford University Press.

Avari, Burjor. 2007. *India: The Ancient Past.* London: Routledge.

Babb, Lawrence E. 1986. *Redemptive Encounters: Three Modern Styles in the Hindu Tradition.* Delhi: Oxford University Press.

Bahal, Ambika. 2015. "Championing Indian Women Who Want to Work." *Forbes,* December 28. https://www.forbes.com/sites/abehal/2015/12/28/championing-indian-women-who-want-to-work/#6753f8571f81.

Bajpai, Kanti, P. R. Chari, Pervaiz Iqbal Cheema, Stephen P. Cohen, and Sumit Ganguly. 1997. *Brasstacks and Beyond: Perception and the Management of Crisis in South Asia.* New Delhi: Manohar.

Bandyopadhyay, D. 2003. "Land Reforms and Agriculture: The West Bengal Experience." *Economic and Political Weekly* 38, no. 9: 879–884.

Bardhan, Pranab. 1984. *The Political Economy of Development in India.* Oxford: Oxford University Press.

Bartolini, Stefano, and Peter Mair. 1990. *Identity, Competition, and Electoral Availability: The Stabilisation of European Electorates, 1885–1985.* Cambridge: Cambridge University Press.

Barua, Anamika, Vishal Narain, and Sumit Vij. 2018. *Climate Change Governance and Adaptation: Case Studies from South Asia.* Boca Raton: CRC Press.

Basham, A. L. 1954. *The Wonder That Was India.* New Delhi: Rupa.

Basu, Aparna, and Bharati Ray. 1990. *Women's Struggle: A History of the All India Women's Conference, 1927–2002.* Delhi: Manmohar.

Basu, Asmita. 2008. "Legislation on Domestic Violence." *Seminar* 583 (March): http://www.india-seminar.com/semframe.html.

Basu, S. 2015. "Bengaluru Water Utility to Launch Door-to-Door Drive to Check Illegal Borewells." *Down to Earth,* July 4.

Bauman, Chad. 2010. "Identity, Conversion, and Violence: Dalits, Adivasis, and the 2007–08 Riots in Orissa." In *Margins of Faith: Dalit and Tribal Christianity in India,* R. Robinson and J. M. Kujur, eds. Washington, DC: Sage.

Baviskar, Amit, and Arjun Singh. 2008. "Malignant Growth: The Sardar Sarovar Dam and Its Impact on Public Health." *Environmental Impact Assessment Review* 14, nos. 5–6: 349–358.

Bayly, S. 1999. "Caste, Society, and Politics in India from the Eighteenth Century to the Modern Age." In *The New Cambridge History of India,* vol. 4. Cambridge: Cambridge University Press.

BBC News. 2019. "Sabarimala: Indian Women Make History by Entering Temple." *BBC News,* January 2. https://www.bbc.com/news/world-asia-india-46733750.

Beg, M. A., S. Pandey, and S. Kare. 2019. "Post-Poll Survey: Why Uttar Pradesh's Mahagathbandhan Failed." *The Hindu,* May 26. https://www.thehindu.com/elections/lok-sabha-2019/post-poll-survey-why-uttar-pradeshs-mahagathbandhan-failed/article27249310.ece.

Beinecke, Frances. 2017. "Truth to Power? India's Renewable Energy Boom." *NRDC Blog.* August 3, 2017. https://www.nrdc.org/experts/frances-beinecke/truth-power-indias-renewable-energy-boom.

Berenschot, Ward. 2011. *Riot Politics: Hindu-Muslim Violence and the Indian State.* New York: Columbia University Press.

Bernard, Steven, and Amy Kazmin. 2018. "The Most Polluted Place on Earth." *Financial Times,* December 12.

Bhaduri, Amit, and Deepak Nayyar. 1996. *The Intelligent Person's Guide to Liberalization.* New Delhi: Penguin.

Bhagwati, Jagdish, and Padma Desai. 1970. *India: Planning for Industrialization.* London: Oxford University Press.

Bharee, Megha. 2006. "The World's Most Powerful Women: India's Most Powerful Businesswomen." *Forbes,* September 1. http://www.forbes.com/2006/08/30/power-women-india.

Bhargava, Rajeev, ed. 1998. *Secularism and Its Critics.* New Delhi: Oxford University Press.

Bharucha, S. P. 1998. "Golden Jubilee Year of the Constitution of India and Fundamental Rights." In *Supreme Court on Public Interest Litigation,* vol. 7, J. Kapur, ed. New Delhi: LIPS.

Bhatt, Ela. 2006. *We Are Poor but So Many: The Story of Self-Employed Women in India.* Oxford: Oxford University Press.

Bhattacharya, Sabyasachi, ed. 2007. *Rethinking 1857.* Hyderabad: Orient Longman.

Bhattacharyya, Debjani. 2019. "Land Acquisition and Dispossession in India." *Oxford Research Encyclopedia of Asian History,* May 23. https://oxfordre.com/view/10.1093/acrefore/9780190277727.001.0001/acrefore-9780190277727-e-189.

Bhuwania, Anuj. 2017. *Courting the People: Public Interest Litigation in Post-Emergency India.* Cambridge: Cambridge University Press.

Bille, Lars. 2001. "Democratizing a Democratic Procedure: Myth of Reality?" *Party Politics* 7, no. 3: 363–380.

Biswas, D., and P. Jamwal. 2017. "Swachh Bharat Mission: Groundwater Contamination in Peri-Urban India." *Economic & Political Weekly* 52, no. 20: 18–20.

Bjorkman, James Warner. 1980. "Public Law 480 and the Policies of Self-Help and Short-Tether: Indo-American Relations, 1965–68." In *The Regional Imperative: The Administration of U.S. Foreign Policy Towards South Asian States Under Presidents Johnson and Nixon,* Lloyd I. Rudolph and Susanne H. Rudolph, eds. Atlantic Highlands, NJ: Humanities Press.

Bjorkman, Lisa. 2015. *Pipe Politics. Contested Water: Embedded Infrastructures of Millennial Mumbai.* Durham: Duke University Press.

Bloom, David E., and Karen N. Eggleston. 2014. "The Economic Implications of Population Ageing in China and India: Introduction to the Special Issue." *Journal of the Economics of Ageing* 4: 1–7.

Bose, Sugata, and Ayesha Jalal. 1997. *Modern South Asia: History, Culture, Political Economy.* London: Routledge.

Bose, Sumantra. 2003. *Kashmir: Roots of Conflict, Paths to Peace.* Cambridge: Harvard University Press.

Brass, Paul R. 2003. *The Production of Hindu-Muslim Violence in Contemporary India.* Seattle: University of Washington Press.

British Petroleum. 2018. *BP Energy Outlook: Country and Regional Insights–India.* http://cdn.ceo.ca.s3-us-west-2.amazonaws.com/1e33chg-bp-energy-outlook-2018-country-insight-india.pdf.

Brown, Judith. 1989. *Gandhi: Prisoner of Hope.* New Haven: Yale University Press.

Buch, Nirmala. 2009. "Reservations for Women in Panchayats: A Sop in Disguise?" *Economic and Political Weekly* 44, no. 40 (October): 8–10.

Burgess, Robin, and Timothy Besley. 2000. "Land Reform, Poverty Reduction, and Growth: Evidence from India." *Quarterly Journal of Economics* 115, no. 2: 389–343.

Bush, Kathleen F., et al. 2011. "Impacts of Climate Change on Public Health in India: Future Research Directions." *Environmental Health Perspectives* 119, no. 6 (June): 765–770.

Capoccia, Giovanni, and R. Daniel Kelemen. 2007. "The Study of Critical Junctures: Theory, Narrative, and Counterfactuals in Historical Institutionalism." *World Politics* 59, no. 3: 341–369.

Carleton, Tamma A. 2017. "Crop-Damaging Temperatures Increase Suicide Rates in India." *Proceedings of the National Academy of Sciences of the United States of America* 114, no. 33: 8746–8751.

Carroll, Lucy, ed. 1988. *Shah Bano and the Muslim Women Act a Decade On: The Right of Divorced Muslim Women to Mataa*. Bombay: Women's Research Action Group.

Center for Developing Societies (CSDS). 2009. "How India Voted: Verdict 2009." *The Hindu* (Chennai), May 26. http://www.hindu.com/2009/05/26 /stories/2009052688880100.htm.

Central Intelligence Agency (CIA). 2019. *World Fact Book: India*. http://www.cia.gov/library/publications/the-world-factbook/geos/in.html.

Chakravarti, Uma. 2005. *Rewriting History: The Life and Times of Pandita Ramabai*. New Delhi: Kali for Women.

Chang, Jen-Hu. 1967. "The Indian Summer Monsoon." *Geographical Review* 57, no. 3: 373–396.

Chatterjee, Partha. 1993. *The Nation and Its Fragments*. Princeton: Princeton University Press.

———. 2004. *The Politics of the Governed: Reflections on Popular Politics in Most of the World*. New York: Columbia University Press.

Chen, Chi, et al. 2019. "China and India Lead in Greening of the World Through Land-Use Management." *Nature Sustainability* 2: 122–129.

Chhibber, Pradeep, and Ken Kollman. 1998. "Party Aggregation and the Number of Parties in India and the United States." *American Political Science Review* 92: 329–342.

———. 2004. *The Formation of National Party Systems: Federalism and Party Competition in Canada, Great Britain, India, and the United States*. Princeton: Princeton University Press.

Chhibber, Pradeep, and Geetha Murali. 2007. "Duvergerian Dynamics in Indian States." *Party Politics* 12, no. 1: 5–34.

Chhibber, Pradeep, and Rahul Verma. 2019. "The Rise of the Second Dominant Party System in India: BJP's New Social Coalition in 2019." *Studies in Indian Politics* 7, no. 2 (December): 131–148.

Chowdhary, Rekha. 2016. *Jammu and Kashmir: Politics of Identity and Separatism*. New York: Routledge.

Coffey, Diane, and Dean Spears. 2017. *Where India Goes: Abandoned Toilets, Stunted Development, and the Costs of Caste*. Delhi: HarperCollins India.

Cohen, Benjamin B. 2019. *An Appeal to the Ladies of Hyderabad: Scandal in the Raj*. Cambridge: Harvard University Press.

Cohen, Stephen P. 2001. *India: Emerging Power*. Washington, DC: Brookings Institution.

Cohn, Bernard S. 1996. *Colonialism and Its Forms of Knowledge: The British in India*. Princeton: Princeton University Press.

Community Forest Rights—Learning and Advocacy (CFR-LA). 2016. "Promise and Performance: Ten Years of the Forest Rights Act in India—Citizens' Report on Promise and Performance of the Scheduled Tribes and Other Traditional Forest Dwellers (Recognition of Forest Rights) Act, 2006, After 10 Years of Its Enactment." https://rightsandresources.org/wp-content/uploads/2017/11/India-Promise-and-Performance-National-Report_CFRLA_2016.pdf.

Corbridge, Stuart, and John Harriss. 2000. *Reinventing India: Liberalisation, Hindu Nationalism, and Popular Democracy.* Delhi: Oxford University Press.

Credit Suisse. 2018. *Global Wealth Report.* Zurich.

Cross, J. 2016. "Off the Grid: Infrastructure and Energy Beyond the Mains." In *Infrastructures and Social Complexity: A Companion,* P. Harvey, C. Bruun Jensen, and A. Morita, eds. New York: Routledge.

Dagli, Vadilal. 1979. *Report of the Committee on Controls and Subsidies.* New Delhi: Ministry of Finance.

Dahl, Robert A. 1998. *On Democracy.* New Haven: Yale University Press.

Dasgupta, Chandrasekhar. 2001. *War and Diplomacy in Kashmir, 1947–48.* New Delhi: Sage.

Dasgupta, Partha. 1993. *An Inquiry into Well-Being and Destitution.* Oxford: Clarendon.

Deaton, Angus, and Valerie Kozel. 2005. "Data and Dogma: The Great Indian Poverty Debate." *World Bank Research Observer* 20: 177–199.

Dev, S. Mahendra. 2010. *Inclusive Growth in India Agriculture, Poverty, and Human Development.* New Delhi: Oxford University Press.

Deviah, M. A. 2016. "Here's Why Women Are Barred from Sabarimala: It Is Not Because They Are 'Unclean.'" *Firstpost,* January 15. https://www.firstpost.com/india/why-women-are-barred-from-sabarimala-its-not-because-they-are-unclean-2583694.html.

DeVotta, Neil. 2012. "Kashmir." In *The Oxford Companion to American Politics,* vol. 2, David Coates, ed. Oxford: Oxford University Press.

———. 2019. "Secularism and the Islamophobia Zeitgeist in India and Sri Lanka." Washington, DC: Middle East Institute, November 20.

Dhar, Prithvi Nath. 2003. *Evolution of Economic Policy in India: Selected Essays.* New Delhi: Oxford University Press.

Dharmadhikary, Shripad. 2013. "Full Report of MoEF's Committee to Review Environmental Laws Confirms Initial Apprehensions: Recipe for Dilution of Environmental Protection Regime." *Manthan Blog,* December 12. http://shripadmanthan.blogspot.com/2014/12/full-report-of-moefs-committee-to.html.

Dhillon, Amrit. 2016. "Will India Open Its Temples and Mosques to Menstruating Women?" *The Guardian,* January 13.

Diamond, Larry. 2019. *Ill Winds: Saving Democracy from Russian Rage, Chinese Ambition, and American Complacency.* New York: Penguin.

"Dirty Work." 2018. *The Economist,* December 8.

Dixon, Annette. 2018. "Women in India's Economic Growth." Paper presented at the Economic Times Women's Forum, Mumbai, March 17. https://www.worldbank.org/en/news/speech/2018/03/17/women-indias-economic-growth.

Dobhal, D. P., Anil K. Gupta, Manish Mehta, and D. D. Khandelwal. 2013. "Kedarnath Disaster: Fact and Plausible Causes." *Current Science* 105, no. 2: 171–174.

Donaldson, Robert. 1974. *Soviet Policy Toward India: Ideology and Strategy.* Cambridge: Harvard University Press.

Doniger, Wendy. 2009. *The Hindus: An Alternative History.* New York: Penguin.

Drew, Georgina. 2017. *River Dialogues: Hindu Faith and the Political Ecology of Dams on the Sacred Ganga.* Tucson: University of Arizona Press.

Dreze, Jean, and Amartya K. Sen. 2002. *India: Development and Participation.* New Delhi: Oxford University Press.

D'Souza, Renita. 2019. "Housing Poverty in Urban India: The Failures of Past and Current Strategies and the Need for a New Blueprint." Occasional Paper no. 187. New Delhi: Observer Research Foundation.

Dubey, S. N., and Usha Mathur. 1972. "Welfare Programmes for Scheduled Castes: Content and Administration." *Economic and Political Weekly* 7, no. 4 (January): 165–176.

Dumont, Louis. 1966. *Homo Hierarchicus.* Paris: Gallimard.

Dupont, Véronique, and N. Sridharan, eds. 2007. *Peri-Urban Dynamics: Case Studies in Chennai, Hyderabad, and Mumbai.* New Delhi: French Research Institutes of India.

Duverger, Maurice. 1963. *Political Parties: Their Organisation and Activity in the Modern State.* New York: Wiley.

Eaton, Richard. 1993. *The Rise of Islam and the Bengal Frontier.* Berkeley: University of California Press.

Eaton, Richard, and Philip Wagoner. 2017. *Power, Memory, Architecture: Contested Sites on India's Deccan Plateau.* Oxford: Oxford University Press.

Elwin, Verrier. 1961. *Nagaland.* Shillong: Adviser Secretariat.

Embree, Ainslie T. 1992. "Christianity and the State in Victorian India." In *Religion and Irreligion in Victorian Society,* R. W. Davis and R. J. Helmstadter, eds. London: Routledge.

———. 1994. "The Function of the Rashtriya Swayamsevak Sangh: To Define the Hindu Nation." In *Accounting for Fundamentalisms,* Martin E. Marty and R. Scott Appleby, eds. Chicago: University of Chicago Press.

Engineer, Asghar Ali. 1987. *Shah Bano Controversy.* Bombay: Sangam.

Epstein, Leon D. 1986. *Political Parties in the American Mold.* Madison: University of Wisconsin Press.

Evans, Peter. 1995. *Embedded Autonomy: States and Industrial Transformation.* Princeton: Princeton University Press.

Farooqui, Adnan, and E. Sridharan. 2014. "Incumbency, Internal Processes, and Renomination in Indian Parties." *Commonwealth and Comparative Politics* 52, no. 1: 78–108.

Farrell, Karen Stoll, and Sumit Ganguly. 2016. *Heading East: Security, Trade, and the Environment Between India and Southeast Asia.* New Delhi: Oxford University Press.

Fernandes, Leela. 2004. "The Politics of Forgetting: Class Politics, State Power, and the Restructuring of Urban Space in India." *Urban Studies* 41, no. 12: 2415–2430.

Finnemore, Martha, and Kathryn Sikkink. 1998. "International Norm Dynamics and Political Change." *International Organization* 52, no. 4: 887–917.

Fisher, Michael H. 2015. *A Short History of the Mughal Empire.* London: I. B. Tauris.

Forbes, Geraldine. 1996. *Women in Modern India.* Cambridge: Cambridge University Press.

Forest Survey of India. 2017. "State of Forest Report 2017." Dehradun: Ministry of Environment, Forests, and Climate Change.

Frankel, Francine. 1989. "Caste, Land, and Dominance in Bihar: Breakdown of the Brahmanical Social Order." In *Dominance and State Power in Modern India: Decline of a Social Order,* vol. 1, Francine R. Frankel and M. S. A. Roa, eds. Oxford: Oxford University Press.

———. 2005. *India's Political Economy, 1947–2004: The Gradual Revolution.* New Delhi: Oxford University Press.

Gadgil, Madhav, and Ramachandra Guha. 1995. *Ecology and Equity: The Use and Abuse of Nature in Contemporary India.* London: Routledge.

———. 1992. *This Fissured Land: An Ecological History of India.* New Delhi: Oxford University Press.

Galanter, Marc. 1979. "Compensatory Discrimination in Political Representation: A Preliminary Assessment of India's Thirty-Year Experience with Reserved Seats in Legislatures." *Economic and Political Weekly* 14, nos. 7–8 (February): 437–454.

———. 1991 [1984]. *Competing Equalities: Law and the Backward Classes in India.* Delhi: Oxford University Press.

Gandhi, M. K. 1997. *Hind Swaraj and Other Writings.* Anthony J. Parel, ed. Cambridge: Cambridge University Press.

"Ganesh Singh's Statement in Parliament." 2019. *Outlook,* December 30.

Ganguly, Sumit. 1991. "From the Defense of the Nation to Aid to the Civil: The Army in Contemporary India." *Journal of Asian and African Studies* 26, nos. 1–2: 11–26.

———. 1997. *The Crisis in Kashmir: Portents of War, Hopes of Peace.* Cambridge: Cambridge University Press.

———. 1999. "India's Pathway to Pokhran II: The Sources and Prospects of India's Nuclear Weapons Program." *International Security* 23, no. 4 (Spring): 148–177.

———. 2001. *Conflict Unending: India-Pakistan Tensions Since 1947.* New York: Columbia University Press.

———. 2017. "The Doklam Dispute in Context." *Foreign Affairs,* August 9.

———. 2019. "Why the India-Pakistan Crisis Isn't Likely to Turn Nuclear." *Foreign Affairs,* March 5.

———. 2020. "An Illiberal India." *Journal of Democracy* 31, no. 1 (January): 193–202.

Ganguly, Sumit, and Dinshaw Mistry. 2006. "The Indo-US Nuclear Accord: A Good Deal." *Current History* no. 105: 375–378.

Ganguly, Sumit, and Rahul Mukherji. 2011. *India Since 1980.* New Delhi: Cambridge University Press.

Garver, John. 2006. "China's Decision for War with India in 1962." In *New Directions in the Study of China's Foreign Policy,* Alastair Ian Johnson and Robert S. Ross, eds. Palo Alto: Stanford University Press.

Geertz, Clifford. 1973. *The Interpretation of Cultures.* New York: Basic.

Ghosh, Jayati, C. P. Chandrasekhar, and Prabhat Patnaik. 2017. *Demonetisation Decoded: A Critique of India's Currency Experiment.* New Delhi: Routledge.

Ghosh, Nilanjan, Jayanta Bandyopadhyay, and Jaya Thakur. 2018. *Conflict over Cauvery Waters: Imperatives for Innovative Policy Options.* Delhi: Observer Research Foundation.

Gill, Gitanjali Nain. 2017. *Environmental Justice in India: The National Green Tribunal.* Abingdon, Oxon: Routledge.

———. 2018. "Mapping the Power Struggles of the National Green Tribunal of India: The Rise and Fall?" *Asian Journal of Law and Society* 7, no. 1: 1–42.

Gilmour, David. 2005. *The Ruling Caste: Imperial Lives in the Victorian Raj.* New York: Farrar, Straus, and Giroux.

Goldman, Michael, and Devika Narayan. 2019. "Water Crisis Through the Analytic of Urban Transformation: An Analysis of Bangalore's Hydrosocial Regimes." *Water International* 44, no. 2: 95–114.

Goldman, Russell. 2020. "India-China Border Dispute: A Conflict Explained." *New York Times,* June 17.

Goldstone, Jack A. 1991. *Revolution and Rebellion in the Early Modern World.* Berkeley: University of California Press.

Gooptu, Nandini. 2009. "Neoliberal Subjectivity, Enterprise Culture, and New Workplaces: Organised Retail and Shopping Malls in India." *Economic and Political Weekly* 44, no. 22: 45–54.

Gopal, S., ed. 1991. *Anatomy of a Confrontation: The Babri Masjid–Ramjan-mabhumi Issue.* Delhi: Penguin.

Gould, Harold. 1987. *The Hindu Caste System: The Sacralization of a Social Order.* Vol. 1. Delhi: Chanakya.

Government of India. 2016–2017. Union Budget Economic Survey. New Delhi: Ministry of Finance. https://www.indiabudget.gov.in/budget2017-2018 /survey.asp.

———. 2019a. "Parliament of India, Lok Sabha." http://164.100.47.194 /loksabha/members/women.aspx.

———. 2019b. Union Budget and Economic Survey, 2018–2019. New Delhi: Ministry of Finance. https://www.indiabudget.gov.in/budgetspeech.php.

Gowda, M., V. Rajeev, and E. Sridharan. 2007. "Parties and the Party System, 1947–2006." In *The State of India's Democracy,* Sumit Ganguly, Larry Diamond and Marc Plattner, eds. Baltimore: Johns Hopkins University Press.

Grofman, Bernard, and Arend Lijphart. 1986. *Electoral Laws and Their Political Consequences.* New York: Agathon.

Grumbine, R. E., and M. K. Pandit. 2013. "Threats from India's Himalaya Dams." *Science* 339, no. 6115: 36–37.

Guha, Ramachandra. 1983. "Forestry in British and Post-British India: A Historical Analysis." *Economic and Political Weekly* 18, no. 45–46: 1940–1947.

———. 1996. "Dietrich Brandis and Indian Forestry: A Vision Revisited and Reaffirmed." In *Village Voices, Forest Choices: Joint Forest Management in India,* Mark Poffenberger and Betsy McGean, eds. Delhi: Oxford University Press.

———. 2007a. "Adivasis, Naxalites, and Indian Democracy." *Economic and Political Weekly* 42, no. 32 (August): 3305–3312.

———. 2007b. *India After Gandhi: The History of the World's Largest Democracy.* London: Macmillan.

Gupta, Akhil. 2015. "An Anthropology of Electricity from the Global South." *Cultural Anthropology* 30, no. 4: 555–568.

Gupta, Charu. 2018. "Allegories of 'Love *Jihad*' and *Ghar Wapsi:* Interlocking the Socio-Religious with the Political." In *Rise of Saffron Power: Reflections on Indian Politics,* Mujibur Rehman, ed. New York: Routledge.

Habib, Irfan. 2015. *Man and Environment: The Ecological History of India.* New Delhi: Tulika Books.

Hall, Peter A. 1993. "Policy Paradigms, Social Learning, and the State: The Case of Economic Policymaking in Britain." *Comparative Politics* 25, no. 3: 275–296.

Hanson, A. H. 1966. *The Process of Planning.* London: Oxford University Press.

Hardgrave, Robert L. 1965. *The Dravidian Movement.* Bombay: Popular Prakashan.

———. 2005. "Hindu Nationalism and the BJP: Transforming Religion and Politics in India." In *Prospects for Peace in South Asia,* Rafiq Dossani and Henry S. Rowen, eds. Stanford: Stanford University Press.

Harrison, Selig S. 1960. *India: The Most Dangerous Decades.* Princeton: Princeton University Press.

Harriss-White, Barbara. 2003. *India Working: Essays on Society and Economy.* New York: Cambridge University Press.

Hasan, Zoya. 1993. "Communalism, State Policy, and the Question of Women's Rights in Contemporary India." *Bulletin of Concerned Scholars* 25, no. 4 (October–December): 5–15.

———. 1999. "Gender Politics, Legal Reform, and the Muslim Community in India." In *Resisting the Sacred and the Secular: Women's Activism and Politicized Religion in South Asia,* Patricia Jeffrey and Amrita Basu, eds. New Delhi: Kali for Women.

———. 2018. "Collapse of the Congress Party." In *Rise of Saffron Power: Reflections on Indian Politics,* Mujibur Rehman, ed. New York: Routledge.

Hawley, John Stratton. 1991. "Naming Hinduism." *Wilson Quarterly* (Summer): 20–34.

Hawley, John Stratton, and Mark Juergensmeyer, trans. 1988. *Songs of the Saints of India.* New York: Oxford University Press.

Herring, Ronald J. 1999. "Embedded Particularism: India's Failed Developmental State." In *The Developmental State,* Meredith Woo-Cummings, ed. Ithaca: Cornell University Press.

Hill, Douglas P. 2013. "Trans-Boundary Water Resources and Uneven Development: Crisis Within and Beyond Contemporary India." *South Asia: Journal of South Asian Studies* 36, no. 2: 243–257.

———. 2016. "Approaching Contemporary India: The Politics of Scale, Space, and Aspiration in the Time of Modi." In *Globalisation and the Challenges of Development in Contemporary India,* S. Venkateswar and S. Bandyopadhyay, eds. Singapore: Springer.

Hill, Douglas P., and Adrian Athique. 2013. "Multiplexes, Corporatised Leisure, and the Geography of Opportunity in India." *InterAsia Cultural Studies* 14, no. 4: 600–614.

Hills, Suzannah. 2013. "Judge Bars Delhi Gang Rape Defendants from Chaotic Courtroom After 150 People Cram Into Space Meant for 30." *Daily Mail*, January 7.

Himanshu. 2015. "Inequality in India." *Seminar* 672: 30–35.

———. 2019. *Inequality in India: A Review of Levels and Trends*. WIDER Working Paper no. 2019/42. Helsinki: United Nations University Press.

"How Vulnerable Are We? Mapping Climate Change in India." 2019. *Down to Earth*, August 16. https://www.downtoearth.org.in/factsheet/how-vulnerable -are-we-mapping-climate-change-in-india-66191.

Husain, S. Abid. 1965. *The Destiny of Indian Muslims*. Bombay: Asia Publishing House.

Hussain, Abid. 1984. *Report of the Committee on Trade Policy*. New Delhi: Ministry of Commerce.

India Briefing. 2018. "India's Solar and Wind Power Industries: Scope for Investors." March 15. https://www.india-briefing.com/news/india-solar -wind-industry-scope-investors-16346.html.

Indu, Bharti. 1992. "Bihar's Bane: Slow Progress on Land Reforms." *Economic and Political Weekly* 27, no. 13: 628–630.

International Monetary Fund. 2018. "World Economic Outlook October 2018: Report for Selected Countries and Subjects." https://www.imf.org/external /pubs/ft/weo/2019/01/weodata/weorept.aspx?pr.x=87&pr.y=17&sy=2013& ey=2023&scsm=1&ssd=1&sort=country&ds=.&br=1&c=924%2C534&s =NGDP_RPCH&grp=0&a=.

Iyer, Ramaswamy. 2003. *Water: Perspectives, Issues, Concerns*. Delhi: Sage.

Jackson, Peter. 1999. *The Delhi Sultanate: A Political and Military History*. Cambridge: Cambridge University Press.

Jaffrelot, Christophe. 2003. *India's Silent Revolution: The Rise of the Lower Castes in North Indian Politics*. New York: Columbia University Press.

———. 2015a. "The Class Element in the 2014 Indian Election and the BJP's Success with Special Reference to the Hindi Belt." *Understanding India's 2014 Elections: Studies in Indian Politics* 3, no. 1: 19–38.

———. 2015b. "What 'Gujarat Model'? Growth Without Development—and with Socio-Political Polarisation." *South Asia: Journal of South Asian Studies* 38, no. 4: 820–838.

———. 2019a. "Class and Caste in the 2019 Indian Election: Why Have So Many Poor Have Started Voting for Modi?" *Studies in Indian Politics* 7, no. 2: 1–12.

———. 2019b. "A De Facto Ethnic Democracy? Obliterating and Targeting the Other, Hindu Vigilantes, and the Ethno State." In *Majoritarian State: How Hindu Nationalism Is Changing India*, Anjana P. Chatterji, Thomas Blom Hansen, and Christophe Jaffrelot, eds. New York: Oxford University Press.

Jaffrelot, Christophe, and A. Kalaiyarasan. 2019. "Quota, Old Plus New." *Indian Express*, March 2. https://indianexpress.com/article/opinion /columns/general-category-quota-dalit-sc-st-reservation-old-plus-new -5607504.

Jaffrelot, Christophe, and Gilles Verniers. 2015. "The Representation Gap." July 24. http://indianexpress.com/article/opinion/columns/the-representation -gap-2.

———. 2019. "Explained: In Hindi Heartland, Upper Castes Dominate New Lok Sabha." *Indian Express,* May 27. https://indianexpress.com/article /explained/in-hindi-heartland-upper-castes-dominate-new-house-5747511.

Jain, S. K., A. K. Lohani, R. D. Singh, A. Chaudhary, and L. N. Thakural. 2012. "Glacial Lakes and Glacial Lake Outburst Flood in a Himalayan Basin Using Remote Sensing and GIS." *Natural Hazards* 62, no. 3: 887–899.

Jeffery, Patricia, and Roger Jeffery. 2006. *Confronting Saffron Demography: Religion, Fertility, and Women's Status in India.* Gurgaon: Three Essays Collective.

Jenkins, Rob. 2019. "India 2019: A Transformative Election?" *Pacific Affairs* 92, no. 3 (September): 475–497.

Jha, D. N. 2005. *Early India: A Concise History.* New Delhi: Manohar.

Jha, Himanshu. 2018a. "Emerging Politics of Accountability." *Economic & Political Weekly* 53, no. 10: 47.

———. 2018b. "State Processes, Ideas, and Institutional Change: The Case of the Right to Information Act in India." *Pacific Affairs* 91, no. 2: 309–328.

Jithesh, P. M. N.d. "Appropriation of Ayyappa Cult: The History and Hinduisation of Sabarimala Temple." *The Wire.*

John, Steven. 2019. "9 Incredible Facts About India's Economy." *Business Insider,* July 23. https://markets.businessinsider.com/news/stocks/india-economy-facts-gdp-agriculture-2019-7-1028376452#agriculture-accounts-for-50-of-jobs-in-india8.

Johnson, Rebecca. 2009. *Unfinished Business: The Negotiation of the CTBT and the End of Nuclear Testing.* Geneva: UNIDIR.

Joshi, Shashi, and Bhagwan Josh. 2011. *Struggle for Hegemony in India.* Rev. ed. New Delhi: Sage Publications India Pvt.

Joshi, Vijay, and I. M. D. Little. 1994. *India: Macroeconomics and Political Economy.* New Delhi: Oxford University Press.

Joshi, Yogesh, and Harsh V. Pant. 2015. "Indo-Japanese Strategic Partnership and Power Transition in Asia." *India Review* 14, no. 3: 312–329.

Juergensmeyer, Mark. 1993. *The New Cold War? Religious Nationalism Confronts the Secular State.* Berkeley: University of California Press.

Kargil Review Committee Report. 2000. Government of India, New Delhi.

Kashyap, Subhash C. 1998. "Ethnicity and Constitutional Reforms in India." In *Ethnicity and Constitutional Reform in South Asia,* Iftekharuzzaman, ed. New Delhi: Manohar.

Kaw, Sanjay. 2010. "The Secret Witness." *Outlook,* October 18.

Kazmin, Amy. 2019. "In Glorifying Gandhi's Killer, Hindu Hardliners Create a New Icon." *Financial Times,* June 11.

Keck, M. E., and K. Sikkink. 1998. "Transnational Advocacy Networks in the Movement Society." In *The Social Movement Society: Contentious Politics for a New Century,* David S. Meyer and Sidney Tarrow, eds. Lanham: Rowman and Littlefield.

Kennedy, Andrew Bingham. 2011. *The International Ambitions of Mao and Nehru: National Efficacy Beliefs and the Making of Foreign Policy.* New York: Cambridge University Press.

Kerr, Ian J. 2007. *Engines of Change: The Railroads That Made India.* Westport: Praeger.

Khan, S., H. Savenije, S. Demuth, and P. Hubert. 2010. "Hydrocomplexity: New Tools for Solving Wicked Water Problems." *IAHS Proceedings & Reports.* Wallingford: IAHS Press.

Khilnani, Sunil. 1997. *The Idea of India.* London: Hamilton.

Khory, Kavita R. 2005. "The Shah Bano Case: Some Political Implications." In *Religion and Law in Independent India,* Robert D. Baird, ed. Delhi: Manmohar.

Khosla, Madhav. 2020. *India's Founding Moment: The Constitution of a Most Surprising Democracy.* Cambridge: Harvard University Press.

Kishwar, Madhu. 1986. "Pro-Women or Anti-Muslim? The Shah Bano Controversy." *Manushi* 32 (January–February): 4–13.

Kochanek, Stanley A. 1980. "India's Changing Role in the United Nations." *Pacific Affairs* 53, no. 1 (Spring): 48–68.

Kosambi, Meera. 1988. "Women, Emancipation, and Equality: Pandita Ramabai's Contribution to Women's Cause." *Economic and Political Weekly* 24, no. 44 (October): 1857–1868.

———. 1993. "An Indian Response to Christianity, Church, and Colonialism: The Case of Pandita Ramabai." Unpublished paper. Bombay: Research Center for Women's Studies, SNDT University.

Kothari, Rajni. 1997. "Caste and Modern Politics." In *Politics in India,* Sudipta Kaviraj, ed. Delhi: Oxford University Press.

Krishnan, Maitrey. 2008. "Sexual Harassment and Law." *Seminar* 583 (March). http://www.india-seminar.com/semframe.html.

Kumar, Radha. 1993. *The History of Doing: An Illustrated Account of Movements for Women's Rights and Feminism in India, 1800–1990.* Delhi: Kali for Women.

Kundu, Amitabh 2011. *Trends and Processes of Urbanisation in India.* London: International Institute for Environment and Development (IIED) and United Nations Population Fund (UNFPA) Population and Development Branch.

Kundu, Debolina. 2014. "Urban Development Programmes in India: A Critique of JnNURM." *Social Change* 44: 615–632.

Lahiri-Dutt, Kuntala, ed. 2014. *The Coal Nation: Histories, Ecologies, and the Politics of Coal in India.* Aldershot: Ashgate.

Lamba, M., and S. Z. Ahammad. 2017. "Sewage Treatment Effluents in Delhi: A Key Contributor of β-Lactam Resistant Bacteria and Genes to the Environment." *Chemosphere* 188: 249–256.

Lateef, Shahida. 2008. "From Shahbano to Sachar." *Seminar* 583 (March). http://www.india-seminar.com/semframe.html.

Lawson, Phillip. 1993. *The East India Company: A History.* London: Longman.

Lele, Sharachchandra Madhukar, and Ajit Menon. 2014. *Democratizing Forest Governance in India:* New Delhi: Oxford University Press.

Levien, Michael. 2012. "The Land Question: Special Economic Zones and the Political Economy of Dispossession in India." *Journal of Peasant Studies* 39, nos. 3–4: 933–969.

Lewis, John Prior. 1995. *India's Political Economy: Governance and Reform.* New York: Oxford University Press.

Lijphart, Arend. 1994. *Electoral Systems and Party Systems.* New York: Oxford University Press.

———. 1996. "The Puzzle of Indian Democracy: A Consociational Interpretation." *American Political Science Review* 90, no. 2 (June): 258–268.

———. 1999. *Patterns of Democracy: Government Forms and Performance in Thirty-Six Countries.* New Haven: Yale University Press.

———. 2007. "Democratic Institutions and Ethnic/Religious Pluralism: Can India and the United States Learn from Each Other—and from the Smaller Democracies?" In *Democracy and Diversity: India and the American Experience,* K. Shankar Bajpai, ed. New Delhi: Oxford University Press.

Linz, Juan J., and Alfred Stepan. 1996. *Problems of Democratic Transition and Consolidation: Southern Europe, South America, and Post-Communist Europe.* Baltimore: Johns Hopkins University Press.

Linz, Juan J., Alfred Stepan, and Yogendra Yadav. 2007. "'Nation-State' or 'State-Nation'? India in Comparative Perspective." In *Democracy and Diversity: India and the American Experience,* K. Shankar Bajpai ed. New Delhi: Oxford University Press.

Lipset, Seymour Martin, and Stein Rokkan. 1967. *Party Systems and Voter Alignments.* New York: Free Press.

Lord, Austin, Georgina Drew, and Mabel Gergan. 2020. "Timescapes of Himalayan Hydropower: Promises, Project Life Cycles, and Precarities." *WIREs Water* 7, no. 6. https://doi.org/10.1002/wat2.1469.

Luce, Edward. 2007. *In Spite of the Gods: The Strange Rise of Modern India.* London: Abacus.

Madan, Tanvi. 2006. "Energy Security Series India." Brookings Foreign Policy Studies. Washington, DC: Brookings Institution, November.

Mandhana, Nikarita, and Anjali Trivedi. 2012. "Indians Outraged by Account of Gang Rape on a Bus." *New York Times,* December 30.

Mani, Lata. 1989. "Contentious Traditions: The Debates over Sati in Colonial India." In *Recasting Women,* Kumkum Sangari and Sudesh Vaid, eds. Delhi: Kali for Women.

Manji, Irshad. 2009. "Changing Lives." *New York Times,* September 17. http://www.nytimes.com/2009/09/20/books/review/Manji-t.html.

Maurya, Nutan, Karthick Radha Krishnan, Kelly D. Alley, Sukanya Das, and Jennifer Barr. 2017. *A Review Report of the Decentralized Wastewater Treatment System (DEWATS) of Kachhpura Agra.* New Delhi. Unpublished.

McDermott, Rachel, Leonard Gordon, Ainslie Embree, Francess Pritchett, and Dennis Dalton. 2015. *Sources of Indian Traditions: Modern India, Pakistan, and Bangladesh.* 3rd ed. New York: Columbia University Press.

Mehta, Aasha Kapur, and Amita Shah. 2003. "Chronic Poverty in India: Incidence, Causes, and Policies." *World Development* 31, no. 3: 491–511.

Mehta, Kalpana. 2008. "Women's Movements in India." *Seminar* 583 (March). http://www.india-seminar.com/cd8899/cd_frame8899.html.

Mehta, Lyla, and Timos Karpouzoglou. 2015. "Limits of Policy and Planning in Peri-Urban Waterscapes: The Case of Ghaziabad, Delhi, India." *Habitat International* 48 (August): 159–168.

Mendelsohn, O., and M. Vicziany. 1998. *The Untouchables: Subordination, Poverty, and the State in Modern India.* Cambridge: Cambridge University Press.

Menon, Manju, and Kanchi Kohli. 2005. *Large Dams for Hydropower in Northeast India: A Dossier.* New Delhi: South Asia Network on Dams, Rivers, and People and Kalpavriksh.

Menon-Sen, Kalyani, and A. K. Shiva Kumar. 2001. *Women in India: How Free? How Equal?* New Delhi: United Nations Office of the Resident Coordinator in India.

Metcalf, Barbara Daly. 1982. *Islamic Revival in British India: Deoband, 1860–1900.* Princeton: Princeton University Press.

Metcalf, Barbara, and Thomas Metcalf, eds. 2008. *A Concise History of India.* Cambridge: Cambridge University Press.

Metcalf, Tom, and Barbara Metcalf. 2001. *A Concise History of India.* Cambridge: Cambridge University Press.

Mickey, Robert, Steven Levitsky, and Lucan Ahmad Way. 2017. "Is America Still Safe for Democracy?" *Foreign Affairs* 96, no. 3 (May–June): 20–29.

Miklian, Jason, and Scott Carney. 2010. "Fire in the Hole." *Foreign Policy* (September–October): 105–112.

Ministry of Tribal Affairs, Government of India. 2019. "Monthly Progress Report on FRA, April 2019." https://tribal.nic.in/MPRnAddit.aspx.

Mitra, Subrata K., and Malte Pehl. 2010. "Federalism." In *The Oxford Companion to Politics in India,* Niraja Gopal Jayal and Pratap Bhanu Mehta, eds. New Delhi: Oxford University Press.

Mohan, Rohini. 2015. "Is Thriving Sugarcane Crop Responsible for Maharashtra's Marathwada and Vidarbha's Water Woes?" *Economic Times,* September 9. https://economictimes.indiatimes.com/news/economy/agriculture/is-thriving-sugarcane-crop-responsible-for-maharashtras-marathwada-and-vidarbhas-water-woes.

Mohanty, Chandra. 1988. "Under Western Eyes: Feminist Scholarship and Colonial Discourses." *Feminist Review* 30 (Autumn): 61–88.

Muirhead, Bruce. 2005. "Differing Perspectives: India, the World Bank, and the 1963 Aid-India Negotiations." *India Review* 4, no. 1: 1–22.

Mukherji, Rahul. 2009. "The State, Economic Growth, and Development in India." *India Review* 8, no. 1: 81–106.

———. 2013. "Ideas, Interests, and the Tipping Point: Economic Change in India." *Review of International Political Economy* 20, no. 2: 363–389.

———. 2014a. *Globalization and Deregulation: Ideas, Interests, and Institutional Change in India.* New Delhi: Oxford University Press.

———. 2014b. *Political Economy of Reforms In India.* New Delhi: Oxford University Press.

———. 2016. "Is India a Developmental State?" In *The Asian Developmental State: Reexaminations and New Departures,* Yin-wah Chu, ed. New York: Palgrave Macmillan.

———. 2020. "India's Illiberal Remedy." *Journal of Democracy* 31, no. 4 (October): 91–105.

Mukherji, Rahul, and Himanshu Jha. 2017. "Bureaucratic Rationality, Political Will, and State Capacity." *Economic and Political Weekly* 52, no. 49: 53–60.

Mukherji, Rahul, Jai Prasad, and Seyed Hossein Zarhani.2020. "Can COVID-19 Malign the Idea of India?" In *The Viral Condition: Identities,* Ravinder

Kaur, ed. https://www.identitiesjournal.com/the-viral-condition-virtual -symposium/can-covid-19-malign-the-idea-of-india.

Mukherji, Rahul, Seyed Hossein Zarhani, and K. Raju. 2018. "State Capacity and Welfare Politics in India: Implementing the Mahatma Gandhi National Rural Employment Guarantee Scheme in Undivided Andhra Pradesh." *Indian Journal of Human Development* 12, no. 2: 282–297.

Mullen, Rani D. 2013. "Panchayat Raj Institutions." In *Routledge Handbook of Indian Politics,* Atul Kohli and Prerna Singh, eds. New Delhi: Routledge.

Nair, Venugopalan. 2018. "'Devotee' Ends Life, BJP Calls for Kerala Shutdown Today." *Times of India,* December 14.

Nandi, Jayashree. 2019. "A Village with Carbon-Positive Tag." *Hindustan Times,* April 1.

Narain, Jai Prakash. 2016. "Public Health Challenges in India: Seizing the Opportunities." *Indian Journal of Community Medicine* 41, no. 2 (April–June): 85–88.

Narain, Sunita. 2014. "Sunita Narain: Breaking the Impasse of 2013." *Business Standard,* January 12.

———. 2018. "Every Drop Matters: Opinion." *Down to Earth,* June 27.

Narasimha Reddy, D., and Srijit Mishra, eds. 2010. *Agrarian Crisis in India.* New Delhi: Oxford University Press.

National Statistical Office. 2019. *Periodic Labour Force Survey (PLFS).* New Delhi: Ministry of Statistics and Programme Implementation, May.

Nehru, Jawaharlal. 1946. *The Discovery of India.* New York: John Day.

———. 2018. *China, Spain, and the War.* Emeryville: Alibris.

Niti Aayog. 2018. *Composite Water Management Index: A Tool for Water Management.* June. http://www.niti.gov.in/writereaddata/files/document _publication /2018-05-18-Water-Index-Report_vS8-compressed.pdf.

Oldenburg, Veena Talwar. 2002. *Dowry Murder: The Imperial Origins of a Cultural Crime.* New York: Oxford University Press.

Omvedt, Gail. 1990. "Women Zilla Parishad and Panchayat Raj, Chandwad to Vinter." *Economic and Political Weekly,* August 4.

———. 1994. "Kanshi Ram and the Bahujan Party." In *Caste and Class in India,* K. L. Sharma, ed. New Delhi: Rawat.

———. 2005. "Farmer's Movements." In *Social Movements in India,* Ray Raka and Mary F. Katzenstein, eds. New Delhi: Oxford University Press.

Oskarsson, Patrik. 2013. "Dispossession by Confusion from Mineral-Rich Lands in Central India." *South Asia: Journal of South Asian Studies* 36, no. 2: 199–212.

Pai, Madhav, and Jaya Dhindaw. 2017. "Unlock Bengaluru: Driving the Next Wave of Urbanisation." *WRI India,* July 7.

Palit, Chittaroopa. 2008. "Combatting Displacement." *Seminar* 583 (March). http://www.india-seminar.com/semframe.html.

Panagariya, Arvind. 2008. *India: The Emerging Giant.* New Delhi: Oxford University Press.

Parashar, Archana. 1992. *Women and Family Law Reform in India: Uniform Civil Code and Gender Equality.* New Delhi: Sage.

Patel, Indraprasad Gordhanbhai. 1987. "On Taking India into the Twenty-First Century (New Economic Policy in India)." *Modern Asian Studies* 21, no. 2: 209–231.

Patel, Sujata. 1993. "Women's Participation in the Anti-Reservation Agitation in Ahmedabad, 1985: Some Issues." In *Women's Participation in Politics,* Kaushik Susheela, ed. Delhi: Vikas.

Pathak, Zakia, and Rajeshwari Sunder Rajan. 1989. "Shahbano." *Signs* 14, no. 3: 558–582.

Phadke, Sheila. 2007. "Dangerous Liaisons: Women and Men, Risk and Reputation, in Mumbai." *Economic and Political Weekly* 62, no. 17: 1510–1518.

Phadnis, Aditi. 2003. "I Wouldn't Mind Being Born Ten Times to Rediscover India." *Business Standard,* July 11.

"Poison of Demographic Prejudice." 2015. *Economic and Political Weekly* 50, no. 35 (August): 7–8.

Pradhan, Jaya Prakash, and Vinoj Abraham. 2005. "Social and Cultural Impact of Outsourcing: Emerging Issues from Indian Call Centers." *Harvard Asia Quarterly* 9, no. 3: 22–30.

Press Trust of India. 2014. "PM Narendra Modi Raises Issue of Incursions with Visiting Chinese President Xi Jinping." *Indian Express,* September 18.

———. 2018. "US Pacific Command Renamed as US Indo-Pacific Command." *Economic Times,* June 2.

———. 2020. "New Education Policy 2020 Highlights: School and Higher Education to See Major Changes." *Hindustan Times,* August 2.

Prime Minister's High Level Committee, Government of India. 2006. *Social, Economic, and Educational Status of the Muslim Community of India: A Report.* New Delhi.

"Quick Take: Women in the Workforce—India." 2018. *Catalyst,* July 11. https://www.catalyst.org/research/women-in-the-workforce-india.

Quraishi, S. Y. 2019. "What It Takes to Run an Election for India." *New York Times,* April 24.

Radhakrishna, Meena, ed. 2016. *First Citizens: Studies on Adivasis, Tribals, and Indigenous Peoples in India.* New Delhi: Oxford University Press.

———. 1995. "Ban on Women of Prohibited Age Group Visiting Sabarimala Shrine Comes Under Scrutiny." *India Today,* January 15.

Radhakrishnan, Sruti. 2019. "New Lok Sabha Has the Highest Number of Women MPs." *The Hindu,* May 27.

Rae, Douglas. 1971. *The Political Consequences of Electoral Laws*, 2nd ed. New Haven: Yale University Press.

Rai, Shirin. 1998. "Class, Caste, and Gender: Women in Parliament in India." In *Women in Parliament: Beyond Numbers.* Stockholm: International IDEA.

Rajalakshmi, T. K. 2019. "Amendments to the Forest Act: Forests over Rights." *Frontline,* July 19. https://frontline.thehindu.com/environment/article285 37157.ece.

Rajshekhar, M., and C. R. Sukumar. 2013. "Hydelgate: We Get Into Projects After Permits and Licenses Are in Place, Says Anil Chalamalasetty, Greenko." *The Hindu,* May 6.

Raju, Saraswati. 2006. "Locating Women in Social Development." In *India: Social Development Report,* Council for Social Development, ed. Delhi: Oxford.

Ramanathan, Swati, and Ramesh Ramanathan. 2017. "The Impact of Instant Universal Suffrage." *Journal of Democracy* 28, no. 3 (July): 86–95.

Ramesh, Jairam. 2018. "India's Role in Ending the Korean War." *The Hindu,* May 3.

Ramusack, Barbara. 1992. "Cultural Missionaries, Maternal Imperialists, Feminist Allies: British Women Activists in India, 1865–1945." In *Western Women and Imperialism: Complicity and Resistance,* Margaret Strobel and Nirad Chaudhuri, eds. Bloomington: Indiana University Press.

———. 2004. *The Indian Princes and Their States.* Cambridge: Cambridge University Press.

Rana, A. P. 1969. "The Intellectual Dimensions of India's Nonalignment." *Journal of Asian Studies* 28, no. 2 (February): 299–312.

Ranganathan, M. 2014. "'Mafias' in the Waterscape: Urban Informality and Everyday Public Authority in Bangalore." *Water Alternatives* 7, no. 1: 89–105.

Rao, Anupama. 2009. *The Caste Question: Dalits and the Politics of Modern India.* Los Angeles: University of California Press.

Reddy, G. Ram. 1989. "The Politics of Accommodation: Caste, Class, and Dominance in Andhra Pradesh." In *Dominance and State Power in Modern India: Decline of a Social Order,* Francine R. Frankel and Rao Madhugiri Shamarao Ananthapadmanabha, eds. Oxford: Oxford University Press.

Repucci, Sarah. 2021. *A Leaderless Struggle for Democracy.* Washington, DC: Freedom House.

Repucci, Sarah, and Amy Slipowitz. 2020. *Democracy Under Lockdown: The Impact of COVID-19 on the Global Struggle for Freedom.* Washington, DC: Freedom House.

Richardson, Shaun D., and John M. Reynolds. 2000. "An Overview of Glacial Hazards in the Himalayas." *Quaternary International* 65–66: 31–34.

Roberts, A. 2010. "A Great and Revolutionary Law? The First Four Years of India's Right to Information Act." *Public Administration Review* 70, no. 6: 925–933.

Robinson, Eva Cheung. 1997. *Greening at the Grassroots: Alternative Forest Strategies in India.* New Delhi: Sage.

Rogaly, Ben, Barbara Harriss-White, and Sugata Bose. 1995. "Sonar Bangla? Agricultural Growth and Agrarian Change in West Bengal and Bangladesh." *Economic and Political Weekly* 30, no. 29: 1862–1868.

Rogaly Ben, Barbara Harriss-White, and Sugata Bose, eds. 1999. *Sonar Bangla? Agricultural Growth and Agrarian Change in West Bengal and Bangladesh.* New Delhi: Sage.

Roy, Aruna, and MKSS Collective. 2018. *The RTI Story: Power to the People.* New Delhi: Roli.

Roy-Chaudhury, Rahul, and Kate Sullivan de Estrada. 2018. "India, the Indo-Pacific, and the Quad." *Survival* 60, no. 3: 181–194.

Rubin, Barnett R. 1985. "Economic Liberalization and the Indian State." *Third World Quarterly* 7, no. 4: 942–957.

Rubinoff, Arthur. 1971. *India's Use of Force in Goa.* Bombay: Popular Prakashan.

Rudolph, L. I., and S. Hoeber Rudolph. 1966. "The Political Role of India's Caste Associations." In *Social Change: The Colonial Situation,* I. Wallerstein, ed. New York: Wiley.

Rudolph, Lloyd I., and Susanne H. Rudolph. 2007. "Iconization of Chandrababu: Sharing Sovereignty in India's Federal Market Economy." In *India's Economic Transition: The Politics of Reform,* Rahul Mukherji, ed. New Delhi: Oxford University Press.

Rudolph, Susanne Hoeber. 1987. Introduction to T. N. Madan, "Secularism in Its Place." *Journal of Asian Studies* 46, no. 4 (November): 747–759.

Saikiran, K. P. 2019. "Two Women Below 50 Claim They Entered Kerala's Sabarimala Temple." *Times of India,* January 2.

Sangari, Kumkum, and Sudesh Vaid, eds. 1989. *Recasting Women: Essays in Colonial Indian History.* New Brunswick, NJ: Rutgers.

Sankhe, Shirish, et al. 2010. *India's Urban Awakening: Building Inclusive Cities, Sustaining Economic Growth.* McKinsey Global Institute. https://www.mckinsey.com/~/media/McKinsey/Featured%20Insights /Urbanization/Urban%20awakening%20in%20India/MGI_Indias_urban _awakening_full_report.pdf.

Sarkar, Tanika. 2002. "Semiotics of Terror: Muslim Children and Women in Hindu Rashtra." *Economic and Political Weekly* 37, no. 28 (July): 2872–2876.

Sarukkai, Sundar. 2009. "Phenomenology of Untouchability." *Economic and Political Weekly* 44, no. 37 (September): 39–48.

Sathyamurthy, Tennalur Vengara, ed. 1995. *Industry and Agriculture in India Since Independence.* Delhi: Oxford University Press.

Savarkar, Vinayak Damodar. 2003 [1923]. *Hindutva: Who Is a Hindu?* New Delhi: Hindi Sahitya Sadan.

Schott, Ben. 2009. "Chikan and Eve Teasing." *New York Times,* September 21. http://schott.blogs.nytimes.com/2009/09/21/chikan-and-eve-teasing.

Sen, Amartya. 2005. *The Argumentative Indian: Writings on Indian History, Culture, and Identity.* New York: Picador.

Sen, Ilina. 2008. "The Livelihood Crisis for Women." *Seminar* 583 (March). http://www.india-seminar.com/semframe.html.

Sen, Lionel Protip. 1994. *Slender Was the Thread: Kashmir Confrontation, 1947–48.* Columbia: South Asia Books.

Sengupta, Arjun. 1984. *Report of the Committee to Review Policy for Public Enterprises.* New Delhi: Ministry of Finance, Government of India.

Sengupta, Debjani. 2005. "Civil Society and Women in Panchayat." *Viewpoint,* August–December. http://webspace.webring.com/people/gh/husociology1 /women7.htm.

Sengupta, Sushmita. 2018. "At Least 200 Cities Are Fast Running Out of Water." *Down to Earth,* March 31.

Shah, Tushaar. 2008. "India's Groundwater Irrigation Economy: The Challenge of Balancing Livelihoods and Environment." In *Handbook on Environmental Economics in India,* Kanchan Chopra and Vikram Dayal, eds. New Delhi, India: Oxford University Press.

———. 2010. *Taming the Anarchy: Groundwater Governance in South Asia.* Washington, DC: Routledge.

Shankar, Soumya. 2019. "Not Everyone Has a Vote in the World's Largest Democracy." *Foreign Policy,* October 22. https://foreignpolicy.com/2019 /10/22/missing-voters-india-elections-muslims-dalits/.

Sharma, Ruchir. 2019. "No Country for Strongmen: How India's Democracy Constrains Modi." *Foreign Affairs* 98, no. 2 (March–April): 96–106.

Sharma, Shalendra D. 2010. "Indian Politics." In *Understanding Contemporary India,* Neil DeVotta, ed. Boulder: Lynne Rienner.

———. 2019. "Modinomics in India: The Promise and the Reality." *Asian Survey* 59, no. 3 (May–June): 548–572.

Shastry, S., et al. 2018. "Towards Smarter Service Provision for Smart Cities: Accounting for the Social Costs of Urban Service Provision." Working paper. Bangalore: World Resources Institute.

Shaurya, Surabhi. 2017. "Triple Talaq: All India Muslim Personal Law Board Issues Code of Conduct—Here's What It Says." April 17. https://www.india.com/news/india/triple-talaq-all-india-muslim-personal-law-board-issues-code-of-conduct-heres-what-it-says-2035881.

Shaw, Annapurna, and M. K. Satish. 2007. "Metropolitan Restructuring in Post-Liberalised India: Separating the Global and the Local." *Cities: The Journal of Urban Policy and Planning* 24, no. 2: 148–163.

Shreyas. 2016. "Jayamala Who Entered Sabarimala in 1986 Now Advocates Women's Rights." *One India,* January 15. https://www.oneindia.com/india/interview.

Shrine, Harikkumar. 2009. "Indian Women Find New Peace in Rail Commute." *New York Times,* September 15.

Siddiqui, Huma. 2020. "Coronavirus Care for Neighbors: India Sends Supplies to Saarc Nations to Fight COVID-19." *Financial Express,* March 20.

Singh, Umesh Kumar, and Balwant Kumar. 2018. "Climate Change Impacts on Hydrology and Water Resources of Indian River Basin." *Current World Environment* 13, no. 1: 32–43.

Sinha, Aseema. 2005. "Understanding the Rise and Transformation of Business Collective Action in India." *Business and Politics* 7, no. 2: 1–35.

Sinha, Mrinalini. 1992. "Chathams, Pitts, and Gladstones in Petticoats." In *Western Women and Imperialism: Complicity and Resistance,* Margaret Strobel and Nirad Chaudhuri, eds. Bloomington: Indiana University Press.

Smith, Donald E. 1963. *India as a Secular State.* Princeton: Princeton University Press.

Soni, Anusha. 2017. "Triple Talaq Undesirable, Worst Form of Dissolution of Marriage Among Muslims: Supreme Court." *India Today,* May 12.

Sood, A. 2019. "Speculative Urbanism." In *Wiley Blackwell Encyclopedia of Urban and Regional Studies,* A. M. Orum, ed. London: Blackwell.

South Asia Network for Dams, Rivers, and People (SANDRP). 2015. "The High-Level Committee Report on Environmental Laws: A Recipe for Climate Disaster and Silencing People's Voice." *SANDRP Blog,* January 8. https://sandrp.in/2015/01/08/the-high-level-committee-report-on-environmental-law-a-recipe-for-climate-disaster-and-silencing-peoples-voice/.

———. 2017. "DRP News Bulletin 16 October 2017: New Groundwater Guidelines Threat to India's Water Lifeline." *SANDRP Blog,* October 16. https://sandrp.in/2017/10/16/drp-news-bulletin-16-october-2017-new-groundwater-guidelines-threat-to-indias-water-lifeline/.

Sridharan, E. 2002. "The Fragmentation of the Indian Party System, 1952–1999: Seven Competing Explanations." In *Parties and Party Politics in India,* Zoya Hasan, ed.. Delhi: Oxford University Press.

Srinivas, M. N. 1995. *Social Change in Modern India.* New Delhi: Orient Longman.

Statista Research Department. 2018. "Reported Rape Cases in India, 2005–2018." July 27. https://www.statista.com/statistics/632493/reported -rape-cases-india/.

Steffen, Will, et al. 2015. "Planetary Boundaries: Guiding Human Development on a Changing Planet." *Science* 347, no. 6223 (February): 736.

Stein, Burton. 1993. *Vijayanagara.* Cambridge: Cambridge University Press.

Subrahmanyam, Sanjay. 2017. *Europe's India: Words, People, Empires, 1500–1800.* Cambridge: Harvard University Press.

Subramanian, Arvind. 2019. *India's GDP Mis-estimation: Likelihood, Magnitudes, Mechanisms, and Implications.* Cambridge: Center for International Development, Harvard University. https://www.hks.harvard.edu/centers/cid /publications/faculty-working-papers/india-gdp-overestimate.

Subramanian, Samanth. 2016. "Mumbai Court Rules Women Can Enter Inner Sanctum of Famous Muslim Shrine." *The National,* August 26.

Subramanian, T. S. R., V. Anand, A. K. Srivastava, K. N. Bhat, B. Sinha, and H. Shah. 2014. *Report of the High-Level Committee on Forest and Environment Related Laws.* Delhi: Ministry of Environment, Forest, and Climate Change.

Sundar, Nandini. 2016. *The Burning Forest: India's War in Bastar.* New Delhi: Juggernaut.

Suri, K. C. 2019. "Social Change and the Changing Indian Voter: Consolidation of the BJP in India's 2019 Lok Sabha Election." *Studies in Indian Politics* 7, no. 2 (December): 234–246.

Swaminathan, Madhura. 2000. *Weakening Welfare: The Public Distribution of Food in India.* New Delhi: Leftword.

Swenden, Wilfried, and Rekha Saxena. 2017. "Rethinking Central Planning: A Federal Critique of the Planning Commission." *India Review* 16, no. 1: 42–65.

Taagepera, Rein, and Matthew Soberg Shugart. 1989. *Seats and Votes.* New Haven: Yale University Press.

Taenzler, Dennis, Lukas Ruettinger, Katherina Ziegenhagen, and Gopalakrishna Murthy. 2011. *Water, Crisis, and Climate Change in India: A Policy Brief.* Berlin: Adelphi.

Talbot, Ian, and Gurharpal Singh. 2009. *The Partition of India.* New York: Cambridge University Press.

Taleb, Nassim Nicholas, and Mark Blyth. 2001. "The Black Swan of Cairo: How Suppressing Volatility Makes the World Less Predictable and More Dangerous." *Foreign Affairs* 90, no. 3: 33–39.

Tankel, Stephen. 2013. *Storming the World Stage: The Story of Lashkar-e-Taiba.* New York: Oxford University Press.

Thaker, J. 2017. "Climate Change Communication in India." *Oxford Research Encyclopedia of Climate Science,* May 10. https://oxfordre.com/climate science/view/10.1093/acrefore/9780190228620.001.0001/acrefore -9780190228620-e-471.

Thakur, Ramesh. 1984. *Peacekeeping in Vietnam: Canada, India, Poland, and the International Commission.* Edmonton: University of Alberta Press.

Thapar, Romila. 2004. *Early India: From the Origins to AD 1300.* Berkeley: University of California Press.

Tian, Hanqin, Kamaljit Banger, Tao Bo, and Vinay K. Dadhwal. 2014. "History of Land Use in India During 1880–2010: Large-Scale Land Transformations Reconstructed from Satellite Data and Historical Archives." *Global and Planetary Change* 121: 78–88.

Tillin, Louise. 2012. *Remapping India: New States and Their Political Origins.* London: Hurst.

Traub, Alex. 2018. "India's Dangerous New Curriculum." *New York Review of Books,* December 6.

Tripathi, Shishir. 2018. "Sabarimala Verdict: SC Upheld Constitution in Letter and Spirit by Giving Preference to Equality in Recent Judgements." *Firstpost,* September 28.

Tully, Mark, and Jacob Satish. 1985. *Amritsar: Mrs. Gandhi's Last Battle.* London: Cape.

Twain, Mark. 1989. *Following the Equator.* New York: Dover.

Ulsrude, K., T. Winther, D. Palit, H. Rohracher, and J. Sandgren. 2011. "The Solar Transitions Research on Solar Mini-Grids in India: Learning from Local Cases of Innovative Socio-Technical Systems." *Energy for Sustainable Development* 15, no. 3 (September): 293–303.

United Nations Department of Economic and Social Affairs (UNDESA), Population Division. 2014. *World Urbanization Prospects: The 2014 Revision.* "Highlights." New York.

United Nations Development Programme (UNDP). 2009. *Human Development Report Profile: India.* New York: Oxford University Press.

———. 2014. *Human Development Report Profile: India.* New York: Oxford University Press.

———. 2018. *Human Development Report: India.* http://www.in.undp.org /content/india/en/home/sustainable-development/successstories/idia-ranks -130-on-2018-human-development-index.

United Nations Economic and Social Commission for Asia and the Pacific. 1997. *Women in India: An Accounting.* New York.

Vagholikar, N., and P. Das. 2010. *Damming Northeast India.* New Delhi: Kalpavriksh, Aaranyak, and ActionAid India.

Vaidya, Ashutosh. 2019. "Unlocking the CNG Challenges for Auto Manufacturers in India." *Tata Technologies,* February 25.

Vaidyanathan, Anantharama. 2010. *Agricultural Growth in India: Role of Technology, Incentives, and Institutions.* New Delhi: Oxford University Press.

Varshney, Ashutosh. 1998. *Democracy, Development, and the Countryside: Urban-Rural Struggles in India.* New York: Cambridge University Press.

———. 2013. *Battles Half Won: India's Improbable Democracy.* New Delhi: Penguin.

———. 2014. "Hindu Nationalism in Power?" *Journal of Democracy* 25, no. 4 (October): 34–45.

———. 2019. "Electoral Vibrancy, Mounting Liberal Deficits." *Journal of Democracy* 30, no. 4 (October): 63–77.

Vatuk, Sylvia. 2009. "A Rallying Cry for Muslim Personal Law." In *Islam in South Asia in Practice,* Barbara Metcalf, ed. Princeton: Princeton University Press.

Verma, Ashok Kalyan. 2002. *Kargil, Blood on the Snow: Tactical Victory, Strategic Failure—A Critical Analysis of the War.* New Delhi: Manohar.

Verniers, Gilles. 2019. "Breaking Down the Uttar Pradesh Verdict: In Biggest Bout, Knockout." *Indian Express,* May 28. https://indianexpress.com /article/explained/lok-sabha-elections-uttar-pradesh-bjp-modi-amit-shah -yogi-5751375.

Vij, Sumit, Vishal Narain, Timothy Karpouzoglou, and Patik Mishra. 2018. "From the Core to the Periphery: Conflicts and Cooperation over Land and Water in Periurban Gurgaon, India." *Land Use Policy* 76: 382–390.

Wagoner, Phillip. 1996. "'Sultan Among Hindu Kings': Dress, Titles, and the Islamicization of Hindu Culture at Vijayanagara." *Journal of Asian Studies* 55, no. 4: 851–880.

Wankhade, Kavita. 2015. "Urban Sanitation in India: Key Shifts in the National Policy Frame." *Environmental and Urbanization* 27, no. 2: 555–572.

Wester, Philippus, Arabinda Mishra, Aditi Mukherji, and Arun Bhakta Shrestha, eds. 2019. *The Hindu Kush Himalaya Assessment: Mountains, Climate Change, Sustainability, and People.* Cham, Switzerland: Springer.

White, King. 2015. "How Big Is the US Call Center Industry Compared to India and the Philippines." Site Selection Group, February 17. https:// info.siteselectiongroup.com/blog/how-big-is-the-us-call-center-industry -compared-to-india-and-philippines.

Whitehead, Andrew. 2007. *A Mission in Kashmir.* New Delhi: Oxford University Press.

Wilkes, Tommy, and Roli Srivastava. 2017. "Protests Held Across India After Attacks Against Muslims." *Reuters,* June 28.

Wilson, John. 2017. *India Conquered: Britain's Raj and the Chaos of Empire.* New Delhi: Simon and Schuster.

World Economic Forum. 2017. "The Global Gender Gap Index." https://en .wikipedia.org/wiki/Global_Gender_Gap_Report.

Wyatt, Andrew. 2017. "Paradiplomacy of India's Chief Ministers." *India Review* 16, no. 1: 106–124.

Yadav, Yogendra. 1999. "Electoral Politics in the Time of Change: India's Third Electoral System, 1989–99." *Economic and Political Weekly* (August): 2393–2399.

Yadav, Yogendra, and Suhas Palshikar. 2009. "Between Fortuna and Virtu: Explaining the Congress' Ambiguous Victory in 2009." *Economic and Political Weekly* 44, no. 39 (September–October): 33–47.

Yang, Anand. 1989. "Whose Sati? Widow Burning in Early-Nineteenth-Century India." *Journal of Women's History* 1, no. 2: 8–33.

Zarhani, Seyed Hossein. 2019. *Governance and Development in India: A Comparative Study on Andhra Pradesh and Bihar After Liberalization.* New York: Routledge.

Zhisheng, An, John E. Kutzbach, Warren L. Prell, and Stephen C. Porter. 2001. "Evolution of Asian Monsoons and Phased Uplift of the Himalaya-Tibetan Plateau Since Late Miocene Times." *Nature* 411, no. 6833: 62–66.

The Contributors

Kelly D. Alley is Alma Holladay professor of anthropology at Auburn University. She is author of *On the Banks of the Ganga: When Wastewater Meets a Sacred River* (2002), which captured the first ten years of her fieldwork. Her second book, *Machines, Digestion and Wastewater Reuse in Contemporary India,* follows a four-year National Science Foundation project on experiments with community-scale wastewater treatment and reuse in India. She has also written about religion and ecology, environmental law, and wastewater management in India.

Chad M. Bauman is professor of religion at Butler University, a senior fellow at the Religious Freedom Institute, and a research fellow at the Center for Religion and American Culture. He is author most recently of *Anti-Christian Violence in India* (2020) and *The Routledge Handbook of Hindu-Christian Relations* (2020). He is currently researching Hindu concerns regarding government interventions in religious affairs and religious liberty in India.

Benjamin B. Cohen is professor of history at the University of Utah. He is author of *An Appeal to the Ladies of Hyderabad* (2019), *In the Club* (2015), and *Kingship and Colonialism in India's Deccan* (2007), and editor of *The Pleasures at Your Side* (2019). In addition, he has authored several articles and book chapters on Hyderabad, the Deccan, and South Asia.

Neil DeVotta is professor of politics and international affairs at Wake Forest University. His research interests include Asian security and politics, ethno-religious nationalism, ethnic conflict resolution, and democratic transition and consolidation. He is author of *Blowback: Linguistic Nationalism, Institutional*

Decay, and Ethnic Conflict in Sri Lanka (2004) and editor of *An Introduction to South Asian Politics* (2016), in addition to the author of numerous articles.

Sumit Ganguly is distinguished professor of political science and holds the Tagore Chair in Indian Cultures and Civilizations at Indiana University, Bloomington. Ganguly is a member of the Council on Foreign Relations and a fellow of the American Academy of Arts and Sciences. He is currently editing the *Oxford Handbook of Indian Politics* with Eswaran Sridharan.

Douglas Hill is associate professor in the School of Geography, University of New Zealand. His geographic focus of research is South Asia, with secondary research interests in a range of sites across Asia, Australia, and New Zealand.

Christophe Jaffrelot is director of research at CERI-Sciences Po/CNRS, professor of Indian politics and sociology at the King's India Institute (London), nonresident fellow at the Carnegie Endowment for International Peace, and president of the French Political Science Association. His most recent book, with Pratinav Anil, is *India's First Dictatorship: The Emergency, 1975–77* (2020).

Rahul Mukherji is professor and head of the Department of Political Science at the South Asia Institute, Heidelberg University. He is also the executive director of the South Asia Institute. His publications include *Globalization and Deregulation: Ideas, Interests, and Institutional Change in India* (2014).

Eswaran Sridharan is academic director and chief executive officer of the University of Pennsylvania Institute for the Advanced Study of India, based in New Delhi. He is author, editor, or coeditor of ten books and has published numerous articles in academic journals and edited volumes. His current research interests include parties and coalitions, political sociology, and international relations of India in comparative perspective. He is editor of *India Review,* a refereed pan–social science journal on contemporary India.

Lisa Trivedi is professor of history at Hamilton College. Her scholarly interests range from the histories of colonialism and nationalism and women and gender in India to photography, medicine, and urban planning. She is author of *Clothing Gandhi's Nation: Homespun and Modern India* (2007) and *Refocusing the Lens: Pranlal K. Patel's Photographs of Ahmedabad, 1937* (2016), as well as numerous scholarly articles.

Seyed Hossein Zarhani is a postdoctoral research fellow and lecturer at the Department of Political Science, South Asia Institute, Heidelberg University. He is author of *Governance and Development in India: A Comparative Study on Andhra Pradesh and Bihar After Liberalization* (2019).

Index

accommodation policies, Nehru's, 11–12
activism: women's mobilization, 230
Adivasis: effects of pollution, 266; uneven development, 43–44. *See also* Tribals
affirmative action, 93–94
Afghanistan: arrival of Islam, 66; outlawing triple talaq divorce, 237; Soviet invasion of, 147
agrarian/lower-caste populist parties, 98
agriculture: agro-ecological zones in a changing climate, 31–32; British *ryotwari* system, 80–81; climate change measures, 265; economic growth in the agricultural sector, 127; food-grains imports, 123; harvest refuse burning, 271; human modification of the environment, 35–37; landlord rape, 243; monsoon and, 28–29; overuse of fertilizers, 264; river systems, 29–31; Vedic Era, 56, 57; water-use management, 262, 263
Ahluwalia, Montek Singh, 127
Akbar (Mughal ruler), 70–72
Alexander the Great, 58
All India Congress Committee (AICC), 111
All India Democratic Women's Association (AIDWA): criminalization of rape, 245

All India Muslim Personal Law Board (AIMPLB), 236–237
All India Services, 96
all-India organizations, women creating, 227–228
Ambassador automobile, 123, 123(fig.)
Ambedkar, Bhimrao Ramji, 168(fig.); caste quotas, 166; constitution, 13; conversion to Buddhism, 196; debate over Untouchables' electoral rights, 86; Independent Labor Party, 169–170; Kanshi Ram, 171–172; lower-caste leadership, 164; Scheduled Castes electoral college, 167; statues controversy, 184(n2)
Ambedkar Villages Scheme, 175–176
Amritsar massacre, 85–86
ancient civilizations: Indus Valley, 54–56; Vedic Era, 56–58
Andhra Pradesh, 2(fig.), 5(table); agro-ecological regions, 32(table); economic transition, 118–119; energy resources, 266; ethnic voting, 180; fertility rate, 39(table); HDI, 41(table); intensifying agriculture, 35–36; *jati* system, 163; land reform, 133; population demographics, 38; poverty reduction, 134; reservation system in politics, 168; right to work, 137; state creation on language lines,

About the Book

Even stronger than its outstanding predecessor, the third edition of *Understanding Contemporary India* provides context for and evaluates more than a decade of challenges and changes in India. Entirely new chapters on geography, politics, the economy, international relations, religion, and environmental challenges, along with updated material throughout (including the impact of the novel coronavirus), result in an indispensable volume that describes and analyzes the paradoxical nature of the world's largest and most diverse democracy.

Neil DeVotta is professor of politics and international relations at Wake Forest University. **Sumit Ganguly** is distinguished professor of political science and holds the Tagore Chair in Indian Cultures and Civilizations at Indiana University–Bloomington.